GLOBAL CULINARY ADVENTURES

Gloria Preston Olson

Global Culinary Adventures

Gloria Preston Olson

© Gloria Preston Olson 2009

Published by 1stWorld Publishing
P.O. Box 2211 Fairfield, Iowa 52556
tel: 641-209-5000 • fax: 641-209-3001
web: www.1stworldpublishing.com

First Edition

LCCN: 2008943715
SoftCover ISBN: 978-1-4218-9060-9
HardCover ISBN: 978-1-4218-9059-3
eBook ISBN: 978-1-4218-9061

All rights reserved. No part of this book may be reproduced or utilized in any form or by any means, electronic or mechanical, including photocopying or recording, or by any information storage and retrieval system, without permission in writing from the author.

This material has been written and published solely for educational purposes. The author and the publisher shall have neither liability nor responsibility to any person or entity with respect to any loss, damage or injury caused or alleged to be caused directly or indirectly by the information contained in this book.

Map Illustrations by Ramona McFarland

CONTENTS

INTRODUCTION 9
IN MY KITCHEN 13
    Foods 13
    Cooking Equipment 16
    Techniques 17

EUROPE 23
    France 23
    Italy 140
    Iberia 205
        Spain and Portugal
    United Kingdom and Ireland 244
    Central Europe 271
        Belgium, Holland, Luxembourg
        Germany, Switzerland, and
        Leichtenstein
    Scandinavia, Russia, and the Baltics 296
        Denmark, Norway, Sweden, Finland,
        Russia, Lithuania, Latvia, and
        Estonia
    Eastern Europe 327
        Poland, Czechoslovakia, Austria,
        Hungary, the Balkans- Yugoslavia,
        Albania, Romania, and Bulgaria
    Greece, Cyprus, Turkey and the Caucasus 361
        Armenia, Georgia, and Azerbaijan

MIDDLE EAST 397
    Iran, Iraq, Syria, Jordan, Lebanon,
    Israel, Persian Gulf, and Yemen

NORTH AFRICA. 433
    Egypt, Libya, Tunisia, Algeria,
    and Morocco

EAST AFRICA 459
    Ethiopia, Eritrea, Djibouti, Somalia,
    Kenya, Tanzania, Zanzibar, Uganda,
    Rwanda, and Burundi

CENTRAL AFRICA AND WEST AFRICA 480
    Senegal, Cote d'Ivoire, Togo,
    Gabon, Sao Tome, and Congo

SOUTHERN AFRICA. 494
    South Africa, Namibia, Botswana,
    Zimbabwe, Zambia, Malawi,
    Angola, Mozambique,
    and African Islands

CENTRAL ASIA 518
    India, Sri Lanka, Maldives, Nepal,
    Pakistan, Afghanistan, and
    the Five Stans

FAR EAST 542
    China, Hong Kong, Taiwan, Bhutan,
    Mongolia, Korea, and Japan

SOUTHEAST ASIA 566
    Philippines, Indochina, Thailand,
    Myanmar, Malaysia, Brunei, Singa-
    pore, and Indonesia

PACIFIC ISLANDS 588
    Australia, New Zealand, Melanesia,
    Micronesia, and Polynesia

SOUTH AMERICA 611
    Chile, Argentina, Uruguay, Paraguay,
    Brazil, Bolivia, Peru, Ecuador, Colombia,
    Venezuela, and the Guyanas

CARIBBEAN ISLANDS 636
    British, Dutch, French, Spanish,
    and American

CENTRAL AMERICA AND MEXICO 654
    Panama, Costa Rica, Nicaragua,
    Honduras, El Salvador, Guatemala, and Belize

INTRODUCTION

FROM THE RUNWAY TO THE RUNWAY..... This could well be the title for this adventurous worldwide collection of recipes with historical notes which show the progression of cooking styles throughout the world. Obtaining this astounding amount of information was not easy, and I think you will appreciate the blood, sweat, and tears that it took to visit everywhere from Timbuktu to Tibet, not to mention Borneo, Afghanistan, Iraq, Iran, and Libya.

During over three decades of exhilarating travel I flew at least a million miles on approximately 2,000 flights. I flew every national carrier in the world, as well as many Mickey Mouse airlines, such as Merpati Nusentera, Air Azerbaijan, and a tiny Nepalese carrier, where I was motioned to sit in the co-pilot's seat next to the robed and bearded Sherpa pilot. Of course, there were also hundreds of buses, trains, and ferries to remote places with no airports, not to mention at least 20 ships, the icebreaker to the North Pole, and the Ilyushin 76 with two great Siberian pilots plus the Twin Otter on skis, which was necessary to get to the South Pole.

This worldly obsession began half a century ago during my tenure as a model in New York, where I discovered the marvel of exotic ethnic restaurants. The restaurateurs were quite amazed that a young and naive Southern lady would ask for the recipes, so they sat down at the table with me and very graciously divulged their culinary secrets. Among them were Sardi's, Lindy's, Gage & Tollner's, Luchow's, Romeo Salta, and the Russian Tea Room.

After reluctantly returning to Nashville, I soon began to resent my modeling calls which took me away from my kitchen, and during a break one day, I even went home to experiment with my first eggplant. Every day since has been a new culinary adventure.

Eventually, I began teaching ethnic cooking in my home, which I did for over three decades, as well as at other schools and cookware shops. Lectures, television commercials and cooking spots, and food and travel articles in local newspapers soon followed. I finally arrived when I was crowned Mrs. Tennessee and participated in the Mrs. America pageant finals in San Diego, but cooking did not prove to be my forte—it was interior design!

By now, the modeling runways gave way to airport runways, as the lure of distant cuisines beckoned. I had a carefully preconceived plan. I covered as many countries in an area as possible, without leaving any pockets, so that I would have a basis for comparison of the foods. Also, before departing on each trip, I prepared all the specialties of the countries to be visited. My family was glad to see me go, especially after a steady diet of Indian, Sri Lankan, Nepalese, and Afghani cooking for three months. I visited markets and ate at humble food establishments, street stalls, and homes, as well as at great temples of gastronomy. Upon returning home, I perfected my recipes and many new ones to add to my repertoire.

In 1978, my cookbook, *Culinary Classics,* which contains the classics from sixty countries, was published, and is still in demand.

Since then, I have been collecting countries, as well as recipes, and have accomplished the incredible feat of visiting 307 countries, one of only about three dozen people to have done so. Many of these countries, of course, have no cuisine, such as Robinson Crusoe, Nauru, Spitsbergen, Fernando do Noronja, Tristan da Cunha, and Lakshadweep, but my culinary knowledge was enhanced by my visits to each and every one.

So now that the runways do not lead to any new culinary destinations and my profound goal is complete, I have endeavored to present the best of old and new recipes, as well as updated classics in this meaningful compilation of recipes. But, it is much more than just recipes, as I have included not only historical information but also pertinent travel notes pertaining to restaurants and hotels, and accounts of these thrilling, but Herculean and sometimes tumultuous culinary adventures.

Hopefully, you may have the opportunity to visit many, if not all of these fascinating destinations, but meanwhile, please enjoy the fruits of my adventures in your own kitchen. The following section, In My Kitchen, will ensure success as it contains invaluable advice on foods, cooking equipment, and techniques.

IN MY KITCHEN

Since I love to test new recipes daily, it is immensely gratifying to have the ingredients I need in my own supermarket kitchen. Except for a few produce items, it is almost always possible to make substitutions, and I have noted many of these in the recipes. For instance, meat, poultry, and seafoods are interchangeable as long as you use the corresponding cuts for roasting, sautéing, grilling, and braising. Many great dishes have evolved this way.

The vast majority of my foods are stored in my upright freezer and in my red Traulsen commercial refrigerator, with its glass door and digital thermometer, the pride of my kitchen. The remaining foods are on a baker's rack placed between the freezer and refrigerator

The following list of foods is in addition to the standard staples which we all use, thus enabling me to prepare dishes from the Caucasus to the South Pacific.

FREEZER ITEMS

Meat, Poultry, and Seafood – Beef brisket or boneless short ribs, lamb shanks, pork tenderloin and boneless loin roasts, country ham or prosciutto; suprêmes (skinless, boneless chicken breasts, to be called as such hereafter), small, whole chickens; cod, salmon, tuna, scallops, and shrimp. Stocks and bones and shells for preparing stocks. Leftover canned escargots.

Breads and Pastry – Baguettes, rye bread, tortillas, pitas, fillo, puff pastry, and assorted flours and yeast.

Fruits and Vegetables – Crystallized fruits (for fruitcake), fresh, pitted cherries, fresh figs and cranberries, chutneys, mushrooms (such as portobello and shiitake), artichoke hearts, and leftover canned hearts of palm. Also, my prepared oven-dried tomatoes, roasted garlic, roasted bell peppers, pesto, tapenade, and freshly peeled and grated coconut. Citrus zest, in strips and julienned.

REFRIGERATOR ITEMS

Dairy – Yogurt and/or sour cream; cheeses, such as chèvre, parmesan (large wheel), Norwegian gjetost, Spanish Idiazabal (similar to Emmenthal), Mexican queso blanco (similar to pot cheese), and Chihuahua (great for melting).

Ricotta, (easily made by heating 1 quart of milk mixed with 1 cup of buttermilk to 180°, then straining when curds rise to top), or mix 2 tablespoons chèvre into 1 pound store-bought ricotta for a creamier product.

Mascarpone, (easily made by mixing 6 ounces cream cheese with 3 tablespoons each heavy cream and sour cream).

Rind of parmesan and other hard cheeses – save for stocks, soups, and stews. Wrap cheeses in paper, then loosely in plastic. Cheeses may also be frozen, as well as butter and lard, which Italian chefs claim has less cholesterol than butter. Also freeze confit fat from duck, chicken, and tuna.

Spices and Herbs – Be sure to include French Four-Spice, Chinese Five-Spice, cardamom, and both dried and powdered saffron. Try adding saffron to water or other liquid for cooking pasta, rice, and potatoes. I keep dried herbs and spices in spice racks in the refrigerator for extended life. Also, store parsley and asparagus in a container of water for extended life. Save stems of each for making vegetable stock or adding to soups for extra flavor.

Grains – Couscous, bulgar wheat, pearl barley, wild rice.

Oils and Vinegars- Olive, truffle, sesame, peanut, and canola. Balsamic, red, Champagne, Sherry or malt vinegar, mirin, and rice wine vinegar.

Dried Fruits and Nuts – Prunes, apricots, figs, dates, and cranberries. Pistachios, almonds, pecans, walnuts, and macadamias.

Dried chestnuts from Allen Creek Farms in Ridgefield, Washington are now a permanent kitchen item, as they keep indefinitely. Be sure to save the soaking water, after reconstituting, for using as part of the liquid in recipes. Quite delicious!

Fresh Fruits and Vegetables – Citrus fruits, a variety of potatoes, beets, and cabbage family members keep well. Be sure to buy sauerkraut in a cryovac bag. Sturdy greens, such as collards, keep well.

Condiments and other ingredients – Preserved lemons, pomegranate syrup or juice, assorted olives, passion fruit juice, dulce de leche, white and red miso (akamiso), oyster sauce, Thai fish sauce, tamarind paste, Chinese fermented black beans, palm sugar, and capers. Also, maple syrup, which I make by boiling equal amounts of water, light corn syrup, and brown and white sugar for about 5 minutes, then adding maple flavoring.

BAKER'S RACK ITEMS

Dried beans – Cranberry, Spanish pink, Japanese azuki, Le Puy, and red lentils.

Pasta – Fusilli, gemelli, etc. Japanese udon, soba, and somen.

Assorted other items – Chestnut honey, sorghum, Cadbury or Schokinag cocoa, potato starch, gallon jug of Mexican-style vanilla, peanut butter, Ducros Poivre Gris (gray pepper) which a former student brought to me from Provence, Fleur de Sel, Brittany sea salt (a natural salt which highlights the natural flavors of food), and Kosher salt. Red and yellow onions, shallots, and garlic.

Liqueurs and Wines – Grand Marnier, Crème de Menthe, Frangelico, and Tiramisu. Madeira, which the French prefer for cooking because the heating process in the making of Madeira makes it a natural, or Marsala or sherry; also red or Tawny Port, as well as a dry red and white. Beer, brandy, and Myer's Jamaica Rum or British Navy Pusser's Rum are always on the rack as well.

The proper cooking equipment is a prerequisite for good food preparation, and it is also very gratifying and pleasurable to work with. Good equipment will last nearly a lifetime. And do look for kitchen items when traveling in foreign countries, as their aesthetic values will provide you with many memorable and sentimental cooking and dining experiences, as will your recipes.

ELECTRIC APPLIANCES

Heavy duty KitchenAid mixer, small and large food processors (my Cuisinart is still processing although it was the first one in Nashville, when Carl Sontheimer sent one to me); immersion blender (so called because it can be placed in a pan or bowl), as well as the beaker which comes with it, something I would not do without; waffle iron with reversible plates, which is a great substitute for a panini grill; yogurt maker; large toaster oven from Cuisinart, which I use more than my large ovens—a must; Bialetti pasta machine, with rollers that roll out the dough (which I make in the food processor) and cut it into spaghetti or fettuccine, much better than a machine which mixes and extrudes the dough.

POTS and PANS

All-Clad copper cookware lined with stainless steel is the ne plus ultra and makes a magnificent addition to kitchen decor when hung on a large copper pot rack. Iron cookware is also excellent when not using acidic ingredients, and colorful enameled iron from Le Creuset is the choice for braising. Stainless steel fish poacher, couscousière used also for steaming rice and as a double boiler; terra cotta casseroles, especially my 4-piece Palyok set from the Philippines, and baking dishes made of Burgundian clay which retain heat better than anything. Stainless steel platters (I have at least half a dozen) make excellent baking sheets for foods to be brought to the table, especially soufflés and entrees with mashed potatoes piped around the edge. A wok with a large bamboo steamer is also a must. A French bread pan with a double convex surface is desirable for achieving the traditional round shape; also use for baguettes.

UTENSILS

My Chinese Big Knife, which I bought in San Francisco's Chinatown in the sixties, is still my most valued tool; also other carbon steel knives, a mandoline for slicing, an Italian mezzaluna (half-moon) for mincing garlic, citrus zest, herbs, etc. a large wooden cutting board, about 5 feet long, and a large marble slab for pastry and candies. Marble rolling pin, French bread rolling pin, and my small birch rolling pin which I bought in the Samarkand, Uzbekistan market for 50 cents. A spaetzle maker for East European tiny dumplings; small and large ravioli molds, dariole molds, cornet molds, and a set of biscuit cutters in graduated sizes. A nutmeg grinder, wooden reamer, zester, and a corer. Also a pizza cutter and a paddle and baking tiles for the oven. Small and large scales, a Donvier ice cream maker in two sizes. Colorful plastic spray bottles for oils, recommended by Thomas Keller of the French Laundry, and my Russian wooden salt box and Welsh ceramic salt jar also give much pleasure. For serving, individual gratin dishes make a simple and lovely presentation, as do colorful platters, instead of bowls, with all the elements of your main course arranged according to color on one platter.

The finest ingredients and cooking equipment do not necessarily make fine cooking, as the proper techniques are de rigueur. These techniques can be applied to simple bourgeoisie cooking as well as haute cuisine.

TECHNIQUES

Reductions and Deglazing – These French techniques are of the utmost importance, and are crucial to the flavor of a dish. Whenever there is too much liquid in a pot of soup or stew, simply cook rapidly to reduce and thus concentrate the liquid, removing any solids which might overcook. If there is too little liquid add a bit more stock, cream, or wine—whatever is most appropriate. This also applies to sauces. When sautéed or roasted foods are removed from the pan, please do not discard these flavorful drippings, except the fat, for they are the true essence of the dish.

Simply add the appropriate liquid, and bring to a boil, scraping up every last bit in the 'dirty' pan (which so many of my students have accidentally washed out in the sink). This deglazing process provides you with a simple sauce, or it can become part of the sauce you may be preparing.

Roux – Contrary to the dictum of other chefs, I find that adding all the liquid at once to the butter and flour mixture, which is called a roux, and whisking until smooth and thickened, is much easier and provides a fool-proof and silky smooth sauce.

Flavor Enhancers – The extraneous parts of meat, poultry, fish, and produce contain the most flavor and should be stored in the freezer for making stocks and sauces. These parts include bones, shellfish shells, citrus zest, parsley stems, and the rinds of hard cheeses.

Reserve pasta water for adding to the sauce to thicken as well as loosen it, reserve potato cooking water for adding to mashed potatoes, and reserve water used for soaking and cooking dried chestnuts to add as part of the liquid in the recipe at hand. Also, keep for later use in innumerable ways. The true flavor of fish is best retained by cooking it in its own habitat, water. This is done by adding fillets to a pan of boiling water, then setting it aside for about 5 minutes. Large fish should be poached slowly. Also, fish of any size can be wrapped in leaves such as romaine, collard, chard, etc., then grilled or baked. Alain Ducasse has a unique technique which is simply placing the fillets between 2 plates, with desired seasonings, and steaming it over a pan of boiling water. It does not lose any of its juices, as it is enclosed between 2 plates. And, do remember to reduce the juices left in the plate for a simple but flavorful sauce. Swirl a bit of butter into sauce to emulsify. For better flavor, toast nuts and spices in an iron skillet or in the oven. Yeast doughs have better flavor if they rise slowly. So I put the metal bowl of dough on the counter underneath an electric lamp. A piano lamp is ideal, and lamps on the counter add an undeniable charm to your kitchen. An added bonus!

We all know that salting your food before sautéing adds flavor, but it is better to add the salt to the pan as it prevents sticking. As we all know, salt brings out the flavor in food, and indeed, is the favorite ingredient of the French Laundry's unsurpassed Thomas Keller. For a most flavorful roast chicken, simply season it well, inside and out, with kosher salt and French gray pepper. Refrigerate overnight.

The Scandinavian method of roasting beef, veal, and lamb shoulders or rounds is my favorite, as these cuts, although less tender, are the most flavorful. After seasoning, roast on a rack, uncovered, at about 375° until browned, then add appropriate liquid, cover, and roast at 320° until tender. If more browning is needed, roast uncovered, a few minutes more.

Country ham, probably the most delicious of all meats, and a great substitute for prosciutto, is undoubtedly the most difficult to cook without drying it out. A long and slow braising in a huge lard can filled with water and covered is a good method, but you need a big, strong man to carry out and empty all those gallons of greasy water. After trying many more methods, I finally discovered the best, recommended by Burgers' Ozark in California, Missouri. No matter what method you use, cover with cold water and soak overnight to remove excess salt. It may need to soak up to 48 hours, depending on your taste. But be careful not to remove too much salt. Scrub well with a brush and remove hock (to cook collards, of course). Place ham in a roaster on a rack, and half fill with water and a cup of brown sugar, honey, or sorghum. Cover, and cook slowly on bottom shelf of oven at 250°, about 20 minutes per pound. I usually cook a 15-pound ham about 5 hours. Remove skin and allow to cool in liquid, even overnight, as long as 18 hours. This kind of ham does not easily spoil. Pull out bones, remove skin and most fat, and score. Place on a large stainless steel platter, and cover with a paste made with 1 cup brown sugar, 2 tablespoons vinegar, and 1 or 2 tablespoons Honey Dijon mustard. Stick with cloves, and bake at 375° about 15 minutes until glazed. Cover loosely and refrigerate, freezing after a couple of months. Slices should be cut thinly and perpendicular to the bone. It is great having this ham for a multitude of purposes year-round.

What do you do if you don't want to bake a huge gratin, cake, or whatever, for a dozen people, yet you are craving it? Use this simple chart, which was figured by the 'pie' method (not my kind of pie), and you can convert pan sizes with ease. To convert from round to rectangular, or vice-versa, simply compare square inches. You can make as little as you wish with this method.

7-inch round pan- 38 square inches

8-inch round pan- 50 square inches

9-inch round pan- 63 square inches

10-inch round pan- 78 square inches

11-inch round pan- 95 square inches.

Also contrary to the dictum of other chefs is my method of mixing ground meats or vegetables with the remaining ingredients. For meatballs, for instance, I whisk the egg, then mix in all but the meat. When thoroughly blended, I mix in the meat, which is a much better way to distribute the flavors evenly. When caramelizing onions, which brings out the flavor, I always add a pinch or more of sugar, as this helps the caramelization, and if there are a lot of onions, I also add a little water, cover the pan, and get it off to a fast start, always uncovering it until it turns golden brown and the water has evaporated. A bit of sugar is always added to peas, in the French style, and brings out the flavor in other vegetables as well.

I use a meat hammer for cracking olives in order to pit them, retaining their shape and juices. I also use it for crushing garlic cloves, either slightly to use whole in oven-drying tomatoes and other procedures, or completely, in lieu of a garlic press. A bit of salt or oil on the counter prevents flying garlic and promotes pulverizing.

The old-fashioned method of making shirred eggs is by far the best way to poach eggs, and other ingredients, such as ham or cheese, can be added to the eggs. I simply butter or oil custard cups or other heat-proof individual dishes to hold 1 or 2 eggs. Add desired seasonings; place them in a shallow pan of boiling water, cover, and let cook until done to your liking. Loosen edges with a knife, and invert. None of the flavor is lost in the water.

I always use 2 buttered iron skillets, 1 larger than the other, for making crêpes. Start with the smaller skillet, and when the crêpe is cooked on the bottom, invert it into the larger skillet to cook on the other side. This method takes half the time.

When slicing celery, carrots, zucchini, etc., always make diagonal slices, as the broader surface will lessen cooking time, thus retaining more flavor. A chiffonade of greens—collards, chard, cabbage, lettuce, etc.—is more pleasing to the eye and cooks more evenly. Simply roll up stacked leaves, and slice.

France

FRANCE

La belle France, the queen of cuisine and a symbol of elegance and all the hedonistic pleasures of life, is the ideal prelude to a culinary tour of the world; but it is imperative that one understands the French mentality, especially that of the Parisian, in order to fully appreciate its splendors. The French are a very proud and distinguished people; therefore, an interest and a basic understanding of their language, food, and wine will assure you a very warm welcome. The warm compassion and generous hospitality that I have received will never be forgotten.

Paris is noted for its culinary refinement and haute cuisine, which are the raison d'être for the Michelin three-star restaurants, the world's greatest. It should be noted that three stars from Michelin are equal or superior to any other rating of four or five stars, as everything from the grounds and the bathrooms to the decor, service, and food must be exemplary. There are rarely more than twenty-two in the entire country. Recently, however, Raymond Sokolov, a renowned Parisian food writer, stated in the International Herald Tribune, "At Least We Still Have Paris." This was in reference to the sometimes ludicrous fusion cuisine that is gripping Paris.

There is a vast range of cooking styles from the English Channel to the Mediterranean, and they have also been influenced by fusion cooking. Home cooking, however, is still quite simple, although French women have access to the finest boucheries, boulangeries, and pâtisseries. As Simone Beck once told me, French women think they were born knowing how to cook, yet microwaves and frozen foods are as much a part of their kitchens as in America.

Alsace, decidedly German, is one of the most scenic areas in

France, especially the quaint wine villages of Ammerschwir, Ribeauville, and Riquewihr. The robust cooking emphasizes pork products, potatoes, sauerkraut, and foie gras, which can equal that of the Périgord in the Southwest. Munster cheese, the best beer, and excellent wines, which are made mainly from Riesling, Sylvaner, Traminer, and Gewurtztraminer, are excellent companions for the rich, hearty food. They are unique among French wines in that their labels do not designate them by vineyard or village names, but by their grape varieties. This is a result of their vineyards having been planted with poor grape varieties by the Germans during their rule. A wine trip through the quaint Alsatian villages is a quintessential experience for the dedicated oenophile, who will find that the German influence penetrates the art, dialect, architecture, family names, and the people as well.

Franche-Comté shares the Jura Mountains with Switzerland and is known for its Kirsch, made from the local cherries. It also specializes in superb omelets, freshwater fish, and the finest mushroom species, cèpes and morilles, along with Savoie, the breathtaking province in the Alps. Savoie produces Reblochon, one of the greatest of all cheeses. Au gratin potatoes had their origin in Savoyarde cooking and also in the Dauphiné. The legendary liqueur, Chartreuse, based on a monk's secret recipe using more than 100 herbs, is still made near Grenoble.

Burgundy is the culinary heartland of France in a two-fold manner, as it produces the finest cooking ingredients and the greatest chefs. Also, Dijon and Lyons are foremost gastronomical centers. Dijon is the home of the world-renowned mustard, made by Grey Poupon since the fourth century, and also Kir, the celebrated aperitif. Historical Beaune, the center of Burgundian wine trade, is noted for its Hospice de Beaune and its famous annual wine auction. Vezelay, a nearby hill town founded by Benedictine monks in the ninth century, is known as the most beautiful village in France.

Among the highlights of the Burgundian table are Bresse chickens, which are fattened on corn, Charrolais, escargots, and, of course, its superior wines. Burgundy has a history of 2,500 years of winemaking, and its best wines are produced in the four major districts of Chablis, Côte d'Or, Beaujolais, and Côtes du Rhone. The major grapes are Pinot Noir for the reds and Chardonnay and Pinot Blanc for the whites.

Chablis produces a dry and flinty wine that is the connoisseur's choice for serving with oysters and shellfish.

The Côte d'Or produces the greatest Burgundian wines, and if you follow the "Route des Grands Crus" which begins in Gevrey-Chambertin, as I did when conducting French wine tours, you can visit the greatest vineyards. Among them are Chambertin, Napoleon's favorite, and Clos de Vougeot, which is the home of the Confrerie des Chevaliers du Tastevin. Madame Pompadour's favorite, Romanée-Conti, is the "queen of Burgundy" and is one of the world's most expensive wines. It was one of the last to succumb to phylloxera, the devastating root disease which almost wiped out the wine industry in the nineteenth century. The grafting of American stock to the French vines saved the vineyards, and it is for this reason that the Burgundians have an especially warm camaraderie with Americans. The most famous whites of the Côte d'Or are Corton-Charlemagne, Montrachet, and Meursault.

Before entering the adjacent Beaujolais area, you should sample Marc de Bourgogne, a byproduct of wine made from the remaining pulp and stems after fermenting the wine. The best I've had was the very special forty-year-old Marc which Madame Terrail so graciously shared with me at her restaurant, L'Escargot-Montorgueil, in Paris, a perfect example of the aforementioned hospitality which I have received in Paris.

Beaujolais wines are produced from the Gamay grape and mature in less than three years. Moulin-à-Vent, the "king of Beaujolais," is the heaviest of the nine grands crus. The others are Brouilly, Fleurie, known as the "queen of Beaujolais," Morgon, Julienas, which was named after Caesar, St. Amour, Chenas, Chiroubles, and Côte de Brouilly.

The firm, fruity wines of the Côtes du Rhone, between Lyons and Avignon, are mostly blended and vintages are not important. Most are not exported because so little is produced, due to the steep hillside plantings on the banks of the Rhone River.

Vienne, the home of the late, great Fernand Point, produces Côte Rotie (roasted slope), a rich, full-bodied red which ages well, and is made from the Syrah grape, introduced by the Crusaders. I can still taste the truffles and raspberries emanating from this wine at the magnificent dinner which Point prepared for us. Château Grillet, made from viognier grapes, is 300 years old, comprises only four acres, and is considered one of the five greatest whites in France.

The Hermitage vineyards in Tain produce reds and whites, dating back to the tenth century, and they were popular with Louis XIV and the Russian czars. The wine firms of Chapoutier and Jaboulet provided me and my group with a memorable lunch and hospitality as warm as their wines. In the Avignon area, Châteauneuf-du-Pape is the Rhône wine best known to Americans and is the largest vineyard. It was favored by Thomas Jefferson. Nearby Tavel produces one of the best rosés from Grenache grapes. It is best chilled and is a good aperitif, as is Lirac, another good local rosé.

Provence, fondly known to the French as the Midi, is so named because the Romans thought it to be like their own provinces, whereas Cologne, Germany received its name from them because they considered it a foreign colony. The Midi has an intense Italianate flavor in its language, cooking, and people, who exhibit much joie de vivre.

The highly seasoned cooking is redolent with garlic, fresh herbs, tomatoes, and olive oil, which was introduced by the Greeks 2,000 years ago. Ratatouille, Salade Nicoise, aioli, and Bouillabaisse (the culinary controversy of Marseille, the oldest city in France) are synonymous with Provence. Cassis, produced nearby, is the finest rosé of the Côte Azure, and is not to be confused with the liqueur of the same name from Dijon.

The Languedoc region, west of the Côte d'Azur, is known for its Cassoulet, which has many versions and is the perfect food for the lusty red wines grown in the vicinity of Castelnaudary and Carcassone. The latter was founded by the Romans in 2 B.C. and has an impressive walled city by the name of La Cité.

The Basque country in the southwest corner of France is the most idyllic and unspoiled part of the entire country, and is home to the best cooks in Europe. Wedged between the Pyrenees and the Bay of Biscay, which is a gulf of the North Atlantic, the Basque country yields the finest dairy products, produce, seafood, poultry, and many varieties of meat and game. The cooking is similar to the Spanish side of the Basque country, both of which feature potatoes much more than rice. There are no significant wines, but Bordeaux is just up the road.

The province of Bordeaux, once known as Aquitania, was under English rule for 300 years as a result of the marriage of Eleanor and Henry II of England. Its aristocratic wines are more legendary than its cuisine, but there is now a surge in gastronomical interest and an even greater appreciation of the astounding riches of the countryside. Consider the Marennes oysters from Arachon, lamprey, lamb from the nearby Auvergne, ortolans, cèpes, roquefort from Rouergue, and of course, Périgord's truffles and foie gras, the ultimate delicacies of the conoisseur.

The two- to three-pound foie gras, or fat liver, is a product of the Périgord goose which endures several weeks of force-feeding on corn before its demise. The remainder of the goose is highly prized for its meat, which is used for unctuous confit, the ancient process of preserving salted meat in its rendered fat. This most delicious of all fats is the cornerstone of much of the cooking of Bordeaux. And the goose down will fill your comforter as you drift off to sleep after your marvelous dinner.

Truffles, those mysterious "black diamonds," are one of the world's costliest foods. They are underground fungi which grow near the roots of oak and other trees, where they are rooted up by dogs and pigs from November to March. Their most notable uses are for the classic dishes Poularde Demi-Deuil, Tournedos Rossini, Sauce Périgourdine, and of course truffled foie gras.

Bordeaux, the most aristocratic of all wines, has been produced since the third century when the Romans planted the first vines. Bordeaux is double the size of Burgundy, but it has half as many wine growers, and it produces one third of all Appellation d'Origine Contrôlée wines, which are highly regulated by the A.O.C., a governmental agency formed in 1935. The most famous are Château Lafite, Château Margaux, Château Latour, Château Haut-Brion, Château d'Yquem, and Château Mouton-Rothschild.

Bordeaux is divided into five major districts, of which the Medoc is the largest and most renowned. The regal Cabernet Sauvignon grape produces subtle, smooth, and mellow wines. The Medoc is the home of Lafite, Margaux, Latour, and Mouton-Rothschild.

Graves produces Haut-Brion, formerly owned by Talleyrand, the great gastronome, and is the best white in Bordeaux. Semillon and Sauvignon are the grapes for this noble wine.

Sautérnes produces the world's best sweet wine, Château d'Yquem. This elegant wine is produced by "noble rot," which is a result of leaving the grapes on the vine until they shrivel, thereby reducing the liquid content and concentrating the sugar.

Tiny St. Émilion produces the fullest and richest reds; they are as earthy as Burgundy, and apropos to bourgeoisie dishes. Château Ausone and Château Cheval-Blanc are designated as premiers crus.

Pomerol, even smaller than St. Émilion, is known for outstanding Château Petrus, and was one of the first known wines in France.

Brandy is a distillation of wine, and only those brandies produced in the area of the town of Cognac may be called Cognac. It has superior finesse due to its long aging in Limousin oak casks. The tannin imparted by this wood produces the mellowness and dark color which is a criterion for Cognacs.

The Touraine, in the Loire Valley, is the "garden of France," as it produces the finest asparagus, artichokes, peaches, prunes, table grapes, and walnuts. The Loire, the longest river in France, provides Tourangeau kitchens with a multitude of fresh fish. The Loire Valley is the oldest civilized area in France and the site of Château de Chenonceaux, the lividly historical setting for Henry II, Diane de Poitiers, and Catherine de Médicis, who was responsible for introducing Italian culinary art to France. It is known not only for its majestic castles but for the best vins du pays in the entire country.

The best wines are Pouilly Fumé, made from the Sauvignon Blanc grape, and Sancerre, Hemingway's favorite, and similar to a white Burgundy. The town of Sancerre is also noted for its outstanding chèvre.

Muscadet, produced both in the Loire Valley and in neighboring Brittany, is named for its grape, and is a light and refreshing wine that is best drunk young with seafood. It is the only A.O.C. wine in Brittany, where the center of wine production is near the ancient capital of Nantes.

Brittany, on the rugged English Channel and the Atlantic, is blessed with an incredible array of seafood, including salmon, perch, pike, lobster, oysters, mussels, and crab. The fertile farmland produces vegetables that rival those of the Loire Valley, and also cabbage, potatoes, and beans to prepare the hearty dishes inspired by the Celts who evangelized the country and gave it its name.

Neighboring Normandy, also on the Channel, is best known for its cider, butter, crème fraîche, and Calvados, an exceptional apple brandy. Among its prized cheeses are Camembert, Pont-l'Evéque, and Neufchâtel.

Champagne, the northernmost of all wine regions, produces the most famous and elegant of all wines. This celebrated libation came into vogue during the gay '90s in Paris. Technically, if not legally, sparkling wine is not entitled to the name of Champagne unless it is produced in the area of Reims and Épernay in the province of Champagne.

Champagne is a blend of both red and white grapes, Pinot Chardonnay and Pinot Noir, as well as a blend of various vintages. The most highly esteemed champagnes are Bollinger, Taittinger, Charles Heidsieck, Piper Heidseick, Krug, Moët & Chandon, and Mumm. They are labeled as Brut, Extra Dry, and Sec, the former being the driest and most expensive. Dom Pérignon, the Benedictine monk, is considered to be the father of champagne making.

RECIPES FROM FRANCE

MEDALLIONS OF AVOCADO WITH TUNA AND LEMON VINAIGRETTE

ZEN RADISH CANAPES

CASSOLETTE D'ESCARGOTS PROVENÇALE

WILD MUSHROOMS AND ESCARGOTS EN CRÔUTE

PALMIERS WITH PROSCIUTTO

BARQUETTES DE CHÈVRE

HERBED CHÈVRE

CHIFFONADE DES FRUITS DE MER (SHELLFISH WITH ROMAINE)

ROASTED RED AND YELLOW TOMATOES WITH CAVIAR, POTATO PURÉE, AND ROASTED SHALLOT VINAIGRETTE

GALETTE DE MESCLUN, TOMATO CONFIT, AND CHÈVRE

OMELETTE BASQUAISE

SOUFFLÉ AU CHÈVRE SUR LE PLAT (CHÈVRE SOUFFLÉ ON A PLATTER)

SOUFFLÉ DE GRENOUILLES (FROG LEGS SOUFFLÉ)

PASTA AU CAVIAR

FETTUCCINE AND SCALLOPS WITH VANILLA CHARDONNAY SAUCE

FETTUCCINE VERDE WITH GRAND MARNIER SAUCE

RAVIOLIS DE CHÈVRE AU SAUCE BASILIQUE (RAVIOLI WITH CHÈVRE AND BASIL SAUCE)

SHRIMP BISQUE

SOUPE EN CRÔUTE À LA BOCUSE

FONDUE DE POULARDE AU PISTOU (BRAISED CHICKEN WITH VEGETABLES AND BASIL)

SOUPE AU PISTOU (PROVENÇALE VEGETABLE SOUP WITH BASIL)

CREAM OF ARTICHOKE SOUP

CREAMY CHESTNUT SOUP WITH MADEIRA

BAGUETTES À LA FRANÇAISE

PAN BAGNAT (TUNA AND VEGETABLE SANDWICH NICOISE)

CLASSIC VINAIGRETTE

SALADE DE POMMES DE TERRE À LA CRÈME DE CAVIAR
(POTATO SALAD WITH CAVIAR CREAM)

SALADE DES TOMATES PROVENÇALE

SALADE DES CRUDITIES (RAW VEGETABLE SALAD)

SALADE DE PIGEON

WARM BACON AND EGG SALAD

SALADE ALSACIENNE

SEA SCALLOPS WITH LETTUCE SAUCE À LA BOYER

FISH FILLETS WITH TOMATO BUTTER À LA BOYER

FISH FILLETS WITH CURRY SAUCE À LA MERE BLANC

SOLE AUX NOUILLES ALSACIENNE

MARINATED TUNA STEAKS WITH BEET PURÉE

BAYONNE WRAPPED SALMON WITH ENDIVE MARMALADE

POACHED SALMON WITH GARLIC AND RED PEPPER SABAYON

SAUMON POCHÉ

POULET SAUTÉ CYNTHIA (SAUTÉED CHICKEN
WITH CHAMPAGNE SAUCE AND FRUIT)

SUPRÊMES AU SAUCE VINAIGRE CARAMELISSE (CHICKEN WITH
CARAMELIZED VINEGAR SAUCE)

SUPRÊMES AU SAUCE VERJUS (CHICKEN WITH GRAPE JUICE)

SUPRÊMES AU SAUCE POIVRONS ROUGE (CHICKEN
WITH ROASTED BELL PEPPER SAUCE)

POULET GRILLÉ AUX HERBES PROVENÇALE
(GRILLÉD CHICKEN WITH PROVENÇALE HERBS)

POULET BRAISÉE À LA CRÈME D'ESTRAGON
(BRAISED CHICKEN WITH TARRAGON CREAM)

POULET À LA BIÉRE D'ALSACE (ALSATIAN CHICKEN WITH BEER)

POULET RÔTI AUX HERBES ET SAUCE DE VEAU ET LIMON
(ROAST CHICKEN WITH HERBS AND LEMON VEAL SAUCE)

MAGRETS AUX RAGOUT DES CHAMPIGNONS
(DUCK WITH MUSHROOM RAGOUT)

CONFIT DE CANARD (PRESERVED DUCK)

DAUBE DE BOEUF PROVENÇALE (PROVENÇALE BEEF STEW)

ENTRECÔTE DE BOEUF AU SAUCE ROQUEFORT
(RIBEYE STEAK WITH ROQUEFORT SAUCE)

BIFTECK À LA CHEVAL (STEAK WITH EGGS)

AU PESTO DE NOIX (VEAL STEW WITH NUTS)

SCALLOPS DE VEAU EN CHEMISE
(VEAL SCALLOPS WRAPPED IN CRÊPES)

FOIE DE VEAU ROTI (ROASTED CALF LIVER)

NOISETTES D'AGNEAU À LA TRUFFE ET POMMES SAUTÉ
(NUGGETS OF LAMB WITH TRUFFLE OIL AND POTATOES)

SAUTÉ D'AGNEAU PROVENÇALE (PROVENÇALE LAMB SAUTÉ)

CASSOULET BOURGEOISE

CHOUCRÔUTE GARNI ALSACIENNE

STUFATU CON MACCHERONI
(CORSICAN MEAT STEW WITH MACARONI)

CIVET DE PORC ET PRUNEAUX (PORK STEW WITH PRUNES)

PORC CARAMELISÉ À LA BASQUAISE

SAUCE ESPAGNOLE (BROWN SAUCE)

SAUCE DEMI-GLACE (BROWN SAUCE REDUCTION)

SAUCE DEMI-GLACE AU CRÈME

GLACE DE VIANDE (MEAT GLAZE)

SAVORY SAUCE CARAMEL À L'ORANGE

SAVORY SAUCE CARAMEL AU CASSIS

SAUCE BASQUAISE

COULIS DE TOMATE (TOMATO SAUCE)

TAPENADE (OLIVE PASTE)

AIOLI (PROVENÇALE MAYONNAISE)

BEURRE BLANC (WHITE BUTTER SAUCE)

BEURRE BLANC ORIENTALE (ORIENTAL BUTTER SAUCE)

BEURRE BLANC À L'ORANGE (ORANGE BUTTER SAUCE)

SAUCE HOLLANDAISE

CRÈME FRAÎCHE

POMMES DE TERRE MACAIRE (SAUTÉED POTATO CAKES)

POMMES DE TERRE SAUTÉE DORDOGNE
(SAUTÉED POTATOES WITH DUCK FAT)

PURÉE OF POTATOES AND BEETS

MACARONI ET FROMAGE AUX CHAMPIGNONS
(MACARONI AND CHEESE WITH WILD MUSHROOMS)

LE PUY LENTILS

GRATIN OF PUMPKIN OR BUTTERNUT

RATATOUILLE PROVENÇALE

TOMATO CONFIT (OVEN-DRIEDTOMATOES)

SORBET CASSIS

SORBET FRAMBOISE (RASPBERRY SORBET)

SORBET AU CHOCOLAT

SORBET PRUNEAUX (PRUNE SORBET)

GLACE AU PISTACHE (PISTACHIO ICE CREAM)

GLACE CARAMEL AU PRALINÉE (CARAMELIZED NUT ICE CREAM)

GÂTEAU MARJOLAINE (MERINGUE CAKE WITH
CHOCOLATE CREAM AND CARAMELIZED NUT CREAM)

LE VACHERIN GLACE AU CITRON (FROZEN LEMON MERINGUE TORTE)

GENOISE (FRENCH SPONGE CAKE)

GÂTEAU AU FRAISES (STRAWBERRY CREAM CAKE)

GÂTEAU AU MOUSSE AU CHOCOLAT (CHOCOLATE MOUSSE CAKE)

PÂTE FEUILLETÉE RAPIDE (RAPID PUFF PASTRY)

CORNETS DE CRÈME (PUFF PASTRY HORNS WITH CREAM)

PALMIERS (PUFF PASTRY PALM LEAVES)

TARTE KIWIS ET FRAISES (KIWI AND STRAWBERRY TART)

MILLEFEUILLE AU CITRON ET PRUNEAUX
(NAPOLEON WITH LEMON AND PRUNES)

TORTE FRANÇAIS

PÂTE SUCRÉE (SWEET FRENCH PASTRY)

TARTES AU CITRON (LEMON TARTS)

TARTE DE NOIX CARAMELISÉ AU CHOCOLAT
(CARAMELIZED NUT AND CHOCOLATE TART)

GALETTES AUX TROIS PRUNEAUX (PASTRY WITH PLUMS)

GALLETTES AUX FIGUES ET FRAMBOISE
(PASTRY WITH FIGS AND RASPBERRIES)

POIRES BELLE DIJONNAISE
(PEARS WITH RASPBERRIES AND SORBET CASSIS)

COUPE AUX MARRONS (VANILLA ICE CREAM AND CHOCOLATE SORBET WITH CANDIED CHESTNUTS)

MARQUISE DE CHOCOLAT
(RICH CHOCOLATE MOLD WITH CRÈME ANGLAISE)

CHOUX-ECLAIRS-SALAMBOS (CREAM PUFFS AND ECLAIRS)

TRUFFES AU CHOCOLAT (CHOCOLATE TRUFFLES)

LEMON CURD

CHOCOLATE BUTTERCREAM FROSTING

CRÈME PÂTISSIÈRE (FRENCH PASTRY CREAM)

FONDANT

GLACE ROYAL (ROYAL ICING)

PRALINÉE AUX NOIX (CARAMELIZED NUT POWDER)

CRÈME CHANTILLY (FLAVORED WHIPPED CREAM)

CRÈME ANGLAISE (ENGLISH CUSTARD SAUCE)

SAUCE FRAMBOISE (RASPBERRY SAUCE)

FIRST COURSES

There is a renaissance of first courses taking place in today's French restaurants, both in France and in other countries. Foie gras will always be the piéce de resistance, but the heavy patés and an excess of butter and crème fraîche are being replaced by amuse-bouches and amuse-gueles, those delightful palate teasers being designed by creative chefs.

MEDALLIONS OF AVOCADO WITH LEMON TUNA

It was a scorching hot day in August 2003, said to be the hottest on record, when I walked 45 minutes to Joël Robuchon's new restaurant, L'Atelier, on the left bank in Paris. After a not-too-brief hiatus since the closing of his magnificent three-star Jamin, Chef Robuchon is once again one of the top players to contend with in the culinary world. This trendy 37-seat counter restaurant, around an open kitchen, offers a creative menu of small plates, and my culinary reward for the long hot walk was this beautifully presented and versatile dish. It may be a starter, salad, or main course. This is my version.

2 small Hass avocados, peeled, pitted, and sliced vertically	1 small can Albacore white tuna, drained and flaked, or ¾ cup flaked crabmeat
3 tablespoons olive oil	
1 tablespoon lemon juice	Watercress leaves & catsup
½ teaspoon sugar	Salt & pepper

Discard outer slices of avocado, and arrange 3 slightly overlapping slices in center of each of 4 plates, with each slice covering the tapered end. Whisk vinaigrette ingredients together, and nap avocados lightly. Mix remaining into tuna. Place a small 1- to 1.5-inch diameter cutter in center of each avocado slice, and fill with tuna, pressing firmly. Garnish plate with small drops of catsup and a scattering of watercress leaves.

Serves 4.

ZEN RADISH CANAPES

This is a beautiful and sophisticated version of the favorite lunch in the bourgeoisie French countryside. Try the baguette and rye slices together.

1 baguette, sliced diagonally, ¼ inch sliced thick, or 24 slices snack rye bread 2-3 dozen radishes, trimmed, and thinly sliced lengthwise	Chopped chives or dill Butter Fleur de Sel & gray pepper

Spread bread with butter, and arrange slightly overlapping slices on top, with each row in the opposite direction. Place on small plates or a large platter with tiny piles of chives or dill, and salt and pepper.

Makes about 2 dozen.

CASSOLETTE D'ESCARGOTS PROVENÇALE
(Provençale Escargot Casserole)

2 dozen escargots	2 tablespoons olive oil
½ cup dry white wine	1 large shallot, chopped
2 tablespoons chopped parsley	1 cup chiffonade of spinach
1 teaspoon grated orange zest	½ cup chiffonade of tender lettuce
2 garlic cloves, crushed	
1 shallot, minced	½ cup watercress leaves
1 bay leaf	¼ cup chopped parsley
¼ teaspoon each of basil, thyme, marjoram, and tarragon	Salt and pepper
	2 tablespoons butter
2 tablespoons diced bacon	2 tablespoons chopped almonds

Mix ½ cup liquid from canned escargots with wine and seasonings, simmer 10 minutes, add escargots, and marinate overnight. Sauté bacon until fat is rendered, add olive oil, shallot, greens, and seasonings. Cover, and let braise about 20 minutes. Remove escargots from marinade, reduce to 1/3 cup, and add to green sauce with escargots, butter, and almonds. Serve hot in small ramekins or in puff pastry shells.

Serves 4-6.

WILD MUSHROOMS AND ESCARGOTS EN CRÔUTE

Another of my favorite escargots recipes, which can be served as in the previous recipe, or on thin slices of toasted French bread, or in this pastry case with sides. A very elegant beginning.

6 ounces wild mushrooms, sliced	2 dozen escargots
3 or 4 shallots, sliced	½ cup crème fraîche
2 tablespoons butter or olive oil	2 tablespoons Glace de Viande
2 tablespoons Marsala or sherry	Salt & pepper, to taste
¾ cup finely chopped herbs (thyme, chives, chervil, parsley, etc.)	1 pound Puff Pastry (see index)

Sauté mushrooms and shallots in butter or oil until tender. Deglaze with marsala, then add herbs, escargots, cream, and seasonings. Cook briskly until thickened, and serve in the following pastry cases. Roll pastry into a rectangle about 1/8-inch thick, and cut 6 ½-inch strips from the long sides, and 4 ½-inch strips from the short sides, using a pastry wheel. Cut remaining pastry into 6 rectangles, about 3 x 4 inches. Brush edges of pastry with cold water, and form a border by pressing strips, cut to fit, around the edges of the rectangles. Prick bottom of rectangles to prevent puffing, and bake at 425° about 20 minutes, or until golden.

Serves 6.

PALMIERS WITH PROSCIUTTO
(Puff Pastry with Prosciutto)

This savory pastry is a version of the dessert that is sprinkled with sugar, then baked. The shape resembles a palm frond. These are great with aperitifs.

1 sheet puff pastry (see index)	1 cup parmesan cheese
3 tablespoons honey mustard	1 egg
4 ounces thinly sliced prosciutto	2 teaspoons water

Roll out a sheet of puff pastry 1/8-inch thick and 18 x 11 inches. Spread with mustard, arrange prosciutto evenly over surface, and sprinkle with parmesan. Press cheese with rolling pin to make it adhere, and roll up each long side toward the center until they meet. With a serrated knife, cut into ½-inch slices, place on a baking sheet, press lightly to flatten, and chill. Brush with the egg and water wash, and bake at 400° about 10 minutes, or until golden brown.

Makes 20 palmiers.

BARQUETTES DE CHÈVRE
(Puff Pastry Tarts with Chèvre)

Barquette molds are elongated oval shapes and are lined with pastry, baked, and filled with both savory and sweet mixtures. Filled with small vegetables, they are a nice garniture for entree platters, or they can be filled with various cold mixtures and passed as an hors d'oeuvres platter.

Puff Pastry (see index) or other pastry ½ pound chèvre or Roquefort	2 eggs 2 tablespoons cream 2 tablespoons minced basil or chives

Line 10-12 small barquette or other molds with your choice of pastry, and place extra molds over them to keep pastry in place, or line with foil. Bake at 425° about 10 minutes and remove liners. Blend cheese with eggs and cream in processor, add basil, and divide among shells. Bake at 350° until puffed and golden. Serve with red pepper marmalade poured around them, or top with the marmalade and pass as an hors d'oeuvres.

For Red Pepper Marmalade

1 red bell pepper, thinly julienned 2 shallots, thinly sliced 2 tablespoons olive oil 1 tablespoon butter	½ teaspoon Herbes de Provence 1 garlic clove, crushed ¼ cup julienned basil

Slowly sweat pepper and shallots in oil and butter, covered, about ½ hour, or until marmalade consistency. Add seasonings, and cool.

Serves 10-12.

HERBED CHÈVRE

A delicious and simple cheese spread from Leon de Lyon, the venerable Burgundian restaurant in Lyon. This was wonderful with the French bread and hot local sausages served with lentils de puys and warm potato salad.

4 ounces chevre	1 tablespoon olive oil
2 tablespoons chopped chives	½ tablespoon champagne vinegar
2 tablespoons chopped parsley	3-4 tablespoons cream
1 small shallot, minced	Salt & pepper, to taste

Whip all ingredients together with a mixer. Spread on Walnut or French bread.

Makes 1 cup.

CHIFFONADE DES FRUITS DE MER
(Shellfish with Romaine)

This is an elegant first course of shellfish with romaine chiffonade and an enlivened version of aioli, French mayonnaise

1 egg yolk	Salt & pepper
1 tablespoon Champagne vinegar	1 cup olive oil
2 teaspoons Dijon mustard	1 tablespoon lemon juice
1 tablespoon tomato paste	2 teaspoons brandy or Marsala
	½ teaspoon tarragon

1 cup cooked shrimp 1 cup cooked crabmeat or lobster	6 Romaine lettuce leaves, cut into fine ribbons (chiffonade) Concassé of 2 medium tomatoes

Blend yolk, vinegar, and seasonings in processor. Gradually add oil until thickened. Add juice, brandy, and tarragon. Fold in shellfish and romaine. Garnish top with concasse.

Serves 6.

ROASTED RED AND YELLOW TOMATOES WITH CAVIAR, POTATO PURÉE, AND ROASTED SHALLOT VINAIGRETTE

Chef Bernd Kessler, chef on a Seabourn cruise of the Red Sea, gave me this intriguing recipe which is representative of today's French cuisine.

3 shallots, peeled ½ cup olive oil 8 ounces Yukon potatoes, peeled, diced, and cooked 2-3 tablespoons cream Salt, pepper, and nutmeg 2 teaspoons rice vinegar	2 tablespoons chopped parsley ½ pint yellow cherry tomatoes ½ pint red cherry tomatoes 2 tablespoons osetra caviar 1 tablespoon chives, cut in 1-inch pieces

Roast shallots in oil at 375° at least an hour, until very soft. Meanwhile, mash potatoes with cream and seasonings, and keep warm. Remove shallots from oil, and slice thinly. Whisk 5 tablespoons of oil from shallots with rice vinegar, and add shallots and parsley. Place tomatoes in pan with remaining oil and roast at 375° until glazed and hot, about 10 minutes. Remove tomatoes and toss with caviar. Place some of potato purée in center of each of four plates, Spoon caviar tomatoes over each, and pour shallot vinaigrette around the plate. Top with the chives.

Serves 4.

GALETTE OF MESCLUN, TOMATO CONFIT, AND CHÈVRE

This stunning red, green, and white salad on a rich pastry galette is great for a Christmas buffet, or you can make individual galettes for a seated dinner.

½ pound Puff Pastry (see index), or other rich pastry	Salt & pepper, to taste
¼ pound mesclun	Tomato confit (see index), use about 1 cup plus several garlic cloves
2 tablespoons olive oil	
½ tablespoon Champagne vinegar	2 ounces chèvre, marinated
	Fresh thyme leaves or basil

Roll out pastry into a 10- or 12-inch circle, place on a baking sheet, and bake at 375° about 20 minutes or until golden brown. Cool, then toss mesclun with oil, vinegar, and seasonings. Arrange on pastry when ready to serve. Place tomato confit quarters in concentric circles, leaving space between them. Garnish with garlic confit, diced chèvre, and fresh herbs.

Serves 6-8.

Egg dishes are of paramount importance in France, but not for breakfast. Instead, they are elegant or bourgeoise first courses, and they frequently are main courses for light lunches or suppers, accompanied by a green salad.

Omelets are a delicious composite of the supreme products in the provinces. Normandy's omelets feature apples, butter, cream, and Calvados, while Savoy's feature potatoes, and Provence omelets feature tomatoes, garlic, basil, and olive oil. Any leftover escargots in my house are marinated in wine and herbs, then added to an omelet. Delicious!

OMELETTE BASQUAISE

After a long train ride from Carcassone I arrived in Biarritz on a dark and rainy night, looking forward to room service at Hotel du Palais, the elaborate summer palace built by Napoleon, on the edge of the savage waters of the Bay of Biscay. This wonderful omelet was my introduction to Basque cooking, the best of France. Prosciutto may be substituted for Bayonne, the renowned ham from the city of the same name just up the road from Biarritz.

¼ cup julienned Bayonne ham	Salt & pepper
2 tablespoons olive oil	3 tablespoons grated Idiazabal cheese
3 eggs	Minced parsley or other herbs

Sauté ham in olive oil over medium heat. Whisk eggs with seasonings add to skillet, and, shaking pan gently, lift edges and let uncooked portion run underneath. Sprinkle with cheese, fold, and slide onto a plate. Garnish with herbs. At the hotel, a huge serving of the most wonderful golden French Fries accompanied the omelet, which is traditional.

Serves 2

SOUFFLÉ AU CHÈVRE SUR LE PLAT

(Chèvre Soufflé on a Platter)

This is a great contemporary method of making soufflées, baking them on a platter.

1/3 cup ground walnuts or almonds	4 egg yolks
¼ cups of butter	Pinch of nutmeg and salt
¼ cup flour	4 egg whites
1 cup + 2 tablespoons milk	¼ teaspoon cream of tartar
3 ounces crumbled chèvre or Roquefort	1 ½ ounces crumbled chèvre or Roquefort

Brush a large oval stainless steel platter, about 16 to 18 inches long, with butter and sprinkle with nuts. Six individual soufflé dishes can be used instead. Make a roux with butter and flour, whisk in milk all at once, and cook until lightly thickened. Remove from heat, and whisk in cheese, yolks, and seasonings. Whisk whites until foamy, add cream of tartar, and whisk until stiff, but not dry. Fold part of whites into mixture, then gently fold in remainder. Pour onto platter, sprinkle with cheese, and bake at 450° about 10 minutes, or until puffed and golden.

Serves 6.

SOUFFLÉ DE GRENOUILLES
(Frog Leg Soufflé)

This soufflé is one of the best dishes I have had in Paris. It was my lunch at Le Grand Vefour, one of the oldest three-star Michelin restaurants, and one of the grandest, with opulent Directoire decor.

2 shallots, finely sliced	5 egg yolks
½ pound frog legs	5 egg whites, stiffly beaten
1 tablespoon butter	Salt & pepper
1/3 cup white wine	Sauce Poulette:
3 cups fish stock	2/3 cup fish stock
Bouquet Garni	2 tablespoons white wine
1/3 cup butter	3 egg yolks
1/3 cup flour	¾ cup cream
	Salt & Pepper

Sauté shallots and frog legs in butter about 5 minutes, add wine, reduce by half, and add stock and bouquet. Simmer until tender, about 5 minutes. Remove bones, and cut meat into dice. Strain stock, reserving 3 cups. Make a roux with flour and butter, add strained stock, and simmer until thickened. Whisk in yolks, and fold in whites. Butter and flour 8 individual soufflé dishes, fill about 2/3 full, place a layer of frog meat, then fill until 2/3 full. Bake at 475° about 10 minutes, and spoon a little sauce over each. To make sauce, bring stock and wine to a boil while whisking yolks and cream together. Whisk hot liquid into yolk and cream mixture, return to heat, and cook gently until thick. Season well. Serves 8.

PASTA

With the advent of nouvelle cuisine, pasta was incorporated more and more in-to the French diet. The following are quite elegant first courses.

PASTA AU CAVIAR

1 pound fettuccine, cooked	Grated zest of 2 large lemons
2 cups crème fraîche, or equal amounts crème & melted butter	Salt & Pepper
	1/3 cup caviar, or more

Drain pasta, and toss with crème and seasonings. Pass caviar (the best you can afford), spooning it onto the center of the pasta.

Serves 6-8.

FETTUCCINE AND SCALLOPS WITH VANILLA CHARDONNAY SAUCE

A delightful buttery pasta with tropical fruits and vanilla, typical of the fusion cuisine in Paris today.

1/3 cup Chardonnay	1 vanilla bean, halved lengthwise
3 tablespoons Champagne vinegar	1 cup cream
1/4 cup thinly sliced shallots	1/2 pound butter
1 bay leaf	Salt & pepper

1 pound sea scallops 1 tablespoon olive oil 1 tablespoon butter 1 pound fettuccine, cooked and drained	1 large mango, peeled and thinly sliced 1 avocado, peeled and thinly sliced

Reduce Chardonnay, vinegar, and seasonings by two-thirds. Add cream, reduce till thickened, and whisk in butter on low heat. Keep warm. Sauté scallops in oil and butter only until opaque. Strain sauce over pasta, arrange on plates, top with scallops, and fan slices of mango and avocado on top of pasta.

Serves 6-8.

FETTUCCINE VERDE WITH GRAND MARNIER SAUCE

2 or 3 oranges 3 tablespoons butter 1/3 cup orange juice 1 ¾ cup cream 1 teaspoon salt	¼ cup orange juice 1 or 2 tablespoons Grand Marnier ¾ pound green fettuccine, cooked Mint Sprigs

Julienne zest, and grate enough to equal 1 tablespoon. Cut pith from oranges, and cut into sections. Sauté grated zest in butter briefly, add juice, and reduce to a glaze. Add cream. Simmer until hot and slightly thickened. Add salt and whisk in juice and liqueur. Pour over drained noodles, and garnish with orange julienne and sections. Top with mint sprigs.

Serves 6-8.

RAVIOLIS DE CHÈVRE AU SAUCE BASILIQUE

(Ravioli with Chèvre and Basil Sauce)

This is an elegant ravioli which I savored at Michel Rostang in Paris. He is the son of Jo Rostang, whose celebrated restaurant, La Bonne Auberge, was the highlight of Antibes. For a first course, use ravioli molds that are about 1-inch square.

6 ounces chèvre	Sauce Basilique:
1 tablespoon cream	20 large basil leaves, blanched & refreshed
1 small egg	
1 tablespoon chopped basil	1 tablespoon white wine
Salt & pepper	2 cups cream, reduced by half
Pasta (see recipe)	2 tablespoons parmesan

Blend filling ingredients in processor, and chill. After rolling pasta, cut into 6 sheets, each a little longer than ravioli mold. Lay a sheet over mold, press gently in each pocket, and fill them with about 1 teaspoon filling. Brush all edges with cold water, lay another sheet on top, and roll firmly with rolling pin to cut them out. Invert on a towel and repeat. Boil in plenty of salted water about 5 minutes, and drain. To make sauce, purée basil with wine in processor, add to hot cream with cheese, season, and pour over hot ravioli. Garnish with small basil leaves.

Serves 6-8.

SOUPS

The quality of a French kitchen is determined by the talent of its saucier, whose domain is soups, as well as sauces, both integral parts of the typical French meal.

An essential caveat in making soup, if you are to avoid the insipid canned taste, is the preparation of excellent homemade stocks. A soup is no better than its base; therefore, I do not recommend bouillon cubes or canned stocks.

__SHRIMP BISQUE__

A shellfish bisque is a traditional, elegant prelude to a French dinner. Lobster can be substituted for the shrimp.

½ pound shrimp, unshelled	Bouquet Garni
3 tablespoons butter	2 tablespoons tomato paste
2 tablespoons brandy	1 cup white wine
½ cup chopped onion	3 cups fish stock
½ cup chopped celery	1 ½ cups veal stock
½ cup chopped carrot	2 egg yolks
1 large shallot, chopped	½ cup crème fraîche
1 garlic clove, crushed	Salt & pepper
	Chopped chervil, to garnish

Sauté shrimp in butter until pink, flame with brandy, and remove. Sauté vegetables until soft, add bouquet, paste, wine, and stocks. Shell shrimp, and add shells to pan, and simmer 30 minutes. Purée in processor, then press through a sieve, and reduce until lightened, as desired. Whisk yolks with cream, whisk gradually into soup, and return to a simmer. Season, add reserved shrimp, and garnish with fresh chervil.

Serves 6.

SOUPE EN CRÔUTE À LA BOCUSE

The most elegant of all soups, this is my version of Paul Bocuse's masterpiece, which was created for President Valery Giscard d'Estaing in 1975 when Bocuse was awarded the Legion d'Honneur. Bocuse is already a legend equal to Escoffier, and his restaurant, Paul Bocuse, in Lyon, is still worth a detour. This dramatic soup will be a spectacular debut for your dinner guests as it was for me when I savored my first meal chez Bocuse in 1975. The recipe is versatile in that any soup without eggs or thickening can be used with the pastry top, and 1 tablespoon truffle oil may be substituted.

¼ cup diced carrots	4 truffles, julienned (optional)
¼ cup diced celery	¼ pound foie gras, diced (optional)
¼ cup diced leeks	
¼ cup diced mushrooms	6 cups chicken or veal stock
2 tablespoons butter	½ cup white wine
1 ½ cups diced chicken breast	½ cup truffle liquid (optional)
½ cup diced country ham	1 ½ pounds Paté Feuilletée (see index)

Braise vegetables in butter until almost tender, about 10 minutes. Add chicken and ham, cooking about 5 minutes. Add remaining soup ingredients, and ladle about 1 ½ cups into each of 8 individual soup tureens, which should be about 4 inches in diameter, and have a capacity of 1 ½ cups. Allow to cool thoroughly. Roll out pastry about 1/8-inch thick, and cut out 8 rounds, 6 inches in diameter. Place over tureens, and press overhang against sides. Chill well, and bake at 400° for 15 to 20 minutes in the lower third of the oven, with the tureens placed on a baking sheet for easy removal. The traditional porcelain French tureens with small lion-head handles and lids are ovenproof, and I love mine for all kinds

of soups. They are quite impressive when served on a napkin, folded like an artichoke, and placed on a plate for presentation.
Serves 8.

FONDUE DE POULARDE AU PISTOU

(Braised Chicken with Vegetables and Basil)

This is my version of the signature dish of Georges Blanc, another great Burgundian chef, whose restaurant, Chez la Mère Blanc, has graced the countryside in Vonnas for many years. His charming rooms are a good reason to stay overnight. This recipe, created by Blanc's grandmother, can be modernized by substituting suprêmes for the whole chicken. Either way, it is outstanding. The term fondue, in this case, refers to the technique of braising vegetables, covered, very slowly until they "melt."

1 3- to 4-pound chicken, cut up	3 garlic cloves, crushed
Salt & pepper	¼ cup olive oil
12 small new potatoes	Concassé of ½ pound tomatoes (see index)
3 tablespoons olive oil	
4 cups chicken or veal stock	½ teaspoon powdered saffron
2 carrots, peeled and diced	1/3 cup torn basil
1 celery rib, diced	1 tablespoon Marsala or sherry
1 large leek, diced	¼ cup butter
1 medium onion, diced	Salt & pepper

Season chicken, sauté in oil until golden, add potatoes and stock, and simmer, covered about ½ hour, or until tender. Meanwhile, braise vegetables in oil very slowly, covered, until very soft. Add tomatoes and saffron, cooking until mixture thickens.

To finish the soup, cut chicken into bite-size pieces, discarding skin and bones. Degrease chicken stock, and add chicken meat, vegetables, basil, and Marsala. Simmer until hot, swirl in butter, and season.

Serves 6.

SOUPE AU PISTOU

A pungent and lively Mediterranean flavor pervades this hearty soup, which is similar to Italian Minestrone. It is highlighted by Pistou, the French version of the Genovese Pesto. I prefer it as a main course.

6 ounces dried pink beans, cooked	1 teaspoon powdered saffron
1 large leek, sliced	6-8 cups chicken stock or water
2 medium carrots, peeled & diced	½ cup small pasta or broken spaghetti
2 or 3 new potatoes, diced	Concassé of ½ pound tomatoes
¼ pound snap beans, broken in half	1-1 ½ cups fresh basil leaves
¼ ounces zucchini, sliced diagonally	¼ cup parsley
	5 or 6 garlic cloves, crushed
¼ cup olive oil	¼ cup olive oil
Salt & pepper	¼ cup Parmesan cheese

Sauté vegetables in oil 20 minutes, until oil is absorbed. Season well, add beans, stock, and pasta. Simmer about 15 minutes, adding about half of the tomatoes to the soup. Purée remaining tomatoes and ingredients in processor, and stir into soup just before serving. Serve with crusty baguettes.

Serves 6.

CREAM OF ARTICHOKE SOUP

This is my version of a modern version of Potage Parmentier, the classic potato and leek soup. Guy Savoy's three-star restaurant in Paris serves this elegant artichoke and Armagnac version.

6 baby artichokes	4 cups veal or chicken stock
2 large shallots, chopped	1 1/3 cups cream
2 celery ribs, chopped	¼ cup Armagnac or brandy
1 medium Yukon potato, peeled and chopped	Salt & Pepper
¼ cup butter	¼ cup walnuts or pistachios, toasted & chopped

Cut off top third of artichokes, and peel off leaves until yellow ones appear. Peel stems. Sauté with remaining vegetables in butter about 5 minutes, then remove artichokes, and cut into quarters, reserving 1 or 2 quarters for each bowl. Add remaining artichokes to vegetables and add stock, cover, and simmer until thickened, about ½ hour. Puree soup in processor, press through a sieve back into pan, add cream, brandy, and seasonings. Bring to a simmer, ladle into bowls, and garnish with nuts and artichoke quarters. Serves 6.

CREAMY CHESTNUT SOUP WITH MADEIRA

Chestnuts roasting over an open fire... This is an aromatic reality on the streets of New York and towns in France during the winter. They are also an earthy and sensuous ingredient in soups, sauces, vegetables dishes, and desserts. Usually found only during the holidays, they are now available year round in the dried form from Allen Creek Farms in Ridgefield, Washington. I love this creamy soup any time of year and have had this classic version in restaurants in Italy, France, and Spain, although the best was at Jean

Joho's very special Everest in Chicago. My version uses dried chestnuts, which has the advantage of using the soaking water in the recipe, and no peeling required!

8-9 ounces dried chestnuts, or 12 ounces vacuum-packed, or 1 pound fresh	3 juniper berries, crushed or ground
1 yellow onion, chopped	½ teaspoon cardamom or nutmeg
3 or 4 large shallots, chopped	2 quarts veal or chicken stock including reserved chestnut liquid
2 large celery ribs, diced	
2 apples, peeled, cored, and cubed	2/3 cup cream
1 teaspoon sugar	3 tablespoons Madeira
2 tablespoons butter, fat from duck confit, or olive oil	Salt & Pepper
	Truffle Oil (optional)
1 bay leaf	

Cover dried chestnuts with water, bring to a boil for about 10 minutes, then let soak for an hour, reserving the liquid. Sauté chestnuts, onion, shallots, celery, apples, and sugar in fat, using a large soup pot, until vegetables are soft. Add seasonings, stock (including chestnut water), and simmer, covered, about an hour, or until chestnuts are very soft.

Remove bay leaf, add cream, and purée with an immersion blender. Reduce if too thin, or add more cream or stock if too thick. Season with remaining ingredients as desired, and serve hot as a first course or a main course.

Serves 4 to 6.

BREADS OF FRANCE

France may not have many bread specialties, but who needs more than baguettes, croissants, and brioche? The latter two ephemeral delights are the pièce de resistance of the French petit dejeuner. I have consumed more croissants in France over the past three decades or so than I can count, but ironically, the best I've ever had were on a UTA flight to Tahiti. Formidable!

An important caveat in working with yeast is that you need not be a slave to the recipe, as you may delay the rising of a yeast dough by punching it down and refrigerating it if you are not ready to bake it when doubled, and actually a slower and cooler rising will develop more flavor. It is important, however, not to let the dough rise too much as the yeast will expend itself. Also, rich breads (with eggs, sugar, and fat) and lean breads (with water) are treated differently. Rich breads cannot tolerate much kneading because the gluten develops to the point that the flour will not absorb large amounts of butter, thus the butter will ooze out during baking. Traditionally, rich breads are glazed with a whole egg, or a yolk beaten with a little milk, and lean breads are simply brushed with water.

BAGUETTES

This wonderful, yet simple, recipe can be made into long, slender baguettes or large loaves, as well as into French rolls of any size.

1 tablespoon dry yeast	4 cups bread flour
1 ½ cups warm water	2 teaspoons salt
1 teaspoon sugar	

Mix yeast with water and sugar in mixer bowl, cover, and let stand 10 minutes or until foamy. Add flour and salt gradually, and knead with dough hook about 10 minutes or until smooth and elastic. Oil bowl, cover, and let rise in a warm place until double, about 1 hour. I find that placing the bowl underneath the table lamp on my counter is perfect for rising.

Divide dough in half, roll out into 2 ovals, and then roll up tightly. Place on a baking sheet, sprinkled with cornmeal, or preferably in a traditional black French bread pan with 2 valley-shaped sections. Either pan can be brushed with olive oil. Brush bread with water, slash top diagonally 3 or 4 times, cover, and let rise until doubled, about 1 ½ hours. Brush with cold water again, and bake at 425° about 15 to 20 minutes. Let cool on a rack before slicing.

Makes 2 baguettes.

PAN BAGNAT

(Tuna and Vegetable Sandwich Nicoise)

This is one of my favorite sandwiches and is a full-flavored Nicoise specialty found at food stalls and sidewalk cafes along the Côte d'Azur.

1/3 cup sliced mushrooms	2 Roma tomatoes, sliced, or ¾ cup oven-dried tomatoes (see index)
4-6 artichoke hearts, sliced	
1 tablespoon red wine vinegar	½ cup sliced Nicoise black olives
½ cup olive oil	
1 teaspoon salt	Capers
1 garlic clove, crushed	1 can white tuna
1 baguette or 4 French rolls halved lengthwise	Anchovies (optional)

Marinate mushrooms and artichoke slices in a vinaigrette made of the oil, vinegar, and seasonings about ½ hour. Drain, and brush the oil on all sides of the bread, using all of it. Layer the bottom half of the bread with the remaining ingredients, and top with remaining bread. Wrap in plastic, and let stand with a heavy weight on top for ½ hour. Enjoy!

Makes 2/4 servings.

SALADS

One of the most refreshing aspects of nouvelle cuisine was the proliferation of ingenious new salads, whereas formerly a variety of lettuces dressed with the same Vinaigrette was ubiquitous. Fruit vinegars became the rage and are still popular. As I always told my students, carefully choose your salad so that it will harmonize with your main course. For instance, do not use a garlicky dressing with a delicate dish, only with a robust one. While on the subject of salad dressings, the French proportions of four parts olive oil to one part vinegar is more palatable than three to one. This is a good example of the French school of thought that no one ingredient should dominate and overpower a dish. That is why chili peppers have not caught on. Thank God!

CLASSIC VINAIGRETTE

2 Tablespoons vinegar (see below)	1 teaspoon salt
1 teaspoon Dijon Mustard	6-8 tablespoons oil (see below)

Mix vinegar, mustard, and salt, then slowly whisk in oil to emulsify.

Vinegars

Champagne vinegar or white wine vinegar

Red wine vinegar

Sherry wine vinegar

Balsamic vinegar

Fruit vinegars

Walnut vinegar

Oils

Olive oil, extra virgin or pure

Walnut oil

Peanut oil

Truffle oil- black or white (1 or 2 teaspoons can be added to other oils)

SALADE DE POMMES DE TERRE À LA CRÈME DE CAVIAR
(Potato Salad with Caviar Cream)

A deliciously glorified potato salad from La Tour Rose in Lyon.

1 to 2 tablespoons lemon juice 1 cup cream 2 tablespoons caviar	18 very small new potatoes, unpeeled 3 cups chicken stock Boston or Bibb lettuce

Whisk juice into cream, and gently add caviar. Simmer potatoes in stock until tender, slice while warm, and arrange on lettuce. Top with dressing.

Serves 6.

SALADE DES TOMATES PROVENÇALE

(Tomato Salad Provençale)

This is the ultimate destiny for summer's finest sun-ripened tomatoes. Roger Verge created this at his Le Moulin De Mougins Restaurant.

6 medium tomatoes, cut into sixths	1 ½ tablespoon kosher salt
1/3 cup raspberry vinegar	Pepper, to taste
3 tablespoons olive oil	Torn fresh basil

Marinate tomatoes with all but basil about 2 hours, and drain. Add basil. Fruit vinegars can be made by adding about ¼ cup berries or diced fruit to 12 ounces Champagne vinegar and letting it stand 1 week or longer.

Serves 6.

SALADE DES CRUDITÉS

(Raw Vegetable Salad)

Crudités are the raw vegetables you usually use for dipping, but this recipe that I had in a tiny cafe perched on top of the village Eze won a handsome set of knives in a recipe contest which I entered.

¼ pound red cabbage, shredded	Concassé of 3 ripe Romas
1 medium beet, cooked, peeled, & julienned	1-2 small cucumbers, peeled, seeded, & julienned
3 small carrots, peeled & shredded	½ cup black Nicoise olives
1 bell pepper, any color, julienned	1 1/3 cups Vinaigrette (your choice)

Toss each vegetable with Vinaigrette separately, and arrange in alternating ribbons on a platter. Pour any remaining Vinaigrette over them, and serve.

Serves 6.

SALADE BAUMANIÈRE

Every French chef had his own version of salade composée during the '70s and '80s, but this was the best, even though not composed. I had this at the wonderful L'Oustau de Baumanière in Les Baux.

1 avocado, peeled & diced	1/3 cup raspberry vinaigrette
1 tomato, peeled & diced	1 head Bibb or Boston or Mesclun
6 artichoke hearts, halved	
8 white mushrooms, sliced	1 tablespoon lemon juice
½ cup diced country ham or prosciutto	½ cup crème fraîche

Toss vegetables and ham with vinaigrette, add lettuce, torn into large pieces. Whisk juice into cream, and serve separately.

Serves 6.

SALADE DE PIGEON

Bernard Loiseau, probably the greatest three-star chef of all and successor to the illustrious Alexandre Dumaine at La Côte d'Or in Saulieu, created this most delicious salad of all. Saulieu is a tiny village, which I reached by open-air train, followed by a long uphill walk to the restaurant, which also has a few overnight rooms, but alas, no vacancy. Bernard, a most wonderful and hospitable host, offered to let me stay in his home. There is an unhappy ending, however, as he took his own life in 2003 after learning that Michelin might take away his third star. This still young chef will be sadly missed.

8 quail or pigeons or 24 chicken wings, tips removed	2 tablespoons raspberry vinegar
¼ cup olive oil	1 teaspoon Dijon mustard
2 tablespoons lemon juice	1 teaspoon salt
1 garlic clove, crushed	½ cup walnut oil
Salt & pepper & thyme	2 tablespoons raspberry vinegar
8 cups salad greens	Concassé of 1 large tomato

Marinate quail, pigeons, or wings in oil with juice and seasonings about 2 hours, turning them occasionally. Roast at 350° about 1 hour, or until done and crisp. Just before done, toss greens with vinaigrette, made with seasonings, vinegar, and oil. Remove quail, pour off fat, and deglaze with remaining vinegar, scraping up brown glaze. Pour over quail, arrange on greens, and garnish with tomatoes.

Serves 6-8

WARM BACON AND EGG SALAD

This salad is comfort food personified, and is found throughout France in many variations. It can be a light meal or a first course before a hearty Alsatian or Basque main course. My version has less bacon fat, and I prefer soft lettuce to the usual chicory or endive.

6 slices bacon, cooked	½ cup olive oil
¼ cup sherry vinegar	6 cups mixed greens or spinach
2 tablespoons bacon drippings	6 poached eggs

Remove bacon from skillet, leaving about 2 tablespoons of drippings. Deglaze with vinegar, whisk in oil, and pour over greens. Top with eggs and bacon.

Serves 6.

SALADE ALSACIENNE

A hearty and robust Alsatian salad which I like to serve as a main course.

¾ cup Vinaigrette	1 pound sauerkraut, rinsed & drained
3 tablespoons mayonnaise	
1 pound boiled potatoes, peeled & sliced	12 ounces smoked sausage, sliced
4 slices bacon	Chopped dill, for garnish

Whisk vinaigrette with mayonnaise, and add ¼ cup to potatoes. Boil sauerkraut in water to cover about 5 minutes. Drain, refresh with cold water, and squeeze dry. Add remaining vinaigrette-mayonnaise mixture. Sauté bacon and sausage until done, and toss sausage with remaining ¼ cup vinaigrette. Mound sauerkraut on a platter, surround with potatoes and sausage, and top with crumbled bacon and dill.

Serves 4-6.

SEAFOOD

France has always had a staggering array of fish and shellfish from its rivers and lakes, the English Channel, the Atlantic, and the Mediterranean. The versatility of the fish is apparent in the infinite number of preparations which are found. Fortunately, the heavy use of cream in their seafood dishes has gone out to sea, which permits the delicate and fresh taste of the fish to survive.

SEA SCALLOPS WITH LETTUCE SAUCE À LA BOYER

My most cherished seafood recipe is a creation of Gerard Boyer at Les Crayères, a magnificent restaurant with elegant overnight rooms located in a bucolic setting outside Reims in Champagne. A short train ride, about 1 ½ hours from Paris, takes you to this three-star restaurant and hotel for one of the most divine culinary adventures in France. This was the first of a succession of great dishes which Chef Boyer sent to my table, and it is quite simple to prepare.

4 ounces Boston Lettuce	2-3 tablespoons browned butter
½ cup chicken stock	20 sea scallops
1 ½ cups chicken stock	¼ cup butter
Salt & pepper	White truffle oil
1 ½ tablespoons cornstarch	

Blanch lettuce in stock, just enough to wilt, refresh under cold water to retain the color, and then purée in processor. Whisk 1 ½ cups chicken stock into cornstarch with seasonings, and bring to a boil, whisking, to thicken. Add lettuce purée and browned butter, which will give it a slightly nutty taste. Sauté scallops in butter until done to your liking, but do not overcook or they will toughen. Place sauce on dinner plates, swirl to cover, and arrange scallops on top. Sprinkle with truffle oil, or add sliced truffles, à la Boyer.

Serves 4.

FISH FILETS WITH TOMATO BUTTER À LA BOYER

This is another elegant, yet simple dish from the master, Gerard Boyer. He serves it with Red Onion Confit (see index), but I prefer it with only the luscious tomato butter, which is adaptable to any seafood and also most meats and poultry. I wrap fish filets in collards to preserve moisture when baked.

2 ½ -3 pounds ripe tomatoes, puréed	2-3 pounds filets: red snapper, salmon, cod, or shellfish
2-4 tablespoons butter	Large collard or other leaves
Salt & pepper	

Press tomatoes through a sieve, using a wooden spoon, into a saucepan. Reduce by 2/3, which should be about 2- 2 ½ cups. Whisk in butter, and season to your taste, adding herbs, if desired. Wrap each filet in a leaf, preferably collard, and place in a roasting pan in one layer, and bake at 350° until tender, about 20 minutes. Pour warm tomato butter around edge of plates, and place unwrapped filets in center. Garnish with herbs, if desired.

Serves 6.

FISH FILETS WITH CURRY SAUCE À LA MÈRE BLANC

Georges Blanc at Chez la Mère Blanc, located in the tiny village of Vonnas near Macon, is a genius at devising seafood dishes and was one of the first to use curry in the new style.

2 shallots, minced	½ teaspoon curry powder
1 garlic clove, minced	1 teaspoon lemon juice
1 tablespoon butter	3 tablespoons water
½ teaspoon minced ginger	3 tablespoons butter
½ cup white wine	2 teaspoons lemon juice
1 teaspoon butter	2-3 pounds filets: red snapper, salmon, angler-fish, or cod
1 teaspoon flour	
2 cups cream	3 tablespoons butter
Salt & pepper	Chopped herbs, to taste

Lightly sauté shallots and garlic in butter, add ginger and wine, and simmer 5 minutes. Whisk blended butter and flour, a beurre manie, into wine mixture, add cream, and simmer until thickened. Season with salt, pepper, curry, and juice. Boil water, whisk in butter gradually to slightly emulsify, and add juice. Whisk into sauce, which lightens it. Sauté filets in butter until done, place on plates, pour sauce over, and sprinkle with herbs.

Serves 6.

SOLE AUX NOUILLES ALSACIENNE

As much as I appreciate the new lighter side of French cuisine, I still yearn for the comforting Alsatian dishes, such as this one which I had at Maison Kammerzell in Strasbourg.

6 filets of sole or flounder	Concassé of 1 tomato
Salt & pepper	1 cup crème fraîche
1 shallot, chopped	1 cup Hollandaise Sauce
¾ cup fish stock	½ teaspoon saffron
¾ cup white wine	8-12 ounces noodles, cooked

Season filets, place in a buttered baking dish, add shallot, stock, wine, and tomato. Simmer about 5 minutes, or until barely done. Remove filets, reduce pan liquid by half, and whisk in half the cream and the Hollandaise. Season with saffron, to taste. Mix remaining cream with noodles, place in a baking dish, top with filets, and cover with sauce. Glaze under the broiler.

Serves 6.

MARINATED TUNA STEAKS WITH BEET PURÉE

The recent fusion cooking in France has produced this Asian influence which is especially adaptable to tuna and salmon.

½ cup light brown sugar	12 ounces beets, cooked & peeled
¼ cup olive oil	2-3 teaspoons sherry vinegar
1 tablespoon tamarind paste	2 teaspoons brown sugar
1 tablespoon catsup	1 ½ tablespoons butter
1 large garlic clove, crushed	Salt & Pepper
6 tuna steaks	Chopped Chervil or parsley

Mix marinade ingredients, add tuna, and marinate at least 2 hours. For the beet puree, place beets in processor with remaining ingredients until smooth, and heat over low heat, while grilling tuna about 5 minutes on each side, taking care not to overcook, which will toughen it. Serve on top of purée, or pour purée over tuna. Garnish with chopped chervil or parsley.

Serves 6.

BAYONNE WRAPPED SALMON WITH ENDIVE MARMALADE

All but the most delicate fish lend themselves to this moist method of fish cookery, especially salmon, tuna, cod, and even scallops. Probably of Basque origin, it is especially good with Sauce Basquaise (see index), and it can also be wrapped in Parma, Serrano, or even country ham. This endive marmalade, the only way I really like endive, is wonderful with pork tenderloin, duck, turkey, and tuna.

6 endives, quartered lengthwise	¼ cup honey
1 ½ cups orange juice	2 tablespoons butter
1/3 cup sherry vinegar	6 6-ounce salmon filets, skinned
½ cup chopped red onion	6 paper-thin slices of Bayonne, Parma, Serrano, or country ham
½ cup golden raisins	

Cover endive with remaining marmalade ingredients in a heavy saucepan, and simmer about 20 minutes, or until tender and very soft. If liquid has not reduced enough, reduce over high heat, watching carefully. Wrap salmon in ham, place on an oiled baking sheet, and bake at 425° about 10 minutes, or until done. Unwrap, if desired, and place on plates with the marmalade spooned over the top.

Serves 6.

POACHED SALMON WITH GARLIC & RED PEPPER SABAYON

Sabayon is traditionally a frothy egg yolk and wine dessert, known as Zabaglione in Italy, but now chefs have discovered that it makes a great savory sauce without the sugar. This version complements the wine-poached salmon.

6 5-ounce salmon filets	2 tablespoons roasted garlic purée (see index)
2 cups red wine	5 egg yolks
½ cup fish stock (see index)	2 tablespoons brandy
1 red bell pepper, roasted (see index)	

Cover salmon with wine, and poach gently about 5 minutes. Remove from heat, and keep warm while making sabayon. Add fish stock to bell pepper and garlic in processor and purée. Pour into a small saucepan and place over very low heat. Whisk yolks and brandy, over very low heat, until lightly thickened, and gradually whisk in warm bell pepper-garlic purée. Drain salmon, place on plates, and pour sabayon over. Mesclun, lightly dressed with oil and vinegar is a perfect accompaniment to place around the salmon.

Serves 6.

SAUMON POCHÉ

This grand old classic is still my favorite for a buffet, a first course, main course, or even a French picnic.

4 to 5 pounds whole salmon	1 bay leaf
2 cups water	Salt & peppercorns
2 cups white wine	1 cucumber, scored & thinly sliced
½ lemon, sliced	Dill, chopped
Leaves of 1 celery rib	Tomato roses
Parsley sprigs	Watercress

To make a court-bouillon, combine water and wine with seasonings, and simmer ½ hour, in a fish poacher if possible, as it has a rack for removing the fish. Otherwise, wrap fish in cheesecloth, and carefully lower into pan of court-bouillon. Simmer about 10 minutes per pound, and chill well in liquid. Remove salmon, remove bones with tweezers, and scrape off skin and dark layer of flesh. Arrange cucumber in overlapping layer down center, and sprinkle with dill. Serve hot with your choice of sauces or cold.

Serves 8-10.

POULTRY

An astounding variety of poultry and game constitutes an integral part of French cuisine, and the most ubiquitous is the highly acclaimed corn-fed Bresse chicken from mountainous Franche-Comte. The famous ducks of Rouen and Nantes are highly prized, as are the renowned geese and their exalted foie gras from Alsace and Périgord. The French are especially partial to ortolans, the delicate game birds I enjoy so much in Bordeaux. Other varieties I frequently encounter are pintadeaux (guinea hen), perdreaux (partridge), faisan (pheasant), becasse (snipe), caille (quail), and grive (thrush). Now you will know what you are ordering!

POULET SAUTÉ CYNTHIA

(Sautéed Chicken with Champagne Sauce and Fruit)

A classic from the days of Escoffier, but the sauce is reduced, à la nouvelle cuisine, and fruit is paired with the chicken as in contemporary cuisine. I have modernized this great dish further by substituting suprêmes for the chicken parts, although the skin and bones do impart more flavor and gelatin which enhance the thickening. Another variation is Poulet Aux Pêches which I had at Hiély-Lucullus in Avignon, a venerable three-star Michelin restaurant.

6 suprêmes	½ cup water
¼ cup butter	¼ cup butter
1 cup champagne	1 cup powdered sugar
2 tablespoons Grand Marnier	3 peaches, peeled & halved
1 tablespoon lemon juice	1 cup orange segments
1 tablespoon Glace de Viande (see index)	1 cup red or black grapes
2 tablespoons butter	¼ cup currant jelly, melted

Sauté suprêmes in butter until golden, add half the champagne, cover, and simmer until done, about 10 minutes. Remove chicken, add remaining champagne, liqueur, juice, and meat glaze, and reduce until syrupy and lightly thickened. Swirl in butter, and pour over chicken. In a skillet, bring water, butter, and sugar to a boil, add peaches, and poach about 10 minutes. Add oranges and grapes, simmering until all fruits are glazed. Remove, and arrange around chicken. Fill peach halves with jelly. A great substitute for the chicken would be magrets, duck breasts.

Serves 6.

SUPRÊMES AU SAUCE VINAIGRE CARAMELISÉE

(Chicken with Caramelized Vinegar Sauce)

Fernand Point created this classic, which has been given many variations by the galaxy of three-star chefs. It has been a favorite since savoring it at Les Frères Troisgros, where Pierre told me how to make it. I prefer this one.

2 ½ cups veal, duck, or chicken stock	3 tablespoons sugar
	1 cup red wine vinegar
6 suprêmes	½ cup cream
¼ cup butter	

Reduce stock by half. Meanwhile, sauté suprêmes in butter until done, remove, and keep warm. Add sugar, caramelize, and add vinegar. Reduce until caramelized again, and add reduced stock. Bring to a boil, add cream, and reduce until lightly thickened. Pour over suprêmes, garnish with desired vegetables. Beef, pork, veal, or duck may be substituted.

Serves 6.

SUPRÊMES AU SAUCE VERJUS

(Chicken with Grape Sauce)

I could easily write an entire book on suprêmes, as they marry well with all fruits, vegetables, stocks, wines, juices, herbs, and seasonings. This recent version incorporates verjus, the unfermented juice of unripe grapes, which is especially popular in Australia as well as California. If unavailable, substitute unsweetened white grape juice.

3 cups chicken or veal stock	½ teaspoon salt
1 1/3 cups verjus	6 suprêmes
¼ cup lemon juice	3 tablespoons butter
2 tablespoons butter	1 ½ cups green or red grapes
¼ teaspoon sugar	¼ - ½ cup butter, softened

Reduce stock to 1 cup, add juice, butter, and seasonings, and reduce to 2/3 cup. Sauté suprêmes in butter until done, add grapes, and sauté briefly. Whisk remaining butter into sauce gradually, until emulsified. Pour over chicken, and garnish with extra sautéed grapes, if desired.

Serves 6.

SAUCE POIVRONS ROUGES

(Chicken with Roasted Bell Pepper Sauce)

Alain Senderens of the legendary Lucas-Carton, on the Place Madeleine in Paris, created this very Parisian version of the Basque classic with roasted red bell peppers.

2 large red bell peppers, roasted (see index)	½ cup white wine
6 suprêmes	1 ½ cups crème fraîche
Salt and pepper	12 ounces Pasta Verde (see index)
3 tablespoons butter	¼ cup julienned basil

Cut ½ pepper into fine julienne, and purée remainder. Sauté seasoned suprêmes in butter until done. Remove from pan, add wine to deglaze, and reduce by half. Add purée, cook until thick, and add cream, reducing again until thickened. Arrange suprêmes on pasta, ribbon with sauce, and garnish with julienne of basil and pepper.

Serves 6.

POULET GRILLÉ AUX HERBES PROVENÇALE
(Grilled Chicken with Herbs)

This unique Provençale classic creates a memorable melange of flavors. Serve with a tomato salad or ratatouille for an alfresco summer dinner.

4 small broiler halves, backbones removed	1 large garlic clove, crushed
Salt and Pepper	1 tablespoon chopped parsley
Thyme or oregano	1 tablespoon chopped basil
1 small onion, sliced	1 tablespoon chopped marjoram
¼ cup lemon juice	¼ teaspoon crushed fennel seeds
¼ cup olive oil	1 lemon, scored & thinly sliced
1/3 cup soft butter	Chopped herbs, to garnish

Global Culinary Adventures

Season chicken well, lay on a bed of onions in a shallow dish, and pour juice and oil over it. Marinate at least 2 hours. Meanwhile, cream butter with herbs, then chill. After marinating chicken, loosen skin and slip butter underneath, spreading any remainder on the outside of chicken. Broil about 6 inches from the heat, on a charcoal grill, turning frequently, about 20 minutes. Baste frequently with lemon-oil marinade. Top with lemon slices and fresh herbs.

Serves 4-6.

POULET BRAISÉE À LA CRÈME D'ESTRAGON

(Braised Chicken with Tarragon Cream)

An old French classic for braising a whole chicken, which renders it extremely succulent, this is my version of the signature dish at Auberge du Père Bise in Talloires. Although not far from Geneva, the trip involved a streetcar, two trains, a bus, and a taxi, as I was coming from Crissier where I had lunch at Fredy Girardet's. Such is the life of an avid recipe collector, but it was worth the detour. Cook this on a cold winter day.

1 3-pound chicken	2 tablespoons butter
Salt and pepper	1/3 cup crème fraîche
1 tablespoon dried tarragon	

Season chicken well, placing tarragon in the cavity, and sauté in butter until golden, using a 3-quart casserole. Braise, covered, at 350° for about an hour. Remove chicken, add tarragon to pan juices, and reduce until lightly thickened. Add cream, strain, and pour over chicken. Serve with noodles.

Serves 4-6.

POULET À LA BIÉRE D'ALSACE

(Alsatian Chicken with Beer)

This is the kind of braised chicken you will find in the home-style restaurants in Colmar and Ammerschwir. The sweet and creamy beer sauce is the piéce de resistance, and is wonderful on noodles.

1 3-pound chicken	½ tablespoon brown sugar
Salt and pepper	2 cups dark beer
2 tablespoons butter	1 tablespoon butter
4 shallots, chopped	1 tablespoon flour
2 cup sliced mushrooms	1 cup cream
1 bay leaf	3 egg yolks
2 tablespoons brandy	Choppd dill

Season chicken well, and sauté in butter on all sides, until brown. Add shallots, mushrooms, and bay leaf, and sauté until wilted. Flame with brandy, add sugar and beer, and simmer, covered, about ½ hour. Remove chicken, degrease liquid, and reduce by 1/3. Make a beurre manie with butter and flour, add reduction, and simmer 10 minutes. Whisk cream and yolks together and gradually whisk into sauce. Place whole chicken on a bed of noodles, pour sauce over, and sprinkle with dill.

Serves 4-6.

POULET RÔTI AUX HERBES & LEMON VEAL SAUCE
(Roast Chicken with Herbs and Lemon Veal Sauce)

I could also write a book about roast chicken, as every country in the world has at least one, and I can't think of a better comfort food unless it's pasta. The French normally stuff the chicken with herbs or a bread and sausage stuffing, and an herb butter under the skin is traditional. Alain Ducasse, the famed chef with the most stars, makes this process easier by spreading the butter on a sheet of wax paper (I use cereal box liners), then covering it with another sheet, and freezing it. Cut into small pieces, and push under the loosened skin.

1 3-pound chicken	1 tablespoon olive oil
Salt and pepper	1 lemon, quartered
5 tablespoons butter	1 small bunch thyme
1 tablespoon each chopped chervil, tarragon, thyme, & chives	1 ½ cups veal stock
4 garlic cloves, thinly sliced	Sautéed baby carrots, peas, and small new potatoes

Season chicken well. Mix butter with herbs and garlic, spread between 2 pieces of wax paper, freeze, and break into small pieces. Loosen chicken skin with your fingers, including the legs, and press butter underneath the skin, pushing it as far as it will go. Place in a roasting pan, rub with oil, place lemon quarters around it, and put thyme in the cavity. Roast at 350° about 45 minutes to an hour, basting with the stock occasionally. When done, remove chicken, degrease the pan, and add remaining stock, deglaze. Squeeze the lemons into the pan, and bring to a boil. Serve with the chicken and place the vegetables around the chicken.

Serves 4-6.

MAGRETS AUX RAGOUT DES CHAMPIGNONS
(Duck with Mushroom Ragout)

Magrets, or duckling suprêmes, can be used interchangeably with chicken in most recipes. This unctuous mushroom ragout would also be great with pork.

8-12 ounces mixed wild mushrooms, sliced	1 cup cream
¼ cup sliced shallots	6 magrets
3 tablespoons butter	2 tablespoons butter
¼ cup brandy	2 tablespoons Glace de Viande (see index)
1 cup veal stock	2 teaspoons white truffle oil
1 cup chicken stock	

Sauté mushrooms and shallots in butter until tender, about 10 minutes, then flame with brandy. Add stocks and cream, bring to a boil, and let reduce until lightly thickened. Sauté magrets in butter until done, about 10 minutes. Deglaze with Glace de Viande, and add mushroom ragout and truffle oil. Simmer briefly to blend flavors.

Serves 6.

CONFIT DE CANARD
(Preserved Duck)

Preserved, salted goose has been a delectable delicacy from Périgord for many years, but duck, as in this recipe, pork, chicken, and turkey may be prepared the same way. Salmon is wonderful this way and can be done with olive oil, as can the others, for a more healthful product.

2 5-pound ducklings	½ teaspoon saltpeter
½ cup kosher salt	1 bay leaf
½ teaspoon pepper	6 cups rendered duck or goose fat or lard
½ teaspoon thyme	

Cut off duck legs and wings and discard wing tips. Cut breast meat away from carcass. Cut off excess fatty skin from all the pieces, and pull off all remaining carcass skin and fat. Reserve carcass for soup or stock. Rub seasonings into duck pieces, and place in a bowl with bay leaf. Cover, and refrigerate 24 hours. Meanwhile, cut skin and fat into small pieces, place in a saucepan with ½ cup water, and cook over very low heat or in a 300° oven for about 1 hour, or until fat is rendered and clear and yellow. Strain, add duck pieces, and simmer over low heat about 2 hours, or until very tender.

Arrange pieces in 2 1-quart terrines, or in a 2-quart terrine, and strain cooking fat over the pieces so that they are completely covered. When cool, cover tightly and refrigerate for 6 months or more. When removing pieces, be sure all remaining pieces are completely covered with fat.

Any leftover fat from the cooking process or from the terrine can be frozen and used for frying the best potatoes in the world, a sublime taste treat. The preserved duck pieces are at their ultimate best when simply grilled, or they may be used in salads, soups, and stews. They are de rigueur in Cassoulet, the famous bean and pork dish from Languedoc.

BEEF, VEAL, LAMB AND PORK

Although seafood and poultry predominate, France is noted for its excellent meat, especially Burgundy's lean and tender beef from the white Charollais cattle, which are grass-fed.

The delicately flavored pale pink veal, especially from Normandy, results from the fact that the calves are milk-fed, and they are slaughtered young as are the exceptional lambs from Pauillac and the pré-salé lambs which graze on the salt meadows in Normandy and Brittany. Pork and ham are a mainstay of the Alsacienne table, and they appear in many different forms at the charcuterie.

DAUBE DE BOEUF PROVENÇALE
(Provençale Beef Stew)

This is my version of the classic and robust stew which is very versatile in that the meat may be whole or cut up and marinated before or after browning.

2 pounds top round or rump roast, cut into 4 to 6 pieces	Salt & pepper
1 tablespoon olive oil	1 ½ cups red wine
1 tablespoon butter	1 ½ cups veal stock
4 shallots, chopped	Concassé of 2 medium tomatoes
4 cloves garlic, crushed	1 tablespoon tomato paste
Bouquet Garni	Chopped basil & marjoram, to garnish
2 or 3 strips of orange zest	

Sauté beef in oil and butter until brown, and add shallots, garlic, and seasonings, sautéeing until translucent. Remove beef, add wine to deglaze, and let cool. Return beef to pan, and marinate at least 6 hours. Add stock, tomatoes, and paste, cover, and let simmer at least 3 hours, or until tender. Remove meat, and reduce until lightly thickened, and about 2 cups of sauce remains. Remove bouquet garni and zest. Sprinkle with herbs.

Serves 4-6.

ENTRECÔTE DE BOEUF AU SAUCE ROQUEFORT
(Ribeye Steak with Roquefort Sauce)

Dominique Ferrière, the young and innovative chef at the Château du Domaine Saint-Martin, perched on a hilltop overlooking the Mediterranean, created this contribution to nouvelle cuisine.

4 ribeye steaks	4 ounces Roquefort
3 tablespoons butter	1/3 cup butter
¼- ½ cup raspberry vinegar	Pepper, to taste
1 cup crème fraîche	

Trim steaks and sauté in butter to desired doneness. Remove from skillet, pour off drippings, and deglaze with vinegar until almost evaporated. Add cream, reducing by half. Cream Roquefort with butter, and whisk into cream. Simmer briefly, season, and serve with steaks.

Serves 4.

BIFTECK À LA CHEVAL
(Steak with Egg)

Steak topped with an egg is an old French classic and is an excellent example of French steak preparation, with or without an egg. The French seldom broil or grill steak, but sauté it in oil or butter, thus the essence of the pan juices is retained as a base for the sauce. After removing the steak, the skillet is deglazed with brandy, or red or white wine, or stock, or even a combination of these liquids and then poured over the steak. An ideal choice for a solo dinner with a glass or two of red wine, and if you have a crêpe or two leftover in the freezer, wrap the steak in the crêpe, cover with the sauce, and you have Steak en Chemise.

1 boneless steak	2 tablespoons butter
Salt and Pepper	1 garlic clove, crushed
2 tablespoons chopped thyme and parsley	½ cup white wine
	1 fried egg

Rub steak with mixed seasonings, and sauté in butter to desired doneness. Remove, deglaze with wine and garlic, reducing until syrupy. Place egg on steak, and pour sauce over it.

Serves 1.

VEAU AU PESTO DE NOIX
(Veal Stew with Nuts)

Veal with a nut pesto sauce is a delicious and simple dish, and is equally good with pork, lamb, chicken, or duck.

2 pounds boneless veal shoulder or leg, cut into 2-inch cubes	3 cups veal stock
2 tablespoons olive oil	¼ cup each walnuts, almonds, and pistachios
2 tablespoons butter	1 tablespoon olive oil
4 shallots, chopped	1 tablespoon butter
4 garlic cloves, crushed	Salt & pepper
	Chopped basil

Sauté veal in oil and butter until golden, and add shallots and garlic, sautéing until translucent. Add stock, cover, and simmer until tender, about 45 minutes. Suprêmes will take less time, and lamb more time. Process nuts with oil in processor until coarsely ground. Reduce cooking liquid to about 2 cups, and whisk in pesto, and simmer until desired consistency. Season, and swirl in butter to finish sauce. Pour over veal, and garnish with basil.

Serves 4-6.

SCALLOPS DE VEAU EN CHEMISE

(Veal Scallops Wrapped in Crêpes)

This is my modern version of a great favorite from the legendary S.S. France. The original version was made with a heavy Sauce Suprême and a chicken filling, whereas this has a truffled veal sauce and a wild mushroom filling.

8 Dill crêpes (see index)	2 tablespoons butter
6 ounces wild mushrooms, sliced	2 tablespoons brandy
3 or 4 shallots, sliced	½ cup crème fraîche (see index)

8 small veal scallops, pounded very thin	2-3 teaspoons truffle oil
3 tablespoons butter	Finely chopped black truffles, optional
3 cups veal stock	½ cup grated Emmenthaler cheese
1 cup mushroom stock (made by simmering mushroom stems in water 15 minutes)	2 tablespoons butter

Sauté mushrooms and shallots in butter until tender, deglaze with brandy, and add cream. Cook briskly until thick. Sauté veal in butter until barely colored, but not cooked through. Arrange 1 on each crêpe.

To prepare sauce, reduce stocks separately by half. Combine, and add truffle oil and truffles. Reduce until syrupy if necessary. Brush each scallop with a little sauce and spread mushroom filling on top. Roll crêpes, place in a baking dish, and drizzle a little sauce on them. Sprinkle with cheese, dot with butter, and bake at 350° until hot, about 15 minutes. Place on plates and pour sauce around edge. Lightly sautéed haricots verts (small green beans) and diagonally sliced baby carrots placed around the edge of the plates make an elegant presentation.

Serves 4-8.

FOIE DE VEAU ROTI

(Roasted Calf Liver)

The French method of roasting calf liver produces a superb texture and flavor unrivaled by the usual sauté.

2 pounds calf liver in 1 piece	6 strips bacon

Wrap liver with bacon, securing it with small picks or skewers. Place on a rack in a drip pan to prevent flareups, and place in a very hot grill. Roast about 10 minutes, turning it once, then lower the heat and cook to desired doneness, about ½ hour for medium rare. The oven may also be used, lowering the heat after about 10 minutes.

Serves 6.

NOISETTES D'AGNEAU À LA TRUFFE ET POMMES SAUTÉ
(Nuggets of Lamb with Truffle Oil and Potatoes)

This is one of several wonderful creations I have enjoyed at Fredy Girardet in Crissier, Switzerland. Although Fredy is no longer there, we can enjoy my version of a truly great dish.

8 noisettes of lamb, small nuggets cut from loin chops	¼ cup minced shallot
Salt & pepper	½ cup sliced mushrooms
1 egg yolk	1 cup veal stock, reduced to 1/3 cup
1 teaspoon water	1 pound thinly sliced potatoes
½ cup minced parsley	3 tablespoons olive oil
1 tablespoon olive oil	Salt & pepper
1 tablespoon butter	Chopped chervil
2-3 teaspoons truffle oil	

Season lamb, coat with yolk mixed with water, and dip into parsley on all sides. Sauté in oil and butter until done as desired, remove, and sauté shallot and mushrooms until done. Add reduced veal glaze. Meanwhile, sauté potatoes in oil until golden and tender, season. Add truffle oil to sauce. Place meat on top of potatoes, and pour sauce over. Garnish with chervil.

Serves 4.

SAUTÉ D'AGNEAU PROVENÇALE

(Provençale Lamb Sauté)

My favorite blend of robust flavors make this dish one of my favorites, and its versatility lends itself to using veal, suprêmes, or pork tenderloin.

2 pounds boneless lamb leg or shoulder, cut into 1-inch cubes	1 ½ cups white wine
3 tablespoons olive oil	1 ½ cups veal stock
4 shallots, chopped	½ cup oven-roasted tomatoes (see index)
1 head garlic, separated into cloves	½ cup Nicoise or Kalamata olives
1 tablespoon chopped thyme	Salt & pepper
1 tablespoon chopped rosemary	2 tablespoons butter

Sauté lamb in oil until well browned, adding shallots and garlic about 5 minutes later. Add herbs and wine. Reduce wine by half, add veal stock, cover, and simmer until lamb is tender, 30 to 45 minutes. Add tomatoes and olives, season, and swirl in butter to finish. This is wonderful on polenta. If the sauce is not thickened, reduce as desired.

Serves 4-6.

CASSOULET BOURGEOISE

In my first book, *Culinary Classics,* I presented the classic and authentic Cassoulet (if there is such a thing—Castelnaudary, Toulouse, and Carcassone cooks endlessly debate this great culinary controversy). Here is a simpler but still great rendition, which is similar to what I savored at the wonderful Hotel de la Cité in Carcassone.

1 pound white beans	1 large onion, chopped
5 cups veal or beef stock	¼ cup chopped parsley
½ pound lamb or pork sausage	1 28-ounce can tomatoes, undrained
2 garlic cloves, crushed	
Bouquet Garni	Salt & pepper
Salt & pepper	Confit de Canard (see index)
4 pounds lamb shanks	1 ½ cups bread crumbs
¼ cup rendered duck fat or olive oil	¼ cup duck fat or olive oil
	½ cup chopped parsley

Soak beans in water overnight, or use quick method, by boiling 1 minute, then letting stand for 1 hour. Bring stock to a boil, add beans, sausage, and seasonings, and simmer, uncovered, about ½ hour. Remove sausage, and simmer ½ hour longer. Discard bouquet.

Meanwhile, sauté lamb in fat or oil until browned, add onion and parsley, and sauté until soft. Add tomatoes, season, and simmer, covered, about 1 ½ hours. Add to beans with confit, using as much as you can spare, place in a 6-quart casserole, and refrigerate overnight. Cover with crumbs mixed with fat, and bake at 350° about 1 hour. A red burgundy or Languedoc red, salad, and baguettes are a must.

Serves 8-12.

CHOUCRÔUTE GARNI ALSACIENNE

One of my most magnanimous culinary memories is that of the incomparable pork and sauerkraut classic which I first savored at Maison des Têtes in Colmar, a small town in Alsace, which I found was worth a detour.

2 pounds sauerkraut	1 bay leaf
1 cup chopped onion	¼ teaspoon caraway seeds
2 garlic cloves, crushed	¼ pound salt pork
¼ cup duck fat or lard	6 smoked pork chops
1 cup Riesling wine	6 knackwurst or other smoked sausage
1 cup chicken or veal stock	
5 juniper berries	1/3 cup soft butter
3 peppercorns	6-12 small new potatoes

Please do not use canned kraut, use only the kraut in cryovac bags, found in the meat department. Soak kraut in cold water about 10 minutes, and squeeze dry. Sauté onion and garlic in fat until soft, add kraut, and mix thoroughly. Add wine, stock, seasonings, and salt pork. Cover, and bake at 325° about 1 hour. Add remaining meat and potatoes, and bake 1 hour longer, or until all the meat is very tender. Arrange on a platter, and serve with the traditional black bread and beer.

Serves 6.

STUFATU CON MACCHERONI

(Corsican Stew with Macaroni)

You may think this is in the wrong section, given its very Italianate flavor, but Corsica is a department of France and the birthplace of Napoleon. The island has an undeniable Italian character, evident in the people, language, and food, because it belonged to Italy until 1768. It is primarily home-cooking, which uses up various leftover meats with their cooking liquids, and then layered with macaroni. My first stufatu was in Bonifacio, at the southern tip of the island, which I reached by ferry from Santa Teresa di Gallura on the island of Sardinia, and it was a very rough and stormy crossing, but I was rewarded with the best comfort food and rough Corsican red wine.

3 strips bacon, chopped	2 cups red wine
¼ cup olive oil	2-3 cups canned tomatoes, or chopped fresh tomatoes
½ pound Boston butt pork	
½ pound beef shoulder or rump	2 bay leaves
	1 tablespoon chopped sage
½ pound lamb shoulder	1 tablespoon chopped rosemary
Salt & pepper	
1 onion, chopped	½ pound macaroni, cooked & drained
4 garlic cloves, chopped	
	1 cup parmesan cheese

Sauté bacon in oil until fat is rendered, then add meats, and sauté until browned. Season, and sauté onion and garlic until soft. Add wine, tomatoes, and herbs, cover, and simmer about 3 hours, or until meats are very tender. Remove meats and slice, while reducing pan liquid until thickened. Layer macaroni, meats, and cheese in a large shallow baking dish, and pour reduced sauce over all. Bake at 350° about 15 minutes.

Serves 6.

CIVET DE PORC ET PRUNEAUX

(Pork Stew with Prunes)

A civet of game or meat was originally thickened with the animal's blood and was considered to be haute cuisine, but now it is thickened by reduction and a little chocolate. Wild boar or rabbit are also done this way, but this is my version, and one of my favorite dishes.

2 pounds boneless pork shoulder or Boston butt, cut into 6 pieces	4 ounces chopped bacon
	3 tablespoons olive oil
2 cups red wine	2 cups veal stock
¾ cup each chopped onion, celery, and carrot	2 ounces semisweet chocolate
	2-4 tablespoons butter
¼ cup olive oil	Salt & pepper
Bouquet Garni of 1 bay leaf, 2 garlic cloves, 1 tablespoon juniper berries, & several parsley stems	18 prunes, cooked in red wine
	Chopped chervil or parsley

Marinate meat in wine, vegetables, oil, and bouquet garni about 2 to 4 hours. Drain meat and vegetables, saving the marinade. Sauté bacon in oil until fat is rendered, and add pork and vegetables, sautéeing until well browned. Add marinade, including bouquet, and stock. Cover, and simmer about 1 ½ hours or until tender. Remove meat, and drain cooking liquid through a sieve into a saucepan. Reduce sauce to about 2 cups, add chocolate, and swirl in butter. Season, to taste. Arrange 1 piece of pork in center of each plate, place 3 prunes at intervals around edge of plates, and cover bottom of plates with the sauce. Garnish with chervil.

Serves 6.

PORC CARAMELISÉ À LA BASQUAISE

Caramelizing meat is a popular trend with French chefs, and the best I've had was at Les Pyrenées, a two-star (should be three) Michelin restaurant in the tiny and serene village of St. Jean-Pied-de-Port, It was a pleasant train ride, only two cars, from Biarritz. This part of France is completely unspoiled and is virtually free of tourists, a place I will return to time and again. The mountain and valley scenery provided a dramatic background for this delicious a1 fresco lunch.

1 pound pork tenderloin, cut into 4 pieces	2 tablespoons sugar
1/3 cup olive oil	2 tablespoons olive oil
3 tablespoons sherry vinegar	2 shallots, sliced
2 garlic cloves, sliced	1 tablespoon brandy
Thyme sprigs	1 tablespoon sherry vinegar
Salt & pepper	1 ½ cups veal stock
	1 tablespoon butter

Marinate pork in oil, vinegar, garlic, and seasonings about 2 hours. Coat all sides with sugar, and sauté in oil until done to taste, about 5 minutes. Remove, add shallots, sauté until tender, and deglaze with brandy. Add stock, reduce until lightly thickened, and finish with butter. Slice pork, arrange on plates, and pour sauce over, covering the plates, and garnish with sautéed seasonal vegetables.

Serves 4.

SAUCES AND STOCKS

The glorious sauces of French cuisine are its foundation, and likewise, the carefully nurtured stocks are the foundation of its classic sauces. One of the best outcomes of nouvelle cuisine, and of utmost importance to fusion cooking, however, is the preparation of simple and quick sauces in the pan in which the seafood, poultry, game, or meat was prepared. As I have always maintained in my classes, a thorough understanding and knowledge of the sauce repertoire insures the mastery of French cuisine.

SAUCE ESPAGNOLE
(Brown Sauce)

This is the most important of all sauces, as many derivative or compound sauces are made from it, and it freezes well. Normally called Brown Sauce, it can be made with any good veal or beef stock base, preferably not bouillon cubes.

1 carrot, cut in chunks	1 garlic clove
1 onion, cut in chunks	1 bay leaf
½ cup butter	½ teaspoon thyme
1 cup flour	2 tablespoons tomato paste
1 quart brown stock	Salt & pepper
1 cup white wine	¼ cup Marsala or sherry

Sauté vegetables in butter until well browned, add flour, and brown further. Add all but Marsala, and simmer, covered, at least 1/2 hour. Add Marsala, and strain well, pressing on the vegetables to extract their juices.

Makes about 1 quart.

SAUCE DEMI-GLACE

(Brown Sauce Reduction)

This half-glaze is especially rich and concentrated, and it may be used in place of Sauce Espagnole. A very simple process.

| 1 quart Sauce Espagnole | 1 quart brown stock (beef or veal) |

Reduce together by half.

Makes about 1 quart.

SAUCE DEMI-GLACE AU CRÈME

(Brown Sauce Reduction with Cream)

Another simple derivative sauce, and the one I turn to when I want an especially rich sauce, and any amount may be made.

| 1 quart Sauce Espagnole | 1 quart cream |

Reduce together until desired thickness is obtained. The thickness of the cream determines the amount of reduction.

Makes about 1 quart.

GLACE DE VIANDE

(Meat Glaze)

Not a sauce per se, but a meat glaze which is essential for enriching sauces, and is simply a reduction of stock.

1 to 2 quarts veal or beef stock	

Place stock in a large wide pan, bring to a boil, skimming the surface. When reduced by half, place in a smaller pan, and continue reducing by 1/4. This may be reconstituted by adding 2 tablespoons of glaze to 1 cup water.

Makes ½ to 1 cup.

SAVORY SAUCE CARAMEL À L'ORANGE

Among the sauces now in vogue are the ones which begin with a caramelization of sugar or even honey. The poultry, meat, or game can also be coated with sugar or honey and sautéed until golden. This is a luscious favorite of mine.

¼ cup sugar or honey	¾ cup veal stock
1 cup orange juice	2 tablespoons butter
¼ cup red wine vinegar, raspberry, or sherry vinegar	2 tablespoons Glace de Viande (optional)

In a small heavy saucepan, heat the sugar over medium heat until caramelized. Do not stir after it comes to a boil. Add juice and vinegar, boiling until reduced slightly. Add stock, and reduce until lightly thickened. Swirl in butter, and add meat glaze if desired.

Makes about 1 ½ cups.

SAVORY SAUCE CARAMEL AU CASSIS

Another version of savory caramel sauces, which is even better if you make it in the skillet's pan drippings after sautéeing suprêmes, duck, veal or pork scallops, or beef tenderloin. Try substituting other vinegars and jellies, such as mint for rack of lamb.

¼ cup red wine vinegar	2-3 tablespoons crème de cassis liqueur or red port
1 tablespoon red currant jelly or black currant preserves	1 ½ cups Sauce Demi-Glace (see index)
1/3 cup dried currants	¼ cup butter

Preferably after sautéeing poultry or meat, deglaze skillet with vinegar, add jelly, and boil until caramelized. Add liqueur and demi-glace, then simmer until reduced by about half. Currants may be added before reducing.

Makes about 1 cup.

SAUCE BASQUAISE

From both sides of the border, this wonderful sauce is used extensively in French and Spanish cooking. It can be used with almost any seafood, meat, poultry, and with egg dishes. I freeze it in small amounts for instant use.

1 small red onion, chopped	¼ cup olive oil
2 medium red bell peppers, chopped	1-1 ½ pounds tomatoes, chopped
6-8 garlic cloves, crushed	2 bay leaves
	Salt & pepper

Sauté onion and peppers in oil about 5 minutes over high heat, add garlic, and cook briefly. Add remaining ingredients, cover, and simmer until thickened. If desired, purée in a food processor.

Makes about 2 cups.

COULIS DE TOMATES

(Reduced Tomato Sauce)

A coulis is generally a thick, reduced tomato sauce, and can be served cold or warm with any seafood, poultry, or meat.

2 pounds tomatoes, peeled & seeded	1 teaspoon salt
¼ cup olive oil	½ teaspoon sugar
2 tablespoons raspberry vinegar (optional)	1 tablespoon chopped parsley
1 garlic clove	1 tablespoon chopped basil

Purée tomatoes in processor, and strain through a sieve into a saucepan. Reduce to 1-1 ½ cups, and whisk in oil, vinegar, and seasonings. Add herbs.

Makes about 1 ½ cups.

TAPENADE
(Olive Paste)

Not a sauce per se, but a highly seasoned Provençale specialty which can be made with black, green, kalamata, or other olives and spread on sandwiches, or added to soups, salads, pastas, and even omelets. Feel free to adjust the amounts to your taste.

1 cup pitted black or green olives	10-12 basil leaves
1 or 2 cloves garlic	1 tablespoon lemon juice
1 or 2 anchovies (optional)	¼ to ½ cup olive oil
1 or 2 tablespoons capers	

Simply place all ingredients in processor, and process until desired consistency is reached, chunky or smooth. Refrigerate several weeks or freeze.

Makes about 1 cup.

AIOLI
(Provençale Mayonnaise)

Mayonnaise, actually French in origin, is a Provençale specialty, made with garlic and olive oil. Roasted garlic is optional, but I love it, and although it took me many years to appreciate aioli, I will not settle for any other kind of mayonnaise now.

2 large egg yolks or 1 large egg	1 to 1 ½ cups olive oil
1 teaspoon Dijon mustard	1 small head roasted garlic (optional)
1 or 2 teaspoons lemon juice	Salt, to taste

Have all ingredients at room temperature. Place yolks or whole egg in processor with mustard and juice, and blend thoroughly. Add oil in a very slow stream until mayonnaise is thickened, adding a little faster near the end. Season and add a little water to diminish the oiliness if desired. Refrigerate up to a week. The garlic can be added at any time, depending on its use.

Makes about 1 ½ cups.

BEURRE BLANC

(White Butter Sauce)

Like mayonnaise, this sauce is an emulsion, but can be tricky to execute, because it is made over low heat. The secret is to be sure that the heat is always very low. If the sauce does break, put it in the processor and that should rectify the problem. This sauce is extremely rich, and has fallen out of fashion, but there is nothing quite as wonderful. It is so versatile that it can be made with any kind of vinegar or wine (even red), any kind of fruit juice with the wine, and your choice of herbs, other seasonings, and a purée of roasted red bell peppers.

¼ cup white wine	2 tablespoons cream
¼ cup champagne vinegar	1 teaspoon Dijon mustard
1 shallot, minced	Salt & pepper
1 cup cold butter	

Reduce wine, vinegar, and shallot to 1 or 2 tablespoons, and gradually whisk in butter over very low heat. If it looks like it's melting, remove from heat until it is emulsifying again. Whisk in cream and seasonings.

Makes about 1 ½ cups.

BEURRE BLANC ORIENTALE

(Oriental Butter Sauce)

Fusion cooking has produced this flavorful variation, which can stand up to robust meat and game.

½ cup veal stock	1 garlic clove, crushed
2-3 tablespoons light soy sauce	¾ cup butter
1 shallot, minced	1 or 2 tablespoons rice vinegar

Reduce stock, soy sauce, shallot, and garlic to about 1 or 2 tablespoons, and gradually whisk in butter over very low heat. Whisk in vinegar, and season with chopped coriander, if desired. This is great with pork.

Makes about 1 cup.

BEURRE BLANC À L'ORANGE

(Orange Butter Sauce)

As an ardent saucier I could give you 101 Beurre Blanc sauces, but I will end with this light, fresh, and fruity variation.

1 cup orange juice	1 tablespoon lime juice
2-3 cup white wine	¾ cup cold butter
¼ cup raspberry vinegar	1 tablespoon minced mixed
1 shallot, minced	herbs, thyme, rosemary, & basil

Reduce juice, wine, vinegar, and shallot to about ¼ cup. Whisk in lime juice and butter over very low heat. Add herbs. This is wonderful with fish or chicken.

Makes about 1 cup.

SAUCE HOLLANDAISE

One of the mother sauces, meaning that many other sauces are derived from it, this is also an emulsion sauce with many possibilities. This creamy version can be seasoned with herbs, spices, or even a few raspberries can be added instead of the concassé. In this case, substitute raspberry vinegar for the juice.

4 egg yolks	¾ to 1 cup softened butter
2 tablespoons cream	¼ cup Tomato confit (see index)
1 tablespoon lemon juice	Salt & pepper

Whisk yolks with cream and juice over very low heat, using a heavy saucepan. When lightly thickened, gradually whisk in butter until emulsified. Add concassé, and season to taste. Hollandaise, like Beurre Blanc, is never served hot (which would cause it to separate), but pleasantly warm.

Makes about 1 cup.

CRÈME FRAÎCHE

Not a sauce, per se, but an essential ingredient for many recipes in the entire French repertoire. Heavy cream may be used but this is thicker and richer. There are various methods of making it, which simulate the natural heavy cream of Normandy with a high butterfat content. For the health-conscious, a very good version is obtained by mixing equal parts of fat-free milk and fat-free sour cream or yogurt. To keep it from curdling when adding it to a hot mixture, simply whisk in about ½ teaspoon cornstarch for each cup.

1 cup heavy cream	½ cup sour cream

Whisk together, heat to lukewarm, and let stand several hours, or until lightly thickened.

Makes 1 ½ cups.

VEGETABLES

In France, vegetables are most often relegated to the status of a garniture for the main course, but the quality of their preparation is outstanding in the culinary world. The exceptional fresh taste and vivid color is retained due to the special technique of boiling them in a large quantity of salted water, only until crisp-tender, and then draining and refreshing with cold water to stop further cooking. This step can be done in advance, and they are reheated by quickly tossing them in hot butter when ready to serve. Also, look for small vegetables for the freshest flavor, contrary to American opinion. Likewise, Americans consider nutmeg to be a dessert spice, but in France it is primarily used for vegetables, especially potatoes.

POMMES DE TERRE MACAIRE
(Sautéed Potato Cakes)

Although a simple and homey dish, these potatoes are a great favorite of chefs because of the pure essence of flavor.

4 large baked potatoes	Salt, pepper, & nutmeg, to taste
¾ to 1 cup butter	1 to 2 teaspoons truffle oil (optional)

Cut potatoes in half, scoop out pulp, and mash rather roughly with a fork. Add half the butter, season, and form into large thick cakes. Sauté slowly in remaining butter until golden on each side.

Serves 4.

POMMES DE TERRE SAUTÉES DORDOGNE

(Sautéed Potatoes with Duck Fat)

Golden, crisp sautéed potatoes are the most sublime tasty treat when fried in your leftover duck fat from Confit de Canard, as they do in Dordogne and the entire Bordeaux and Basque areas.

2 pounds new potatoes	6 garlic cloves, crushed
Salt & pepper	2 tablespoons chopped parsley or chervil
½ cup olive oil or duck fat	

Boil potatoes until barely tender, peel, and slice. Sauté in oil or duck fat, using a large sauté pan, until golden on each side, adding the garlic when almost done, about 20 minutes total. Sprinkle with parsley.

PURÉE OF POTATOES AND BEETS

Puréed vegetables were a symbol of nouvelle cuisine, and this is the one worthy of anyone's repertoire.

1 ¼ pounds Yukon potatoes, peeled & cooked	Salt & pepper
2 teaspoons raspberry vinegar	1 ¼ pound beets, peeled & cooked
¼ to ½ cup cream	Salt & pepper
¼ to ½ cup butter	2 tablespoons chives

Whip potatoes in electric mixer until smooth, add vinegar, cream, butter, and seasonings. Purée beets in processor, season, and whisk into potatoes. Sprinkle with chives.

Serves 6.

MACARONI ET FROMAGE AUX CHAMPIGNONS

(Macaroni and Cheese with Wild Mushrooms)

Macaroni and cheese, the old childhood staple, has become the darling of chefs around the world and is the new comfort food. The mushrooms are optional, but they give the dish a new depth.

6 ounces small macaroni or shells	2 tablespoons olive oil
1 ½ cups cream	Salt, pepper, & thyme
Salt, pepper, & nutmeg	2 cups grated Emmenthaler cheese
8-12 ounces mixed wild mushrooms	

Cook macaroni until done, drain, and mix with cream. Refrigerate several hours or overnight. Season well. Sauté mushrooms in oil until tender, about 5 minutes, and season well. Place half the macaroni in a buttered 6-cup gratin dish, and cover with half the cheese. Place mushrooms over the cheese, and add remaining macaroni and cheese. Bake at 350° about 15 minutes. This is quite elegant if baked in individual gratin dishes.

Serves 4-6.

LE PUY LENTILS

No collection of French recipes is complete without Le Puy Lentils. My only problem with them is that they tend to have tiny pebbles mixed in, so you may use red or brown lentils instead of these green ones.

4 shallots, chopped	2 cups light veal or chicken stock
4 garlic cloves, crushed	Salt & pepper
2 tablespoons duck fat or olive oil	Thyme branches
1 cup green, red, or brown lentils	2 tablespoons butter
	1 tablespoon balsamic vinegar

Sauté shallots and garlic in duck fat, preferably left from your Confit de Canard, until tender, add lentils, toss to coat with fat, and add stock and seasonings. Simmer, about 20 minutes, or until done. Add butter and vinegar.

Serves 4.

GRATIN OF PUMPKIN OR BUTTERNUT

Pumpkin is prepared this way in Provence, but I prefer butternut squash.

2 pounds pumpkin or butternut	¼ cup chopped parsley or chervil
¼ cup flour	Salt, pepper, & nutmeg
2 tablespoons turbinado sugar	¼ cup parmesan cheese
1 tablespoon chopped sage	1/3 cup olive oil
6 garlic cloves, crushed	

Peel squash, remove seeds, and cut into medium cubes. Place in an oiled gratin dish. Mix flour with all but oil and mix thoroughly with squash. Drizzle oil over squash, and bake at 350° about 45 minutes, or until squash is tender and the top is crusty.

Serves 4.

RATATOUILLE PROVENÇALE

This lusty vegetable stew from the Côte d'Azur has numerous variations, but this one is truly fantastic. I like to serve this with the Gratin of Pumpkin that preceded this recipe.

¾ pound onions, thinly sliced	1 teaspoon sugar
1 green pepper, cut into long narrow strips	1 bay leaf
	6 garlic cloves, crushed
1 red pepper, cut into long narrow strips	1 round eggplant, peeled & cut into chunks
¼ cup olive oil	1 pound zucchini, cut into chunks
1 ½ pounds tomatoes, peeled, seeded, & chopped	1/3 cup olive oil
2 tablespoons tomato paste	Salt & pepper
1 teaspoon thyme	2 tablespoons each chopped basil & cilantro

Sauté onion and peppers in oil, using a large sauté pan, until very soft. Add tomatoes, paste, and seasonings, and cook briskly until excess liquid evaporates. Sauté eggplant and zucchini in oil, using a large skillet, until tender. Add to tomato mixture, season, and serve warm or cool. Sprinkle with herbs.

Serves 6-8.

TOMATO CONFIT

(Oven-Dried Tomatoes)

Instead of sun-dried tomatoes, those dull, dried-up things you pay a fortune for, I use these oven-dried tomatoes which are satiny, sweet, sensuous, and bursting with intense flavor. You can make any amount, but I make a lot because they keep refrigerated about 2 weeks, or they may be frozen with no loss of quality. Use them almost anywhere, in sandwiches, salads, pasta, soups, sauces, and sautés.

4 pounds ripe Roma tomatoes, halved & seeded	2 teaspoons kosher salt
6 garlic cloves, unpeeled	1 teaspoon turbinado sugar
6 sprigs thyme	1/3 cup olive oil

Cover a jelly roll pan with parchment or aluminum foil. Toss tomatoes with all ingredients and place cut side down. Bake slowly at 200° to 275°, depending on your oven, about 2 to 3 hours, or longer, until very soft and shiny. They may be turned over after an hour. Place in a container, covering with more oil if necessary. Be sure to add the herbs and garlic, as they will continue to flavor the tomatoes, and the garlic is a sublime tasting treat.

Makes about 1-2 cups.

DESSERTS

Fabulous dessert creations are the "pièce de resistance" of the French restaurant kitchen, and are really not as complicated as they seem. I have always maintained that cooking students must learn the classic foundations of French desserts—puff pastry, genoise, meringues, pastry creams, butter creams, and crêpes—for an infinite array of delicacies can be created from these basics.

SORBET CASSIS

An old favorite of mine from Dijon, where I first enjoyed it at the legendary Hôtel de la Poste in Beaune. Sorbet presentations during the seventies and eighties were phantasmagorical and one had colored lights under the plate to cast a surreal glow on the sorbets. An elegant presentation needs no more than an attractive grouping of 3 sorbets with a mint sprig in the center. Essentially a palate cleanser, sorbets are generally served before the main dessert, but they are great anytime, especially in hot weather.

2 cups water	1 pound package frozen blackberries thawed & puréed, or 3 pints fresh blackberries, or black currants
1 cup sugar	
3 tablespoon crème de cassis	

Boil water and sugar 5 minutes, and chill. Add berries and cassis, and process in an ice cream freezer.

Makes 1 quart.

SORBET FRAMBOISE
(Raspberry Sorbet)

3 cups water 1 cup sugar 1/3 cup lemon or lime juice	3 tablespoons Chambord liqueur (raspberry) 1 pound frozen raspberries, thawed

Boil water and sugar 5 minutes, and chill. Purée raspberries, strain, and add to syrup with juice and liqueur. Process in ice cream freezer.

Makes 1 quart.

SORBET AU CHOCOLAT

Technically a sherbet because of the milk, this sorbet is more appealing to me than ice cream, and is especially good when paired with fruit sorbets.

1 ½ cups milk ¾ cup sugar 2/3 cup Cadbury cocoa powder	4 ounces semi-sweet chocolate 2 to 3 tablespoons Tiramisu liqueur

Slowly bring milk, sugar, and cocoa to a boil. Add liqueur and chocolate, stir until melted, and chill well. Freeze in an ice cream maker.

Makes about 1 pint.

SORBET PRUNEAUX

(Prune Sorbet)

If you can find good ripe plums this is truly great, otherwise, I find that Concord grapes are a perfect alternative.

2 pounds very ripe plums, pitted, or Concord grapes 1 cup light brown sugar	¼ cup honey 3 tablespoons lemon juice

Simmer plums with remaining ingredients about 10 minutes, then purée and chill. Process in an ice cream freezer.

Makes 1 quart.

GLACE AU PISTACHE

(Pistachio Ice Cream)

This is one of the few ice creams which I truly love, along with the following caramel variety, and it is especially compatible with figs, dates, and oranges, all with their roots in Persia, but more about that in the Middle East section. Pistachios also pair well with chocolate.

6 egg yolks ½ cup sugar 1 cup milk 1 cup cream	¼ cup pistachios, coarsely ground in processor ¼ cup finely chopped pistachios Green food coloring, if desired

Whisk yolks with sugar until thick and pale. Scald milk, cream, and pistachio paste, and whisk in yolk mixture, cooking only until lightly thickened. Add chopped nuts, and green coloring, to achieve the desired color. Chill and freeze.

Makes 1 quart.

GLACE CARAMEL AU PRALINÉE

(Caramelized Nut Ice Cream)

2 vanilla beans, split & seeds scraped out	1 ½ cups milk, scalded
1 cup sugar	6 egg yolks
¾ cup cream	1/3 cup Pralinée aux Noix (see index)

Place vanilla pod and beans in a heavy saucepan with sugar, and cook over medium heat until sugar is deeply caramelized. Whisk in cream off the heat. Whisk hot milk into yolks slowly, then whisk into caramel cream, cooking gently until lightly thickened. Chill and freeze in ice cream maker, adding pralinée just before firm.

Makes 1 quart.

GÂTEAU MARJOLAINE

(Meringue Cake with Chocolate Cream and Caramelized Nut Cream)

The ultimate dessert, Gâteau Marjolaine is a luscious melange of meringues layered with chocolate ganache and pralinée buttercream. It was created by the great Fernand Point at La Fyramide in Vienne, and the pyramidial design stenciled on the gâteau is the restaurant's logo, derived from the town square's ancient obelisk.

It was a dinner never to be forgotten.

This is a derivation of the great classic, La Dacquoise, which is simply 3 round layers of meringue, each spread with chocolate buttercream frosting and garnished with pralinée. If you really want to go over the top, Le Succès, you'll need it, is composed of meringue layers, a puff pastry layer, and chocolate buttercream with pralinée butter and crushed macaroons.

1 ½ cups blanched almonds	3 tablespoons cornstarch
1 cup hazelnuts	8 egg whites
1 ½ cups sugar	

Roast nuts at 425° about 15 minutes, rub off hazelnut skins, and grind nuts finely in processor, but not until pasty or oily, because the whites have an aversion to fat. Add sugar and cornstarch. Whisk whites until stiff, but not dry, and fold in nut mixture. Cover a baking sheet with parchment paper, and spread meringue into 4 rectangles, 4 x 12 inches. Bake at 250° about 45 minutes, or until crisp but still pliable. Cool.

1 cup cream, scalded	12 ounces semi-sweet chocolate
¼ cup soft butter	

Mix cream with chocolate and butter, stirring until melted, and chill.

½ cup very soft butter	2 cups cream, whipped
2 tablespoons vanilla	1 cup Pralinée aux Noix (see index)

Whisk butter and vanilla into whipped cream, divide cream in half, and add pralinée to half of cream.

To assemble the gâteau, spread 1 meringue layer with 1/3 of the chocolate cream, add a second meringue layer, and spread with all the plain buttercream, add a third meringue layer, and spread with all the pralinée buttercream. Add fourth meringue layer, and spread entire gâteau with remaining chocolate cream. Press extra pralinée or grated chocolate on the sides. Place 3 pyramid stencils with short columns on top, sift heavily with powdered sugar, and remove stencils. Chill, and enjoy with champagne!

Serves 12-16.

LE VACHERIN GLACE AU CITRON

(Frozen Lemon Heringue Torte)

In *Culinary Classics,* I gave a recipe for making the elaborate and ornate meringue shell, which is the classic Vacherin, but this simplified version is just as delicious and versatile. The basic meringue layers may be used with your choice of various ice creams, sorbets, flavored whipped creams, and other fillings. This lemon version is my favorite, but the Vacherin made with layers of pralinée ice cream that I had at La Maison des Têtes in Colmar is a delicious example of the Alsatian style.

4 egg whites	1 cup sugar
Pinch of salt	6 tablespoons butter
¼ teaspoon cream of tartar	1/3 cup lemon juice
1 cup sugar	1 ½ tablespoons grated lemon zest
1 teaspoon vanilla	
2 whole eggs	1 pint vanilla ice cream or sorbet
2 egg yolks	Powdered sugar

To make the vacherin meringue layers, beat whites with salt and cream of tartar until foamy, gradually add sugar, and beat until shiny and stiff. Cover 2 inverted 9-inch cake pans with parchment paper, cut to fit, and spread with meringue. Bake at 225° for 1 hour, turn off oven, and let meringues dry for at least an hour before removing. In a saucepan, beat eggs with sugar, and gradually beat in butter, juice, and zest. Cook over moderate heat, whisking, until thick and smooth. Chill. Place a meringue layer in a 9-inch springform pan and spread with softened ice cream and lemon filling. Add remaining meringue layer, cover, and freeze until firm. Sift powdered sugar over top before serving, or if you are in an elegant mood, you can decorate the Vacherin with whipped cream, piped through a pastry bag, and fruit. Raspberry Sauce is delicious with this version. Now you know the basics for this wonderful and easy dessert, which is great during hot weather.

Serves 8.

GENOISE

(French Sponge Cake)

Theoretically a spongecake, Genoise is the most important of all French cakes and is the base for many elaborate as well as simple creations. Like many French classics, it originated in Italy where it is known as Genoese. The layers may be used with meringue layers, pastry creams, buttercreams, whipped cream, and fruit. Since there is no leavening, the key to rising is to whip the eggs over hot water until triple in volume. A hot-water attachment for a KitchenAid mixer is ideal, otherwise, heat eggs with sugar in a very low oven or place bowl over hot water on the stove while whisking.

6 eggs	6 tablespoons melted butter
1 cup sugar	1 tablespoon lemon juice
1 cup flour	1 teaspoon vanilla

Heat eggs with sugar over hot water until lukewarm, then whisk at high speed until triple in volume. Gently fold in flour, then gradually fold in butter mixed with flavorings. Bake at 350° in a buttered and floured 10-inch cake pan about ½ hour, or until done. Alternatively, the batter may be baked in 2 9-inch cake pans, but 1 large cake can be cut into layers, eliminating the number of crusty surfaces. Invert onto a rack to cool, and use in the following recipes.

Makes 1 large or 2 small layers.

GÂTEAU AUX FRAISES

(Strawberry Cream Cake)

This glorified strawberry shortcake was inspired by many, including the specialty at Auberge du Père Bise in Talloires.

1 cup cream	6 tablespoons soft butter
3 tablespoons powdered sugar	1 egg yolk
Raspberry or strawberry liqueur, to taste	2 cups powdered sugar
1 pint strawberries, halved	Raspberry or strawberry liqueur
2 layers Genoise	

Whip cream with sugar until stiff, add liqueur, and fold in strawberries, reserving about 1 cup for decorating. Spread over 1 layer, add remaining layer, and frost with a simple buttercream made by beating remaining ingredients together until smooth. A little red coloring may be used to add a pale pink tint to the frosting. Use a pastry bag if desired. Decorate with remaining berries.

Serves 8.

GÂTEAU AU MOUSSE AU CHOCOLAT

(Cake with Chocolate Mousse)

This triple chocolate cake is an all-time favorite of chocoholics everywhere but can be made with plain Genoise if desired. The various elements of the dessert can be used interchangeably with other desserts, and the chocolate mousse is the best you will ever find.

Genoise au Chocolat:

6 eggs	½ cup flour
1 cup sugar	½ cup cocoa
1 tablespoon Grand Marnier	½ cup melted butter

Beat eggs with sugar over hot water until at least double in volume. Add liqueur, sift flour and cocoa over mixture, and fold in gently. Gradually fold in butter. Bake in 2 buttered and floured 9-inch cake pans at 350° about 20 minutes, or until done. Invert onto racks to cool.

Mousse au Chocolat:

6 ounces semi-sweet chocolate	¼ cup Grand Marnier or coffee
¼ cup coffee, rum, or brandy	¾ cup soft butter
4 egg yolks	4 egg whites
¾ cup sugar	Pinch of salt
	2 tablespoons sugar

Melt chocolate in coffee over low heat. Beat yolks with sugar until thick and pale. Beat in chocolate, liqueur, and butter. Fold in whites which have been beaten with salt and sugar until stiff. Chill well.

Glace au Chocolat:

3 ounces unsweetened chocolate	1 tablespoon corn syrup
1 cup cream	1 egg, beaten
1 cup sugar	1 teaspoon vanilla

Simmer chocolate with cream, sugar, and syrup about 5 minutes, add egg gradually, and simmer until lightly thickened. Add vanilla, and chill.

1 cup cream, whipped	Crystallized lilacs or rosebuds

To assemble, spread mousse on 1 layer, add remaining layer of genoise, and place on a rack over a pan. Pour chocolate glaze over cake, spreading it evenly. Chill, and garnish base and top of cake with cream, forming large fleur de lys or other designs, using a pastry bag. Arrange lilacs over cream.

Serves 12.

PÂTE FEUILLETÉE RAPIDE

(Rapid Puff Pastry)

Puff Pastry, especially this rapid variety, should be a staple in every cook's kitchen, for its uses are varied and numerous. It is used for Bocuse's Soupe en Croûte, to envelop salmon, Beef Wellington, veal, and lamb, and for topping creamed dishes. Save the trimmings for cutting decorative fleurons (shapes) to decorate soups, casseroles, and desserts. It freezes beautifully.

3 cups flour	1 teaspoon salt
1 ½ cups cold butter, cut in chunks	¼ to 1/3 cup cold water

Blend flour, butter, and salt in food processor until crumbly, add water, and run machine briefly. The mixture should be slightly crumbly and not wet or sticky. Chill 10 minutes in the freezer. Roll into a rectangle about ½ inch thick, fold into thirds starting at the narrow edge, and with the open end at your right, roll out and fold again. This is a double turn. Chill again, and give the dough another double turn. The dough is now ready to be chilled again and used, or it may be refrigerated for a week, or frozen. Always use plastic wrap for chilling and freezing.

Makes 1 ½ pounds.

CORNETS DE CRÈME

(Puff Pastry Horns with Cream)

Cream horns are an ideal and delicious way to use leftover puff pastry and may be filled with flavored whipped cream, pastry creams, lemon curd, or savory fillings, such as chicken salad for hors d'oeuvres.

½ pound Pâte Feuilletée	1-1 ½ cups filling

Roll puff pastry into a rectangle, about 7 or 8 inches wide and 1/8 inch thick. Cut into 8 lengthwise strips, about 1 inch wide, using a pastry wheel. Starting at the tip end of 8 cream horn molds, wrap pastry around them, slightly overlapping the strips. Roll in sugar, or paint with an egg glaze, if desired, and bake at 425° about 15 minutes. Slip off of molds, cool, and fill, using a pastry bag for a decorative appearance.

Makes 8.

PALMIERS

(Puff Pastry Palm Leaves)

A simple cookie made from leftover puff pastry.

½ pound Pâte Feuilletée	Sugar

Sprinkle pastry with sugar, place on a surface sprinkled with sugar, and give the pastry 2 turns, as in the basic recipe, but rolling it ¼ inch thick. Roll into an 8-inch wide rectangle, and fold in each side to the center. Sprinkle with sugar, fold in half, forming 4 layers of dough. Cut into slices almost ½ inch thick. Lay them on their sides, curve the ends inward or out- ward, and chill. Sprinkle with sugar, and bake at 425° about 8 minutes.

Makes about 18.

The French method of shaping pastry for tarts is quite versatile as they may be free-form, without the use of a pan, or they may be made by placing the dough over an inverted baking pan of any size or shape, and then baked. Individual tart pans or dariole molds are also used. The baked shapes or shells are then spread or filled with your choice of filling and topped with fruit glazed with melted jelly or preserves. The following is a favorite.

TARTE AUX KIWIS ET FRAISES
(Kiwi and Strawberry Tart)

A stroll by the window of Fauchon, the great and inimitable food store on the Place de Madeleine, gave me this inspiration. I also make it in a 4- x 13-inch tart pan with a removeable bottom. Regular pastry may be used, if desired.

1 pound Pâte Feuilletée	1 pint strawberries
1 recipe Crème Pâtissière or Lemon Curd (see index)	Apricot preserves, melted
5 kiwis, peeled & sliced	Crème Chantilly (see index)

Roll out puff pastry into a large circle, square, or rectangle, about 1/8 inch thick. Place on a large baking sheet, sprinkled with cold water, prick well with a fork, and chill. Bake at 425° about 25 minutes, or until golden. Cool on a rack, and spread with pastry cream or lemon curd. Arrange fruit on top, brush with glaze, and garnish with cream, using a pastry bag.

Serves 6.

MILLEFEUILLE AU CITRON ET PRUNEAUX
(Napoleon with Lemon and Prunes)

Probably the most important and outstanding creation using puff pastry is the Napoleon, made up of several rectangular layers with pastry cream and icing on top. Fredy Girardet made a strawberry Napoleon with an ethereal combination of pastry cream, whipped cream, raspberry liqueur and purée, and strawberries. It is one of my favorites, and it inspired this lemon and plum variation.

1 pound Pâte Feuilletée	2 cups Lemon Curd (see index)
10-12 ripe plums, sliced	Powdered Sugar or Glace Royal (see index)
½ cup water	
¼ cup water	

Roll out pastry into a rectangle about 12 inches long and 1/8 inch thick. Place on a wet baking sheet, and bake at 400° about 15 minutes. Cook plums with water and sugar in a sauté pan until very tender and almost like a marmalade. Chill well. Cut cooled pastry into 4 rectangles about 12 inches long. To assemble, place a layer of pastry on a long and narrow platter, cover with 1/3 of lemon curd and plums. Repeat with 2 more layers of each, and top with final layer of pastry. Sift with sugar or spread with Glace Royal. Chill well.

Serves 6 to 8.

TORTE FRANÇAIS

This phantasmagorical creation is an example of how you can combine many of the French dessert components and achieve a most delectable taste sensation. This is related to Fernand Point's Gâteau Margolaine.

Meringue Layers:

5 egg whites	½ cup Pralinée Butter (see index)
1 cup sugar	
2 tablespoons cornstarch	1 cup coarsely crushed macaroons (see index)
1 ½ tablespoons cocoa powder	
2 cups ground almonds	½ cup cream, whipped
½ pound Pâte Feuilletée (see index)	2 teaspoons Grand Marnier
	Powdered sugar & cocoa powder
Chocolate Butter Cream (see index)	

For meringue layers, whisk whites with sugar added gradually until thick. Beat in cornstarch, and fold in almonds. Spread into 2 12-inch squares on a baking sheet lined with parchment paper. Bake at 250° ½ hour until dry. Turn squares over in pan and cool before removing paper.

Roll out puff pastry into a 12-inch square, place on a baking sheet, chill, prick all over with a fork, and bake at 350° about 45 minutes, until golden. To assemble torte, mix pralinée butter and half the macaroons into the chocolate butter cream, and spread about ½ cup on 1 meringue layer. Cover with pastry layer. Mix cream with remaining macaroons and liqueur, and spread on pastry layer. Add remaining meringue layer, and spread entire torte with remaining butter cream. Sift powdered sugar over top, lay any stencil design on the torte, and sift powdered sugar over the openings.

Serves 8 to 10.

PÂTE SUCRÉE

(Sweet French Pastry)

This very flaky and tender pastry contains sugar and egg yolks, and is the most popular for French desserts. One of the glories of the food processor is its ability to produce an excellent pastry with the greatest of ease, and with a minimum of handling and a minimum of water, both of which produce a more tender dough. A good flaky pastry is delicate and should be rolled up on the rolling pin to facilitate moving it to the pie plate. Remember that all pastry must be made with cold ingredients to insure flakiness and ease of handling. When I was a very young cooking teacher at Watkins Institute in Nashville, an older student of mine said that the pastry I was demonstrating was going to fall apart because it was so crumbly, so you can imagine her surprise when I deftly placed it in the tart pan. She later claimed it was the most outstanding pastry she ever had.

1 ¼ cups flour	2 egg yolks
1/3 cup powdered sugar	1 tablespoon cold water (I use orange juice, don't tell the French)
½ cup cold butter	

Blend flour, sugar, and butter in food processor only until crumbly. Add yolks and water, running machine briefly. Gather into a ball, enclose in a plastic wrap, and chill. After you become proficient you can do without the chilling. Roll out on a floured surface, preferably marble, roll up on the rolling pin, and place in tart shell. Press a square of foil over pastry to hold in place, and bake at 400° about 10 minutes, remove foil, and bake about 10 more minutes, or until golden. Or bake individual shells about 12 minutes.

Makes 1 9-inch or 10-inch tart shell or 6 individual shells.

TARTES AU CITRON

(Lemon Tarts)

Lemon tarts are my weakness, especially when made with British lemon curd, the richest and most unctuous filling imaginable. This was inspired by the one made by Roger Vergé in Mougins. One large tart may be made instead, and a variety of contrasting fruits may used to garnish the tarts.

10 3 ½ -inch tart shells, baked	Crème Chantilly
1 recipe chilled Lemon Curd (see index)	Crystalized violets or lilacs

Fill tart shells, garnish with cream using a pastry bag, and place violets on top.

Makes 10 individual tarts or 1 large.

TARTE DE NOIX CARAMELISÉE AU CHOCOLAT

(Caramelized Nut and Chocolate Tart)

Another of my numerous favorite tarts, this caramelized nut and chocolate delight was originally created by a Provençale country inn, Le Mas des Serres, and has reappeared in many variations.

1 cup sugar	2 cups walnuts, broken into pieces
1/3 cup water	Double recipe Pâte Sucrée (see index)
9 tablespoons butter	
9 tablespoons cream	6 ounces semi-sweet chocolate
1/3 cup honey	¼ cup butter

Dissolve sugar in water, then boil until caramelized. Remove from heat, and gradually add butter and cream. Simmer 15 minutes, or until slightly reduced and thickened. Add honey and nuts, and cool to room temperature. Roll 2/3 of dough into a 12-inch round, and press into a 9-inch tart pan with removeable bottom, letting dough extend above top of pan. Spread filling in pan, and roll out remaining dough into a 10-inch circle. Fold extended pastry over filling, and top with remaining pastry, sealing well. Make several slashes in dough, and bake at 450° in lower third of oven about 20 minutes, or golden brown. Cool, invert onto a platter, remove pan. Melt chocolate with butter, and pour over tart, spreading evenly. Garnish with walnuts, if desired, and serve at room temperature.

Serves 8.

GALETTES AUX TROIS PRUNEAUX

(Pastry with Plums)

Galettes are flat circles of pastry and may be used in place of tart shells in many recipes. A luscious plum marmalade is spread on the pastry and is topped with a variety of cooked plums for an outstanding dessert inspired by Alain Senderens of Lucas Carton, one of my favorites in Paris.

1 ½ pounds ripe Italian plums, sliced and pitted	2-2 ½ pounds assorted small, ripe plums, red, purple, & black
½ cup sugar	1 cup powdered sugar
¼ cup water	½ teaspoon French 4-spice powder
1 vanilla bean, halved lengthwise	1 recipe Pâte Sucrée

Simmer plums with sugar, water, and vanilla bean in a large sauté pan until the consistency of marmalade. Chill well. Halve and pit assorted plums, place on a baking sheet, cut side down, and sift powdered sugar and 4-spice over them. Bake about 10 to 15 minutes at 375°, or until tender and glazed, removing smaller ones when tender. Chill well.

Roll dough into 6 5- to 6-inch rounds about 1/8 inch thick. Place on a baking sheet, prick, and bake at 400° until golden. Cut any remaining dough into triangles, and bake alongside the rounds for decoration. Spread plum marmalade on pastry rounds, and alternate plums in concentric circles. The triangular fleurons are to be placed on top at an angle. Crème fraîche is divine with this.

Serves 6.

GALETTE AUX FIGUES ET FRAMBOISE

(Pastry with Figs and Raspberries)

Another of the numerous variations on fruit pastries, which I dearly love. Try pineapple with kiwis or rhubarb marmalade with strawberries.

1 recipe Pâte Sucrée	12 ripe Black Mission figs, halved
1/3 cup black currant preserves	¼ cup melted butter
1 pint raspberries	
2 tablespoons honey	¼ cup Demarara or brown sugar

Roll out pastry into 6 5- or 6-inch rounds. Spread with preserves. Toss raspberries with honey and place over preserves. Arrange 4 fig halves on top, and sprinkle with butter and sugar. Bake at 400° about 15 to 20 minutes, or until pastry is golden.

Serves 6.

POIRES BELLE DIJONNAISE

(Pears with Raspberries and Sorbet Cassis)

My rendition of this luscious classic from Dijon includes poached pears, raspberry sauce, and Sorbet Cassis. I like to have this as an elegant and refreshing finale for Thanksgiving or Christmas dinner.

2 cups water	2 tablespoons crème de cassis
1 1/3 cups sugar	Sorbet Cassis (see index)
2 tablespoons crème de cassis	Sauce Framboise (see index)
4 pears, peeled & halved	1 pint raspberries
1 cup cream	

Boil water, sugar, and cassis about 10 minutes. Add pears, poach until tender, and chill in syrup. Whip cream, adding cassis, and fill well-drained pears, using a pastry bag. Unmold sorbet in center of large platter, and pour sauce around it, completely covering bottom of platter. Arrange pears on sauce, and decorate platter with raspberries. Enjoy! If desired, sorbet may be frozen in 8 ½-cup molds for individual presentation.

Serves 8.

COUPE AUX MARRONS

(Vanilla Ice Cream and Chocolate Sorbet with Candied Chestnuts)

A memorable Black Sea cruise on Swan Hellenic's Minerva II gave me the inspiration for this elegant adaptation of a great classic. I found wonderful marrons glacées, glazed chestnuts in syrup, on the north coast of Turkey, in Sochi, Russia, and the Crimea.

6 small scoops Vanilla ice cream	6 tablespoons marrons glacées
6 small scoops Sorbet au Chocolat	¾ -1 cup chocolate sauce
	1/3 cup chopped pistachios

Place ice cream and sorbet on individual plates, top with marrons, and pour sauce around the plate. Garnish with pistachios.

Serves 6.

MARQUISE DE CHOCOLAT

(Rich Chocolate Mold with Crème Anglaise)

This very rich and divine molded chocolate dessert was made famous by Taillevant, one of the most highly esteemed Parisian restaurants. My version is enriched with cocoa powder and flavored with Tiramisu liqueur.

8 ounces semi-sweet chocolate	½ cup Cadbury cocoa powder
¾ cup butter	1 cup cream, whipped
¾ cup powdered sugar	Crème Anglaise or Sauce Pistache, or Cherry Sauce (see index)
4 egg yolks	
2 tablespoons Tiramisu liqueur	

Melt chocolate with butter and sugar in a heavy saucepan over low heat, stirring until smooth. Whisk in yolks, liqueur, and cocoa. Fold in cream, and pour into a buttered 8-inch springform pan, a soufflé dish lined with wax paper, or a 4-cup terrine lined with wax paper. Chill 6 to 8 hours, or overnight. Unmold, cut into wedges or slices, and serve with your choice of sauce.

Serves 8-12.

CHOUX-ECLAIRS-SALAMBOS

(Cream Puffs and Eclairs)

Cream puffs, eclairs, and salambos (ovals), along with chocolate truffles, are among my favorites as Mignardises, the little pick up desserts so popular in today's restaurants. Actually, the best I've had were on Air Cameroon from Libreville to Douala, but we must remember the great culinary legacy left by the French in Africa. One of my ardent cooking fans said, "Only in New York can you find cream puffs and eclairs this wonderful."

Pâte à Chou:	1 teaspoon sugar
½ cup milk	¾ teaspoon salt
½ cup water	1 cup flour
½ cup butter	4 large eggs

Bring milk, water, butter, sugar, and salt to a boil. Quickly beat in flour with a wooden spoon until dough leaves side of pan. Turn off heat, and continue beating a minute or so to dry out dough. Put in food processor, and add eggs one at a time, running machine only until well blended. Put dough in pastry bag, fitted with a large plain tip, and pipe onto a baking sheet lined with parchment paper, forming small 1-inch rounds, 1 ½ -inch rectangles, and 1 ½ -inch ovals, spacing them about 1 inch apart. Bake at 425° for 10 minutes, lower heat to 400°, insert a wooden spoon in oven door to hold it slightly open, and bake 10 minutes. Cool on racks, pack in tins, and refrigerate 1 week, or freeze 1 month. Defrost in refrigerator overnight, and fill and frost the day of serving.

Lemon curd or Crème Pâtissière:

Lemon Curd or Crème Pâtissière (see index) Fondant (see index)	2 tablespoons semi-sweet chocolate ½ teaspoon vegetable oil

Fill each, using a pastry bag fitted with a Bismarck tube inserted in the side, which does not require cutting them in half. Dip cream puffs in pink, green, and yellow fondant. Dip eclairs in chocolate melted with oil, which gives them a nice gloss.

Makes about 5 or 6 dozen.

TRUFFES AU CHOCOLAT

(Chocolate Truffles)

French chocolate truffles have always been the ultimate mignardise. The name is derived from their resemblance to the savory truffle found underground. Truffles also make an elegant addition to the dessert plate, or served at cocktail parties.

Basic directions for truffles: After preparing the following mixtures, whip them over ice water, preferably using a heavy duty mixer with a water jacket, until thick enough to hold their shape. Place in a pastry bag, fitted with a ½-inch plain tip, and pipe onto wax or parchment paper or into small foil bonbon cups. After chilling, traditional truffles are rolled into balls, which are then rolled in imported cocoa (I love Cadbury), or they may be dipped in a melted chocolate couverture or tempered chocolate. If desired, the American method of melting chocolate with paraffin, using proportions of 3 to 1, may be used. In either case, use a fork or wooden pick for dipping, and place on wax or parchment paper. Store in refrigerator a week or in freezer in tins. The following truffle varieties are among the best I've sampled. Probably, the best are in Toronto's Four Seasons Hotel, where their restaurant is aptly named Truffles. They are brought to your table in an elegant chocolate box.

Chocolate Cream Truffles:

¼ pound semi-sweet chocolate, chopped ½ cup cream 2 tablespoons butter	1 tablespoon honey 1 tablespoon brandy, rum, or liqueur

Melt chocolate with cream, butter, and honey over low heat. Add brandy, and proceed as in basic directions.

Makes about 1 ½ dozen.

Pralinée Cream Truffles:

¼ pound semi-sweet chocolate, chopped ¾ cup cream	¼ cup Pralinée aux Noix (see index) 1-2 tablespoons brandy or Frangelico

Melt chocolate with cream over low heat, add flavorings and proceed as in basic directions. These may be rolled in extra pralinée, if desired.

Makes about 1 ½ dozen.

Fruit Truffles:

4 ounces semi-sweet chocolate, chopped	¼ cup orange marmalade & 1 tablespoon Grand Marnier, or
3 tablespoons butter	¼ cup finely chopped marrons glacées & 1 tablespoon drained chestnut syrup
¼ cup black currant preserves & 1 tablespoon Chambord liqueur, or	

Melt chocolate with butter over low heat, and add your choice of flavorings. Follow basic directions. These may be rolled in cocoa, coconut, or pistachios.

Makes about 1 ½ dozen.

Minted White Chocolate Truffles:

¼ pound white chocolate, chopped	1 tablespoon crème de menthe
2 tablespoons cream	1 tablespoon finely chopped mint
2 tablespoons butter	¼ pound semi-sweet chocolate, melted

Melt chocolate with cream and butter over very low heat, as white chocolate is very sensitive to heat, and add flavorings. Follow basic directions, and dip in melted chocolate for a delightful contrast in flavors and colors. Makes about 1 ½ dozen.

The following fillings, frostings, icings, and sauces are used in a number of the previous recipes and others in this book:

LEMON CURD

My favorite filling for cakes, tarts, meringues, all kinds of pastries, and for serving with fruits. Lime or orange juice may be substituted.

3 eggs 3 egg yolks 1 cup sugar	½ cup lemon juice (or lime juice) 3 tablespoons grated lemon zest ½ cup soft butter

Whisk eggs, yolks, and sugar until blended, add juice and zest, and cook gently over medium heat until thickened. Gradually whisk in butter, and cool.

Makes about 2-2 ½ cups.

CHOCOLATE BUTTERCREAM

Another luscious and unctuous filling or frosting good enough to eat with a spoon.

1 cup sugar ½ cup water ¼ teaspoon cream of tartar 5 egg yolks	½ pound soft butter 2 ounces semi-sweet chocolate, melted Vanilla or liqueur, to flavor

Dissolve sugar in water with cream of tartar, and boil to 238°. Beat yolks until thick and light in color. Add syrup gradually, beating until thick and cool. Beat in remaining ingredients gradually.

Makes about 2 ½ cups.

CRÈME PÂTISSIÈRE

(French Pastry Cream)

The most important of French fillings for cakes, tarts, cream puffs, and even in such American classics as Banana Pudding.

¾ cup sugar	6 egg yolks
2 ½ tablespoons flour	6 tablespoons butter
2 tablespoons cornstarch	1 teaspoon vanilla
2 cups milk	1 tablespoon Grand Marnier

Mix dry ingredients in heavy saucepan, add milk gradually, and bring to a boil. Add a little to yolks, return to pan, and cook gently until thick. Beat in remaining ingredients, and chill.

Makes about 3 cups.

FONDANT

An essential component in the serious pastry kitchen, especially for cream puffs, or any time you want a better icing than the ordinary powdered sugar type.

1 cup sugar	Food coloring
1/3 cup warm water	Almond, orange, or lemon extract
Pinch of cream of tartar	

Stir sugar, water, and cream of tartar until dissolved, then boil to 238°, and turn out onto a lightly oiled marble slab. Let cool about 5 minutes, then scrape it back and forth onto itself with a spatula until it is white and opaque. Blend in food processor until creamy. Store in tightly covered container indefinitely in refrigerator. To use, heat very slowly with 1 or 2 teaspoons hot milk, water, or coffee for each ½ cup fondant and heat until pourable. Add a few drops of coloring and extract, as desired.

Makes about ¾ cup.

GLACE ROYAL
(Royal Icing)

Another important icing for pastries, especially Napoleons.

1 egg white 1 cup powdered sugar	1 ½ teaspoons lemon juice

Beat white, adding sugar gradually, and when stiff, add juice. Makes about 1 cup.

PRALINÉE AUX NOIX
(Caramelized Nut Powder)

Always keep a container of this versatile caramelized nut powder in the refrigerator of freezer, for it is indispensable for garnishing desserts of all kinds and for flavoring frostings, ice cream, and mousses.

1 cup sugar 1/3 cup water	1 cup walnuts, pecans, almonds, or hazelnuts

Dissolve sugar in water, boil until caramelized, and add nuts. Pour onto an oiled baking sheet or marble slab, cool until hardened, and break into pieces. Pulverize in processor until crumbly, or process to a paste for pralinée butter.

Makes about 2 cups powder or 1 cup butter.

CRÈME CHANTILLY

(Flavored Whipped Cream)

This flavored and sweetened whipped cream, piped through a pastry bag, will be an elegant addition to your desserts.

1 cup cream 2 tablespoons powdered sugar	1 teaspoon vanilla or liqueur

Whip cream until stiff, gradually adding sugar, and flavor.

Makes 2 cups.

CRÈME ANGLAISE

(Custard Sauce)

English cream, a rich custard sauce which originated in England, is used extensively in French desserts, and is the forerunner of American custard.

1 cup milk	5 egg yolks
1 cup cream or crème fraîche	½ cup sugar
½ to ¾ cup chopped marrons glacées (optional)	2 tablespoons Grand Marnier or other liqueur

Bring milk and cream to a simmer. Beat yolks with sugar until light and fluffy, add a little hot milk mixture, then return to pan, and cook gently until lightly thickened. Add flavorings and chill.

Makes about 2 cups.

SAUCE FRAMBOISE

(Raspberry Sauce)

A darling of nouvelle cuisine that is here to stay, as it has infinite uses, especially with sorbets, fruits, and tarts.

1 package frozen raspberries, thawed	1-2 tablespoons Chambord or Crème de Cassis
¼ cup currant jelly or black currant preserves, melted	

Purée raspberries in processor, sieve to remove seeds, and add remaining ingredients.

Makes about 1 ½ cups.

ITALY

My extensive travels throughout France and Italy, to remote villages and cosmopolitan cities, have confirmed my opinion that there are many interesting parallels between their cuisines and their people. The southern parts of both countries are the most similar, although on different latitudes. Olive oil, garlic, tomatoes, and herbs dominate the cooking of the vivacious and romantic Latin types, while butter and cream dominate the more refined and elegant cuisines of the serious and dignified northerners, although there are exceptions to the rule.

Italy had the first fully developed cuisine in Europe, and became the mother of French cuisine when Catherine de Medici, with her cooks in tow, went to France to marry the future King Henri II. Pâte à Choux, Genoise, and ice creams were among the many preparations of Italian cuisine that made the historic journey.

Piedmont, a region of spectacular mountain scenery, retains much French influence from the era when it was ruled by the court of Savoy, and the beautiful city of Turin is considered to be the Paris of Italy. The pride of Piedmontese cooking is the white truffle, more flavorful than the black truffle of France, and it attains sublimity when savored in Fonduta, the local version of Swiss Fondue. Butter and cream, staples of the elegant Piedmontese cusine, are the primary ingredients of Bagna Cauda, an unctuous hot dip for crudités (raw vegetables) and grissini (bread sticks), which were conceived in Turin. Zabaglione, the Italian version of French Sabayon, is an elegant finale to a Piedmontese dinner. The foremost wines are vermouth and Asti Spumante, both aperitifs, and the renowned Barolo, a great red wine made from the Nebbiolo grape, as is Barbaresco.

Lombardy is known for its languid and beautiful lake resorts of Como, Lugano, and Garda, especially the majestic Villa d'Este on Lake Como, which is one of my favorites in the entire world. Milan is noted for Savini, the venerable restaurant in the Galleria Vittorio Emanuele, the world's largest glass-covered arcade, and La Scala, one of Italy's most renowned opera houses. An elaborate feast for the eyes is provided by the window displays of Milan's famed food emporiums, such as Gastronomia Peck, which is Italy's answer to London's Harrods and Paris's Fauchon. The most irresistible of Lombardy's specialties are bresaola (very superior dried beef), mostarda di fruta (mustard-fruit relish) from Cremona, and my favorite Italian cheeses—Gorgonzola, Mascarpone, and Bel Paese. Butter and saffron are important elements in Risotto alla Milanese, which is an ideal accompaniment to Osso Buco, the unctuous and garlicky veal shank dish that I could dine on eternally. Minestrone is an important soup, and Pannettone, a rich bread with crystalized fruit is the pride of the baker. Lombardy produces good red and white wines.

Liguria is quintessentially Italian, from the moment the train crosses the border at Ventimiglia and begins its coast-hugging route through the Italian Riviera, where La Dolce Vita reigns. It is always a temptation to disembark at Portofino, the most posh of all resort areas, but the aficionado of Italian cuisine must visit the Museum of Spaghetti at Pontedassio and the Italian Academy of Cooking at Savona before progressing to Genoa, Italy's most important seaport for over 2,500 years. The best restaurants are located in the colorful waterfront area in the old city. The rest of Genoa is almost perpendicular, as it is built on steep stone cliffs, which rise abruptly from the sea. The aroma of basil pervades the entire area, as it is grown even on windowsills in the labyrinth of winding alleyways in the old city, and it is the most important element of Ligurian cooking. Pesto, basil's most divine destination, is the traditional pasta sauce, and it adds a fillip to Minestrone, which the Ligurians claim to have invented, as well as ravioli.

Although the Veneto region boasts of the great university town of Padua and the historical literary town of Verona, it is personified by Venice, once the most splendiferous city in the world, reaching its pinnacle in the sixteenth century. The Queen of the Adriatic, still replete with its ornate palaces in the Gothic, Byzantine, and Renaissance styles, is a delight to explore via vaporetti or romantic gondolas on its 160 canals. Or you can lose yourself, literally, in the charms of Venice by walking through its 120 islands, connected by 400 stylized bridges. The Grand Canal, which Goethe called the most beautiful street in the world, leads you to the regal Piazzo San Marco, the area where the riches of Venetian cuisine can be sampled at their best. Seafood is foremost, especially the scampi dishes. Polenta and Risotto, sans saffron as in the Milanese style, are ubiquitous. As for wines, Prosecco is a good sparkling wine from Friuli, north of Venice, and Soave, probably Italy's most famous but uninteresting white wine, is produced in Verona, along with Valpolicella, their best known red. Both are to be drunk young, and are good companions to Venetian food.

Bologna, the heart of Emilia-Romagna, is to Italy what Lyon is to France—the gastronomic center of the country. Its rich calorific cooking has bestowed it with the name of "la grassa" or "the fat one." Alleged to be the center of Italian Communism, Bologna, nevertheless, is a charming city to explore under the porticos which line the streets, and it is mercifully free of mass tourism. Bologna is somewhat of an oasis in the rice-dominated north, as it excels in pasta-making. Synonymous with Bologna is tortellini, Lasagna Verde, cappelletti, pappardelle, and tagliatelle, which are indigenous to this area. Ragu, the rich and creamy meat sauce for pasta and polenta, is the pride of the Bolognese. Rivaling pasta are the numerous pork products, which can be seen hanging in the salumeria. Our bologna is an undeserving namesake for the most highly esteemed of Bologna's sausages, mortadella. Last, but not least is Parma ham, or prosciutto, from Parma, which is also renowned for its universally famous Parmesan cheese. The perfect wine to drink with these sinfully rich dishes is the local Lambrusco, a somewhat paradoxical wine in that it is a dry but sparkling red. The priceless art and riches of Tuscany, whose name is derived from its ancient Etruscan origin, have produced an incessant flow of tourism in its cities of Pisa, Siena, and especially

Florence, the art capital of the world. Known for its writers, artists, and sculptors, Florence was the leader of the Renaissance era under the rule of the Medicis, and its eternal culture is kept alive by constant reminders of Dante, Michaelangelo, da Vinci, Boccaccio, Petrarch, Machiavelli, and others.

As priceless as Tuscany's art is its cuisine—pure, simple, and uncomplicated, the result of excellent ingredients prepared with skill. An interesting parallel is that classic simplicity is the main objective of the new cooking of the past several decades, yet today's Tuscan cuisine is as old as the tables of the Medicis, who had a vast influence on France. The most important Tuscan ingredient is its light olive oil from Lucca, which produces the best. Tuscan beef is also the best in Italy, and when accompanied by Fagioli all'uccelletto, the classic bean dish, a comforting and memorable dinner like this will need nothing more than the greatest of all Italian wines, Chianti Classico. The best Chiantis are in Bordeaux-type bottles, those with a high neck. Brunello di Montalcino is another great wine, and is a big one.

Umbria is a rugged, hilly area that is relatively undiscovered. This is Italy as it should be, and the best cooking here is that in the homes, where simplicity reigns, and one-dish meals are common. The golden city of Perugia is perched on a hill, and Assisi is the only other city of any size. Spit-roasting, especially porchetta, a whole suckling pig, is the most important specialty. Verdicchio is a famous white wine from the Marches, a coastal area. Orvieto is either sweet or dry, and is the best white.

Also in central Italy is Abruzzo, a rugged and mountainous land well worth exploring. Lamb is supreme here, along with game. Pecorino cheese and scamorza, which is roasted over an open fire, are excellent with the Trebbiano whites and especially the Montepulciano reds which have been exported much more in recent years. Aurum, an orange flavored liqueur, is also produced here, and it rivals the orange liqueurs of France.

Roma, the eternal city of almost three millenia, has classic sights as numerous as its great restaurants. Even the most avid epicurian must see the Colosseum, the Vatican City's Basilica of St. Mark, the world's largest church, and the famous piazzas. Piazza Navona is the place to stop for tartufi, the white truffle ice cream, at the sidewalk cafe of Tre Scalini. The equally famous Piazza di Spagna, with its 137 steps leading to the Villa Borghese gardens, rises from Via Condotti's irresistible luxury shops of Gucci, Pucci, Valentino, and Bulgari, not to mention Caffe Greco, the venerable coffee house. Do as the Romans do; stroll on the Via Veneto, throw a coin in the Trevi fountain, and dine, dine, dine!

All the great regional dishes of Italy may be sampled in Rome, but for typical Roman food, one must eat at the trattoria of Trastevere, the colorful quarter across the Tiber. Romans indulge in pasta, young roasted lamb, and exquisite vegetables, such as artichokes, peas, and beans. Frascati, made since ancient times, is a wonderfully assertive and dry white wine and the best.

The colorful and scenic Campania region is a delight to explore, and the warm-hearted hospitality of the Neapolitans is memorable. Naples is synonymous with pizza and spaghetti, as tomatoes were introduced here in the sixteenth century and had a lasting influence on the cooking. My cookbook, *Culinary Classics,* has an authentic recipe for Spaghetti and Meatballs, which I obtained from Tony Tomaso, my aunt's husband from Naples, and it is still my best pasta dish.

The highlight of the entire area, however, is not Capri, but the spectacular Amalfi Drive along the precipitous cliffs between Positano and Vietri, above the Gulf of Salerno. Ancient Ravello, about 1,200 feet above the coast, is my favorite hideaway, and the source of several great recipes in this book. The cooking of Campania, as well as Calabria and Apulia, reveal the influence of the Greeks, Turks, Albanians, and Arabs who infiltrated the area in earlier times. Olive oil, garlic, tomato paste, and eggplant are the cornerstones of the cooking, along with the indigenous mozzarella and the abundant seafood.

Sicily probably has the best cooks in all of Italy, and the pasta is the most outstanding of all their specialties. Pasta was cooked here first and then spread to the rest of Italy. Palermo, Siracusa, and Catania all have great restaurants with wonderful fish, especially tuna and swordfish. Cannoli and ice cream originated here also. Sicilians are noted pastry chefs, which was a result of the Arab influence. Marsala, a fortified wine similar to sherry and Madeira, originated in the town of the same name on the west coast of Sicily near Trapani. The Arabs left their culinary legacy on the west coast, and the Greeks were dominant on the east coast.

Sardinia, Italy's other large island, is my favorite, as it is sparsely populated and is a wild land of craggy rocks and dramatic scenery. It is also the site of Costa Smeralda, the beautiful people's playground for the rich and famous, developed on the northeastern coast by Aga Khan in 1962. Cala di Volpe, Pitrizza, and Romazzino are the most unique, exclusive, and private hotels I know of, and they all have wonderful food. An outdoor pool barbecue had table after table loaded with salads, pastas, pizzas, and grills ready to cook your choice of succulent lamb chops, lobster, and anything else you desired. The King of Sweden was there at the time, and is a regular. Native to Sardinia is a flat bread called carta di musica, because its crisp flat shape looks like a sheet of music. A mullet caviar, called bottarga, was quite good, as were the caprino and robiole cheeses. Vernaccia, an amber wine with an aroma of orange zest, is Sardinia's most important wine and complements the delicious food.

RECIPES FROM ITALY

CARPACCIO ALLA CIPRIANI

INVOLTINI DI PROSCIUTTO CON PATÉ
(PROSCIUTTO ROLL WITH PATÉ)

FICHI CON PROSCIUTTO E GORGONZOLA
(FIGS WITH PROSCIUTTO AND GORGONZOLA)

ANTIPASTO ALLA SWAN

HARRY'S BAR CHICKEN SALAD

INSALATA DI POLLO CON GORGONZOLA
(CHICKEN AND GORGONZOLA)

PANZANELLA (TUSCAN BREAD SALAD)

INVOLTINI DI PESCE CON COUSCOUS
(SICILIAN FISH ROLLS WITH COUSCOUS)

CRESPELLE CARUSO BELVEDERE

ZUPPA ALLA TOSCANA (TUSCAN COUNTRY SOUP)

ZUPPA DI MELANZANE ARROSTO (ROASTED EGGPLANT SOUP)

BRUSCHETTA CON OLIO DI TARTUFA
(GRILLED BREAD WITH TRUFFLE OIL)

BRUSCHETTA CON POMODORI
(GRILLED BREAD WITH TOMATOES)

FOCACCIA

GRILLED VEGETABLES, PESTO, AND MOZZARELLA SANDWICHES

MALTESE TUNA SANDWICHES

PIZZA MARGHERITA

PIZZA DOUGH

PASTA DOUGH

SPAGHETTI ALLA NORMA

TAGLIOLINI CON SALSA DI POMODORI FRESCA
(TAGLIOLINI WITH FRESH TOMATO SAUCE)

PASTA CON CREMA DI LIMONE (PASTA WITH LEMON CREAM)

FETTUCCINE AL LIMONE (LEMON FETTUCCINE DOUGH)

LINGUINE CON CREAM DI QUATTRO NOCI
(LINGUINE WITH CREAM OF FOUR NUTS)

PASTA CON ZUCCHINI

FARFALLE CON UOVO E BRESAOLA
(FARFALLE WITH EGGS AND BRESAOLA)

PAPPARDELLE CON PEPERONI E SALCICCIA
(PAPPARDELLE WITH PEPERONI AND SAUSAGE)

RAVIOLI DI FUNGHI E SPINACI ALLA SWAN
(RAVIOLI WITH MUSHROOMS AND SPINACH)

RAVIOLI DI ZUCCA CON BUTTER E SALVIA
(RAVIOLI OF SQUASH WITH BUTTER AND SAGE)

RAVIOLI CON UOVO E SPINACH
(RAVIOLI WITH EGG AND SPINACH)

TIELLA (BAKED APULIAN FISH)

PESCE ALLA SICILIANA (SICILIAN STYLE FISH)

POLLO AL SALE (BAKED CHICKEN WITH A SALT CRUST)

POLLO AL LIMONE (LEMON CHICKEN)

POLLO CON FAGIOLI (CHICKEN WITH DRIED BEANS)

ITALIAN SAUSAGE

MAIALE CON LATTE (PORK COOKED IN MILK)

POLPETTE ALLA SARDEGNA (SARDINIAN MEATBALLS)

CARNE ALLA TIELLA (TERRA COTTA ROASTED MEAT)

AGNELLO BALSAMICO (LAMB WITH BALSAMIC)

OSSO BUCO MODERNE

OSSO BUCO ORIENTALE

PESTO WITH ROASTED GARLIC

CREAMY PESTO

SALSA DI POMODORI SICILIANA (SICILIAN TOMATO SAUCE)

RED AND YELLOW TOMATO SAUCE

HONEY-BALSAMIC GLAZE

LEMON-ORANGE SICILIAN MARINADE

ROASTED GARLIC

CAPONATA (SICILIAN VEGETABLE STEW)

FAGIOLI ALLA UCCELLETTO (BEANS COOKED IN OLIVE OIL)

FAGIOLI DI BORLOTTI (ITALIAN BORLOTTI BEANS)

BORLOTTI CON POMODORI (BORLOTTI BEANS WITH TOMATOES)

VERDURE ALLA AGRODOLCE
(SWEET AND SOUR VEGETABLES SICILIAN STYLE)

POLENTA CON FORMAGGIO (POLENTA WITH CHEESE)

POLENTA CON RAGU DI FUNGHI
(POLENTA WITH WILD MUSHROOM RAGOUT)

RISOTTO DI ZUCCA (PUMPKIN RISOTTO)

RISOTTO ALLA POMODORI E OLIVE
(TOMATO AND OLIVE RISOTTO)

MONTE BIANCO

SOUFFLÉ DI LIMONE E CIOCCOLATO
(LEMON AND CHOCOLATE SOUFFLÉ)

CRESPELLE AU RHUM PALUMBO (RUM CRÊPES PALUMBO)

ANANAS CARAMELLATO CON GELATO
(CARAMELIZED PINEAPPLE WITH ICE CREAM)

MASCARPONE ICE CREAM

TORTA DI CIOCCOLATA E NOCCIOLA
(CHOCOLATE HAZELNUT TORTE)

AMARETTI OR MACAROONS (ALMOND COOKIES)

ANTIPASTO

Antipasti has come a long way since the days of arranging cheese, salami, olives, artichoke hearts, hard-cooked eggs, and myriad other ingredients on a platter. Elegance and a sensible salute to fusion cooking have entered the culinary picture. These first courses also include salads, crespelle (crêpes), bruschetta, and soups.

CARPACCIO ALLA CIPRIANI

Hotel Cipriani, on its own private island, a private boat ride away from St. Mark's Square in Venice, offers some of the best food to be found in Italy, and this was my favorite dish, although I do not recommend raw beef unless you know your source. This is a classic originating at Harry's Bar.

½ pound beef tenderloin, sliced paper-thin	1 ½ teaspoons lemon juice
½ cup mayonnaise	1 teaspoon Dijon mustard
1 ½ teaspoons worcestershire	3 tablespoons veal stock

Drape beef slices on each of 6 plates. Whisk mayonnaise and seasonings together, and drizzle over meat.

Serves 6.

INVOLTINI DI PROSCIUTO CON PATÉ
(Prosciutto Roll with Paté)

An unusual but simple and delicious version of a paté. This paté is rolled in prosciutto, served on lettuce, and is garnished with your choice of traditional antipasto items. This is a classic from northern Italy.

1 small leek, sliced	3 tablespoons Marsala or brandy
1 small carrot, sliced	
1 small celery rib, sliced	2 tablespoons chopped sage
¼ cup olive oil or butter	2 tablespoons chopped pistachios
¼ teaspoon French 4-spice powder	8-10 slices prosciutto
1 ½ teaspoons salt	Red leaf lettuce or mesclun
3 suprêmes & 6 ounces pork tenderloin	Black olives, grape tomatoes, artichoke hearts, figs, etc
6 ounces butter, softened	¼ cup Vinaigrette (see index)

Sauté vegetables in oil or butter lightly, add seasonings, chicken, and pork. Simmer, covered, until tender, about 20 minutes. Cool, discard vegetables, and grind meats in processor. Whip butter, add meats, seasonings, and nuts. Form a rectangle with slightly overlapping slices of prosciutto on a large piece of plastic wrap. Form meat mixture into a log, place in center, and with the help of the plastic wrap, roll up. Chill well, slice, place on lettuce, and garnish as desired with vegetables. Drizzle with vinaigrette.

Serves 6.

FICHI CON PROSCIUTTO E GORGONZOLA

(Figs with Prosciutto and Gorgonzola)

Figs, prosciutto, and cheese are an old standby in Italy, but this is currently a popular presentation by Italian chefs everywhere. I recently enjoyed this in a Virgin Atlantic Upper Class lounge.

6 ounces gorgonzola or chèvre	1 ½ cups ruby Port
1-2 tablespoons cream	¼ cup Balsamic vinegar
8-10 slices prosciutto	2 tablespoons honey
1 pound fresh figs, preferably Black Mission	¼ cup mint leaves

Mash cheese with cream to spread easily. Arrange half the prosciutto slices in a rectangle, overlapping slightly, forming 2 rows. Spread with cheese, and repeat with remaining prosciutto. Cut figs in half, and simmer in combined remaining ingredients for about 15 minutes. Drain and cool, then arrange across the prosciutto rectangles, end to end. Roll tightly, chill, and slice on the diagonal, about 3 inches long. Serve as part of an antipasto platter or on plates, with the reduced braising liquid. For an interesting variation, replace the cheese with an equal amount of the paté from the previous recipe.

Makes 8-12.

ANTIPASTO ALLA SWAN

The most impressive and delicious antipasto was the one I had in the Swan Restaurant on the Minerva II, an elegant but relaxing Swan Hellenic ship. The creative chef, Niranjan Taste, was an Indian, the ship is British, and we were in the Black Sea, but what a great Italian dinner!

6 artichoke hearts	¼ cup Herbed Chèvre (see index)
2 tablespoons Tapenade (see index)	18 small asparagus spears, blanched
6 small slices baguette	
6 tablespoons Pesto (see Index)	6 slices prosciutto
Shaved Parmesan cheese	¼ pound gruyere, cut into strips
½ cup oven-dried tomatoes (see index)	2 tablespoons butter

Flare out the artichoke hearts with a fork and top with tapenade. Spread baguette slices with pesto, and sprinkle with cheese shavings. Place each of these on 6 plates. Arrange several pieces of tomatoes on plates, top them with a rosette of chèvre, using a pastry bag. Place 3 asparagus spears on each prosciutto slice diagonally, place most of cheese on top of asparagus, dot with some butter, roll up, and place in a shallow buttered baking dish. Place remaining cheese and butter on top and bake at 325° about 15 minutes, or just until cheese is melted. Place on plates with other antipasto.

Serves 6.

HARRY'S BAR CHICKEN SALAD

One of the world's most venerable and notable restaurants is Harry's Bar in Venice. The cognoscenti have been enjoying the food and ambiance here for over five decades. This is my version of the best thing I've eaten there.

6 suprêmes, poached & julienned	4 large Romas, sliced or 1 pint cherry or grape tomatoes
4 cups chiffonade of romaine	Worcestershire

Salt & pepper 1 ½ cups mayonnaise	2-3 tablespoons veal stock 3 hard-cooked egg yolks Nicoise or Kalamata olives

Place lettuce in center of platter, arrange chicken on lettuce, and place tomatoes around edge of lettuce. Season chicken with worcestershire and salt and pepper. Thin mayonnaise with stock and spread over chicken. Sieve yolks over mayonnaise, and garnish with olives.

Serves 6.

INSALATA DI POLLO CON GORGONZOLA

(Chicken and Gorgonzola Salad)

This is a wonderful warm chicken salad inspired by Valentino, the best Italian restaurant in Los Angeles.

6 suprêmes, grilled 4 ounces gorgonzola, sliced 1 cup Vinaigrette (see index) 3 tablespoons veal stock	12 ounces mesclun or arugula Nicoise or Kalamata olives Cherry or grape tomatoes

When almost done, place a few slices of cheese on suprêmes to melt. Slice suprêmes diagonally, and keep warm. Add remaining gorgonzola to vinaigrette and stock, heating until cheese melts. Toss with lettuce, arrange suprêmes on top, and garnish with olives and tomatoes.

Serves 6.

PANZANELLA

(Tuscan Bread Salad)

This Tuscan bread salad is eaten throughout central Italy, and has many versions. The bread can be sourdough, ciabatta, or any kind of country bread, and it can be grilled, fried, baked, and even soaked in water. It can be sort of a tossed salad, but I think the true flavors of the bread and tomatoes come forth if the salad is kept simple. This is the best I've come across in my travels, and you'll love it.

½ pound Rosemary Olive Oil bread	2 garlic cloves, crushed
2 tablespoons olive oil	Salt & pepper
1 pound very ripe Roma tomatoes	½ cup torn basil leaves
½ cup olive oil	2-4 ounces shaved Asiago cheese
1 tablespoon Balsamic or red wine vinegar	Fleur de Sel & gray pepper, at table
	Olives (optional)

Tear bread into approximately 2-inch chunks, sprinkle with oil, and toast at 400° about 5 minutes, until crusty on the outside. I love using my Cuisinart toaster oven for this. Place in a large salad bowl, cut tomatoes in half, and squeeze half of them over the bread to extract the juices. Cut remainder into smaller pieces. I have also used very ripe cherry or grape tomatoes with great success. Add vinaigrette made with oil, vinegar, and seasonings. Toss well and add basil, cheese, and seasonings.

Serves 4.

INVOLTINI DI PESCE CON COUSCOUS

(Sicilian Fish Rolls with Couscous)

This is one of my favorite recipes from Sicily, and is a good example of the Arab influence. The fish rolls are filled with golden couscous, raisins, and almonds. This was inspired by a dish I savored at Ristorante Jonico in Siracusa, on the rocky Ionian coast. Stemperata, an assertive mixture of olive oil, vinegar, garlic, and mint is the cornerstone of Siracusan cooking.

1/3 cup couscous	1/4 cup golden raisins
1 cup water	1/4 cup currants
1/4 cup chopped red bell pepper	2-3 tablespoons chopped mint
1/4 cup chopped green bell pepper	1/3 cup Marsala
2 tablespoons olive oil	Salt & pepper
1 large garlic clove, minced	6 thin slices swordfish or snapper
1/4 cup sliced almonds or pine nuts	Arugula & lemon slices

Add couscous to boiling salted water, cover, and let stand about 5 minutes or until water is absorbed. Sauté peppers in oil until soft, add garlic, nuts, raisins, currants, and mint. Add marsala, and reduce until evaporated. Season, and add couscous. Spread on fish, roll up, place in a shallow baking dish, and bake at 400° about 10 minutes, or until fish is done. Place on a bed of arugula, and garnish with lemon. Add a bit of wine to pan to deglaze, and pour over fish with extra oil, if desired.

Serves 6.

CRESPELLE CARUSO BELVEDERE

(Crêpes Caruso Belvedere)

Crespelle, Italian crêpes, are either sweet or savory, and the best I've had were in Ravello, perched on top of the Amalfi coast. Caruso Belvedere was a legendary hotel, and its owner, Signor Caruso, was quite a gastronome, as well as a distinguished old gentleman. The grand hotel is now open again.

3 tablespoons butter	¼ cup parmesan
3 tablespoons flour	1 tablespoon chopped parsley
1 cup milk	Salt & pepper
¼ cup diced prosciutto	1 egg, beaten
¼ cup diced mozzarella	2 or 3 8-inch crespelle
¼ cup ricotta cheese	(crêpes-see index)

Make a roux with butter and flour, add milk all at once, and whisk until thick. Add prosciutto, cheeses, seasonings, and egg, cooking again until thick. Chill, spread on crêpes, roll up, and chill again. Slice about 1-inch thick, arrange in a buttered baking dish, and bake at 375° about 15 minutes, or until golden. Everybody loves these.

Serves 6-8.

ZUPPA ALLA TOSCANA

(Tuscany Country Soup)

Tuscany's country soup, and all of Italy's peasant soups, are the supreme comfort food and the purest example of Italian food at its best. Ribollita is the name commonly used when greens are added, but dried borlotti beans and good peasant bread are the principal ingredients, so use whatever your garden offers. I like to use my Thanksgiving turkey stock.

½ pound dried borlotti, cranberry, or October beans, soaked overnight	1 carrot, peeled & chopped
	1 celery rib, chopped
¼ cup chopped bacon or pancetta	1 pound chard, kale, or collards, cut into a chiffonade
¼ cup olive oil	2 quarts strong chicken stock
5 garlic cloves, crushed	¼ cup red wine
1 tablespoon chopped sage	Salt & pepper
1 tablespoon chopped rosemary	6 slices Foccaccia or other peasant bread, grilled or toasted
1 large onion, chopped	½ cup parmesan cheese

Drain beans, cover with cold water, and cook until half done, about 1 hour. Older beans take longer. Save the cooking liquid, if desired, for the soup. Sauté bacon in oil until golden, add garlic and herbs, cook briefly, and add chopped vegetables, cooking until well coated with oil, and the greens are wilted. Add the beans and broth, using part of the bean cooking liquid, if desired. Cover and simmer about 1 ½ to 2 hours, or until the beans are very soft. Add wine and seasonings. Place a slice in each soup plate, sprinkle with cheese, and ladle soup over. In true Italian style, drizzle more oil over soup at the table.

Serves 6-8.

ZUPPA DI MELANZANE ARROSTO
(Roasted Eggplant Soup)

This roasted eggplant soup has the robust and concentrated flavors of Sicily and Campania, where eggplants and tomatoes were first introduced to Italy.

2 eggplants, about 12 ounces each	6 ounces tomato paste
1 ½ cups chopped onion	1 cup torn basil leaves
6 garlic cloves, crushed	Salt & pepper
2 tablespoons olive oil	½ cup oven-dried tomatoes (see index)
2 quarts chicken or veal stock	½ cup torn basil leaves
	Parmesan, to pass at the table

Cut eggplants in half, oil, and season, and grill over high heat about 10-15 minutes, cut-side down. Or they may be roasted at 375° about 10-15 minutes, or until tender. Meanwhile, sauté onion and garlic in oil, using a large soup pot, until soft. Scoop out eggplant, add to soup pot, and cook briefly. Add stock, tomato paste, and basil, simmer about 20 minutes, or until lightly thickened. Season, purée, and garnish with oven-dried tomatoes and shredded basil.

Serves 6-8.

BREADS AND PIZZAS

Pane, Italian bread, is probably my favorite as its crusty exterior and coarse-grained interior make it extremely versatile. When slightly stale, it is the perfect cushion for soup, or for making the endless varieties of bruschetta, now so popular in the United States, and crostini (croutons). Foccaccia, with its mouth-watering toppings, and Ciabatta are great with meals as well as the perfect bread for sandwiches. Pizza, a worldwide favorite found on every room service menu, is the pride and glory of Naples.

BRUSCHETTA CON OLIO DI TARTUFA
(Grilled Bread with Truffle Oil)

Bruschetta with Piedmont's white truffle oil is an elegant accompaniment to a glass of Prosecco or Asti Spumante, at any time of day or night.

6 slices Italian country bread	Balsamic vinegar
Olive oil	2 tablespoons white truffle oil
Fleur de sel	¼ cup shaved Parmesan or Asiago
1 garlic clove, slightly crushed	

Sprinkle bread with oil and salt, then grill or toast until golden. Rub with garlic, sprinkle with vinegar and truffle oil, then top with cheese. Top with more Fleur de Sel and truffle oil, as desired.

Serves 6.

BRUSCHETTA CON POMODORI
(Grilled Bread with Tomatoes)

This rustic bruschetta with tomatoes and basil is great with country soups and pastas. Try spreading the bread with Tapenade or especially pesto!

6 slices Italian country bread	3 garlic cloves, minced
Olive oil	½ cup torn basil leaves
Salt & pepper	Salted anchovies, chopped (optional)
1 cup Oven-dried Tomatoes (see index)	Fleur de Sel & gray pepper

Sprinkle bread with oil and seasonings, then grill or toast until golden. Mix tomatoes, with plenty of their oil, and remaining ingredients. Let marinate briefly, and dollop on top of bread.

Serves 6.

FOCACCIA

Try your choice of toppings on this crisp and golden flat bread. I also love to add escargots, basil, diced Romas, chèvre, and garlic to the top.

1 package yeast	Cornmeal
1 cup lukewarm water	¼ cup olive oil
1 tablespoon sugar	1 large garlic clove, minced
1/3 cup olive oil	2 tablespoons chopped rosemary
1 teaspoon salt	
2 ¾ cups bread flour	2 teaspoons coarse salt

Proof yeast in water with sugar. Using a mixer with a dough hook, add oil, salt, and half the flour, beating until absorbed. Add remaining flour gradually until dough is smooth and elastic. Oil bowl and let rise until double, covered, about 1-1 ½ hours. Punch down and let rise again. Oil a 12- x 16-inch baking sheet, and sprinkle with cornmeal. Roll out slightly, then place in pan, spreading it over entire surface, and let rise about ½ hour. Mix oil with garlic and rosemary, spreading over dough, and making indentations with your fingertips. Sprinkle with salt, and bake at 400° about 20 minutes, or until crisp and golden. Cut into squares.

Serves 6-8.

GRILLED VEGETABLE, PESTO, AND MOZZARELLA SANDWICHES

This big, beautiful, and lusty sandwich is one of my favorites, as it was in my cooking classes.

1 eggplant, about 10 ounces	½ cup Creamy Pesto (see index)
2 large Romas	½ pound sliced mozzarella
Olive oil	½ cup torn basil
1 large loaf Italian bread, halved horizontally, brushed with oil	Coarse salt and gray pepper

Slice eggplant and romas about ¼-inch thick, brush with oil, and grill until tender, turning occasionally, about 5 minutes. Grill bread until crusty and golden on both sides. Spread bread with pesto, arrange vegetables and cheese on top, and grill until cheese melts. Top with basil, and cut into halves or quarters. Season, as desired, adding more pesto.

Serves 4-8.

MALTESE TUNA SANDWICH

The island of Malta, located between Tunisia and Sicily, does not belong to Italy, but its cooking is highly influenced by Italy. Although I have visited Malta twice, I haven't been especially impressed with the food, except for this very easy, quick, and delicious openface sandwich which I enjoyed at the Hilton's outdoor dining terrace overlooking the Mediterranean. This is a typical local luncheon dish.

2 thick slices country bread	Olive oil
Mayonnaise or Aioli (see index)	Capers
2 small cans white tuna, drained	Kalamata olives
	Cherry tomatoes & hard-cooked eggs
Red leaf lettuce	

Spread bread with mayonnaise, or brush with olive oil, and sauté or grill. Mound tuna on top, one can per person, and place on lettuce leaf. Pour as much oil over top as desired, and garnish with your choice of capers, very traditional, olives, tomatoes and eggs. Every Maltese cook has his own way.

Serves 2.

PIZZA MARGHERITA

Like most Americans, I've had many more pizzas in the United States than I've had in Italy, but when I was in Naples, I made my required gastronomic visit to the Santa Lucia waterfront, across from the best hotels, to try the legendary pizza named after Queen Margherita when she visited Naples. This is my updated version of the red, white, and green pizza symbolic of Italy's flag. Be sure to use a pizza peel or paddle and pizza tiles.

1 recipe Pizza dough (see below)	1 cup Oven-roasted tomatoes (see index)
½ cup Pesto (see index)	½ cup sliced fresh basil
1 cup grated Mozzarella	

When dough is ready, roll out into 4 circles about 7 to 8 inches in diameter. Place on a wooden paddle sprinkled well with cornmeal. Spread most of pesto on each one, leaving a little for the top. Sprinkle with cheese, tomatoes, and basil. Bake at 450° to 500°, depending on your oven, about 15 minutes. Slide peel under pizzas to remove, and dribble remaining pesto on top.

Makes 4 7- to 8-inch pizzas.

PIZZA DOUGH

1 cup warm water, 105° to 110°	1 teaspoon salt
1 envelope dry yeast	2 tablespoons olive oil
1 tablespoon sugar	3-4 cups all-purpose flour

Using an electric mixer with a dough hook, proof yeast in water with sugar about 5 minutes, When foamy, add salt, oil, and flour, 1 cup at a time. Knead with dough hook, and when shiny and elastic, oil bowl, cover, and let rise about an hour, or until double in bulk.

Makes 2 12-inch or 4 7- to 8-inch pizzas.

PASTA   PASTA   PASTA

Oh yes, I could write volumes about pasta, my most favorite comfort food of all and the one I would request for my last meal on earth. Pasta is undoubtedly the most versatile food of all, as all vegetables, fruits, fish, meat, poultry, and seasonings of all kinds complement the supple yet assertive consistency of pasta, and its variety of shapes is infinite. A must for making good pasta is a machine which does not mix the dough or extrude it. The processor makes an excellent dough quite easily, and the pasta machine is needed only to roll out and cut the pasta. I love my Bialetti, made in Italy, which I have had for many years.

PASTA DOUGH

This is a good basic dough, and with the addition of spinach you have Pasta Verde or green pasta. The recipe can easily be doubled or tripled.

¾ cup all-purpose flour 1 egg ½ teaspoon salt	¼ 10-ounce package frozen chopped spinach, thawed & well drained

Blend ingredients (use spinach for green pasta) in processor until still slightly crumbly. If too moist, add more flour, or if too dry, add a little water. Process until a smooth dough forms. Press into a rectangle, and put through widest setting of pasta machine roller several times, folding in half after the first time. Run through successively narrower settings until pasta is as thin as you want. Put through noodle or spaghetti cutter, or cut into desired shape with a knife. Spread out in 1 layer on dish towels until ready to cook.

Makes 6 ounces.

SPAGHETTI ALLA NORMA

When I discovered this famous pasta dish in Catania, Sicily, I had it two nights in a row, and couldn't wait to get home to perfect it for my cooking classes. It is still one of my favorites.

1 or 2 eggplants, about 12 ounces each, peeled & sliced ½ inch thick, lengthwise	2 cups canned crushed tomatoes
1 quart water	2 tablespoons tomato paste
1 tablespoon salt	Salt & pepper
Flour	1 teaspoon sugar
½ -1 cup olive oil	1 tablespoon butter
4 garlic cloves, crushed	1 pound spaghetti, cooked
½ cup chopped parsley	1 cup diced mozzarella
½ cup chopped basil	¼ cup parmesan
2 tablespoons olive oil	¼ cup chopped parsley

Soak eggplant in water and salt solution at least ½ hour, drain, and dry well. Dredge in flour, and fry in hot oil until tender, turning once. Sauté garlic and herbs in oil, add tomatoes and seasonings, and simmer ½ hour. Add butter and toss with hot pasta and cheeses. Arrange eggplant on top, and garnish.

Serves 4 to 6.

TAGLIOLINI CON SALSA DI POMODORI FRESCA

(Tagliolini with Fresh Tomato Sauce)

Pasta with a marinated sauce of tomatoes, olive oil, garlic, basil, and cheese is the epitome of Italian summer pastas. Feel free to substitute whatever herbs and cheese you desire.

1 ½ -2 pounds very ripe tomatoes, cubed (or cherry or grape tomatoes)	2 or 3 garlic cloves, crushed
	1 teaspoon salt
	Gray pepper, to taste
½ pound mozzarella or chèvre, diced	1 pound fettuccine or spaghetti, cooked
1 cup olive oil	Parmesan, freshly grated
½ cup basil chiffonade	
½ cup olives	

Mix tomatoes and cheese with oil and all seasonings. Let marinate in a large pasta platter at room temperature at least 2 hours. Add hot pasta, toss, and pass parmesan at the table. Serve with a lusty Montepulciano and a good country bread for a terrific and simple summer meal.

Serves 6.

PASTA CON CREMA DI LIMONE

(Pasta with Lemon Cream)

This is another pasta that I love during the summer as it is redolent with lemon, both the pasta and the sauce.

2 teaspoons grated lemon zest	2 teaspoons lemon juice
¼ cup butter	¼ cup butter
2 tablespoons white wine	1/3 cup Parmesan
1 2/3 cup cream	Salt & gray pepper
1 pound fettuccine, cooked	1/3 cup Oven-dried Tomatoes (see index)
Fettuccine al Limone (see below)	Mint sprigs

Sauté zest in butter briefly, add wine, and reduce slightly. Add cream, bring to a boil, add pasta, and toss well. Add butter and cheese, toss again. Garnish with tomatoes and mint.

Serves 6.

FETTUCCINE AL LIMONE

(Lemon Fettuccine)

1 ½ cups flour	1 tablespoon warm water
1 egg	1 tablespoon olive oil
2 tablespoons lemon juice	½ teaspoon salt
1 tablespoon grated lemon zest	

Place all ingredients in processor, and blend until it can be formed into a ball. Use standard procedure as in Pasta Dough (see index).

Makes 12 ounces.

LINGUINE CON CREMA DI QUATTRO NOCI

(Linguine with Cream of Four Nuts)

This is a most unique version of the classic Fettuccine.

¼ cup each walnuts, almonds, pistachios, and pine nuts	6 ounces Gorgonzola
2 tablespoons butter	½ cup Parmesan
2 garlic cloves, crushed	Salt & gray pepper
1 cup cream	12 ounces linguine, cooked
2/3 cup chicken stock	1/3 cup Pesto (see index)

Roast nuts at 350° about 5 minutes. Sauté garlic in butter briefly, add cream and stock, reducing until thickened. Add cheeses over low heat, season and when melted add pasta and toss well. Garnish with nuts and drizzled pesto.

Serves 4-6.

PASTA CON ZUCCHINI

Some of the best pasta I've had in Italy and throughout Europe has been zucchini pasta in humble hotels and restaurants, where the Europeans eat. One was at the Top Hotel Post near the Frankfort airport, and another was at the Best Western on Lake Como. This is a composite of both.

1 pound zucchini, sliced diagonally, about ¼ inch thick	½ cup Parmesan
	Salt & gray pepper
2 tablespoons butter	½ cup chiffonade of basil
2 tablespoons olive oil	12 ounces fettuccine or pappardelle (pasta cut into ¾ inch ribbons)
1 ½ cups cream	

Sauté zucchini in butter and oil, tossing until barely tender. Meanwhile, reduce cream slightly, add cheese, seasonings, basil, and cooked pasta. Gently fold in zucchini, and some of the pasta water if too dry.

Serves 4-6.

FARFALLE CON UOVO E BRESAOLA
(Farfalle with Eggs and Bresaola)

This glorified pasta with bresaola, a dried beef or venison specialty from the Alpine region of Italy, was inspired by the superb appetizer of melon, figs, and the best bresaola I've ever experienced. The setting was the magical and majestic Villa d'Este on Lake Como. You can substitute pancetta or prosciutto, but do try to find bresaola.

2 cups cherry tomatoes or 1 cup Oven-dried Tomatoes (see index)	Salt & gray pepper
	12 ounces farfalle or pappardelle
2 garlic cloves, crushed	1/3 cup parmesan
¼ cup olive oil	4 poached or fried eggs
20 asparagus tips, cooked	

Sauté tomatoes and garlic in oil until cherry tomatoes are softened, or just briefly for the oven-dried. Add asparagus, season, and toss with pasta and cheese. If too dry, add a spoon or two of the pasta water. Place eggs on top, and if a more elegant presentation is desired, save asparagus tips for arranging in spokes around the eggs, using 5 tips per person. This would be a great breakfast dish with Prosecco, with or without Lago di Como.

Serves 4.

PAPPARDELLE CON PEPERONI E SALSICCIA

(Pappardelle with Pepperoni and Sausage)

A vivid red, yellow, and green bell pepper sauce over yellow and green pasta is a visual delight. Yellow pasta can easily be made by adding powdered saffron to the pasta dough, or saffron powder or whole saffron can simply be added to the pasta cooking water. You may use store-bought Italian sausage, or you can follow my recipe, which I use for just about all recipes requiring sausage, adapting it by changing the herbs and seasonings.

3 bell peppers, 1 each red, yellow, and green, roasted (see index)	¼ cup olive oil
	2 tablespoons butter
3 medium tomatoes, diced	12 ounces each yellow & green pasta (see index)
3 garlic cloves, crushed	
½ pound Italian sausage (see index)	2/3 cup parmesan
	Chopped fresh basil or sage
Salt & gray pepper	

Sauté roasted peppers (peeled and cut into 2-inch squares), tomatoes, garlic, and sausage with seasonings in oil and butter, over medium heat, until very tender and juicy, about 10 minutes. Add cooked and drained pasta and cheese. Toss well, and garnish with basil or sage.

Serves 4-6.

RAVIOLI DI FUNGHI E SPINACI ALLA SWAN
(Ravioli with Mushrooms and Spinach)

After you prepare Antipasto alla Swan in the previous section, you must have this luscious ravioli which I savored on the Minerva's Black Sea cruise. The Swan Restaurant, named after Swan Hellenic, served excellent cuisine. If possible, try to find Hen of the Woods mushrooms, absolutely delicious, otherwise use shiitake or porcini.

4 ounces Hen of the Woods mushrooms, or others, sliced	1 tablespoon diced pancetta or bacon
1 shallot, sliced	1 tablespoon butter
1 tablespoon olive oil	1 tablespoon flour or parmesan
2 tablespoons white wine	¼ cup cream
1 small egg yolk	4 ounces cooked, chopped spinach, well drained
1 tablespoon parmesan	
Salt & gray pepper	Salt & gray pepper
1 teaspoon finely chopped sage	24 wonton wrappers
	1 quart veal stock

Sauté mushrooms and shallot in oil about 5 minutes, deglaze with wine, and when evaporated, chop mushrooms. Add yolk, cheese, and seasonings. Moisten edges of 12 wonton wrappers, place about 2 teaspoons of filling in center, and fold in half, pressing edges together firmly. Make spinach ravioli by rendering pancetta in butter, add flour to thicken, add cream, and cook until thickened. Add spinach, season, and fill remaining 12 ravioli as before. Add all ravioli to boiling stock, and simmer until they rise to the top. Drain, and serve with a simple sauce made by reducing 2 cups cream slightly, then adding 1 or 2 tablespoons white truffle oil. The chef, Niranjan Taste, served 2 ravioli of each kind with the sauce poured around them.

Serves 4-6.

RAVIOLI DI ZUCCA CON BURRO E SALVIA
(Ravioli of Squash with Butter and Sage)

Ravioli with butternut squash, sage, and browned butter is a great dish for fall or any time, and it can be so easy with wonton wrappers, as in the previous recipe. Yes, I have finally succumbed to buying something ready-made, so the secret is out. These freeze beautifully and can be folded into rectangles, triangles, or tortellini, in addition to placing another on top for squares, or cutting out circles. I also keep large eggroll wrappers in the freezer for even greater versatility.

½ pound butternut squash or pumpkin, halved & seeds removed	¼ cup parmesan
	½ cup butter
	8 large sage leaves
3 Amaretti or macaroons, crumbled (see index)	24 to 30 wonton wrappers
	Freshly grated nutmeg
2 tablespoons Fig or Cranberry Chutney (see index)	Parmesan & small sage leaves

Place squash on an oiled baking pan, and roast at 375° about ½ hour, or until tender. Scoop squash from the skin into a bowl when cool. Add amaretti, chutney, and parmesan. Brown the butter with sage until it emits a nutty aroma, and add 2 tablespoons to the filling. Brush edge of wrappers with water, and place about 2 to 3 teaspoons on each. Fold as desired. Cook in boiling salted water until they rise to the top. Strain remaining brown butter over them, and season with freshly grated nutmeg, parmesan and sage.

Serves 4-6.

RAVIOLI CON UOVO E SPINACI

(Ravioli with Egg and Spinach)

These large yellow ravioli are filled with spinach and cheese, on top of which is a yellow egg yolk. This is an old Italian method and is a signature dish of Valentino, the best Italian restaurant in the United States. This is my version, which I prefer because of the truffle oil and the green and yellow pasta.

¼ cup cooked spinach, with water pressed out	3 ounces green pasta dough (see index)
¼ cup mascarpone cheese	3 ounces yellow pasta dough, made by adding ¼ teaspoon powdered saffron when making dough
½ cup Parmesan	
1 large egg	
1 teaspoon white truffle oil	½ cup melted butter
Freshly grated nutmeg	1 or 2 teaspoons white truffle oil
4 egg yolks	
	¼ cup Parmesan

Mix spinach with cheeses, egg, and seasonings. Roll out green pasta, cut into 4 4-inch rounds, and roll out yellow pasta, cutting into 4 5-inch rounds. Divide filling between green pasta rounds, brush edges with water, and make a depression in top of filling in which to place yolks. Top with yellow pasta round, pressing firmly to seal edges. Gently boil the pasta in a very wide large pot, cooking only a few at a tune so that they do not overlap, about 3 to 4 minutes only. Remove carefully with a wide slotted spatula. Add truffle oil to butter, pour over ravioli, and add parmesan. This is such a special and elegant pasta, I would only drink champagne with it, and it would make a perfect romantic meal at any hour.

Makes 4 for 2 romantic diners.

SECONDI

Secondi, the main course of the meal, frequently does not have the zest or the element of surprise that the previous dishes do, because of the tremendous variety and importance of antipasti and pasta. Fish, however, is proliferous throughout most of the country as the Adriatic and the Mediterranean, as well as rivers and lakes produce numerous varieties. Eel, pike, carp, squid, and shellfish, (especially mussels, clams, and shrimp), are quite popular, as are sea bass, tuna, and swordfish. Meat is usually prepared in a simple manner. Roman lamb is legendary, as are the pork products from Bologna, such as the famous Parma ham and other pork products. Florentine beef from Tuscany has been grilled since ancient times, and the veal from Piedmont and Lombardy is of the highest quality. Poultry is less important, but chicken, rabbit, and turkey are prepared in several exceptional ways.

TIELLA

(Baked Apulian Fish)

I love almost any version of the Apulian baked fish casserole prepared in an unglazed terra cotta covered dish, a tiella, also used by ethnic groups in many parts of the world.

1 pound Yukon Gold potatoes, peeled & thinly sliced	¼ cup chopped basil or sage
1 large onion, sliced	Salt & pepper
4 ripe Romas, sliced	1/3 cup olive oil
4 artichoke hearts, canned or from cooked fresh artichokes	1 cup Parmesan cheese or Asiago
6 garlic cloves, thinly sliced	4 salmon, cod, or halibut fillets
¼ cup chopped parsley	½ cup each white wine & fish stock

Using a 3-quart casserole, preferably a terra cotta one, oil generously, and add alternate layers of half the vegetables and seasonings. Add half the oil, half the cheese, and all the salmon. Repeat layers, leaving the potatoes, oil, and parmesan for the top. Pour wine and stock over, cover, and bake at 375° about 1 hour, or until potatoes are tender. Uncover about half way through baking to brown the top slightly.

Serves 4-6.

PESCE ALLA SICILIANA
(Sicilian Style Fish)

When I think of Italian fish preparations, the Sicilian style is always paramount because of the simplicity and the robust flavor. As for cooking fish, its own habitat, water, is considered to be the best by many chefs.

4 ripe Romas, seeded & diced	2 tablespoons rinsed capers
½ cup black or Kalamata olives	¼ cup olive oil
¼ cup currants	¼ cup chopped mint or parsley
¼ cup golden raisins	4 salmon, cod, or halibut fillets
¼ cup sliced almonds or pistachios	4 preserved lemon quarters (see index)

Sauté first 6 ingredients in oil about 15 minutes and add herbs. Place fish in a pan of boiling water, turn off the heat, cover, and let stand about 5 to 10 minutes depending on thickness of the fish. Drain well, and serve with the sauce. Numerous kinds of fish and shellfish are great with this sauce, cold or hot. Garnish with lemon, a nice touch of fusion influence.

Serves 4.

POLLO AL SALE

(Baked Chicken with a Salt Crust)

Chicken, covered with salt and baked, is an old Italian method which produces the most tender, succulent, and flavorful chicken imaginable. There are recipes which mix beaten egg whites with the salt to make the chicken hermetically sealed, but you just may not be able to get the salt crust out of your pan! This chicken is eaten without the skin and is perfect for any recipe requiring the best cooked chicken, especially salads, sandwiches, and soups.

1 3-pound chicken	Rosemary & sage sprigs
1 garlic clove	2 pounds Kosher salt

Fill cavity with garlic and herbs, and place in a 3-quart terra cotta casserole with a thick layer of salt of salt on the bottom. Cover chicken completely with remaining salt, and cover casserole. Bake 10 minutes at 300°, then bake 1 ½ hours at 400°. Crack the hard crust, remove chicken, and brush off excess salt.

Serves 4-5.

POLLO AL LIMONE

(Lemon Chicken)

Another simple yet superbly flavored chicken, this one is roasted with lemons and is served with a luscious lemon sauce.

1 3-pound chicken	2 lightly crushed garlic cloves
2 lemons, halved	Salt & pepper
Rosemary and sage sprigs	Olive oil

2 large garlic cloves, sliced	2 tablespoons rinsed capers
2 tablespoons olive oil	Grated zest of 1 lemon
2 tablespoons chopped basil or sage	1 tablespoon lemon juice
	1/3 cup yogurt or cream

Fill chicken cavity with lemons, herbs, and garlic. Season chicken, rub with oil, and bake at 350° about 15 minutes to allow lemons to baste the breasts. Turn chicken over, and bake about 45 minutes, or until done. Meanwhile, sauté garlic in oil briefly, add herbs, capers, and lemon. When chicken is done, strain off pan juices, remove fat, and reduce until glazed. Add to basil and caper mixture, and whisk in yogurt. Serve with chicken.

Serves 4.

POLLO CON FAGIOLI

(Chicken with Dried Beans)

Chicken cooked with dried beans is popular throughout Italy and is a wonderful homey dish. You can use any combination of Italy's most popular beans-borlotti, also known as cranberry or October, cannellini, chickpeas, or lentils.

6 chicken breasts, boned & skinned	1 ½ cups chicken or beef stock
¼ cup olive oil	1 tablespoon chopped rosemary
2 slices pancetta or bacon, diced	3 cups cooked, dried beans (see above)
1 red onion, chopped	1 Roma, seeded & diced
2 garlic cloves, sliced	Chopped parsley
½ cup white wine	

Sauté chicken in oil with pancetta until golden. Remove chicken, add onion and garlic, and sauté until tender. Deglaze with wine, reducing slightly. Add stock, rosemary, and beans. Simmer until lightly thickened, add chicken, and simmer until heated through. Season, and garnish with tomato and parsley.

Serves 6.

ITALIAN SAUSAGE

Sausage, an integral part of everyday Italian cooking, is so easy and versatile to make. You can use beef, pork, lamb, veal, or poultry, or any combination. Garlic and salt are de rigeur, and you can add a combination of fresh herbs to blend with whatever ethnic recipe you're using. Most chefs like to use extra fat for flavor and texture, usually a ratio of 3 parts meat to 1 part fat. This is optional, and I must admit I usually make a quite good and healthful sausage using only pork tenderloin.

1 pound pork shoulder or tenderloin	1 tablespoon chopped sage or 1 teaspoon poultry seasoning
3 garlic cloves, crushed	¼ cup red wine (optional)
2 teaspoons kosher salt	

Grind pork in food processor with seasonings, or use a meat grinder. Add wine, if desired, and let ripen overnight in the refrigerator. Freeze, dividing it as desired, or form into sausage shapes or patties, and sauté or cook on a grill.

Makes 1 pound.

MAIALE CON LATTE

(Pork Cooked in Milk)

If you've never cooked pork in milk, you are in for a wonderful and flavorful taste treat. Again, in the interest of healthful cooking, you may use pork loin instead of pork shoulder, but the latter is definitely more succulent.

2 pounds boneless pork loin	1 tablespoon butter
2 garlic cloves, slivered	1 tablespoon olive oil
Coarse salt	2 cups milk, or more to cover
1 teaspoon chopped rosemary	

Trim excess fat from pork, make small incisions, and insert garlic. Rub with salt and rosemary, and sauté in butter and oil, and add enough milk to cover pork, using a pan just large enough to hold the pork. Cover, and simmer about 2-3 hours or until tender. Remove pork, and if milk is too thin reduce until thickened and caramelized. The sauce may be lumpy, so purée it until smooth. The pork may also be baked at 300° the same length of time.

Serves 6.

POLPETTE ALLA SARDEGNA

(Sardinian Meatballs)

Meatballs have always been synonymous with Italy, but they have come a long way since the time they were always drowned in tomato sauce and served on spaghetti. My version of the local meatballs which I had at the Cala di Volpe on Sardinia's Costa Smeralda are fresh tasting and versatile enough to be served with polenta, pasta, risotto, or on their own.

½ pound each ground beef and veal	¼ cup olive oil
1 egg, beaten	1 red onion, thinly sliced
1 tablespoon each chopped mint & parsley	1 tablespoon sugar
	1 tablespoon capers
1 or 2 cloves garlic, crushed	2 tablespoons pine nuts or sliced almonds
Salt & pepper	3 tablespoons red wine vinegar
½ cup each bread crumbs & parmesan	3 tablespoons water
2 tablespoons golden raisins	2 tablespoons chopped mint & parsley

It is much easier to mix ground meat with other ingredients if you start with the beaten egg, adding seasonings, and then the meat. Form meatballs. Sauté in oil until almost done and well browned. Remove from skillet, and add onion, sautéeing until almost soft. Add sugar, and cook until caramelized. Add remaining ingredients and meatballs, cover, and simmer about 5 minutes or until hot. Garnish with herbs. These may be served hot or cold.

Serves 4-6.

CARNE ALLA TIELLA

(Terra Cotta Roasted Meat)

Meat cooked in a tiella, the unglazed terra cotta casserole for which I gave a fish recipe in the previous section, is especially juicy and tender. Any meat can be prepared this way, as long as it is a cut meant for stewing or braising. This is found throughout central Italy and is the epitome of a simple but delicious peasant dish.

2 pounds boneless veal, pork, lamb, or beef shoulder or shank	Several sprigs of basil or sage
Salt & pepper	Sangiovese, Lambrusco, or Chianti, enough to cover meat, about 3 cups
1 small head of garlic, peeled	

Cut meat into large chunks, and place in 3-quart terra cotta casserole or an enameled Dutch oven. Add all other ingredients, cover, and bake at 350° about 2 ½ to 3 hours, or until tender. Reduce sauce to thicken, if necessary. This is great with polenta.

Serves 4-6.

AGNELLO ALLA BALSAMICO

(Lamb with Balsamic Vinegar)

Lamb and balsamic vinegar are a heavenly pair in this quite simple dish which is typical of Modena in Emilia Romagna.

2 pounds center cut lamb leg steak	1 garlic clove, sliced
3 tablespoons olive oil	1 teaspoon each chopped rosemary, sage, and mint
Salt & pepper	1/3 cup Balsamic vinegar

Using a sauté pan just large enough for the lamb, sauté in oil until well browned. Add seasonings and vinegar, cover, and simmer very slowly about 1 hour or until very tender. Add a little water if vinegar evaporates too much. Remove fat, reduce if necessary, and pour over lamb.

Serves 4.

OSSO BUCO MODERNE

Osso Buco has always been one of my favorites, and now the chefs in Lombardy, its birthplace, are doing their thing with fusion cooking. According to many in the culinary field, the Italians have not quite mastered it yet. A recent issue of *Slow*, the magazine of the slow food movement, states that Italy is peopled by sorcerer's apprentices who unleash terrifying concoctions on the restaurant-going public. There are, however, great exceptions such as these new renditions of the classic braised veal shank which have inspired me.

4 small veal or lamb shanks, floured	½ teaspoon saffron, crushed
¼ cup olive oil	2 large Romas, seeded & diced
½ pound cippollini onions, cut into halves	2 tablespoons tomato paste
	1 1/3 cups Lambrusco or Chianti
4 garlic cloves, crushed	2/3 cup orange juice
2 tablespoons each chopped rosemary and thyme	1 1/3 cups veal stock
	¼ cup Marsala
Salt & pepper	1 cup pitted prunes

Sauté veal or lamb, which I prefer, in oil, using an oval Dutch oven if possible, so that the pan is just large enough for the shanks. When golden, remove, and sauté onions until golden, adding garlic briefly. Add remaining ingredients, cover, and simmer or bake at 350° about 2 hours, or until shanks are very tender. If braising liquid is not thick enough, remove shanks and prunes, and reduce. These are absolutely the best shanks of all.

Serves 4.

OSSO BUCO ORIENTALE

Fusion cooking originally got its name from combining Oriental and Western ingredients, and this is one of the most successful creations, one of my favorites.

4 small veal or lamb shanks, floured	1 or 2 teaspoons Five-spice powder
Salt & pepper	¼ cup chopped chervil or savory
¼ cup peanut oil	2 cups veal stock
1 red onion, chopped	2/3 cup Marsala
4 garlic cloves, crushed	1/3 to ½ cup soy sauce
2 tablespoons turbinado or brown sugar	

Season shanks, brown in oil, using an oval Dutch oven if possible, so that the pan is just large enough for the shanks. When well browned, remove, and add onions until softened, adding garlic briefly. Add sugar, and cook until onions are caramelized. Add remaining ingredients, cover, and simmer or bake at 350° about 2 hours, or until shanks are very tender. If braising liquid is not thick enough, remove shanks, and reduce. Serve with rice.

Serves 4.

The following sauces, marinade, and roasted garlic are used in many Italian recipes as well as other ethnic dishes. These are frequently the essence of the dish and may be kept frozen:

PESTO WITH ROASTED GARLIC

Pesto can be made in an infinite number of ways, and it does not always have to be based on basil. Parsley, spinach, sage, arugula, and even mesclun can be used alone or in combination with each other.

1 cup packed basil	¾ cup olive oil
1 cup packed parsley	Salt & pepper
¼ - ½ cup parmesan	½ cup Roasted Garlic (see index)

Place herbs in food processor with parmesan. Gradually add oil, and purée. Add seasonings and garlic, process until smooth.

Makes about 1 ½ cups.

CREAMY PESTO

This variation is milder than the usual pesto and is wonderful on pasta as well as eggs, polenta, salads, fish, and chicken.

1 cup packed basil	¼ - ½ cup parmesan
1 cup packed spinach	1/3 cup olive oil
¼ cup walnuts or almonds	1/3 cup cream
1 garlic clove, crushed	Salt & pepper

Place herbs in processor with nuts, garlic, and cheese. Gradually add oil processing until smooth. Add cream, and season.

Makes about 1 ½ cups.

SALSA DI POMODORI SICILIANA

(Sicilian Tomato Sauce)

This is a variation of the tomato sauce which is part of the Spaghetti Alla Norma recipe (see index), and it is sensational with pasta, polenta, and seafood.

¼ cup chopped parsley	1 cup red wine
4 garlic cloves, crushed	1 cup black or Kalamata olives
¼ cup olive oil	½ cup dried currants
3 cups canned Italian tomatoes, drained	¼ cup sliced almonds or pine nuts
2 tablespoons tomato paste	

Sauté parsley and garlic in oil until soft, add tomatoes and paste, and simmer ½ hour, covered. Add remaining ingredients, and simmer about 10 minutes or until thickened to desired consistency.

Makes about 4 cups.

RED AND YELLOW TOMATO SAUCE

This is a beautiful fresh sauce which can be made with a combination of tomatoes or whatever your garden offers.

1 pound ripe red, yellow, or cherry tomatoes, or a combination ¼ cup olive oil	2 garlic cloves, sliced Salt & pepper ¼ cup chiffonade of basil

Remove seeds from tomatoes, chop, and sauté in oil over high heat until they release their juice. Add garlic, and simmer about 5 minutes. Add seasonings, and simmer briefly.

Makes about 1 ½ cups.

HONEY-BALSAMIC GLAZE

This glaze is especially good on swordfish, salmon, or meat.

½ cup Balsamic vinegar ½ cup red wine	¼ cup honey ½ cup dried currants

Reduce vinegar and wine with honey by about 2/3 or until it becomes a thick and shiny glaze. Add currants.

Makes about ½ cup.

LEMON-ORANGE SICILIAN MARINADE

½ cup olive oil 2 rosemary sprigs 2 garlic cloves, lightly crushed	Salt & pepper Zest of 1 orange and 1 lemon, cut off in wide strips ¼ cup lemon juice

Bring oil and seasonings to a simmer to develop flavor, then add juice and let cool. This is great for fish or lamb.

Makes about ¾ cup.

ROASTED GARLIC

A brief simmer in milk renders these garlic cloves milky-white and creamy in texture. You can make less, but this freezes beautifully. Just remember that 1 bulb of garlic yields about 3 tablespoons of purée. If you do roast garlic in the usual manner of roasting with olive oil, be sure you cover the cloves with oil to prevent burning. Save the oil for using in any dish where garlic is compatible.

4 garlic bulbs, separated	1/3 cup olive oil
1 ½ cups milk, enough to cover garlic	

Cover garlic with milk, and bring to a slow simmer for about 5 minutes, Drain, place garlic in a very small dish, and cover with oil. Cover, and bake at 325° about 1 hour or until very soft, checking occasionally. Cool, then squeeze out of skins.

Makes about ¾ cup.

VEGETABLES   POLENTA   RISOTTO

Italian vegetables are of utmost importance and are of the highest quality, so much so that they are eaten on their own quite frequently. Likewise, polenta and risotto are always a separate course unless part of the main dish, while we think of them as an accompaniment like mashed potatoes.

CAPONATA

(Sicilian Vegetable Stew)

Caponata is undoubtedly my most favorite vegetable, actually a sort of stew, and is an important Sicilian specialty which can be used as part of the antipasti, or it can be served hot with the main course. This sweet and sour combination is known as agrodolce in Italy, and the flavors and textures are incomparable because of the separate cooking of the vegetables.

1 rib celery, sliced diagonally	Salt & pepper
1 small red bell pepper & 1 small yellow bell pepper, seeded & sliced	1 large garlic clove, crushed
	¾ cup canned crushed tomatoes
½ cup Roasted Garlic oil (see index)	1/3 cup mixed currants & golden raisins
1 medium red onion, diced	¼ cup each black & green olives
Salt, pepper, & sugar	1 tablespoon capers, rinsed
1 or 2 tablespoons Balsamic vinegar	1 teaspoon cocoa (optional)
1- 1 ½ pounds eggplant, peeled, cubed, & sprinkled with coarse salt	1 tablespoon each chopped basil & parsley

Sauté celery and peppers in a small amount of the garlic oil, using a large sauté pan. Season, remove from pan, and sauté onion with seasonings in a small amount of garlic oil. Add to celery mixture when almost caramelized. Dry eggpant, and sauté in remaining garlic oil until tender, turning, and add garlic when almost done. Season, and add previously cooked vegetables, along with all remaining ingredients. Simmer about 5 to 10 minutes to blend flavors, and correct seasonings, if necessary, adding more sugar if desired, or more vinegar to suit your taste.

Serves 6.

The most unique caponata presentation I've seen was on the SilverSea ship, the Shadow, on a cruise of the Chilean fjords. They placed a layer of caponata between 2 3-inch layers of polenta and served it with a simple sauce of caramelized sugar, vinegar, and tomato paste. The garnish was short chives, in a criss-cross pattern. Quite impressive!

FAGIOLI ALLA UCCELLETTO

(Beans Cooked in Olive Oil)

Probably the most important dish in Tuscany, these dried white beans are cooked in olive oil, which produces the most flavorful and tenderest of beans. This is a good method for garbanzos, especially canned ones which are not always ideal. Oil is all you need and a few herbs for simmering about ½ hour.

1 pound dried navy beans, soaked	3 garlic cloves, crushed
2/3 cup olive oil	Salt & pepper
6 sage leaves	Water or veal stock, to cover beans

Place drained beans in a 3-quart casserole with oil, seasonings, and enough water or stock to cover by an inch. Cover and bake at 300° about 3 hours, or until tender, adding more liquid if necessary. They may be served hot, but are even better if chilled a day or so, seasoned with more sage and oil, and served at room temperature. They are a great antipasto when served in roasted and skinned red, yellow, and green bell peppers.

Serves 6-8.

FAGIOLI DI BORLOTTI

(Italian Borlotti Beans)

My favorite Italian bean is borlotti, a very close cousin to cranberry and even October beans. They are mottled pink and red in color, and can be cooked in canned tomatoes, any kind of stock, and even coffee.

1 cup dried borlotti beans, soaked	½ cup chopped red onion
4 garlic cloves, crushed	1 cup carrots, peeled & diced
2-4 ounces pancetta or bacon, chopped	½ cup Sangiovese or Chianti
1 quart water or stock	2 cups veal or duck stock
3 tablespoons olive oil or pork fat or duck fat	1 tablespoon butter
	1 tablespoon chopped sage or rosemary

Add beans and garlic to pancetta which has been rendered in a 3-quart soup pot, and cook until beans are well coated with fat. Add water, cover, and simmer about 2 hours, or until tender. Heat oil or other fat in a skillet, and sauté onion and carrots until browned, deglaze with wine, and add to drained beans with stock, and simmer until lightly thickened. Add butter and herb.

Serves 4-6.

BORLOTTI CON POMODORI

(Borlotti Beans with Tomatoes)

This tomato version of borlotti is quite simple and equally good.

½ pound dried borlotti beans, cooked	2 garlic cloves, crushed
¼ pound pancetta or bacon, chopped	1 tablespoon chopped sage or rosemary
¼ cup olive oil	1 ½ cups canned crushed tomatoes
½ cup chopped onion	Salt & pepper
	1 tablespoon butter

Add drained beans to pancetta, which has been rendered with olive oil. Add onion and cook until beans are coated with fat, add garlic and rosemary, cooking briefly to infuse flavors. Add tomatoes butter, and seasonings, and simmer about 15 minutes or until lightly thickened. These are especially good with Italian Sausage added to the cooked beans.

Serves 4-6.

VERDURE ALLA AGRODOLCE

(Sweet and Sour Vegetables Sicilian Style)

Italians have always loved their vegetables and through necessity have always combined in a pot whatever the garden yielded, with the result being a tasty and healthful stew for dinner. This is a lusty combination typical of the south, especially Sicily.

1 large eggplant, cut into large cubes, sprinkled with 1 tablespoon salt, and placed in a colander to drain ½ cup barley, cooked & drained 1 red onion, thinly sliced 2-3 garlic cloves, sliced ¼ cup olive oil	2 cups canned, crushed tomatoes ¼ cup lemon juice ¼ cup honey, preferably chestnut ¼ cup chopped basil 1 ½ cups cooked cannellini or navy beans, or canned Salt & pepper

Sauté onion and garlic in oil until soft, add eggplant, turn to coat with oil, and add tomatoes and seasonings. Cover, and simmer until eggplant is tender, about 10 minutes. Stir in barley, beans, and seasonings.

Serves 4-6.

POLENTA CON FORMAGGIO
(Polenta with Cheese)

Polenta, made in northern Italy since ancient times, is extremely versatile in that it may be made with any kind of stock, milk, cream, or water, the choice of purists, or any combination thereof. Also, many different cheeses may be used, preferably parmesan, fontina, or mascarpone, or a combination. It may be layered with a tomato sauce or a ragu, and it may be chilled, sliced and fried or grilled, then topped with a sauce. As you can see there are infinite choices, but I especially like the following two versions.

1 cup polenta or yellow cornmeal	½ cup parmesan
1 quart water or chicken stock	½ cup mascarpone cheese or gorgonzola
Salt & pepper	1 tablespoon minced sage or basil
¼ cup butter or olive oil	

Gradually whisk cornmeal into boiling liquid with seasonings, and simmer about ½ hour, stirring occasionally, until smooth and thick. Meanwhile, mix cheeses together with sage, and whisk into cooked polenta.

Serves 6.

POLENTA CON RAGU DI FUNGHI

(Polenta with Wild Mushroom Ragu)

This is a most elegant polenta with wild mushrooms and truffle oil. For a rustic dish, add half a pound or so of Italian sausage and some red wine.

1 cup polenta or yellow cornmeal	1 pound Hen of the Woods mushrooms, (or other variety) sliced
2 cups milk	
1 cup cream	2 tablespoons olive oil or butter
1 cup veal or chicken stock	¼ cup chopped shallots
Salt & pepper	1 cup veal stock
1 or 2 teaspoons truffle oil	¼ cup julienne of bresaola (optional)
Salt & pepper	

Gradually whisk cornmeal into boiling liquids, and simmer about ½ hour, stirring occasionally, until thick and smooth. Season, and add oil. While cooking, sauté mushrooms in oil until almost tender, about 5 minutes. Add shallots and sauté until tender. Add stock, and cook briskly until lightly thickened and glazed. Add bresaola, season, and serve over polenta.

Serves 6.

RISOTTO DI ZUCCA

(Pumpkin Risotto)

Pumpkin risotto is just one of a plethora of northern Italy's famous rice dish. Like polenta, it may contain a variety of ingredients and be cooked in various stocks. In Italy it is usually eaten as a separate course. I do not find that arborio rice, as many purists insist on, is necessary. Any short- or long-grained rice will suffice. This risotto with pumpkin is one of my favorite Thanksgiving side dishes.

12 baby pumpkins, about 4 inches in diameter	½ cup white wine
1 medium onion, chopped	5 to 6 cups chicken stock
¼ cup butter or olive oil	½ cup parmesan
1 ½ cups diced baby pumpkin	¼ cup butter
2 cups rice	2 tablespoons chopped sage or thyme
	Salt, pepper, & fresh nutmeg

Cut about a ½-inch thick slice off the top of the pumpkins to form lids. Scoop out seeds, then enough pumpkin to leave ½-inch shells. Dice enough pumpkin to make 1 ½ cups. Steam pumpkins about 15 to 20 minutes, and keep warm. Sauté onion in butter until tender, add pumpkin, and sauté briefly. Add rice, coat well with butter, then add stock in ¾ cup increments, simmering and stirring until evaporated, and rice is rich and creamy. Add parmesan and butter, mixing well, and add seasonings. Fill each pumpkin, heaping full, arrange lids at an angle, and keep warm. Children appreciate this as much as adults. Of course, you may use a 2-pound pumpkin or butternut squash and prepare one large dish.

Serves 12.

RISOTTO ALLA POMODORI E OLIVE

(Tomato and Olive Risotto)

Risotto with a southern flair is an example of the new cooking.

1 small onion, finely chopped	¼ cup parmesan
2 tablespoons butter or olive oil	1 cup small green olives, pitted & halved, or 1 cup tiny peas
1 cup rice	
½ cup white wine	½ cup oven-dried tomatoes (see index)
2-3 cups chicken stock, boiling	
½ teaspoon saffron, crushed or ½ teaspoon powdered	Salt & pepper
	Minced chervil or parsley

Sauté onion in butter until tender, add rice, coat well with butter, then add wine, cooking until almost evaporated. Add stock in ¾ cup increments, simmering and stirring until evaporated, and rice is rich and creamy. Add saffron, stirring until color is distributed. Add parmesan, olives, and season well, adding all of the tomatoes, or encircle rice with tomatoes. Sprinkle with chervil.

Serves 4-6.

RISOTTO ROSSO

(Red Risotto)

Another colorful risotto, this one has a northern flair.

1 large shallot, chopped	2 cups veal stock
2 cups chiffonade of radicchio	2 tablespoons butter
2 tablespoons butter	¼ cup parmesan
1 cup rice	Salt & pepper & white truffle oil
1 cup red wine	Minced chervil or parsley

Sauté shallot and radicchio in butter until wilted, and remove. Add rice, coating well with butter, and add wine. Boil until almost evaporated, and add stock in ¾ cup increments, simmering and stirring until evaporated and rice is rich and creamy. Add butter, parmesan, and seasonings. Garnish with chervil. Radicchio may be mixed into rice or placed around it.

Serves 6.

DESSERTS

Italian desserts, such as fresh fruit, gelati, and granite, tend to be simple, especially at home. In the great restaurants you will find elegant cakes, soufflés, crespelle (crêpes), and many concoctions incorporating ricotta (such as cannoli), mascarpone, chocolate, and amaretti. Pastry has never been an important element in Italian desserts. And, of course, there are always the recent favorites of Tiramisu and Panna Cotta.

MONTE BIANCO

An old classic, especially in Piedmont and Lombardy, Monte Bianco or Mont Blanc, the Alpine mountain's namesake, is a luscious combination of chestnut purée, chocolate, and cream.

1 ½ pounds chestnuts or 2 cups canned purée	2 to 4 tablespoons brandy, rum, or Tiramisu liqueur
2/3 cup sugar	½ cup cream, whipped & flavored
¼ cup water	
2 to 4 ounces semi-sweet chocolate, melted	1 ounce semi-sweet chocolate, grated
3 tablespoons soft butter	

If using fresh chestnuts, slash the shells on the flat side, cover with cold water, bring to a boil, then remove shells and skins before they cool. Cover with milk and simmer until very tender, then drain. Press through a potato ricer or purée in a food processor. Boil sugar and water to the soft ball stage, then beat into the purée with the chocolate, butter, and brandy. While still warm, force through a potato ricer or a colander onto a large platter, forming the shape of a mountain. Do not pack it down. Cap the top of the mountain with the cream, and sprinkle with chocolate.

Serves 6-8.

SOUFFLÉ DI LIMONE E CIOCCOLATO

(Lemon and Chocolate Soufflé)

Hotel Caruso Belvedere, perched on top of the Amalfi coast in Ravello, was reached by bus, accompanied by none other than Signor Caruso, who was a most delightful Italian gentleman and gourmand. This was just one of the great dishes which we enjoyed while at his hotel.

1/3 cup sugar	2 egg whites, stiffly beaten
1 teaspoon cornstarch	3 egg whites
1 teaspoon grated lemon zest	3 tablespoons sugar
3 tablespoons lemon juice	2 tablespoons cocoa powder
3 tablespoons water	3 egg yolks
½ tablespoon butter	1/3 cup cherry or black currant preserves
2 egg yolks	

Mix first 6 ingredients in a medium saucepan, and whisk until thick. Whisk in yolks, and cook briefly. Fold in egg whites gently, and set aside. To make the chocolate soufflé, beat whites until frothy, gradually add sugar and cocoa, and beat until stiff. Beat in yolks. Spread preserves in a buttered and sugared 4-cup oval baking dish or in 4 to 6 individual baking dishes. Spoon soufflé mixtures side by side in baking dish, and bake at 375° about 20 minutes for the large or 10 minutes for individual ones, or just until set but still creamy.

Serves 4 to 6.

CRESPELLE AU RHUM PALUMBO

(Rum Crêpes Palumbo)

Hotel Palumbo, just down the street form Hotel Caruso, was a lovely old mansion with another delightful host and more excellent food. Crespelle, or crêpes, are endowed with a light lemon custard and enlivened with a rum sauce.

2 egg yolks	2 cups water
¼ cup sugar	1 cup sugar
2 tablespoons flour	¼ cup rum
1 ¼ cups milk	2 tablespoons lemon juice
Grated zest of 1 lemon	½ teaspoon vanilla or almond extract
3 tablespoons butter	
16 crespelle (see below)	1/3 cup powdered sugar or turbinado

Whisk eggs with sugar and flour in a small saucepan, and then whisk in milk, cooking until thick. Add zest and butter, and divide among crespelle. Roll up, and place side by side in a buttered baking dish just large enough to hold them. Make rum syrup by boiling water and sugar about 15 minutes. Add flavorings, pour over crespelle, and sift powdered sugar over them. No sifting is necessary for the turbinado, which is a coarse natural sugar. Bake at 400° until sugar caramelizes.

Serves 8.

Crespelle or Crêpes:

3 eggs	Dash of salt
¾ cup flour	2 tablespoons butter, melted
2 cups milk	

Blend all ingredients together in food processor or blender until smooth. Chill an hour or so for better texture. Butter a 6- to 8-inch iron skillet, place over fairly high heat, and pour in about 1 tablespoon of batter, immediately tilting pan so that the entire bottom is thinly coated. Cook about 1 minute, loosening edges, then flip over into another larger skillet to cook the other side. This two-skillet method allows you to make the crêpes in half the time. Continue in this manner, stacking the crêpes. They may be refrigerated or frozen and do not need wax paper squares between them. They are very easy to make and can be used for desserts as well as savory dishes.

Makes 2 ½ to 3 dozen.

ANANAS CARAMELLATO CON GELATO
(Caramelized Pineapple with Ice Cream)

This fantasy of caramelized pineapple, Mascarpone Ice Cream, and glazed oranges is wonderful at any time and takes the traditional fruit and ice cream combination to new heights.

1 ripe pineapple, peeled, cored, & cut into 8 slices ½ inch thick	½ cup brown sugar
1/3 cup butter	¼ cup Aurum orange liqueur
	8 scoops Mascarpone Ice Cream

Melt butter in a large skillet, add sugar, stirring to melt, and add pineapple. Cook about 10 minutes, turning once. When caramelized, remove and boil juices until thick. Add rum. Serve warm with a scoop of ice cream on each slice, and with the following glazed oranges and zest over all.

Mascarpone Gelato:

6 ounces Mascarpone or Neufchâtel cheese ¾ cup sugar 1 cup sour cream	1 cup cream 3 tablespoons lemon juice 1 teaspoon vanilla

Whisk cheese with sugar in electric mixer, and gradually beat in the rest until smooth. Chill, whisk again, and freeze in an ice cream freezer.

Makes about 3 cups.

Glazed Oranges and Zest:

1 cup orange juice 2 tablespoons sugar	2 oranges, zest julienned & fruit segmented 2 tablespoons grenadine

Dissolve sugar in juice, and boil to 230°. Reserve 1 tablespoon, and add oranges to remainder. Chill well. Blanch zest in water about 5 minutes, drain, and refresh under cold water. Add to reserved syrup with grenadine, and simmer gently until candied. Drape over a wire rack until dry.

Serves 8.

TORTA DI CIOCCOLATA E NOCCIOLA

(Chocolate Hazelnut Torte)

Milan's food shops never cease to amaze and inspire me with their elaborate chocolate creations. This is an updated Italianate version of the French Marquise. Delicious served with Amaretti.

2 egg yolks	¼ cup each cream & sour cream
3 tablespoons cream	6 ounces semi-sweet chocolate
2 tablespoons Frangelico liqueur	¼ cup butter
1 tablespoon sugar	1 ounce white chocolate
3 ounces semi-sweet chocolate	6-8 roasted hazelnuts
3 ounces white chocolate	Coconut Cream Sauce (see Index) or Cherry Sauce (see Index)
½ cup butter	
3 tablespoons light corn syrup	Amaretti (see below) (optional)
½ cup roasted hazelnuts, finely chopped	

Whisk egg yolks with cream, liqueur, and sugar in a small saucepan over low heat until warm, and add chocolates, butter, and corn syrup. Whisk until chocolate is melted, and add nuts. Whip creams together until stiff, and fold into chocolate mixture. Pour into a 3-cup mold lined with plastic wrap, and chill until set, then unmold. Melt chocolate with butter, pour over mold, spreading on all sides. Melt white chocolate. Dip nuts, and arrange at intervals on top of torte. Pipe any remaining glaze on top of torte. Pour sauce around torte or individual slices.

Serves 6-8.

AMARETTI OR MACAROONS

(Almond Cookies)

Whether Italian or French, these cookies are indispensable in dessert making.

2 cups almonds	3 egg whites
2/3 cup sugar	½ tablespoon Amaretto liqueur
¾ tablespoon powdered sugar	

Grind almonds with sugars in processor until fine, add whites and liqueur, processing until blended. Drop with a tablespoon on a parchment-lined baking sheet. Bake at 350° about 20 minutes. Cool in the open oven, and store in a tin.

Makes 20.

IBERIA

From the mystical Pyrenees in the North to the central plains of Don Quixote's La Mancha, to the Andalucian beaches in the South, Spain's varying scenery is reflected in its wide-ranging cuisine. Also, the cuisine is not spicy, as is commonly thought, but simple and refined. And, it is not all rice, even in Andalucia and Valencia, where rice is king.

The 700-year Moorish occupation provided citrus fruits, almonds, sweet baked goods, and, of course, rice, while Latin America introduced tomatoes, corn, potatoes, peppers, and chocolate. Spain was the first to receive these foods, and they were later introduced to the rest of Europe. England, for instance, can thank Spain for its marmalade, made from Seville's oranges. Combined with the native ingredients, such as the renowned Serrano ham, chorizo sausage, seafood, and garlic, an outstanding cuisine was created, and Spain reciprocated by having a far-reaching influence on the cuisines of other lands, including Latin America, the Philippines, and the destinations of the Sephardic Jews who took their highly regarded cuisine with them when expelled from Spain.

The national dish of Spain is probably Paella, but it is the tortilla, or omelet, made from potatoes, which is found throughout the country, and is eaten by peasants and nobility alike, as is La Mancha's Manchego cheese.

Castile, an inland province, elevates the art of roasting, as it is renowned for its baby lamb and suckling pig which are only two to six weeks old when they reach the table. In Madrid's Botin Restaurant, they have been roasted in their ancient ovens for almost 300 years. Cocido Madrileño is the national dish here and is known by different names throughout the country. It is a soup with many kinds of meats, vegetables, and dried beans. Although Madrid serves all Spanish dishes, its great restaurants also serve other ethnic cuisines as well. I highly recommend afternoon tea in the garden of the elegant Ritz Hotel.

Andalucia, along the southern coast, is known for its flamenco, sangria, gazpacho, and its historical cities of Seville, Granada, and Cordoba. But it is Jerez, the town for which Sherry is named, that places Spain on the cuisine map of the world. This golden aperitif is one of the oldest and most highly respected wines in the world, and is also a dessert wine and a cooking wine. The adjoining Valencia is noted for its citrus fruits as well as Paella, but it is farther north in Catalonia that you seem to be entering another country.

The Catalans are a vital, creative, passionate, and even violent people, who along with the Basques, would like to be independent of Spain. Among the most famous Catalonians is Gaudi, whose remarkable architecture in Barcelona rivals the food, wine, and scenery. South of Barcelona is the Penedès, one of the world's great sparkling wine areas, where Cordiniu is produced. North of Barcelona is the Costa Brava, where terraced vineyards cling to the rugged coastal hillside, much like the Côtes du Rhône. It was like déjà vu, visiting these vineyards where very good red and white wines are made in limited quantities. The fishing villages along the coast offer great seafood, and I remember a very special multi-course lunch at Casa Gallego in Empuria Brava.

This was a day of wining and dining with no equal—that night I partook of a twenty-six-course extravaganza accompanied by eleven wines, if I remember correctly, at El Bulli in the Catalonian countryside, near the town of Roses. This is where the controversial new food movement began back in the early eighties, and it has as many harsh critics as it does avid admirers. The owner and chef, Ferrán Adrià, has been called the most impressive and creative chef of the century, but when I was there with a Chaîne des Rôtisseurs group, we were not all titillated by his palate shockers, especially the layered purées, which were not identifiable. His gelatinization of many ingredients, such as truffle gelatin replacing pasta, is another surprise!

At the other end of the Pyrenees, in the Basque country, is a famous comrade of Ferrán Adrià. Juan Marie Arzak and his daughter Elena are the third generation at the charming and comfortable Arzak Restaurant in San Sebastien, one of the most sophisticated resort areas in Europe, and I had an excellent lunch there. Elena showed me her laboratory, where she and her father create new masterpieces, and I was amazed at the small room with hundreds of herbs, spices, and seasonings for experimentation. Arzak is one of three Michelin three-star restaurants in San Sebastien. I also had great meals at Martin Berasategui in the suburb of Lasarte and Akelare, both with three stars. In fact, the Basque country has a total of more Michelin stars than any other area of its size in Europe, and this is not surprising since the Basques have long been known for being the best cooks in Europe.

The Basques are a stubborn and fiercely independent people and are also determined to become independent. They are proud of their five thousand year history and their language, although their origin is not known. As on the French side of the Basque Pyrenees, the sea and the mountains provide them with a plethora of foodstuffs. Seafood of all kinds is of utmost importance, especially salt cod, which the Basques have been given credit for discovering on Newfoundland's outer banks. One of my favorite cheeses, Idiazabal, is from the Basque country and is especially good for melting. As for wines, Txacoli or Chacoli is made along the coast and is a great white for summer or for drinking with pinchos, the Basque form of tapas. Red wines are the most popular, especially those from the inland Rioja region, which is world famous. Aside from the San Sebastien region, Bilbao, the capital, also has excellent restaurants and the world famous Guggenheim museum.

I am drawn to the entire Cantabrian coast, so called because the land lies between the Cantabrian mountains and the Bay of Biscay, which is west of the Basque country, where I will return to time and again. Asturias is a beautiful mountainous province first settled by the Vikings, and it was never invaded by the Muslims. This is where the wonderful Cabrales, a blue cheese, is produced, along with the excellent cider which is drunk with everything. The national dish here is Fabada, made with fava beans and pork.

Galicia, the most northwestern point in Europe, is a mysterious, foggy land and as green as Ireland. Its Atlantic coast provides the most scenic drive in Europe because of the rias, or fjords, which cut into the high land during the geologic formation of Galicia, which was the first part of Spain to emerge from the sea.

Since this area was founded by the Celts, it is no surprise to find kilts and bagpipes along with people who eat pork, potatoes, and turnip greens, and who resemble those in the United Kingdom. The most important food, however, is the astonishing array of seafood with more varieties and a greater volume than the entire Mediterranean coast provides. The fertile Bay of Biscay supplies the most highly prized catch of all, the percebes, or goose barnacles, which are scraped off of the rocks on the rugged coastline. Also of note is that scallops are found here and nowhere else in Spain. Caldo Gallego, a soup of pork, white beans, and turnip greens, is the national dish, as well as empanadas, very similar to the Cornish Pasties in Cornwall, England.

The capital, Santiago de Compostela, and its illustrious ninth century cathedral are the final destinations for those who follow the Pilgrim's Way, which begins in St. Jean Pied de Port in the French Pyrenees. Spain's most glorious parador, Hostal Reyes des Catolicos, was where I stayed prior to boarding the El Transcantabrico for my fascinating gastronomical pilgrimage along the coast and through the Cantabrian mountains to San Sebastien. For those on a wine pilgimage, La Coruña, on the northwestern tip of Galicia, is the starting point for the scenic drive along the Atlantic which leads to the villages on the rias, or fjords, where the extraordinary Albariño wines are made. The Albariño grape is grown only here in Rias Baixas, near the Portuguese border, and produces a white wine which is elegant, dry, and aromatic. They are a wonderful aperitif and the perfect choice for seafood.

When you cross the border into Portugal, you will be in the

province of Minho, the poorest part of the country, and yet the culinary capital. The national dish, Caldo Verde, is at its best here, as is its fresh vinho verde wine.

Portugal has mainly the same food products as Spain, but the major difference is the intense spices and seasonings which were brought from the country's colonies in India, Mozambique, Angola, Brazil, and even Macao, which is near Hong Kong. In fact, I have had wonderful Portuguese meals in all these places, so apparently the explorers reciprocated. Vasco da Gama brought curry spices from Goa in southern India in 1497, and of course coffee was brought from Brazil, which caused the proliferation of coffee houses. Another difference in the cooking is the use of butter and cream, and also the juxtaposition of many foods and seasonings provides a more unique cuisine. Like Spain, salt cod is of utmost importance, and is brought from the Grand Banks of Newfoundland because it is not found in Portuguese waters. Desserts are very rich with the extensive use of egg yolks.

Oporto, famous for its namesake wine, which is one of the world's oldest and most highly esteemed, is now famous for something else. The chefs in Oporto and Lisbon have followed the lead of Spanish chefs in developing a new cuisine, which I was told is not well received by the people. On a visit to the world famous Sandeman wine lodge, I was a guest at a magnificent luncheon, and we were all very impressed with the food as well as the port. We were served white port, red port, tawny port, and the crème de la crème, the vintage port. The grapes are grown inland, then taken to these port lodges in Vila Nova de Gaia, near Oporto, to be aged as long as fifty years, both in wood and the bottle, then shipped.

South of Lisbon, still one of the most magnificent cities in Europe, is the Baixa Alentejo, which is famous for its unique Porco con Ameijoas, pork with clams. Farther south is the Algarve, land of the Moors and fabulous beaches. There is a proliferation of almond trees, which supply the Potuguese with their favorite nut, and also an abundance of fig trees.

Portuguese islands supply fresh tropical fruits, but it is in the

Azores that the best bread is found. Massa Sovada, made from cornmeal, was one of my great culinary discoveries. It was on the island of Sao Miguel, one of seven beautiful and unspoiled islands, that I learned about this tender and flavorful bread. Of all the islands in the world, the Azores are my favorite.

The beautiful island of Madeira, 400 miles west of Morocco, is known for its Madeira Cake, as well as the famous fortified wine of the same name. Most of it is produced in the area around Funchal, capital of the island, and the home of Reid's Hotel, one of the classics of the world. It was designed by the same architect as the Polana Hotel in Maputo, Mozambique, and I immediately recognized the similarity, as both are perched on a cliff over the sea, and have impressive floral gardens. The food is excellent, especially when accompanied by the wines. Sercial, an aperitif wine, is the driest, and Malmsey, a dessert wine, is the best and sweetest with a characteristic caramel flavor which is achieved by its unusual aging process with the use of heat. This is also the reason the French favor Madeira as a cooking wine.

RECIPES FROM IBERIA

EMPANADAS CON IDIAZABAL

CROQUETAS DE POLLO Y JAMON
(CHICKEN AND HAM CROQUETTES)

SIZZLING GARLIC SHRIMP

SERRANO AND IDIAZABAL TERRINE

SALADA PORTUGUESA

ENSALADA VALENCIANA

ENSALADA DE BACALAO CON NARANJA
(COD SALAD WITH ORANGES)

ENSALADA ESPARRAGOS BLANCOS Y JAMON DE SERRANO
(WHITE ASPARAGUS AND SERRANO HAM SALAD)

PINK BEAN SALAD WITH ARTICHOKE HEARTS

ROAST PURPLE POTATO SALAD WITH TUNA AND EGGS

SOPA DE TOMATE À LA BERASATEGUI
(TOMATO SOUP BERASATEGUI)

FABADA ASTURIANA (ASTURIAN BEAN SOUP)

AZOREAN FISH CHOWDER

AZOREAN CORNBREAD

ENSAIMADAS (MALLORCAN SWEET ROLLS)

TORTILLA EL TRANSCANTABRICO

WILD MUSHROOMS, SCRAMBLED EGGS, AND CAVIAR

BONITO EN ROLLO (ROLLED TUNA)

SEA BASS WRAPPED IN FILLO WITH SPICY BEURRE BLANC

PIQUILLO RELLEÑOS DE BACALAO
(RED PEPPERS STUFFED WITH COD)

COD WITH BANANA ALMOND SAUCE ALGARVE STYLE

ZARZUELA DES MARISCOS CON SALSA BASQUAISE À LA CREMA
(SHELLFISH MEDLEY WITH CREAMY BASQUE SAUCE)

FRANGO PORTUGUESA À LA MAROC
(PORTUGUESE CHICKEN MOROCCAN STYLE)

POLLO À LA CANARIA (CANARY ISLAND CHICKEN)

PORCO CON AMEIJOAS ALENTEJANA
(PORK WITH CLAMS ALENTEJANA STYLE)

GLAZED ASIAN-STYLE PORK WITH PRUNES AND GRAINS

COCHIFRITO ARAGONESE (FRIED MEAT ARAGON STYLE)

ROASTED PEPPERS

PATATAS ESPAÑOL (SPANISH FRIED POTATOES)

PATATAS CON CHORIZO Y QUESO
(POTATOES WITH SAUSAGE AND CHEESE)

TORTA DE NARANJA (ORANGE CAKE)

OLIVE OIL ICE CREAM

MEDLEY OF TINY AMBROSIAL FRUITS

CARAMEL ICE CREAM

TAPAS AND PINCHOS

Tapas and Pinchos, the Basque version, are a daily tradition when the sun goes down and the bars fill up. These appetizers can be pickup food or eaten on small plates, and can be as simple as little bowls of shrimp, anchovies, hard cooked eggs, olives, almonds, and chorizo sausage. Or, you may prefer my favorites, which are delicious and quite versatile.

EMPANADAS CON IDIAZABAL

Empanadas, known throughout Latin America, are also quite popular in Spain, and this is my version of the varieties that I enjoyed on the El Transcantabrico gastronomical train journey from Galicia to the Basque country. These may also be a main course when made larger.

½ cup chopped onion	¼ cup sherry
½ cup chopped red bell pepper	¼ cup chopped parsley
4 ounces chopped mushrooms	¼ cup bread crumbs
2 tablespoons olive oil	¼ cup chopped Spanish olives
4 ounces Serrano ham, chopped	1 ½ cups grated Idiazabal cheese
4-6 marinated artichoke hearts, chopped	Pie Pastry (see Index)

Sauté onion, pepper, and mushrooms in oil until soft, and add ham, artichokes, and sherry. Simmer until juices evaporate, and add parsley, crumbs, and olives. When cool, stir in cheese. Roll out pastry into 10 or 12 5-inch circles, distribute filling among them, fold in half, and brush edges with water, crimping well. Bake at 400° about 10 minutes or until golden.

Makes 10-12.

CROQUETAS DE POLLO Y JAMON

(Chicken and Ham Croquettes)

Fried croquettes are something I remember from my childhood, so you can imagine my surprise when they turned up time and again on the gastronomical El Transcantabrico train trip. They were always small appetizers or pinchos, but can be made into larger ones as a main course. The best were from Hostal des Reis Catolicos in Santiago de Compostela and Hotel Londres y de Inglaterra in San Sebastien. The elegant Hotel Infantado in the breathtaking Picos de Europa National Park also served excellent croquetas.

1 ½ tablespoons butter	1 ½ cups chopped Serrano ham or prosciutto
1 ½ tablespoons flour	
¾ cup milk	1 cup grated Idiazabal cheese
Salt, pepper, & nutmeg	1 egg, beaten
2 tablespoons chopped cilantro	2 cups bread or cracker crumbs
1 ½ cups chopped cooked chicken	Olive oil

Make a thick roux with butter, flour, and milk. Season well, and add cilantro, chicken, ham, and cheese. Form into small ovals, or large ones for a main course, and dip in egg, then crumbs. Chill well. These may be deep-fat fried, but I prefer to sauté them in olive oil. If used as a main course, they are great served with a Bechamel Sauce with Idiazabal cheese.

Makes about 12 small or 6 large croquettes.

SIZZLING GARLIC SHRIMP

Santander is one of the most beautiful cities on the Bay of Biscay, and Posada del Piar, owned by Tomás Merendón, is one of the best restaurants I experienced on the El Transcantabrico trip. The dinner and wines were outstanding, but his Sizzling Garlic Shrimp were the best ever.

1 pound shrimp, peeled	1 tablespoon sherry vinegar
1 or 2 tablespoons minced garlic	1 tablespoon sherry
	Chopped parsley
1 small red pepper, halved & seeded	Sea Salt
	Country Bread, torn into pieces
¼ cup olive oil	

Toss the shrimp, garlic, and pepper in very hot oil, using an iron skillet. When shrimp are done, splash with vinegar and sherry. Top with parsley and salt, and serve immediately with plenty of bread for dipping.

Serves 4-6.

SERRANO HAM AND IDIAZABAL TERRINE

This is my version of an incredibly easy and delicious specialty of Gerald Hirigoyen, an accomplished Basque chef in San Francisco. It may be used as a tapa or on a salad, and especially in an omelet.

1 pound thinly sliced Serrano or Prosciutto ham	1 pound thinly sliced Idiazabal cheese
Flour	Olive oil

Line a 1-quart terrine or loaf pan with plastic wrap. Place alternate layers of ham and cheese in terrine, pressing firmly. It does not matter how filled up the pan is, so you can make as much as you want. Cover, and chill. Unmold, cut into vertical slices, dip in flour, and sauté until golden.

Serves 6-8.

SALADS

Salads have always been a rather simple affair in both Spain and Portugal, but with the advent of nueva cocina, or new cooking, chefs are becoming more creative—though the finest and freshest local ingredients are of primary importance.

SALADA PORTUGUESA

A port wine vinaigrette adds new flavor to a traditional salad.

3 tablespoons tawny port	1 bunch watercress
3 tablespoons lemon juice	2 medium ripe tomatoes, sliced
1 garlic clove, crushed	1 small red onion, sliced
Salt & pepper	1/3 cup black olives
½ cup olive oil	2 hard-cooked egg yolks, sieved
4-5 cups chiffonade of romaine	

Whisk vinaigrette ingredients together, then toss with greens. Place on a platter or individual plates, and arrange tomatoes around the greens. Place onion rings and olives on top, and sprinkle yolks over.

Serves 6.

ENSALADA VALENCIANA

This has been a longtime favorite of my cooking students, but I have added a few new touches for an updated version.

¼ cup sherry vinegar	1 small red onion, thinly sliced
1/3 cup olive oil	1 or 2 oranges, segmented
Salt & pepper	Chiffonade of romaine & spinach
¼ cup roasted red bell pepper strips (see Index)	Black olives

Whisk vinaigrette ingredients together, add onion and oranges, and marinate 1 hour. Add salad greens and olives, and toss.

Serves 6.

ENSALADA DE BACALAO CON NARANJA

(Cod Salad with Oranges)

In the Basque country, salt cod is used in every course except desserts, but due to the lack of good salt cod in this country, I have found fresh cod to be equally good. This is one of my favorite salads, and can also be a main course.

1 pound cod, cut into 4 pieces	Salt & pepper
1 ½ cups milk	4 cups red-leaf lettuce
½ cup mayonnaise	2 oranges, peeled and cut into sections, and zest julienned
¾ cup orange juice, reduced by half	1/3 cup black olives
1/3 cup olive oil	Chopped chervil
2 tablespoons sherry vinegar	

Cover cod with milk, gently bring to a simmer, cover, and let stand 10 minutes. Whisk mayonnaise with juice. Whisk vinaigrette ingredients together, and toss with lettuce. Place on plates, top with cooled cod, spoon mayonnaise over cod, and garnish with orange zest and sections and olives. Sprinkle with chervil.

Serves 6.

ENSALADA ESPARRAGOS BLANCOS Y JAMON DE SERRANO
(White Asparagus and Serrano Ham Salad)

White asparagus is one of the specialties in northern Spain, and both the Basque country and Catalonia excel at using it in diverse ways. Hostal de la Gavina, a Relais & Châteaux hotel in S'Agaro, on the Costa Brava, is one of Spain's most elegant and aristocratic hotels, and it has a most romantic candlelit outdoor dining terrace where I savored this salad. This is my version.

12-16 white or green asparagus spears, trimmed & cooked	1/3 cup olive oil
2 red bell peppers, roasted (see Index) & cut in halves, trimmed	1 garlic clove, crushed
	Salt & pepper
12-16 thin slices of Serrano ham or prosciutto	1 hard-cooked egg, finely chopped
1 ½ tablespoons sherry vinegar	Red bell pepper trimmings, chopped

Place a bell pepper half on 1 side of each of 4 plates, and place 3 or 4 asparagus spears on each. Drape 3 or 4 slices of ham on the other side of each plate. Whisk vinaigrette ingredients together, and stir in egg and reserved bell pepper trimmings. Drizzle vinaigrette over all. This is an elegant and beautiful salad for a special dinner, but I actually like to have it as a main course with a fried or poached egg placed between the asparagus and ham.

Serves 4.

PINK BEAN SALAD WITH ARTICHOKE HEARTS

Dried pink beans have become my favorite, as they are very tender and have a beautiful rosy hue. Goya sells them, but they can be hard to find. This is an especially delicious salad or main course, which can have marinated tuna, shrimp, or scallops. In Spain, dried beans are usually cooked with aromatic vegetables and butter.

2 cups dried pink beans, soaked overnight	¼ cup sherry vinegar
2 tablespoons butter	1 teaspoon Dijon mustard
1 tablespoon chopped garlic	Salt & pepper
1 tablespoon lemon juice or sherry vinegar	1 cup olive oil
6-8 artichoke hearts, quartered	Cherry or grape tomatoes
	Black and green olives
	Chopped chervil

Cover beans with cold water, add butter, garlic, and juice or vinegar, and cook, covered, about 1 hour or until tender. Drain, and add artichoke hearts. Make vinaigrette, heat until warm, and pour over beans. This may be made in advance and reheated slightly or served at room temperature. Place a ring of tomatoes around the base of the beans, and garnish with olives and chervil.

Serves 6.

ROAST PURPLE POTATO SALAD WITH TUNA AND EGGS

High in the Andes, purple potatoes have been around for hundreds of years, and now we have them, along with many other types. In Spain, roasted (not baked, per se) potatoes are a wonderful method for flavor enhancing. This salad is a wonderful luncheon dish on a hot day, or it can accompany a main course. This is a good example of la nueva cocina on the Andalucian coast showing the Moroccan influence with preserved lemons.

1 pound purple potatoes, halved	2 or 3 hard-cooked eggs, sliced
¼ cup olive oil	1 preserved lemon, pulp removed (see Index)
2 garlic cloves, lightly crushed	½ cup olive oil
½ -inch wide strips from 1 lemon	1 tablespoon capers
Salt & pepper	Green & black olives
1 6-ounce can Albacore white tuna, drained	Chopped chervil or parsley
	Sea Salt

Toss potatoes with oil, garlic, lemon strips, and seasonings. Roast on a pan covered with parchment paper at 375° about 20 to 30 minutes, or until tender. When cool, slice and place in a wide shallow bowl or on a platter. Arrange tuna and eggs over potatoes. Make vinaigrette by puréeing preserved lemon with oil. Pour over salad, and garnish with remaining ingredients. Taste for salt at each stage, as preserved lemons can be quite salty.

Serves 4-6.

SOUPS AND BREADS

Spanish and Portuguese soups are generally very robust, such as the cocidos chock full of dried beans, potatoes, and meat. The exception, of course, is the ubiquitous Gazpacho. Rye and cornbread are eaten along the Bay of Biscay, while typical European country breads are eaten in Castile, where the finest flour and baking are found. Sweet breads of Arab influence are of utmost importance.

SOFA DE TOMATE À LA BERASATEGUI

(Tomato Soup Berasategui)

My wonderful lunch at Restaurant Martin Berasategui in the leafy suburb of Lasarte, near San Sebastien, was enhanced by having a table with a fabulous view of formal gardens and the emerald green rolling countryside. This creative Michelin three-star chef presented me with a most unusual tapas platter consisting of an anchovy atop a piece of puff pastry of the same shape and the most delicious tomato soup I've ever encountered, among other items. The soup was served in a small white demitasse in the current avant-garde shape, on a rippled white plate with the other creations. This is my interpretation.

2 pounds very ripe tomatoes, coarsely chopped	Salt & pepper
2 large garlic cloves, lightly crushed	1 tablespoon Spanish brandy or sherry
1 teaspoon sugar	1 cup cream, reduced to 2/3 cup
½ teaspoon saffron threads	

Simmer tomatoes with garlic, sugar, and seasonings about 20 to 30 minutes, or lightly thickened and reduced. Purée, strain to remove seeds and skins, and add brandy and cream. Adjust seasoning, adding more cream, if desired. An elegant touch would be to add a small dollop of caviar on top.

Serves 6-8 in small cups.

FABADA ASTURIANA

(Asturian Bean Soup)

The most important Asturian dish is this fava bean and pork stew, which can be a soup as well. Anxious to compare mine with the one on Asturian soil, I am pleased to say that mine is even better than that at Casa Fermin, one of the most renowned restaurants on the Bay of Biscay, and in the capital of Oviedo. Good quality dried fava beans are not always available, but I have found that small dried lima beans or kidney beans are acceptable substitutes.

1 cup dried fava or small lima beans, soaked overnight	½ pound Serrano ham or prosciutto
1 onion, chopped	½ pound chorizo or blood sausage
2 large garlic cloves, crushed	1 teaspoon paprika
2-4 ounces slab bacon	½ teaspoon saffron threads
2 tablespoons olive oil	Salt & pepper

Sauté onion, garlic, and bacon in olive oil until onion is translucent. Add drained beans and enough water to cover by an inch. Cover, and simmer about 1 hour, then add remaining ingredients. Simmer about 1 hour, or until beans are tender. Serve as a soup, or drain off most of the liquid and serve on plates. I like to drizzle extra virgin olive oil over the top.

Serves 6.

AZOREAN FISH CHOWDER

The quiet deserted streets of São Miguel, in the Azore islands, were filled with the aroma of the best fish chowder I've had. It is very simple, yet flavorful. Serve with Azorean cornbread

1 cup chopped onion	½ cup Madeira or port
2 garlic cloves, crushed	1 ½ teaspoons dried coriander
4 ounces salt pork or bacon, diced	½ teaspoon powdered saffron
	Salt & pepper
1 pound potatoes, peeled & cubed	2 pounds monkfish, cod, or halibut
6 cups fish stock	

Sauté onion and garlic in rendered salt pork, using an iron pot. Add potatoes, stock, and wine. Simmer until potatoes are tender, then add seasonings and fish. Shellfish can also be added. Simmer about 10 minutes, or until fish is just done, and garnish with lots of fresh chopped cilantro.

Serves 4-6.

AZOREAN CORNBREAD

The Azoreans make this delicious bread with white cornmeal, but I prefer yellow. It is one of my favorite breads and is always served with the fish chowder, but I find it is especially good with any hearty meal, and also with breakfast, as I had in my hotel in São Miguel.

¼ cup warm water	2 teaspoons salt
1 package dry yeast	¾ cup yellow or white cornmeal
2 tablespoons sugar	2 ½ cups all-purpose flour
1 ¾ cups warm water	2 ½ cups bread flour
¼ cup soft butter	

Add water to yeast and sugar in a large electric mixer bowl, and let stand until foamy. Using a dough hook, add remaining water, butter, salt, and cornmeal. Gradually add flour, and knead with dough hook until smooth and elastic, adding more flour if dough is sticky. Let rise in a buttered bowl, covered, for about 1 ½ hours, or until doubled. Punch dough down, form into 2 balls, and place in 2 9-inch cake pans or pie plates that have been buttered and sprinkled with cornmeal. Cut a deep cross in the top of each with a very sharp knife, and let rise again until doubled, about 1 hour. Bake at 350° about 45 to 50 minutes, or until golden brown. Cool on racks, and serve.

Makes 2 8-to 9-inch loaves.

ENSAIMADAS

(Mallorcan Sweet Rolls)

Normally, I don't eat breakfast, but on the island of Mallorca, it was my favorite meal because of the luscious sweet rolls slathered with butter and honey that were served with my Café au Lait at La Residencia, a luxury resort hotel in Deya on the north side of the island. It is a 400-year old manor house that was lovingly restored, and is a Relais & Châteaux.

½ cup warm milk	1 egg & 1 egg yolk
1 package dry yeast	1 teaspoon orange flower water
2 tablespoons sugar	3 cups all-purpose flour
¼ cup warm water	Chestnut honey
¼ cup soft butter	Powdered sugar
1/3 cup sugar	Melted butter

Add milk to yeast and sugar in a large electric mixer bowl, and let stand until foamy. Beat in water, butter, sugar, eggs, flower water, and flour, mixing until dough is smooth. Separate into 16 pieces, and roll them into long ropes, about 18 inches long. Coil them into spirals, brush with melted butter and honey, and place on a large buttered baking sheet. Cover and let rise about 1 hour, or until doubled. Bake at 350° about 10 to 15 minutes. Cool on rack, and brush again with butter and honey. Sift powdered sugar over them.

Makes 16.

TORTILLA EL TRANSCANTABRICO

El Transcantabrico, the deluxe gastronomical tour train, also had a buffet breakfast worth waking up for, especially their potato omelet (called a tortilla all over Spain), which is somewhat of a national dish. Many chefs add chopped onions, ham, or sausage, but I prefer only potatoes and eggs. This can also be eaten for lunch or a light dinner, and cut into small pieces for tapas.

½ pound potatoes, peeled & thinly sliced	4 or 5 large eggs, whisked
½ cup olive oil	2 or 3 ounces Serrano ham or prosciutto, very thinly sliced
Salt & pepper	

Using a large iron skillet, sauté potatoes in hot olive oil until tender, turning occasionally. Season, and with a slotted spatula, add to eggs. Let stand about 10 minutes, then cover bottom of same iron skillet with ham. Add egg and potato mixture, and cook over moderate heat, shaking pan occasionally until barely set. Loosen bottom, and invert onto a round platter.

Serves 2.

WILD MUSHROOMS, SCRAMBLED EGGS AND CAVIAR

Another fabulous breakfast buffet worth going back for was that at the legendary and palatial Maria Cristina Hotel in San Sebastien. Champagne and caviar, in copious amounts, were part of the buffet.

½ pound chanterelles, or other wild mushrooms, trimmed & sliced	Salt & pepper
	2 tablespoons cream
	2 tablespoons butter
1 or 2 shallots, chopped	1 tablespoon sherry or port
1 tablespoon butter	4 slices country bread, brushed with oil & grilled or toasted
1 tablespoon olive oil	
4 eggs	Caviar

Sauté mushrooms and shallots in butter and oil about 5 minutes, or until tender. Whisk eggs with seasonings and cream, and cook gently in butter until soft and creamy. Stir in sherry. Place mushrooms over bread, top with eggs, and add caviar, as you desire. Be sure to have plenty of champagne for this romantic breakfast.

Serves 4.

MAIN COURSES

Spain and Portugal undoubtedly eat more seafood than poultry or red meats, especially since they have the longest coastline in Europe. Game is found throughout the mountains and is more popular than chicken. As for beef, the mountainous land is more conducive to providing veal, and pork is the meat of choice in the south.

BONITO EN ROLLO
(Rolled Tuna)

Mirador de Toro is a wonderful restaurant in Llanes, Asturias, and it serves a truly outstanding rolled tuna dish with a delicious and light caramelized lemon butter sauce. I prefer to use salmon instead.

1 pound tuna or salmon fillets, about ¼-inch thick	2 tablespoons olive oil
1/3 cup chopped red bell pepper	1/3 cup chopped mint or parsley
1/3 cup chopped shallot	½ cup butter
2 garlic cloves, crushed	2 tablespoons sugar
	¼ cup lemon or lime juice

The length and width of the fillets do not matter, as they are sliced ½-inch thick when rolled, and if they are narrow and long, you will simply end up with slices that are of a greater diameter and fewer of them. If you want to serve several smaller slices, simply cut wider and shorter fillets. Sauté pepper, shallot, and garlic in oil about 5 minutes, or until tender. Add mint, which I prefer, and stir until wilted. Spread on the fillets, roll up, slice ½-inch thick, and sauté lightly in a little extra oil, if necessary, about a few minutes on each side. Do not let them brown. For the sauce, heat butter with sugar in a heavy small skillet, and stir until caramelized. Add juice, and swirl until sauce thickens. Pour over and around salmon spirals.

Serves 4.

SEA BASS WRAPPED IN FILLO WITH SPICY BEURRE BLANC

Helio Loureiro, the chef at the Sandeman Port Lodge in Oporto and one of the most creative in Portugal, prepared this visually stunning and delicious fish course for the Chaîne des Rôtisseurs members, as part of a most memorable lunch. I use cod and the following folding of fillo to achieve the unique effect of fish fins.

12 half-sheets of fillo, each about 9 x 14 inches	1 tablespoon butter
½ cup melted butter	¼ cup sliced almonds
Salt & pepper	Beurre Blanc (see index) made with white port and seasoned with cumin, red pepper, & powdered saffron
4 5-ounce cod or sea bass fillets	

Brush fillo sheets with butter, stacking 3 at a time. Season fillets, place in center of each stack so that the long side is perpendicular to the long side of the fillo. Sprinkle with almonds, sautéed in butter. Fold in long edges of fillo, brush with butter, and bring short edges together over fish, sealing them together. Pleat down the length of the fish to resemble fins. This is easier than it sounds and is very effective. Brush all of exposed fillo with melted butter, place on baking sheets, and bake at 375° about 20 minutes or until golden. Serve with the Beurre Blanc poured around them.

Serves 4.

PIQUILLO RELLEÑOS DE BACALAO

Red Peppers Stuffed with Cod)

This is a classic dish in both Spanish and French Basque country, and it has many interpretations. I arrived in St. Jean Pied de Port by train on market day, and all the ladies of the tiny village were selling their jars of small roasted piquillos on the sidewalks. They are grown in southern Basque country in Navarre on the Spanish side. I have found that our bell peppers are a fine substitute. Also, fresh cod can be used instead of salt cod.

4 small Roasted Red Bell Peppers, peeled, & left whole (see Index)	2 tablespoons flour
	1 ½ to 2 cups milk
	Salt (if needed) & pepper
¾ pound salt cod or fresh cod	Sauce Basquaise or Salsa Vizcaina (see index)
½ cup chopped onion	
2 garlic cloves, crushed	Chopped parsley
¼ cup olive oil	

If using salt cod, soak in several changes of water at least 24 hours in refrigerator. Cut cod of either type into ½-inch strips, and sauté with onion and garlic in oil about 5 minutes. Add flour, blend well, and add milk. Simmer, stirring often, about 15 minutes, or until very thick. Season, and fill peppers, folding over any torn edges to enclose filling. Place in oiled individual gratin dishes, and cover with Sauce Basquaise. Bake at 350° about 15 minutes, or until very hot. Sprinkle with parsley.

Serves 4.

COD WITH BANANA ALMOND SAUCE ALGARVE STYLE

The Algarve and Andalucia both share an Arab legacy and a similar cuisine. This is an example of the new style which the chefs are creating.

6 cod fillets	½ cup toasted sliced almonds
Flour, for dredging	¼ cup Madeira or sherry
2 eggs, beaten	Salt & pepper
½ cup butter	Chopped cilantro or mint
6 fresh figs, quartered	3 lemon slices, scored & halved
2 small bananas, sliced diagonally	

Dredge cod in flour, dip in eggs, and sauté in butter on both sides until just done, about 5 minutes. Remove fillets, and sauté figs, bananas, and almonds briefly. Deglaze pan with Madeira or sherry, and pour over cod. Garnish with cilantro or mint and lemon slices.

Serves 6.

ZARZUELA DES MARISCOS CON SALSA BASQUAISE À LA CREMA

(Shellfish Medley with Creamy Sauce Basquaise)

This is my memory of a delightfully refreshing cold plate of shellfish with a creamy but light version of Sauce Basquaise. This was part of a multi-course seafood feast at Casa Gallego in Empuria Brava, located on the Costa Brava in Catalonia. You can use any kind of seafood and grill, broil, sauté, or steam it. Garnish to your heart's content, and enjoy on a hot summer night with plenty of cava.

2 lobsters, boiled, halved, and meat removed	4 cups watercress
1 dozen large shrimp, boiled & shelled	¾ cup cream
	2 cups Sauce Basquaise (see Index)
8 sea scallops, cooked	Black olives
Clams and mussels (optional)	Hard-cooked eggs, quartered

Arrange cold shellfish on watercress. Whisk cream, as much as desired, into cold puréed Sauce Basquaise, and pour over shellfish. Garnish with olives and eggs.

Serves 4.

FRANGO PORTUGUESA À LA MAROC

(Portuguese Chicken Moroccan Style)

This rich and creamy sauté of suprêmes with olives, figs, and preserved lemons shows the contemporary influence of Morocco.

4 suprêmes	3 or 4 figs, quartered
Salt & pepper	½ cup green and black olives
2 tablespoons butter	1 preserved lemon, pulp removed & rind quartered (see index)
1 garlic clove, crushed	
¼ teaspoon crushed or powdered saffron	
	½ cup cream
¼ cup Madeira or port	2 tablespoons chopped mint or cilantro
¾ cup chicken stock	

Season suprêmes, sauté in butter on both sides, about 5 minutes, until golden. Add garlic and saffron, sauté briefly, and deglaze with port. Add stock and fruits, and simmer until chicken is done, about 10 minutes. Remove chicken and fruits, add cream, and simmer until lightly thickened, and pour over chicken. Garnish with mint.

Serves 4.

POLLO À LA CANARIA

(Canary Island Chicken)

The food of the Canaries pales in comparison to the friendliness and generosity of the people. My first visit was on one of my whirlwind trips, involving at least 3 dozen flights, ferries, trains, and buses, when I was collecting countries and on my way to Western Sahara. My overnight stay at the old-world Hotel Mencey ended early in the morning with a constant cock-a-doodle-doo, so chicken was destined to be my lunch. This wonderful country dish was a perfect end to my visit to Las Palmas in Grand Canary. Not only was it gratis, but it was prepared especially for me.

1 chicken breast, with skin & bones	2 lemon slices, or ¼ preserved lemon, pulp removed, & rind chopped
1 chicken thigh, with skin & bones	1 garlic clove, crushed
Salt & pepper	½ teaspoon paprika
Flour	1/3 cup sherry
2 tablespoons olive oil	¼ cup chicken stock
1 small sausage, chopped	1 tablespoon chopped cilantro
	½ cup garlicky fried croutons

Season and flour chicken, and sauté in oil over high heat until well browned. Add sausage, lemon, garlic, and paprika. Lower heat and cook about 5 minutes. Add sherry and stock, and simmer, half covered, about 20 minutes or until chicken is done, adding a little water if necessary. Garnish with cilantro and croutons, and serve over rice.

Serves 1.

PORCO CON AMEIJOAS ALENTEJANA

(Pork with Clams Alentejana)

Grand old Aviz is the jewel in Lisbon's restaurant crown, and this is my version of the savory pork with clams that is a specialty of Alentejo.

1 ½ pounds pork tenderloin, sliced diagonally about ½ inch thick	Salt & pepper
	2 tablespoons olive oil or lard, which is traditional
1 ½ cups white port	1 ½ dozen clams in the shell, washed & scrubbed
2 garlic cloves, lightly crushed	
½ tablespoon paprika	1/3 cup Roasted red bell pepper strips, (see index)
1 bay leaf	
	Chopped cilantro

Marinate pork in port with seasonings about 2 or 3 hours. Drain and dry well, and sauté in oil until well browned. Remove pork, add marinade, and deglaze skillet, reducing to about 1 cup. Return pork, add clams, and simmer, covered about 6 or 8 minutes, until clam shells open. Discard those that do not open, and also discard garlic and bay leaf. Serve garnished with peppers and cilantro.

Serves 4.

GLAZED ASIAN STYLE PORK WITH PRUNES & GRAINS

If there ever were a fusion recipe, this would be it. Created by a young genius, Ramon Freixa, in Catalonia. This is my interpretation.

1 small pork tenderloin	½ cup hot cream
8 prunes, marinated in Madeira	½ teaspoon curry powder
3 tablespoons soy sauce	¼ cup cooked dried apricots, diced
3 tablespoons chestnut honey	
1 tablespoon peanut butter	¼ cup golden raisins
1/3 cup couscous	2 tablespoons slivered almonds, roasted
1/3 cup bulgar wheat	
2 cups hot veal stock	Chopped Cilantro

Cut a pocket along 1 side of the tenderloin, and stuff with prunes. Marinate in soy sauce and honey about 2 hours, turning frequently. Sauté in an oval sauté pan until golden brown, then coat with peanut butter, and roast in a 350° oven about 10 minutes, or until just done. Cover couscous and bulgar wheat separately with hot stock, and let stand about 10 minutes. Stir cream and curry into couscous, and stir dried fruits and nuts into bulgar wheat. Keep both warm while slicing pork into 4 diagonal sections. Arrange on 4 plates with couscous and bulgar wheat. Garnish with cilantro.

Serves 4.

COCHIFRITO ARAGONESE

(Fried Meat Aragon Style)

This classic lamb dish from Aragon is equally good when made with veal, and ideally either should be from young animals. I have added a new twist with the addition of preserved lemons. Chopped rosemary is also excellent.

1 tablespoon butter	2 garlic cloves, crushed
1 tablespoon olive oil	1 teaspoon paprika
2 pounds cubed lamb or veal foreshank or shoulder	2/3 cup veal stock
Salt & pepper	Preserved lemon, pulp removed & rind diced (see Index)

Heat butter and oil in a sauté pan, and sauté lamb or veal, seasoned, about 10 minutes, or until golden brown. Add seasonings, stock, and lemon. Cover and simmer about 1 hour, or until tender. Add more stock if necessary, or if too much remains, reduce to desired consistency.

Serves 4.

ROASTED PEPPERS

The Basque country has the best of all vegetables, but it is peppers, especially piquillos, that are of utmost importance. Roasted Peppers are used alone, as a garnish, and as an integral part of many dishes. They are really very easy to roast in any number of ways. They may be grilled, roasted, put directly over a gas flame, broiled, or placed on a hot ridged iron stovetop grill, which I prefer. Turn them until blackened all over, or cut in half, and press skin side down with a spatula. In either case, remove core and seeds before blackening. When done, either place in a plastic or paper bag, or immerse in a bowl of water. This will loosen the skins, which you will be able to peel off easily. I put them in plastic bags and freeze them, preparing lots of them when the price is right. Any kind of pepper can be used.

PATATAS ESPANOL

(Spanish Fried Potatoes)

The most common way to prepare potatoes in Spain, other than as a tortilla or omelet, is to fry them thinly sliced. They may be embellished with roasted bell peppers, onion, herbs, chorizo, or ham. My favorite comfort food is to cook eggs over the top of the potatoes, by covering the skillet until done as desired. Grated Idiazabal over the eggs is sheer heaven. Enjoy!

1 ½ pounds Yukon Gold potatoes, peeled & sliced thinly	¼ pound julienned Serrano ham or Prosciutto (optional)
¼ cup olive oil	4 eggs, (optional)
Salt & pepper	Chopped parsley
4 or 5 garlic cloves, crushed	

Turn and toss potatoes in hot oil, using an iron skillet, until almost done. Then season, add garlic, toss again, and add ham. Cover, and cook gently until done, adding eggs if desired. Cover until eggs are done. Add parsley.

Serves 4.

PATATAS CON CHORIZO Y QUESO

(Potatoes with Sausage and Cheese)

This is a new Spanish dish, quite rich with cream and cheese, but absolutely delectable. It was inspired by the incomparable Martin Berasategui, whose restaurant in Lasarte, near San Sebastien, is one of my favorites.

2 ounces chopped chorizo or bacon	2 tablespoons butter
½ cup chopped onions	3 garlic cloves, crushed
¼ cup sherry vinegar	1 ½ pounds Yukon Gold potatoes, peeled & diced
1/3 cup white wine	1 cup veal or chicken stock
1 cup cream	¾ cup grated Idiazabal cheese
Salt & pepper	¼ cup Tetilla cheese or Mascarpone

Sauté chorizo or bacon with onions until golden brown, add vinegar, and deglaze. Add wine, reduce slightly, then add cream, and reduce until lightly thickened, season. Melt butter in sauté pan, and sauté garlic and potatoes until golden. Add stock, and simmer until potatoes are tender, about 15 minutes. Stir in cheese, and pour cream sauce over.

Serves 4.

DESSERTS

Spain and Portugal have quite simple desserts, except in the luxury hotels and restaurants. The most popular are the custard ice creams. I noticed on my gastronomical train trip that the Spaniards made a production of peeling and carving their fresh fruits for dessert. The Moorish influence is quite evident in the use of almonds and eggs. There are excellent fried pastries, such as many kinds of doughnuts and fritters which are eaten for breakfast. Chocolate candies and hot chocolate drinks are ubiquitous.

TORTA DE NARANJA
(Orange Cake)

Not a Spanish classic, but a classic at the Hotel Kitz, a venerable luxury hotel in Madrid, which is always my favorite option. This is my idea of what a cake should be-fruit and pastry cream, as well as buttercream, with the cake itself being a mere catalyst for these. You can use the French Sponge Cake.

1, 8- or 9-inch cake layer, sliced into 3 layers	

Orange Syrup:

½ cup sugar ½ cup orange juice	1 tablespoon orange flower water

Orange Pastry Cream:

½ cup orange juice	1/3 cup sugar
4 egg yolks	1 tablespoon reduced juice
2 tablespoons cornstarch	Chocolate Buttercream (see Index) or Orange Buttercream
1 cup milk	

Orange Buttercream:

1 cup sugar	1 ½ cups soft butter
1/3 cup water	1 tablespoon reduced juice
6 egg yolks	1 tablespoon orange liqueur

Garnish:

½ cup sliced almonds, toasted	1 cup red currants or grapes
2 or 3 oranges, peeled & segmented	½ cup orange marmalade
	2 tablespoons orange liqueur

Heat syrup ingredients until sugar dissolves, cool, and brush over cut layers of cake.

For pastry cream, reduce juice to 2 tablespoons. Whisk yolks with cornstarch, gradually whisk in milk, add sugar, and cook gently until thick. Add 1 tablespoon reduced juice, and chill well.

To make buttercream, dissolve sugar in water, and boil to 238°. Meanwhile, beat yolks in electric mixer until they are pale and form a ribbon. Add syrup gradually, beating until cool, then gradually add butter, and beat in remaining tablespoon of reduced juice and liqueur.

To assemble cake, spread ½ cup buttercream over each of 2 layers, and spread half the pastry cream over each layer. Stack them, add top layer, and spread entire cake with buttercream, reserving about ¾ cup for decorating. Press almonds onto side of cake, and arrange fruit on top. Mix marmalade with liqueur, and brush over fruit. Using a pastry bag with a decorative tip, decorate edge of cake with a border of reserved cream.

Chill well. Serves 8-10.

OLIVE OIL ICE CREAM

Olive oil ice cream, believe it or not, is simply delicious, and it has become quite the rage in southern France as well as in Spain. I even had one that had chopped olives in it. The best were at El Bulli in Catalonia and at La Balette in Collioure, France. Cheese ice cream is also spreading, the best being made with Idiazabal, the great Basque cheese, which I had at Hotel Londres y Inglaterra in San Sebastien.

4 egg yolks	3 cups half & half or light cream
2/3 cup sugar	1 or 2 tablespoons lemon juice
½ cup mild olive oil	½ teaspoon powdered saffron (optional)

Whisk yolks with sugar in an electric mixer until pale and a ribbon forms. Gradually whisk in oil, cream, and seasonings. Freeze in an ice cream maker.

Makes about 1 quart.

MEDLEY OF TINY AMBROSIAL FRUITS

One of my greatest dessert finds ever, this is good enough to eat on its own, but European chefs are using it in many diverse ways. On my visit to the Sanderman Port Lodge near Oporto, Portugal, the chef, Helio Loureiro, told me he mixes whatever fruits are available, usually including currants, with a little liquid. He served his with an almond cake and raspberry sorbet. Walter Blakemore, the chef on the Silver Cloud, had just recently served this fruit medley around molded chocolate mousse, with chocolate sauce and cocoa over everything. Absolutely delicious! The following is my version and presentation.

3 tablespoons dark corn syrup	¼ cup golden raisins
½ tablespoon cocoa powder	10 or 12 cherries or raspberries
½ tablespoon port or your choice of liqueur	1 pint Caramel Ice Cream (see Index)
¼ cup dried currants	½ pint Chocolate ice cream or Sorbet au Chocolat (see Index)
¼ cup chopped pistachios	

Mix syrup, cocoa, port, and fruits together. If cherries and raspberries are large, cut into halves or quarters. Let stand so that juices are released from fruit. Line a 4-5 cup terrine or loaf pan with plastic wrap. Soften both ice creams by leaving in refrigerator about an hour or whip in an electric mixer or processor. Spread half the caramel ice cream in the terrine, freeze until firm, and add all the chocoate ice cream over it. Freeze again until firm, and spread remaining caramel ice cream over top. Cover and freeze. When ready to serve, unmold, remove plastic, and slice about ½-inch thick. Place on 6 plates with an arc of fruit medley around it.

Serves 6.

CARAMEL ICE CREAM

This is a simpler version than the Caramelized Nut Ice Cream in the French section and is my favorite of all.

1 cup sugar	1 cup sour cream or yogurt
¾ cup water	5 egg yolks
2 cups cream	2 tablespoons dessert port wine

Melt sugar in a 9-inch skillet over fairly high heat (I use high) and stir only occasionally, until caramelized. Do not stir after it bubbles, or it will crystalize. Add water, and stir until dissolved over medium heat. Add cream, whisking, and bring to a simmer. Whisk sour cream into yolks, and warm with a little of the hot caramel mixture. Whisk gradually into remaining caramel, and cook until it coats the back of the spoon. Freeze in an ice cream freezer, after chilling well.

Makes 1 quart.

UNITED KINGDOM AND IRELAND

What can be said about British food that hasn't been said before? Plenty! Some of the most highly acclaimed and innovative chefs in the European area are in London, Dublin, Belfast, and other cities in the United Kingdom, which also includes the Isle Of Man, and the Channel Islands. It certainly hasn't hurt that these young chefs have French training, now that they are the progenitors of fusion cooking along with the United States, Australia, and South Africa. It is not ironic that they all speak English, but it is ironic that the British are just now becoming great chefs, when one considers that they have had some of the world's greatest food writers—Elizabeth David, Jane Grigson, Patience Gray, and let us not forget the highly esteemed André Simon, an incomparable writer of gastronomy and wine.

Also, Harrod's Food Halls in Knightsbridge is undoubtedly the largest and most impressive food purveyor in existence. From its origin as a humble grocery in 1835, it was selling prepared foods by 1900, what we now call "takeout." The current 45,000 square feet of lavish food displays purvey at least 500 kinds of cheese, 100 kinds of chocolates made on site, 150 kinds of breads, and 60 salami varities, and enough else to fill a book.

Of course, they have always been noted for their hearty and delicious breakfasts of the world's best oatmeal with Lyle's Golden Syrup, York and Irish ham and bacon, Scottish Scones with Dundee marmalade, and butter to die for. And, let's not forget Teatime or High Tea, where one partakes of more scones (now in many variations including chocolate), crumpets, cakes, and the great rival to crème fraîche, the wickedly rich Devonshire clotted cream.

Other exceptional food products include their renowned Roast Beef, lamb, and the best duck I've ever eaten, the Aylesbury from Aston Clinton, which has no equal. The Emerald Isle has excellent produce, and is known for its oysters and other shellfish, while Scottish salmon is among the world's best. And, although there are not many cheeses, the Stilton is my favorite of all blue cheeses because of its mellow creaminess. I also like Cheshire, Cheddar, and the delectable Welsh Caerphilly, a soft, creamy cheese that I discovered on the Silver Cloud, while on a Silversea cruise. The chef, Walter Blakemore, is from London, and apparently he is one of the finest from England.

No eminent wines are yet produced in the British Isles, but the cheeses have great companions in the imported Portuguese wines. Also, there is Irish cream Liqueur, Irish and Scotch whiskys, Beefeater gin, and Guinness Stout.

Let's not forget that the British created a number of great classics, namely Cornish Pasties, steamed puddings, Trifle, Steak and Oyster Pie, and fruitcake. The current cuisine is being influenced by the growing Indian, Pakistani, and other ethnic groups, along with the very competent new chefs. Heston Blumenthal, who practices his molecular gastronomy at the Fat Duck, is already a culinary icon and is Britain's answer to Spain's Ferran Adria.

Other great British chefs who have placed Britain on the culinary map are Raymond Blanc of Le Manoir aux Quat Saisons, Anton Mosimann, and the Roux brothers of Le Gavroche and Waterside Inn. In 2008, Britain actually received more Michelin stars than France, although not as many restaurants received the top award of three stars.

And now, a wee bit o' Scotland, which is like a totally different country than England, and actually more like Ireland, also Gaelïc. It is known for its enchantingly beautiful heather-clad highlands, Loch Ness, lilting bagpipes and, of course, Scotch whisky.

But it was the fabulous four-night journey on the Royal Scotsman, an Orient Express train, followed by a stay at the incomparable and luxurious Prestonfield House, just outside Edinburgh, where my family originated 1,000 years ago, that proved what a treasure of great food and chefs Scotland has to offer. I dined on succulent Shetland lamb; Aberdeen Angus beef; the freshest of seafood from the North Sea and the surrounding islands of Shetland, Orkney, and the Hebrides; and produce to equal that of France.

Raspberries are exquisite and the centerpiece of the dessert table, especially when served with clotted cream, heather honey, and Scotland's original Butterscotch Sauce. Kale is ubiquitous and prepared in numerous ways, as are butter beans. Oats are used extensively, not just for the morning porridge, but as a thickener for soups, coating fish and meats, baked goods, stuffings called skirlie, and always in Haggis, the controversial and dreaded national dish.

The Normans definitely left a culinary legacy, as the French influence is dominant, although the Romans and Vikings introduced many new foods and influenced the cooking style. Home-style cooking is a unique blend of all three, but the nomenclature is strictly Scottish—skirlie, clapshot, cock-a-leekie, bannocks, rumbledethumps, cranachan, champit, tatties, crowdie, and cloutie must all be tried.

RECIPES FROM UNITED KINGDOM AND IRELAND

PECAN PANCAKES WITH HONEY-PECAN BUTTER

CURRANT SCONES

ENGLISH HERB BREAD

SCRAMBLED EGGS ON TOAST

SAVORY HERB CRÊPES WITH CREAMED MUSHROOMS

EGG SALAD SANDWICHES

ENGLISH WHITE FRUITCAKE

BLINI WITH CAVIAR AND EGG SALAD

COCKALEEKIE SOUP

POACHED EGGS WITH RICE AND SAUCE MESSINE

IRISH PARSLEY SAUCE

ORANGE-BAKED SEA BASS WITH ORANGE BASIL BUTTER

FILLET OF SEA BASS WITH FINGERLING POTATOES, HARICOTS VERT, OVEN-DRIED TOMATOES, AND LEMON VINAIGRETTE

SEABASS WITH CREAMY BUTTER SAUCE

IRISH HAM WITH WHISKY SAUCE

YORK HAM WITH CUMBERLAND SAUCE HOTEL SAVOY

HAGGIS

HAGGIS IN PUFF PASTRY

CONFIT DE CANARD WITH SHREDDED BRUSSEL SPROUTS AND PEANUT PESTO

ENGLISH SUMMER PUDDING

IRISH FLAMING GRAPE CAKE

BUTTER SPONGECAKE

SCOTTISH SHORTBREAD

STICKY DATE PUDDING WITH BUTTERSCOTCH SAUCE

DEMITASSE OF CHOCOLATE WITH MASCARPONE CREAM

BREAKFAST AND TEATIME

PECAN PANCAKES WITH HONEY-PECAN BUTTER

The best English breakfast I can remember was prepared by Chef Walter Blakemore on the Silver Cloud the day I disembarked. I didn't even use any butter, only lots of maple syrup. I do like Honey-Pecan Butter, so I have added it.

1 ¼ cups soft wheat flour	½ teaspoon salt
1/3 cup cornmeal	2 eggs
2 tab1espoons sugar	1 ½ cups buttermilk
2 teaspoons baking powder	¼ cup melted butter
1 teaspoon baking soda	1 cup chopped pecans, or more, roasted

Honey-Pecan Butter:

½ cup soft butter	1/3 cup chopped pecans, roasted
¼ cup chestnut honey	

Mix dry ingredients in a large bowl. Whisk eggs with buttermilk and butter, and stir into dry ingredients lightly, leaving slightly lumpy to achieve very light pancakes. Fold in pecans. Cook on a hot, lightly greased griddle or iron skillet, dropping batter with a large spoon. Cook until golden on both sides. Mix butter with honey and pecans, and serve over pancakes, with plenty of maple syrup also.

Serves 4.

CURRANT SCONES

Scones, like biscuits, have taken on many different disguises recently, but British purists will have none of this. Some of the best I've had were on the St. Helena mail ship, which makes about 3 or 4 trips a year from Cardiff down the Atlantic to the British islands of Ascension, St. Helena, where Napoleon was in exile for six years, and Tristan da Cunha, where only about 200 people live, with no roads, phones, or television. My two voyages were several weeks long, so I had many great breakfasts, English-style. These scones were the best because of the Demarara sugar which they also use in their tea.

2 cups soft wheat flour	1/3 cup dried currants
¼ cup Demarara sugar or brown	2/3 cup milk or cream
2 teaspoons baking powder	Milk & brown sugar for glaze
½ teaspoon salt	Clotted cream or crème fraîche (see Index)
½ cup cold butter	Marmalades & Preserves

Mix dry ingredients in electric mixer bowl, then cut in butter. Add currants and stir in cream until barely blended, like the pancakes. Form into 1 large cake, round or square, about ½-inch thick. Brush with milk, sprinkle sugar on top, and bake at 350° about 20 minutes, or until just done. Otherwise, you can cut out 3-inch circles, and bake the same way. Serve with the cream and marmalades and preserves for breakfast or afternoon tea.

Makes about 15.

ENGLISH HERB BREAD

This yeast bread is perfect for toasting and topping with eggs, or in the manner of many St. Helena passengers, eating with the ubiquitous finnan haddie, herring, mackerel, or even smoked salmon that are always served at breakfast. I prefer it as a toasted base for little tea sandwiches.

½ tablespoon dry yeast	1 ½ tablespoons melted butter
1 tablespoon sugar	2 ½ cups bread flour
1/3 cup warm water	1 ½ teaspoons salt
½ cup creamy cottage cheese	1 teaspoon baking powder
1 egg, beaten	¼ cup mixed, chopped chives & chervil

Proof yeast in mixture of sugar and water in an electric mixer bowl with a dough hook. When foamy, add cheese, egg, butter, and flour, adding it gradually with salt and baking powder. Knead until smooth and elastic, then work in the herbs. Place in a 9-inch loaf pan, let rise, covered, for about an hour, or until doubled. Bake at 350° about ½ hour, or until done. Turn out onto a rack, and slice when almost cool.

Makes 1 9-inch loaf.

SCRAMBLED EGGS ON TOAST

A typical British treat at breakfast, lunch, or afternoon tea.

2 tablespoons soft butter	3 tablespoons cream
1 tablespoon anchovy paste	Salt & pepper
1 teaspoon English mustard	2 tablespoons butter
6 slices English Herb Bread (see Index)	1/3 cup grated Cheddar or Cheshire
6 eggs, beaten	2 tablespoons melted butter
	Worcestershire sauce

Mix butter with anchovy paste and mustard. Toast bread and spread with the mixture eggs with cream and seasonings, then scramble gently in butter, using an iron skillet. Place on top of toast, and top with cheese, butter, and Worcestershire. Place under broiler until cheese melts. Serve hot.

Serves 6.

SAVORY HERB CRÊPES WITH CREAMED MUSHROOMS

1 large egg	3 tablespoons whole wheat flour
1 cup milk	Salt & pepper
1 tablespoon melted butter	1 tablespoon chopped chives, chervil, or dill
½ cup flour	

Place all ingredients in processor, and blend until smooth. Heat 2 iron skillets, one larger than the other, brush with butter, and pour just enough batter into pan, tilting it, until the bottom is covered.

Cook briefly, loosening the sides, then flip over into larger pan to cook the other side. This enables you to makes the crêpes twice as fast. Stack them and keep warm. When mushroom filling is done, place about 2 or 3 tablespoons on each crêpe, and roll them. If desired, they can be sprinkled with grated Cheddar and placed under the broiler until cheese melts.

Creamed Mushrooms:

6 slices bacon	3 tablespoons flour
1 pound mushrooms, stemmed	1 ½ cups light cream
¾ cup water	2 tablespoons sherry
2 shallots, chopped	Salt & pepper
3 tablespoons butter	1 tablespoon chopped chives, chervil, or dill

Cook bacon in a large skillet until done, remove, and reserve fat. Boil mushroom stems in water until about 5 cup of stock remains. Sauté sliced mushroom caps in bacon fat with butter until tender, and liquid evaporates. Add flour to make a roux, and when smooth whisk in cream and mushroom stock. When thickened, add sherry, and seasonings. Also add crumbled bacon, and fill crêpes. These luscious mushrooms, my favorite, are also great served in puff pastry shells, tart shells, or on toast points, such as the English Herb Bread. Serve hot.

Makes about 12 7-inch crêpes & about 2 cups mushroom filling.

EGG SALAD SANDWICHES

My most enjoyable teatime sandwich was at the lovely seaside DeVere Hotel in St. Helier, Jersey, in the Channel Islands. I had just returned from a very long day trip by ferry to the tiny island of Sark, which belongs to Guernsey. The only method of transportation on the idyllic isle is by horse and buggy or on foot, and I had chosen the latter to see the scenery.

4 eggs	1 tablespoon chopped chives or chervil
¼ cup mayonnaise	
½ teaspoon curry powder	6-8 slices whole wheat bread or English Herb Bread
2 tablespoons dried currants	

For perfect hard-boiled eggs, place in a pan of cold water, bring to a boil, and cook 10 minutes. Drain, and immediately cover with cold water. Peel, crush with a pastry blender or a large fork. Mix in mayonnaise and seasonings. Spread on bread slices, cut off crusts, and cut into smaller sections, as desired. Or, spread on half the slices, add remaining slices, and cut in half diagonally, if you are really hungry as I was when returning from Sark.

Makes 3 or 4 sandwiches.

ENGLISH WHITE FRUITCAKE

This fabulous fruitcake was served every day at teatime on the St. Helena voyages to St. Helena and Tristan da Cunha. The chef, Danny, is a native St. Helenian and quite accomplished in the kitchen.

1 cup crystalized cherries, halved	1 cup white or light brown sugar
1 cup crystalized pineapple, sliced	3 eggs
1 cup golden raisins	1 ½ cups all-purpose flour
½ cup crystalized orange peel	1 teaspoon baking powder
½ cup sliced almonds	1 teaspoon salt
¼ cup flour	2 teaspoons each lemon & orange juice
½ pound soft butter	2 or 3 tablespoons brandy or rum

Lemon Glaze:

1 ½ cups powdered sugar	1 tablespoon each lemon & orange juice
Crystalized fruit for garnishing	

Toss fruit and almonds together with the flour, which will keep the fruit separate and prevent it from sinking to the bottom. Cream butter with sugar until very pale and fluffy, then beat in eggs one at a time. Add dry ingredients gradually, and beat only until barely blended. Add juice, brandy, and fruit. Butter an 8- or 9-inch cake pan, about 3 inches deep, and line bottom with wax or parchment paper. Bake at 300° for about 1 hour and 20 minutes, or only until a tester comes out clean and top is light golden in color and not crisp around the edge. Cool slightly, then invert onto a rack. Whisk sugar with juices until smooth or blend in processor. Add a little hot water if not thin enough. Drizzle over cake, letting it run down the sides, or spread it over entire cake. Decorate with extra crystalized fruit.

Makes 1 8- or 9-inch cake.

LUNCH AND DINNER

Lunch and dinner share many of the same dishes, especially potatoes. When I was a passenger on the St. Helena, would you believe two kinds of potatoes were served both at lunch and dinner? And one voyage lasted three weeks! Even with substantial breakfasts and teatime, lunch and dinner are not lacking in sustenance.

BLINI WITH CAVIAR AND EGG SALAD

This elegant first course on the Silver Cloud was so special, I ordered a second serving. Walter Blakemore, the chef, created a perfect example of fusion cooking by combining a Russian classic and British egg salad.

1/3 cup all-purpose flour	2 tablespoons melted butter
1/3 cup sifted buckwheat flour	1 egg
1 teaspoon dry yeast	Egg Salad, without currants (see Index)
1 tablespoon sugar	
Dash of salt	Caviar, preferably Beluga or Osetra
2/3 cup warm milk	
	Garnitures: Sour cream, chives, & sieved hard-cooked egg yolk

Mix dry ingredients in bowl of electric mixer, add milk, butter, and egg. Beat until well blended, cover, and let rise about 1 hour, or until doubled. Heat a large iron skillet, grease lightly, and add large spoons of batter to make blinis about 4- to 5-inch in diameter. Cook only about 1 minute on each side, and keep warm. This makes about 1 dozen. Spread egg salad on 6 blinis, top with another blini, and spread with caviar. Place on center of 6 plates, and add small drops of sour cream on plates at random. Sprinkle with chives and sieved yolks, placing a bit on top of caviar, if desired. Serve with your best champagne.

Serves 6, using 2 blini per person.

COCKALEEKIE SOUP

A wonderful hearty Scottish soup which dates back to medieval times, I first tasted this at the old North British Hotel, located over Waverley Station in Edinburgh. This is the way I remember it, except I decided to reinvent it with the addition of prunes which were in the original.

2 ½ -3 pound whole chicken	¼ cup pearl barley
2 quarts chicken stock	10 or 12 prunes, pitted
4 or 5 leeks, with 2 inches of green tops, well washed, cut into ½ -inch slices	Salt & pepper
	Chopped chervil or parsley

Place chicken in a pot just large enough to hold it, add stock, bring to a simmer, and skim the surface. Add leeks and barley, and simmer, partially covered, until chicken is tender, about 1 hour. Remove chicken, remove skin and bones, and cut meat into bite-size pieces. Return to soup pot, and add prunes. Season well, and simmer briefly. Garnish with chervil.

Serves 6 to 8.

POACHED EGGS WITH RICE AND SAUCE MESSINE

This classic herb sauce is very versatile and can be used on fish, chicken, vegetables, and especially potatoes.

2 shallots, chopped	1 cup cream
4 tablespoons butter	2 tablespoons lemon juice
½ teaspoon curry powder	4 poached eggs
1 tablespoon mixed chopped thyme, chives, and chervil	½ cup rice, cooked
2 egg yolks	Cooked peas, asparagus, or snap beans to garnish

Sauté shallots in butter, using a small sauce pan. Add seasonings, and yolks beaten with cream, whisking over low heat until lightly thickened. Add lemon juice. Place eggs on bed of rice, and pour sauce over eggs. Garnish with vegetables, as desired, or sprinkle with extra herbs.

Serves 6.

IRISH PARSLEY SAUCE

Ireland does not have many sauces except for the heavy white sauces, but this popular one is exceptionally good and can be interchanged with the preceding Sauce Messine. It is traditional to poach a chicken with part of the water that ham has been poached in, and then use it in making this sauce, but you can use chicken stock only or add a little beef or veal stock.

1 bunch parsley, about 1 cup	2 tablespoons flour
1 cup each milk and chicken stock	Dash of nutmeg or mace
	Salt & pepper
2 tablespoons butter	1 tablespoon lemon juice

Blanch parsley in milk and stock until wilted, strain stock into another pan, and chop parsley finely. Make a roux with butter and flour, and whisk in stock, boiling until lightly thickened and smooth. Season and add parsley.

Makes about 2 cups.

ORANGE-BAKED SEA BASS WITH ORANGE BASIL BUTTER

This is an example of the new and lighter cuisine taking place in Scotland and especially with the oranges and marmalade in Dundee.

4 4- to 5-ounce sea bass or tilapia fillets	1 teaspoon grated orange zest
	1 tablespoon chopped basil & extra leaves
Olive oil	
Salt & white pepper	4 tablespoons soft butter
3 tablespoons orange juice	3 cups hot cooked rice
1 tablespoon grated orange zest	2-3 tablespoons orange marmalade
2 tablespoons orange juice	

Place fillets in a baking dish just large enough to hold them, rub with oil, season, and top with juice and zest. Bake at 350° about 10 minutes or just until done. While baking, make orange basil butter by whisking juice, zest, and basil into soft butter. Place rice on plates, pour pan juices over rice, top with the fillets, and dollop basil butter and marmalade over them. Garnish with basil.

Serves 4.

FILLET OF SEA BASS WITH FINGERLING POTATOES, HARICOTS VERT, OVEN-DRIED TOMATOES AND LEMON VINAIGRETTE

This is my version of a delicious and beautiful presentation devised by Chef Ian on the great Royal Scotsman, an Orient Express train which does superb tours of the Scottish Highlands between even more superb meals in the elegant dining cars. Chef Ian serves a Beurre Blanc sauce with this dish, but I prefer the juxtaposition of the creamy mayonnaise with the tangy lemon vinaigrette. I also prefer oven-dried tomatoes to a concassé.

4 Roma tomatoes, oven-roasted, diced	¼ cup mayonnaise
2 tablespoons olive oil	2 teaspoons roasted garlic
½ tablespoon lemon juice	4 4- to 5-ounce fillets sea bass or tilapia
2 tablespoons chopped basil	¼ pound haricots vert
Salt & gray pepper	1 tablespoon butter
12 ounces fingerling potatoes, cooked & sliced ¼-inch thick	1 cup watercress
	½ cup Lemon Vinaigrette (see Index)

Mix tomatoes with oil, juice, basil, and seasonings. Mix potatoes with mayonnaise and garlic. Sear fish in a heavy non-stick pan, such as an iron skillet, then turn and cook briefly until just done. Simultaneously, toss haricots in butter until tender but still bright green. Place potato salad on plates in a thin layer, place fish on top, then add tomatoes, and top with beans. Place watercress around edge of plate, and drizzle vinaigrette over all.

Serves 4.

SEABASS WITH CREAMY BUTTER SAUCE

Although this is a new style of British sauce, butter and cream are still very much in evidence. This great dish was actually served to me on Virgin Atlantic in Upper Class, definitely the way to and from London. Their Upper Class Lounges, where I had the privilege to see Richard Branson, also serve great buffets, as well as menu service. Simply the best!

4 5- or 6-ounce seabass fillets	¼ cup Oven-Dried Tomatoes (see Index)
¼ cup chopped shallots	¼ cup chiffonade of spinach
¼ cup champagne vinegar	1/3 cup soft butter
¼ cup white port	Garlic Mashed Potatoes (see Index)
½ cup cream	
½ teaspoon curry powder	

Bring a pan of water to a boil, add fillets, cover, and remove from heat. Let stand about 10 minutes. This method of cooking fish in its natural habitat is my favorite, especially when served with an important sauce. In a small saucepan, boil shallots in vinegar until evaporated. Add port and evaporate again. Whisk in cream and curry powder. Stir in tomatoes and spinach, and whisk in butter. Drain fish, place on a bed of potatoes, and pour sauce over all. Garnish plates with vegetables of your choice.

Serves 4.

IRISH HAM WITH WHISKY SAUCE

One of the most memorable foods I have had in Ireland, however prepared, was the ham, both in Belfast and at Dromoland Castle in County Clare. Housed in an ancient Gothic building, their wonderful restaurant was my introduction to Irish ham as well as vegetables as fresh as possible.

1 ham steak, ¾ inches thick, about 1 ½ pounds, trimmed of fat Flour, for dredging 2 tablespoons butter ¼ cup Jameson Irish Whiskey	1 apple, peeled, cored, & diced 2 tablespoons honey ½ cup cream ½ cup Brown Sauce (see Index) or gravy

Dredge ham in flour, then sauté on both sides in butter until golden brown. Flame with whiskey, remove ham, and sauté apple in remaining pan juices. Return ham to skillet, and add remaining ingredients. Cover, and simmer gently until ham is done, about 20 minutes. Serve with any kind of potatoes.

Serves 4.

YORK HAM WITH CUMBERLAND SAUCE HOTEL SAVOY

My first encounter with English ham was at the lovely and venerable Hotel Savoy before I took the Orient Express to Venice, but it was only recently that I learned the best English ham is from up north in Yorkshire. This was on my Black Sea Cruise on the incomparable Minerva II of Swan Hellenic.

1 ½ pounds ham steak, trimmed	½ cup Reduced Brown Stock (see Index)
2 tablespoons butter	½ cup Cumberland Sauce (see below)

Sauté ham in butter on both sides until done. Remove, and keep warm. Add both sauces to skillet, and simmer until lightly thickened.

Cumberland Sauce:

1 orange & 1 lemon, zest julienned, & blanched in water	¼ cup Tawny Port
	1/3 cup currant jelly
Juice of orange & lemon	½ teaspoon dry mustard

Place juice of orange and lemon in small saucepan with wine, jelly, and dry mustard. Simmer until smooth and lightly thickened, and stir in zest. Makes about 1 cup.

Serves 4.

HAGGIS

Scotland's much maligned national dish is in a quite controversial renaissance, as there are now actually vegetarian versions, but I would not go quite that far since there are many substitutes for the traditional sheep's stomach, lungs, liver, heart, and suet. The USDA, in fact, will not permit them since they are not deemed fit for human consumption. Oatmeal and various meats with fat (I substitute bacon) are the only prerequisites, and it can be made into sausages, using casings, or baked, steamed in a covered mold or wrapped in a towel or cheesecloth. It can be used in a multitude of ways, as can sausage, such as with fried eggs, in lasagna, crêpes, biscuits, or as an elegant hors d'oeuvre in puff pastry shells as in the following recipe. The Royal Scotsman serves a slice under beef filet. The serving of haggis is traditional on Robbie Burns's birthday, January 25, so if you are a die-hard Scot, be sure to bring into the dining room accompanied by the bagpipes and the waiters in kilts. Then it is slashed open with a dagger, and consumed with much Scotch whisky.

1 pound ground lamb, veal, or beef	Salt & pepper, to taste
¼ pound calf or chicken livers	½ teaspoon Five-Spice powder
3 or 4 slices chopped bacon	1 cup old-fashioned oats
½ cup chopped onion	1/3 to ½ cup Scotch or meat stock

Mix thoroughly in food processor, wrap in a towel, or put in a loaf pan or pudding mold, and steam about 1 to 1 ½ hours, or until firm.

Makes about 1 ½ pounds.

Haggis in Puff Pastry:

¾ pound Haggis, warmed	1/3 cup Italian boule bread crumbs
12 2-inch puff pastry shells	¼ cup coarsely chopped oregano, basil, and rosemary

Fill pastry shells with haggis, then grind crumbs with herbs in processor. Put on top of tart shells. These can also be served as a dinner accompaniment.

Makes 12.

CONFIT DE CANARD WITH SHREDDED BRUSSEL SPROUTS AND PEANUT PESTO

My most meaningful travel experience was my stay at the luxurious and dramatic Prestonfield House in Midlothian County, Scotland, where my family originated 1,000 years ago. Only three miles outside Edinburgh and on 20 acres, it is undoubtedly the most idyllic place imaginable, and their Rhubarb Restaurant, so named because it was the first place to grow rhubarb in the United Kingdom, is widely known for its great food. This is my version of my memorable dinner.

1 piece Confit de Canard (see Index) 4 ounces Brussel sprouts, shredded in food processor	2 tablespoons butter Creamy Pesto (see Index), using peanuts instead of other nuts

While warming confit, sauté sprouts in butter until barely tender and bright green. Season as desired, place in center of plate, top with confit, and place dabs of pesto around edge of plate.

Serves 1.

DESSERTS

Cream and butter still figure prominently in British and Irish desserts, as well as a plethora of fools, puddings, and rich baked goods, such as Eccles Cakes from Lancashire. The following are my all-time favorites, especially the South Pole specialty.

ENGLISH SUMMER PUDDING

There is nothing better in the summertime, when you have lots of fresh berries. This is similar to Gâteau Allard, which is made from strawberries, brown sugar, and sour cream. Sadly, Allard, once one of the best restaurants in Paris, is now gone. This Summer Pudding is similar to the one I had at Rule's, which, like at Allard in Paris, is where you can find the best traditional food.

2 cups strawberries, quartered	1 8-ounce package frozen raspberries, thawed, puréed, & strained
¾ cup blackberries, quartered	
½ cup sugar	
½ cup water	8 slices Vienna bread, crusts removed
1/3 cup sugar	
1 ½ teaspoons vanilla	Crème Anglaise (see Index)

Cook berries with sugar until sugar dissolves, then chill. Boil water with sugar, until sugar is dissolved, and chill. Add vanilla, and stir into purée. Line a 6-cup mold or bowl with cheesecloth. Dip bread into purée, and line mold completely. Add alternate layers of berries and bread, dipping each slice in purée, ending with bread. Cover top with plastic wrap, place a plate just large enough to cover mixture, and place a weight on top to compress it. Chill several hours, until juices are absorbed, then mold, and serve with Crème Anglaise or sour cream.

Serves 6.

IRISH FLAMING GRAPE CAKE

This unusual cake can be made with a variety of berries or other fruit and different liqueurs or brandies. An obbstorten pan is German, and it has a depression in the top to hold the filling. I especially like to use it for Strawberry Shortcake.

1 8-or 9-inch Butter Spongecake	1 teaspoon vanilla
1-1 ½ cups black and red grapes, halved	2 tablespoons sliced almonds, roasted
3 tablespoons crème de cassis	3 tablespoons brown sugar
1 cup cream	2 or 3 tablespoons crème de cassis
½ cup brown sugar	

Marinate grapes in cassis about ½ hour, then fill obbstorten with them. If you do not have an obbstorten pan, simply make cake in an 8-inch pan, and remove about ½ inch of cake from the top, leaving a ½-inch rim. Whip cream with sugar and vanilla until stiff, and spread over grapes. Sprinkle almonds with sugar on top of cream, and pour flaming cassis over it, using a platter with a rim.

Serves 6.

BUTTER SPONGECAKE

This is the most used cake in the British Isles and in most of Europe. It can be used for many purposes, with a variety of frostings and fillings.

3 large egg yolks	1 teaspoon vanilla
2/3 cup sugar	¾ cup soft wheat flour
1/3 cup scalded milk	1 teaspoon baking powder
	3 tablespoons melted butter

Beat yolks with sugar in an electric mixer until light and fluffy. Beat in milk and vanilla. Fold in dry ingredients, then fold in butter very gently. Bake in a buttered and floured 8-inch cake pan or in a German 9 ½-inch obbstorten pan, the kind with a depression in the center, at 350° for about 20 minutes, or until a tester comes out clean.

Makes 1 8- or 9-inch layer.

SCOTTISH SHORTBREAD

This is the traditional shortbread, which dates back to the sixteenth century. It is normally a cookie, but the chef at the South Pole Amudsen-Scott Station created a fantastic sort of bar with it. When the shortbread comes out of the oven, cover with a pound of sliced strawberries that have been macerating with sugar. Pour a frosting of 8 ounces of chocolate melted with ¾ cup cream over the top. Fantastic! They thought I was going to eat the whole thing,

½ pound soft butter	2 ½ cups soft wheat flour
½ cup sugar	

Beat butter and sugar in electric mixer until light and fluffy. Beat in flour gradually until well blended. Roll out about ¼- to ½-inch thick, and cut out desired shapes, such as a star for Christmas. Place on a baking sheet, and bake at 350° about 20 minutes, or until golden. Cool on racks. These can be made well in advance and kept in tins for Christmas.

Makes about 15.

STICKY DATE PUDDING

This must be my prize for sleeping in a tent at Patriot Hills base camp, when it was 40° below, for a week. I arrived on a Russian Ilyushin 76, a cargo aircraft which is supposed to be the world's most dangerous, but we had great Siberian pilots. A Twin Otter on skis took six of us to the South Pole, but it was at the base camp where I was privileged to get this wonderful recipe from Mairi, the young chef from northern Scotland. We had lots of hearty and wholesome food, and there were always plenty of chocolate bars, other snacks, and beverages around the clock, with Chilean wine for dinner.

4 ounces dates, cut in thirds	1 egg
1 cup water	1 ¾ cup flour
½ teaspoon baking soda	1 tablespoon baking powder
¼ cup butter	1 teaspoon salt
¾ cup sugar	Butterscotch Sauce (see below)

Soak dates in water with baking soda overnight. Cream butter and sugar with an electric mixer, and beat in egg. Add dry ingredients alternately with dates and their soaking water. Bake in a buttered 10-inch round cake pan or a 9-inch square pan at 375° about 20 to 25 minutes. Pour Butterscotch Sauce on top when it comes out of the oven.

Butterscotch Sauce:

2 cups brown sugar	½ cup cream or sour cream
½ cup butter	2 teaspoons Balsamic vinegar

Simmer sugar, butter, and cream until thickened and smooth, about 10 minutes. Add balsamic to temper the sweetness. Makes about 3 cups.

Serves 6-8 or 2 South Pole trekkers.

DEMITASSE OF CHOCOLATE WITH MASCARPONE CREAM

Chef Ian of the Royal Scotsman serves this elegant dessert with Hazelnut Biscuits, but it is absolutely delicious alone. This is my version.

1 ½ cups semi-sweet chocolate	½ to 1 tablespoon Grand Marnier
5 tablespoons butter	½ pound Mascarpone cheese, softened
6 egg yolks	
¼ cup powdered sugar	1 cup heavy cream, whipped
6 egg whites, whipped until stiff with powdered sugar	¼ cup Demarara sugar
1 to 2 tablespoons Drambuie	1 teaspoon vanilla

Melt chocolate with butter in heavy small saucepan, then whisk in yolks over low heat to barely cook them. Gently fold in whites with liqueurs. Pour into 12 demitasse cups and chill. Gently fold cheese and cream together with sugar and vanilla. Top each demitasse with mascarpone cream, piling it high. Dust with sieved cocoa powder.

Serves 12.

CENTRAL EUROPE:

BELGIUM HOLLAND LUXEMBOURG GERMANY SWITZERLAND LEICHTENSTEIN

The common culinary bond between these cold and northerly countries is the simplicity and heartiness of their cuisines, and above all, the enormous quantities of food eaten. How well I know, as my maternal grandfather was from Emden, Germany, on the North Sea, and he was known for saying to his 11 children, "Eat, children, eat."

From London's Waterloo Station, the Eurostar will take you in grand style to Brussels in only 2 hours and 20 minutes. The Grand Place, with its magnificent Gothic and Baroque architecture, is truly the grandest in all of Europe, and is in the center of the best restaurants. The streets beckon you with their names—Rue du Beurre (butter), Rue de Bouchers (butchers), and even Rue des Harengs (herring). Come Chez Soi and Villa Lorraine are still two of the finest Michelin-starred restaurants, and they offer cuisine equal to the best in Paris.

Besides being known for its French influence, Belgium is noted for its mussels, which are eaten straight out of the shell and then thrown into plain tin buckets on the floor. The North Sea provides an abundance of eels, another favorite. Other notable Belgian specialties are endive, black grapes, and chocolate, of which my favorite is Callebaut. Beer is the national drink, except with French cuisine, when copious amounts of wine are consumed instead.

Holland, home of windmills, tulips, and wooden shoes, also has some wonderful cooking to offer, as well as numerous canals for scenic cruising. My travels have taken me as far as Groningen in the northeast, and I have discovered that Indonesians and their cooking pervade the entire country still, a result of the seventeenth century spice trade with Indonesia. Likewise, the strong connection still exists, as I was surprised to see Dutchmen doing business in remote Indonesian places such as Borneo.

As in Belgium, eels and herring are of utmost importance in Holland, as are Gouda and Edam cheeses. The national drink is beer, but jenever or gin, and Curacao liqueur are also specialties.

Germany's cuisine, considered by some to be one of the world's best, is now producing some of the world's greatest chefs and has its share of Michelin restaurants. The cuisine is vast and varied, with the north specializing in substantial and solid dishes, much like the people who eat them. Dumplings and noodles, as well as potatoes, accompany a vast array of pork products, such as hams and sausages, goose, and duck. Sauerkraut, pickles, and dried fruits are eaten extensively. We know Muenster and Limburger cheeses, but it is Quark cheese that is the most admired, and also bestowed its name on Quark Expeditions.

We also know the Delikatessen (good eating), and Dallmayr in Munich is an exceptional one offering everything from caviar to gifts in its boutique. Munich is also the home of Heinz Winkler, the mastermind of Germany's new cuisine. The Konditerei, or bakeries, are famous for their kugelhopf, lebkuchen, stollen, and jelly doughnuts, especially at Christmas.

German wines are some of the oenophile's favorites, notably the Rhines, in brown bottles, and the Moselles, in green bottles. Virtually all the better wines are white and grown from the riesling grape. The wine districts are along the Rhine and Mosel Rivers, and the best are the Mosel, Saar, Ruwer, and Rheingau. Among Germany's finest wines are Schloss Vollrads, Piesporter Goldtropfchen, and Bernkasteler Doktor. German beer is equally popular especially in Munich's famous beer halls.

Tiny Luxembourg, only 1,000 square miles in size, is a Grand Duchy and one of the world's wealthiest countries. Its capital city, of the same name, features moats, castles, 91 bridges, and a medieval atmosphere, as well as some excellent restaurants. The culinary influence is German, Belgian, and French, with the addition of trout, pike, and crayfish from mountain streams. When I was there, Um Bock was one of the leaders of the new cooking, which is in contrast to the typical restaurants that pile huge amounts of potatoes and everything else on your plate. Their own Moselle wines and beer wash it all down. The famous Villeroy & Boch china factory is located in Luxembourg and a tour of it can be taken, followed by a visit to their shop with excellent values. I will always cherish the beautiful green platter that I bought there.

Switzerland, the land of the Alps and the world's most scenic train rides, has a cuisine which varies according to the proximity of its neighbors. The Valais is influenced by France, and Lausanne is the home of one of the greatest chefs in the past century, Fredy Girardet, who is now retired. I made a very worthwhile detour to dine at his restaurant in Crissier, near Lausanne, and dined on foie gras, rouget, langoustine, baby lamb with truffles, and six sorbets, among other specialties, for lunch.

We all know of the renowned Tobler, Lindt, and Nestle chocolates, as well as the Emmenthaler and Raclette cheeses from the Valais, but the cured meats of all types from the Grisons in the western part of the country are worth a detour. The Ticino in the south, of course, is the gateway to Lombardy and Piedmont in Italy, and the food reflects this proximity. It also produces red wine made from the Merlot grape. Most of the best wine, however, is produced in the areas of Neufchâtel, Valais, and Vaud, all near the French border. Kirsch, the renowned cherry liqueur, is also valued in cooking.

I reached another tiny country, not often visited, by train from Zurich, followed by the postal bus from Sargans on the border. Leichtenstein, a Kingdom of only about 3,000 people, is best known to connoisseurs of fine food for Hotel Real, owned by Felix Real, grandson of Viscount Real of Spain. I will be eternally grateful to Felix, as he was responsible for my last-minute reservation at Fredy Girardet's. My dinner at Torkel (wine press), owned by the

Prince, was especially interesting because of the emphasis on wine, which is 95% red and made from pinot noir grapes. The Hotel Real Restaurant serves its own wine which is excellent, especially the Vaduzer Reserve Felix Real 1982. Martin Real, the chef, served me his specialties of Foie Gras terrine; noodles with cèpes and chanterelles; an ingenuous version of the Swiss classic, Emincé de Veau, with curry and fruits; and the Terrine de Soufflé Glace Real. This was definitely worth a detour and a longer visit.

RECIPES FROM CENTRAL EUROPE

NOODLES WITH WILD MUSHROOMS

SPÄTZLE OMELET

BAVARIAN BEER AND CHEESE SOUP

SOUP D'ESCARGOTS

LAUSWOLT NORTH SEA SALAD

LOBSTER SALAD WITH MANGO SAUCE

SWEET AND SOUR POTATO SALAD

COD À LA FLAMANDE

FISCHLABSKAUS (NORTH SEA FISH, POTATOES, AND ONIONS)

SUPRÊMES WITH GRAPES

ROAST PORK WITH CARAMELIZED BEER SAUCE

MEDALLIONS OF PORK WITH CHERRIES

DUTCH BROWN BEANS AND BACON

KÖNIGSBERGER KLOPSE (GERMAN MEATBALLS IN CAPER SAUCE)

STOEMP (BELGIAN POTATOES WITH SPINACH AND BACON)

STEAMED BRUSSEL SPROUTS AND GRAPES

BELGIAN ENDIVES WITH ORANGE HONEY BUTTER

SWISS CHARD SAUTÉ

SWEET AND SOUR RED CABBAGE

STRAWBERRIES WITH RHUBARB

RHUBARB SORBET

RÖTE GRUTZE (GERMAN RED FRUIT PUDDING)

APPLE STRUDEL

SWISS PLUM TART

FLAMBÉED CHERRY CRÊPES

NOODLES WITH WILD MUSHROOMS

Although the people of Leichtenstein eat hearty and humble food at home, Hotel Real serves sophisticated specialties which reflect the cuisines of Germany, Austria, Italy, and France. This can be a first course or main course.

1 pound cèpes & chanterelles, de-stemmed & sliced, or other mushrooms	1 teaspoon Glace de Viande (see Index)
1 cup water	Reserved mushroom stock
¼ cup butter	1 tablespoon brandy
1 shallot, chopped	Salt & pepper
½ cup sour cream	1 pound noodles or linguine, cooked
½ cup heavy cream	Chopped dill & chives

Simmer stems in water about 10 minutes, drain, and reduce water to about ½ cup of condensed mushroom stock. Sauté mushrooms in butter about 10 minutes, or until tender, adding shallot the last few minutes. Stir in both creams, seasonings, and stock. Simmer until thickened, and add to hot pasta. Garnish with herbs. The Reals serve this with a Riesling.

Serves 6.

SPÄTZLE OMELET

These soft and tender little dumplings, relatives of pasta, are found in many guises throughout central Europe-in Germany, Switzerland, and Austria, among other countries. They can be dropped by a spoon into boiling water or stock, but I wouldn't be without my spätzle maker, which I bought in a Zurich department store. Chicken and Dumplings are a wonderful destination for them, but I still remember them as an omelet at the stately 400-year old Krone Hotel in Assmannshausen, located on the most beautiful part of the Rhine.

½ cup milk	6 eggs, beaten
1 cup flour	¼ cup butter
1 egg	Chopped parsley
Salt, pepper, & freshly grated nutmeg	

Blend milk, flour, and egg in food processor until smooth, and season. Pour into a spätzle maker, or a colander with fairly large holes. Press into boiling stock or water and simmer briskly until they rise to the top. Drain, and sauté about 1 ½ cups of them in butter until golden, using a large iron skillet. Add eggs, and cook gently until barely set. Fold, or serve flat. Garnish with parsley. If desired, cooked egg noodles may replace the spätzle.

Serves 6.

BAVARIAN BEER & CHEESE SOUP

Munich is the place to enjoy a hearty soup like this, especially the Hofbrauhaus. On our first trip to Germany, we had a four-hour layover, so we took a taxi in a rainstorm and had this soup along with Bockwurst and sauerkraut. Thus is the manner of travel with an avid recipe and country collector. I think this soup recaptures the flavor and the ambience.

1 small onion	1 cup beer
1 small celery rib	½ pound Muenster cheese, grated
1 small carrot, peeled	
¼ cup butter	Salt & pepper
¼ cup flour	Chopped dill
1 cup chicken stock	Chopped cooked bacon or sausage
1 cup light cream	

Finely chop vegetables in a food processor, and sauté in butter, using a 6-cup soup pot, about 10 minutes. Add flour, cook until smooth, add stock and light cream, and simmer about 5 minutes, or until thickened. Purée in food processor, return to pan, and over very low heat, stir in beer and cheese. When melted, season, and garnish with dill and bacon. Serve with dark bread.

Serves 6 in soup cups or 4 in soup plates.

SOUPE D'ESCARGOTS

Hotel Beau Rivage, in Lausanne, is an elegant and traditional hotel reminiscent of the old world, and it has an excellent French-inspired kitchen. This soup was an exceptional addition to my repertoire.

2 large shallots, minced	1 cup crème fraîche
2 garlic cloves, crushed	1 small can escargots
¼ cup butter	2 tablespoons butter
½ pound wild mushrooms, chopped	2 tablespoons flour
	2 tablespoons anise liqueur
1 cup white wine	1 tablespoon each chopped chervil, parsley, and thyme
1 cup chicken stock	
1 cup veal stock	

Using a 6-cup soup pot, sauté shallots and garlic in butter briefly, then add mushrooms, and sauté until any liquid evaporates. Add wine, stocks, cream, and liquid drained from can of escargots. Simmer about 20 minutes and add chopped escargots. Make a roux with butter and flour and whisk into soup, cooking until thickened. Add liqueur and herbs.

Serves 6.

LAUSWOLT NORTH SEA SALAD

Beetsterswaag is a tiny and tranquil town in the cold northwest, known as Freisland, Holland. But, it is the site of Langoed Lauswolt Hotel, one of the most aristocratic in Europe. Located on many acres of landscaped grounds, it also has an excellent restaurant, where I had this simple but wonderfully fresh salad of North Sea seafood. This is definitely worth the detour it takes to get here.

1 head Bibb lettuce, separated	½ pound eels or salmon, cooked
½ cup Lemon Vinaigrette (see index)	½ pound smoked salmon
	4 sea scallops, cooked
2 cups tiny shrimp, cooked	1 lobster, cooked & meat removed
4 teaspoons caviar	

Toss Bibb with vinaigrette, arrange in 2 large pasta bowls, and fill with shrimp. Arrange remaining seafood, in bite-size pieces on top, dividing the caviar among the scallops. A very thin slice of fried cheese topped with pesto adorned the top of the salad. What divine fusion!

Serves 2.

LOBSTER SALAD WITH MANGO SAUCE

Another of my favorite hotels in this part of the world is the Vier Jahreszeiten in the old Hanseatic city of Hamburg, which is very close to both the North Sea and the Baltic Sea. We had a marvelous stay in a suite overlooking the Alster before a Royal Viking cruise to the North Cape of Norway. While at the hotel, we learned that it had been owned and operated by the Haeberlin family since 1897, but now, alas, it has been sold because the fourth generation does not want to continue. At least I have the beautiful historical volume which was given to us, and this delicious salad, which was one of the first fusion dishes in Europe.

1 ½ pounds cooked lobster or shrimp	Salt & pepper
Lemon Vinaigrette (see Index)	1 large ripe mango, peeled, pitted, and chopped
3 cups Mesclun	¾ cup cream
18 asparagus spears, cooked	2 tablespoons lemon juice
12 cherry tomatoes	1 tablespoon brandy

Toss lobster, in a small amount of vinaigrette, and arrange on mesclun placed in center of 6 plates. Toss asparagus and tomatoes in vinaigrette, season, and arrange around plate. Purée mango with remaining ingredients, and drizzle over lobster and vegetables. Serve remaining sauce separately.

Serves 6.

SWEET AND SOUR POTATO SALAD

Hamburg, being an epicurean city, has a number of great restaurants, and we especially enjoyed Fischereihafen, located in the port. This potato salad is very simple and one of the best. I enjoyed it with the freshest of fish from the sea.

2 pounds potatoes, cooked, peeled, & cubed	¼ cup white wine vinegar
1 cup mayonnaise	1 tablespoon pickle relish
½ cup sugar	Minced dillweed
	Bibb or Boston lettuce

Mix potatoes with combined mayonnaise, sugar, vinegar, and relish. Add a little dill, place over lettuce, and sprinkle with more dill.

Serves 6.

COD À LA FLAMANDE

Flanders, in northern Belgium, specializes in cooking fish, game, meat, and almost anything else in beer. I gave a recipe for the Belgian national dish, Carbonnade de Boeuf à la Flamande, in Culinary Classics. For a richer dish, they sometimes add cream to the beer.

1 onion, thinly sliced	1 cup Belgian beer
¼ cup butter	4 cod fillets
1 bay leaf	1 lemon, sliced
1 teaspoon fresh thyme	1 teaspoon each minced chervil, chives, and parsley
Salt & pepper	

Sauté onion in butter until golden brown, add seasonings and beer, and bring to a boil to evaporate the alcohol. Place cod on top, baste with beer, and top with lemon slices and herbs. Bake 20 minutes at 350° or until done. Serve with Stoemp, the classic potato dish, which appears with the vegetables that follow the meat recipes.

Serves 4.

FISCHLABSKAUS

(North Sea Fish, Potatoes, and Onions)

One of the easiest and most delicious ways to cook fish and potatoes, this very old fisherman's classic probably originated in the Baltics, and it is a favorite throughout the North Sea area. Also, this is a good example of how a very unhealthful dish made with lots of pork fat can be modified. Simply substitute vegetable oil for the lard or bacon fat. Meat is also prepared in the same manner, sometimes with cabbage.

1-1½ pounds Yukon potatoes, peeled & sliced about ¼-inch thick	Water, to cover potatoes
	Salt & pepper
	1 bay leaf
¼ cup lard, bacon fat, butter, or canola oil, or a combination	1 pound fish fillets: flounder, cod, halibut, or mackerel
½ to ¾ pound onions, sliced	

Sauté potatoes in fat, using a large iron skillet, until barely golden. Add onions, toss, and cook briefly. Add water, seasonings, and fillets. Cover, and simmer until potatoes are done and water is evaporated. Cook until the bottom is crusty. I like this with a sweet and sour slaw.

Serves 4.

SUPRÊMES WITH GRAPES

A strong French influence pervades this elegant dish, but the addition of grapes is a very Belgian practice. This is very similar to the one served at my favorite restaurant in Brussels, the Villa Lorraine.

4 suprêmes	½ cup chicken or veal stock
Salt & pepper	¼ cup chestnut honey
2 tablespoons butter	1 ½ cups green and black grapes
2 large shallots, finely chopped	
2 tablespoons brandy	1/3 to ½ cup cream
½ cup white wine	Green & black grape clusters

Season suprêmes and sauté in butter, using a sauté pan, until golden. Add shallots, sauté briefly, and flame with brandy. Deglaze with wine, reducing by half. Add stock and honey, and simmer, covered, about 10 minutes, or until chicken is done. Remove chicken, add grapes, and simmer until lightly thickened. Add cream, and bring to a simmer. Pour over suprêmes, and garnish with grape clusters. If desired, grapes can be dipped in lightly beaten egg white, then dipped in sugar, for a crystallized effect. Serves 4.

ROAST PORK WITH CARAMELIZED BEER SAUCE

La Grappe d'Or in Lausanne serves quite elegant fare with a French accent, as well as a lighter version of the standard beer sauces which accompany so many of the meat and game dishes in this region of Europe. My first course was fettuccine topped with white truffles shaved at the table.

1 medium onion, thinly sliced	2 tablespoons sugar
2 apples, peeled & thinly sliced	1 cup light beer
2 pounds boneless pork loin	½ tablespoon red wine vinegar
Salt, pepper, & thyme	1 or 2 tablespoons red currant jelly (optional)
1 tablespoon flour	
1 cup veal stock	Chopped chives & chervil

Place onion and apples in roasting pan just large enough to hold the pork. Season pork, place on onion and apples, and roast at 350° about 1 hour, or until done as desired. Remove pork, add flour to pan, and cook on the stove until lightly browned. Deglaze with stock. Caramelize sugar in a small heavy pan, remove from heat, and add beer. Stir until smooth, add to apple and onion sauce with wine vinegar and jelly. If necessary, boil until reduced to thickness desired. Slice pork, cover with sauce, or place sauce underneath, and garnish with herbs. Mashed potatoes are definitely the side dish to serve, along with fresh green asparagus.

Serves 4.

MEDALLIONS OF PORK WITH CHERRIES

Landhaus Scherrer, located in an elegant nineteenth century house in Hamburg, served us this light and refreshing dish with wild mushrooms, but I prefer not to. Suprêmes, duck suprêmes, or calf liver would all be good substitutes to this versatile dish. I had a similar dish at the Ritz in Berlin many years ago.

1 ½ pounds pork medallions, cut from pork loin or tenderloin	Chopped sage
	3 tablespoons butter
Salt & pepper	1 large shallot, chopped
Flour	

1/3 cup red wine or kirsch	¼ cup cherry preserves
2 cups veal stock, reduced to 1/3 cup	2 tablespoons butter
1 cup fresh cherries, pitted	Chopped fresh sage
	Wild Rice

Season pork, dredge in flour mixed with sage, and sauté in butter on both sides until done, as desired. Remove from pan, and deglaze with red wine. Add stock, cherries, and preserves, bring to a boil, and swirl in butter. Serve over pork, garnish with sage, and alongside wild rice.

Serves 4.

DUTCH BROWN BEANS AND BACON

On my first trip to Holland, several decades ago, my first meal was at Die Port Van Cleve on Dam Square. It is probably the oldest hotel in Amsterdam, if not Holland, and this wonderful comforting bean dish is probably the oldest. It makes a great main course with fried eggs on top, or leftover cooked meat can be added. This made for a memorable rainy night dinner after arriving by train.

½ pound dried brown beans or large kidney beans, soaked overnight	1 red onion, chopped
	Salt & pepper
6 to 8 slices bacon, chopped	Chestnut honey, Lyles Golden Syrup, or maple syrup
1 large leek, washed & sliced	

Drain beans, and cover well with cold water. Cover, and simmer about 2 hours or until tender. Fry bacon in a wide casserole dish, preferably an iron pot, until fat is rendered. Add leeks and onion, and sauté until tender. Add drained beans, and season. I like to stir in about 1/4 cup of honey at this time and serve more at the table. These beans are even better the next day.

Serves 4.

KÖNIGSBERGER KLOPSE
(German Meatballs in Caper Sauce)

The year was 1871, during the Franco Prussian war, when Prince Otto von Bismarck achieved the unification of Germany and, in effect, formed the first true German cuisine. Formerly composed of many duchys and kingdoms, all these areas now accepted each other's cuisines as their own. Königsberg, on the Baltic Sea, in East Prussia, was one of these kingdoms, and its luscious, tender meatballs are now eaten all over Germany; however, after World War II, this area became Kaliningrad, and now belongs to Russia. I had the opportunity to visit Kaliningrad on the Maria Kristina, a Finnish ship, in the early nineties, and was impressed by its renowned amber museum, as well as Emmanuel Kant, who was a great philosopher and one of their favorite sons. If you want to enjoy this specialty on its home ground, Kaliningrad is between Lithuania and Poland, and is best reached by way of Gdansk or Vilnius. There are also flights from Russia.

2 eggs, beaten	1 pound each ground veal & pork, or only veal
1 teaspoon anchovy paste	
2 teaspoons salt	¾ cup chopped red onion
½ teaspoon pepper	½ cup chopped parsley
1 teaspoon grated lemon zest	2 tablespoons butter
1 teaspoon worcestershire	½ cup butter
1 hard roll, soaked in water & squeezed dry	½ cup flour
	1 quart veal stock

1 cup white wine	½ cup sour cream
¼ - ½ cup capers	1 tablespoon lemon juice
2 egg yolks	Mashed Potatoes

Mix eggs with seasonings, roll, and meat. Sauté onion and parsley in butter until tender, add to meat mixture, and form into 16 meatballs. Make a roux with butter and flour, whisk in stock, and simmer until smooth. Add wine, simmer 10 minutes, and add meatballs. Simmer about 45 minutes, partially covered. Add capers, beat yolks with cream, and add to sauce. Simmer gently until lightly thickened. Add juice, and serve over lots of mashed potatoes.

Serves 6-8.

STOEMP

(Belgian Potatoes with Spinach and Bacon)

As in Holland, my first meal in Brussels was a very hearty peasant dish. Stoemp, at Auberge des Chapaliers, became a favorite of mine instantly, and it is quite similar to dishes in other central European countries, as well as Colcannon in Ireland. It can be a main course or served with meat.

1 onion, chopped	2 pounds Yukon potatoes, peeled
½ pound bacon, chopped, or ½ pound sausages or ham	1 cup hot milk
2 cups chopped, cooked spinach	½ cup butter
	Salt & pepper

Sauté onion with bacon until both are cooked, and add spinach. Boil potatoes until tender, drain, and mash. Add milk, butter, seasonings, and bacon and spinach mixture. Great comfort food on a cold night.

Serves 4-6.

STEAMED BRUSSEL SPROUTS AND GRAPES

Brussel sprouts were never a favorite of mine until I tasted this fresh and fruity combination. The secret is not to overcook, the same as with cabbage.

1 pound brussel sprouts, trimmed	2 teaspoons lemon juice
1 ½ cups red or black grapes	Salt & pepper
2 tablespoons butter	Freshly grated nutmeg

Steam brussel sprouts about 15 minutes, or until just barely tender, adding grapes about the last 5 minutes. Toss with butter, juice, and seasonings.

Serves 4-6.

BELGIAN ENDIVES WITH ORANGE HONEY BUTTER

Like brussel sprouts, endives have never been a favorite, but a little sweetness does wonders for them. Known as witloof in Belgium, they are used in endless ways, and are also good cooked in beer with chicken or pork.

4 Belgian endives, halved lengthwise & slightly cored	¼ cup chestnut honey
¼ cup butter	1 tablespoon lemon juice
1 cup orange juice, reduced to ½ cup	Salt & pepper
	Freshly grated nutmeg

Sauté endives in butter, using a small sauté, about 5 minutes, or until golden. Add juice, honey, and lemon juice, and simmer, covered, about 15 minutes, or until almost tender. Remove cover, and simmer briskly until liquid is syrupy. This is excellent with game, pork, and ham.

Serves 4.

SWISS CHARD SAUTÉ

Frequently the simplest preparation is the best, as I discovered at Fredy Girardet's in Crissier. This is my interpretation, as I prefer not to cook chard in water, but rather to treat it like spinach. Also, I love to use the multi-colored chard which is available now.

8 ribs Swiss chard, multi-colored	¼ cup cream (optional)
¼ cup butter	Salt, pepper, & nutmeg

Cut leaves away from stems, and cut into a chiffonade. Slice stems diagonally about ¼-inch thick, and sauté them in butter, partially covered, until almost tender, about 5 minutes. Add chiffonade of leaves, cover, and cook until wilted, only a few minutes. Season. If using cream, sauté ribs and leaves separately, and add cream to leaves. Season ribs and leaves, placing ribs around edge of the plates, with the leaves in the center. Place sautéed fish, chicken, or meat on leaves.

Serves 4.

SWEET AND SOUR RED CABBAGE

Red cabbage definitely needs a sweet touch, and I now prefer chestnut honey to the usual currant jelly treatment. This idea came to fruition after having red cabbage with chestnuts in Luxembourg and Germany.

2 pounds red cabbage, cut into a chiffonade	1 cup red wine
	1 bay leaf & 3 cloves
¼ cup butter or duck fat	2 red apples, diced
1 red onion, chopped	¼ cup chestnut honey, or to taste
2 tablespoons red wine vinegar	
1 cup veal stock	Salt & pepper

Melt butter, and sauté onion until wilted, add cabbage and sauté until well coated with fat. Add vinegar, stock, wine, and seasonings. Cover and simmer about 1 hour, add apples, and simmer until cabbage is tender and liquid is almost evaporated. Add honey and adjust seasonings. Even better the next day.

Serves 6.

STRAWBERRIES WITH RHUBARB

Chef Eckert Witzigmann of Aubergine in Munich created this wonderfully refreshing fruit dessert back in the eighties, which is still reflective of German cuisine, even though it is not heavy or rich. I have lightened it even more by replacing the pastry cream and whipped cream with rhubarb sorbet.

1 pound rhubarb, diced 2/3 cup sugar 1 pint strawberries, thinly sliced	1 quart Rhubarb Sorbet (see below) To garnish: powdered sugar & mint sprigs

Cook rhubarb with sugar, covered, about 15 minutes, or until soft. Purée in food processor, and chill. Pour about 1/3 cup of purée on each of 6 plates, tilting to cover bottom. Arrange berries in an overlapping petal design, beginning at the outer edge of the plates. The points face toward the edge of the plates. Place a scoop of sorbet in the center, and sift powdered sugar over all, decorating with mint sprigs.

Serves 6.

RHUBARB SORBET

The first rhubarb sorbet I ever had was one of six that adorned my enormous plate at the incomparable restaurant of Fredy Girardet in Crissier, Switzerland. This is my version, very creamy and full of flavor.

1 pound rhubarb, sliced 1 ¼ cups sugar 1 cup water	2 tablespoons crème de cassis 1 egg white

Boil rhubarb with sugar and water about 10 minutes, purée, and add cassis and egg white. Blend well, chill, and then freeze in an ice cream freezer.

Makes 1 quart.

ROTE GRUTZE

(German Red Fruit Pudding)

A perennial at my Thanksgiving dinner, this cold and fruity dessert actually means "red grits," and is an old favorite from northern Germany. I was pleased to discover that mine was so much like that which I had at the Post Hotel in Emden, on the North Sea, the town where my maternal grandfather was born. It is delicious with ice cream, cake, and custard.

1 pint black currant juice or cranberry juice	1 vanilla bean, split
2 cups frozen blackberries	2 tablespoons lemon juice
2 cups frozen cherries	½ -1 cup sugar
1 10-ounce package frozen raspberries	1/3 cup cornstarch
	1/3 cup water

Mix juice with all fruits and any juices in a large saucepan. Scrape seeds from vanilla bean, and add both to fruit with lemon juice and sugar. Bring to a boil, and add cornstarch mixed with water, stirring until thick. Chill, remove bean, and serve chilled. If red currants are available in your area, they may replace the blackberries for an even more authentic version.

Serves 6-8.

APPLE STRUDEL

Ubiquitous and claimed throughout middle Europe-especially in Germany, Switzerland, Hungary, and Austria-strudel can also be made with cherries, which I love, and there is even a savory potato strudel.

1 pound apples or cherries	¼ cup dried cranberries or cherries
1 cup sugar	½ cup melted butter
1 teaspoon grated lemon zest	¾ cup bread or cake crumbs
Freshly grated nutmeg	1/3 cup ground hazelnuts
¼ cup golden raisins	4 sheets phyllo pastry

Peel, core, and thinly slice apples, or pit cherries. Mix with sugar, seasonings, and fruits. Brush 1 sheet of phyllo with butter, sprinkle with ¼ cup of crumbs and nuts, and repeat with another sheet on top. Place half the filling along 1 edge of the pastry, turn in the sides, and roll up. Brush with butter, place on a buttered baking sheet, and make another strudel with remaining ingredients. Bake at 350° about 45 minutes, or until crisp and golden. Sift powdered sugar over strudels.

Makes 2 strudels, serving 4 to 6.

SWISS PLUM TART

Rich tarts are very much in vogue in Switzerland, due to the French influence, and this is one of my favorites.

Pâte Sucre (see Index)	2 tablespoons lemon juice
¾ cup cake crumbs	3 tablespoons butter
1/3 ground hazelnuts	½ cup plum jelly, melted with 1 tablespoon plum brandy: Mirabelle, Quetsch, or Kirsch
12 black or purple plums, pitted and halved	
¼ cup sugar	

Roll out pastry and line a 9-inch pie pan. Sprinkle crumbs and nuts over the bottom. Arrange plums, cut side down on the top, and sprinkle with sugar and juice. Dot with butter, and bake at 375° about ½ hour. Brush with jelly, and when cool, sift powdered sugar over the tart.

Serves 6.

FLAMBÉED CHERRY CRÊPES

Cherries are enormously popular from Belgium to Germany and beyond, and they are my favorite fruit, so much so that I buy at least 6 pounds every summer that I pit, stem, and freeze in large containers. They thaw out beautifully. The French influence is evident in this dessert, which is reminiscent of those at the grand old hotels-the Ritz in Berlin, Brenner's Park Hotel in Baden-Baden, the Baur-au-Lac in Zurich, and the Amstel in Amsterdam. This is a composite of my favorites.

12 crêpes (see Index)	1/3 cup butter
3 ounces Neufchâtel cheese	1/3 cup sugar
1/3 cup sour cream	1 ½ cups Bing cherries, fresh or frozen
½ cup German cherry preserves	¼ to ½ cup kirsch

Mix softened cheese with sour cream and preserves. Spread about 2 tablespoons on each of the crêpes, and roll up. Caramelize butter and sugar in a chafing dish or in a sauté pan, add cherries, and heat until bubbly. Add crêpes, turning to coat with sauce, then flame with kirsch. More cherry preserves can be added to the sauce before or after flaming. The contrast in texture and flavor adds another dimension to the dessert.

Serves 6.

Scandinavia, Russia & the Baltics

SCANDINAVIA
RUSSIA and the BALTIC STATES

The Danes live to eat, the Norwegians eat to live, and the Swedes eat to drink. This adage lives on, and I might add that the Russians and Baltic peoples live to eat and drink, as vodka and beer are the consummate beverages. My extensive travels through these harsh and northerly climes have taken me to such far outposts as Iceland, about 600 miles west of Denmark; and farther along the Viking trail, to Greenland on a semi-circumnavigation aboard the Columbus Caravelle, a Russian ship. Spitsbergen, on the large and remote island of Svalbard, 400 miles north of Norway, offered a pristine diet, but my voyage on the powerful Russian icebreaker, the Yamal, to the ethereal North Pole provided an abundance of delicious meals. To the East, I traveled 5,000 miles from Moscow to Khabarovsk, through Siberia, on the Trans Siberian Express. This memorable trip offered not only excellent train-made soups but ethnic "fast food" at the several dozen stops. Then there was the Kristina Regina, a Finnish ship which took me to Estonia, Latvia, and Lithuania.

This vast and remote area has a common culinary heritage, as I noticed a particular fondness for herring, dark bread, sour cream, mushrooms, cucumbers, cabbage, potatoes, and beets, not to mention the ever present aquavit or vodka and beer. There are subtle differences, however, as the topography and other ethnic influences have an effect on the cooking.

Denmark, a green and rolling land of pastures, abuts the top of Germany, whose baking skills are equally matched across the border in the form of the world-renowned Danish pastries. The

French and Swedish influence produced a more refined cuisine than in other Scandinavian countries. Also, more meat is eaten in Denmark, along with eels, shrimp, haddock, and plaice. Its pastures produce excellent dairy products, which are an integral part of the cuisine.

Norway has always had a simple and unsophisticated cuisine because of its fjords, glaciers, and mountains, which made transportation difficult. Thus, preservation in the form of salting, drying, smoking, and pickling were a necessity. They have a variety of game and the outstanding salmon and cod. Now, however, the new wave of cooking has reached this country of magnificent scenery, and Norway is collecting its share of Michelin stars, as far north as Tromso.

Sweden, like Denmark, has a highly developed cuisine with a German and French influence. The outstanding Smörgåsbord at the venerable Operakälleren is justly famous. The double-tiered sixty-foot long table is laden with dozens of cold and hot dishes. Cardamom, dill, and horseradish are favorite seasonings along with curry powder, a fairly recent addition to the cuisine due to the large number of central Asians that have emigrated to both Norway and Sweden. Tropical fruits, such as mango, are now proliferous, and you will have no trouble finding fusion cooking in the restaurants. Stockholm now has the best marketplace in Europe, with a vast array of every imaginable kind of food—even caviar cream in a tube. I had a most impressive lunch consisting of beautifully arranged fresh vegetables, fruits, and a variety of shellfish when I took Lindblad's wonderfully unique expedition on the Swedish Islander to Lake Mällaren, home of the Swedish Vikings. Unfortunately, the trip is no longer offered, but you can still go to the Östermalm Market for lunch and shopping.

Finland, a land of forests and saunas, has a cuisine which has been influenced by the east as well as by the west. The Karelian influence is the most outstanding, as Karelia, once a part of Finland and now a part of Russia, is famous for its savory rye pastries with many variations. Under the Swedish crown for 600 years, this influence has endured in Finland, both in cooking and in statistics.

Both Sweden and Finland vie for the highest alcohol consumption in Europe. The Finnish forests yield an enormous amount of fresh vegetables, especially mushrooms, while the Arctic yields the cloudberries and lingonberries which are also important in Sweden. Reindeer is another Arctic specialty, but the lakes and the Baltic supply the Finns with an infinite array of seafood, as you will see on Market Square on Helsinki's waterfront.

Although the Soviet Union is now obsolete, Russia is still an immense country which borders on the Arctic, Atlantic, and Pacific Oceans, as well as the Baltic, Black, and Caspian Seas. The terrain is a vast expanse of fields and forests with the Ural mountains forming a border with Asian Russia, and many nationalities influence the diversified cooking. Slavic cooking predominates, but there is a distinct Mongol influence from the East, notably in tea, spices, and pasta. Moscow and St. Petersburg have a multitude of ethnic restaurants featuring the cuisine of all major countries as well as the former Soviet republics. The elegant and lavish lifestyle and cuisine of Russia's Czarist days is now returning, and French cuisine, originally introduced by Antonin Carême in the eighteenth century, is once again in vogue, as is the current European craze for fusion cooking. The vast majority, however, still endure a plebeian lifestyle and diet.

Estonia, one of the three Baltic states that were formerly a part of the Soviet Union, has close ties with Finland, but its cuisine is most influenced by Denmark and Sweden. Its capitol, Tallinn, actually means Danish City, and its architecture is distinctly Scandinavian. The landscape is a vivid green dotted with white birch trees and evergreens, and like their neighbors across the sea, the meadows yield excellent dairy products, while the sea provides the much-loved and ubiquitous herring. But, there is a different flair to their meatballs, pancakes, pastries, and cream cakes, as these people cling to their heritage. Coffee houses have always been a symbol of their lifestyle.

Latvia, like Estonia, has been invaded by Vikings, Slavs, and Mongols, and occupied by Danes, Swedes, Germans, Poles, and Russians, but the proud Latvians have retained their own style of cooking. There is a preference for salty, sour, and spicy foods; and herring, of course, is a daily staple in many forms. Eels, sprats, pork, bacon, and pickles are widely eaten. Riga, the ancient capitol, is an enchanting city with copper church steeples and cobbled streets.

Lithuania's capitol of Vilnius was reached by a beautiful drive through the Latvian and Lithuanian countryside. Also proud and independent, the country once extended to the Black Sea, and then became a part of Poland. Thus, the culinary influences were Mongol, Ottoman, Polish, German, Russian, and Jewish. The Jews once formed half the population, and there is still a similarity in some of the foods. Meat patties, meat pies, and dumplings filled with mashed potatoes and topped with butter and sour cream are the memorable and deeply satisfying dishes that I savored while in Vilnius.

RECIPES FROM SCANDINAVIA AND RUSSIA AND THE BALTICS

GRAVLAX WITH MUSTARD DILL SAUCE

CUCUMBER SALAD

RUSSIAN POTATO SALAD

SIBERIAN SOLYANKA (FISH SOUP SIBERIAN STYLE)

TSENTRALNAIA BORSCHT

NORTH POLE CREAM OF GARLIC SOUP

BALTIC HERRING WITH RED ONION SAUCE

GRATIN OF COD WITH GJETÖST SAUCE

SWEET AND SOUR FISH WITH TOMATO PURÉE SAUCE LATVIAN STYLE

SCANDINAVIAN MEAT PATTIES

NORWEGIAN ROAST LAMB WITH GJETÖST SAUCE

SWEDISH ROAST BEEF WITH COFFEE GRAVY

LATVIAN ROAST PORK WITH SAUERKRAUT

KARELIAN PASTIES WITH SOUR CREAM PASTRY

DANISH CARAMELIZED POTATOES

SWEDISH SWEET AND SOUR BEANS

NORWEGIAN RED CABBAGE WITH SYRUP

SWEDISH GRIPSHOLM EGGS

GRIPSHOLM WAFFLES

SWEDISH SAFFRON COFFEECAKE

SWEDISH PLÄTTAR

STRAWBERRIES WITH PASSION FRUIT

PASCHKA (RUSSIAN EASTER CHEESE MOLD WITH FRUITS AND NUTS)

ALEKSANDER TORTE

NORGE TÖRTA WITH STRAWBERRIES

OPERATÖRTA WITH CARAMEL AND CHOCOLATE FROSTINGS

CHOCOLATE BEET CAKE

GRAVLAX WITH MUSTARD DILL SAUCE

This delicious salty-sweet cured salmon is the star of Scandinavian cooking, as well as of Russia and the Baltics. It is surprisingly easy and is versatile in that it may be an elegant first course or a main course. Be sure to buy very fresh salmon. Some prefer to use more sugar than salt and more spices, as well as an annointment of aquavit.

1 ½ -2 pounds center-cut salmon fillet	1 tablespoon mixed grated zest of lemon, lime, & orange
½ cup kosher or sea salt	Dill sprigs
½ tablespoon white or gray pepper	Mustard Dill Sauce
	1/3 cup sugar

Wash salmon, pat dry, and remove any stray bones with tweezers. Score skin lightly several times. Mix salt and sugar with seasonings and dill sprigs. Spread half the mixture on a stainless steel or glass platter, and place salmon on top. Spread remaining salt mixture on top, and press plastic wrap over and around it. Place another platter, large enough to cover salmon on top, and place several large cans or other weights on top. I keep a couple of foil-wrapped bricks in a cabinet for this purpose. Place in refrigerator for two to three full days, depending on the depth of flavor desired. Wipe off excess marinade, and slice very thinly on the diagonal, removing skin. Serve with the Mustard Dill sauce for a traditional Scandinavian presentation, or for an elegant French presentation, serve with mesclun dressed in a caviar vinaigrette, and roll salmon slices into cornucopias to place over mesclun.

Mustard Dill Sauce:

1 egg yolk	¾ cup canola oil
1 tablespoon sugar	1-2 tablespoons white wine vinegar
1-2 tablespoons Dijon mustard	¼ cup chopped fresh dill

Blend egg with seasonings in an immersion blender, and gradually add oil. When thickened, add dill, and check for seasoning. Chill.

Serves 8 to 12 as an appetizer.

CUCUMBER SALAD

Another ubiquitous smörgåsbord item that belongs to every country in this part of the world. The Finns and Russians would add sour cream.

2 English-style cucumbers, scored & very thinly sliced	2-4 tablespoons sugar
½ cup white wine vinegar	Salt & gray pepper
	Fresh chopped dill

Marinate with all but dill about an hour in the refrigerator. Sprinkle with dill. This is great with the gravlax or as a salad.

Serves 8.

RUSSIAN POTATO SALAD

This very versatile salad can also contain chicken, as it does in the excellent Salat Olivet in my book, *Culinary Classics,* so feel free to interchange ingredients.

1 ½ pounds small red new potatoes	1 teaspoon salt
½ cup mayonnaise	½ teaspoon sugar
½ cup sour cream	3 hard-cooked eggs, cut in quarters
1 tablespoon lemon juice	1 jar pickled beets, sliced or quartered
1 tablespoon capers	
1 tablespoon chopped dill pickle	Chopped dill or parsley

Cook potatoes in salted water, and keep warm while preparing dressing. Mix mayonnaise and cream with all seasonings. Cut potatoes into quarters, and stir in dressing. Mound on a platter, and place eggs and beets around the potatoes. Sprinkle with herbs. Russians love stuffed eggs, so these would be an option instead of the plain eggs.

Serves 6.

SIBERIAN SOLYANKA

(Fish Soup Siberian Style)

Early in the morning, as the legendary Trans Siberian Express sped clickety-clack through the birch forests of Siberia, the aroma of fresh bread baking in the galley wafted through the train. The rotund female cook provided delicious train-made breads and soups daily, and this fish soup was one of the best. She also prepared it with meat, when available.

2 onions, thinly sliced	6-8 cups fish stock
¼ cup butter	2 pounds sturgeon or salmon, cut into small chunks
1 English cucumber, peeled & diced	½ cup chopped sour pickles
2 tomatoes, diced	2 tablespoons lemon juice
1 bay leaf	Chopped dill

Sauté onions in butter, using a 4-quart soup pot, until translucent. Add cucumber, tomatoes, and bay leaf. Sauté about 10 minutes, add stock and fish, and simmer until fish flakes easily. Add pickles and juice, and serve with lots of dill sprinkled on top. Black rye bread is a must for sopping up the stock.

Serves 8.

TSENTRALNAIA BORSCHT

The year was 1975, and my first Russian meal was at the still elegant old-world Tsentralnaia Restaurant on Gorky Street. Borscht, the Russian national dish, was a light version without meat, and this is the way I remember it. I also remember that we always shared a table with warm and convivial Russians, who made our meals memorable occasions.

1 red onion, thinly sliced	¾ cup tomato purée
2 tablespoons butter	2 cups thinly sliced cabbage, blanched
2 garlic cloves, crushed	
¾ cup thinly sliced celery	1 tablespoon red wine vinegar
¾ cup thinly sliced carrot	½ tablespoon sugar
1 pound beets, peeled & shredded	Salt & pepper
	Sour cream
6 cups chicken or beef stock	Chopped dill

Sauté onion in butter, using a 3-quart soup pot, until translucent, and beginning to caramelize. Add garlic, celery, carrot, and beets, and sauté briefly. Add stock and purée, and simmer until vegetables are tender, about 20 minutes. Add cabbage and seasonings, simmering briefly. Serve with lots of sour cream, dill, and the camaraderie of Russians.

Serves 6-8.

NORTH POLE CREAM OF GARLIC SOUP

The date was July 25, 1999, a delightful sunny day at 90° north, and we were celebrating our late arrival at the North Pole with copious amounts of Russian champagne and a barbecue on the ice, while others took a plunge into the Arctic Ocean. The Yamal, the most powerful Russian icebreaker, had the thickest and hardest ice cap in many years to crash through. It was an exhilarating experience and one of my most memorable adventures that also provided excellent food of many kinds, including the best hamburger ever. From the departure in Murmansk, still a very secretive and high-security port, to the arrival in Spitsbergen by helicopter, I was enchanted by the ever-changing patterns of the ice floes as far as the eye could see, and I was deeply saddened to leave this ethereal beauty. But I was able to bring home this outstanding garlic soup, compliments of Gunter Walder, the Austrian executive chef who served it for lunch on that magical and unforgettable day of July 25, 1999.

1 medium onion, chopped	1 teaspoon worcestershire, or to taste
4 large garlic cloves, crushed	
¼ cup butter	2 teaspoons salt
1/3 cup flour	White pepper & nutmeg, to taste
¼ cup white wine	½ cup cream, partially whipped
5 ½ cups chicken stock	Chopped parsley, bacon, croutons
1 tablespoon lemon juice	

Using a 2-quart soup pot, sauté onion and garlic in butter until soft, add flour and blend well. Deglaze with wine, add stock and seasonings, and simmer 10 minutes. Fold in cream, and garnish with your choice of parsley, bacon, and croutons.

Makes about 6 cups.

BALTIC HERRING WITH RED ONION SAUCE

Herring, in its preserved form, has never appealed to me, but when prepared fresh, as I had it on the Kristina Regina's Baltic cruise, it is a very mild and delicious fish. A simple sweet and sour marinade is also quite good.

1 pound herring fillets, or other small white fish, such as trout	½ tablespoon flour
Salt & pepper	½ cup sour cream
Rye flour	½ tablespoon Dijon mustard
2 tablespoons each canola oil & butter	½ tablespoon capers
	1 teaspoon lemon juice
½ cup finely chopped red onion	Salt & pepper

Season fillets, dredge in flour, and sauté in oil and butter until golden and done. Remove from skillet, and keep warm. If necessary, add more butter, and sauté onions until translucent. Add flour, blend well, and whisk in sour cream and seasonings. Cook briefly, until bubbling, and pour over herring.

Serves 4.

GRATIN OF COD WITH GJETÖST SAUCE

Simple and homey cod gratins have always been eaten throughout Norway, and I remember a particularly robust variation which was worth the mile-long walk from my "dormitory" room to the only restaurant nearby in Spitsbergen, on the large island of Svarlbard, 400 miles from the North Pole. Polar bears and Arctic temperatures are the only dangers in this remote area, which has not yet entered the realm of new European cooking. The heavy white sauce that I savored in Svarlbard is quite a contrast to this deliciously light sauce made with gjetöst, my favorite Norwegian cheese, which is made from goat's milk. This sauce is also adaptable to pork tenderloin and other meats when made from chicken or veal stock. The Pakistani influence is evident in the curry powder.

2 tablespoons butter	Salt & pepper
1 tablespoon flour	Turbinado or plain sugar
1 cup fish stock	¼ cup butter
½ cup sour cream	1 ½ pounds Yukon potatoes
1-2 tablespoons aquavit	¼ cup each butter and sour cream
Salt & pepper	
¼ cup diced gjetöst cheese	1 teaspoon curry powder, or to taste
4 cod fillets	

Make a roux with butter and flour, whisk in stock, and simmer until thickened. Whisk in sour cream, seasonings, and cheese, and whisk until cheese melts. Sprinkle cod with seasonings and sugar, then sauté in butter on both sides until done, and fish begins to flake. The sugar caramelizes, thus making it compatible with the caramel flavor of the cheese. Whisk hot cooked potatoes with butter, sour cream, and curry powder. Spread in a buttered 4- to 6-cup gratin dish, place cod on top, and cover with sauce. Bake about 10 minutes at 350°, or place under the broiler briefly. If a true gratin effect is desired, sprinkle dry rye bread crumbs on top before placing it in the oven.

Serves 4.

SWEET AND SOUR FISH WITH TOMATO PURÉE LATVIAN STYLE

A sweet, sour, and salty tomato marinade, which becomes the sauce, is quite typical in the Baltics, and I prefer it to the usual sugar and vinegar marinade for herring. I especially like to serve this with the Finnish rye pasties that are in the vegetable section. If there were currants and pine nuts in this recipe, you would think it belonged with the Sicilian fish recipes.

1 cup diced red onion	½ teaspoon 5-spice powder (Chinese)
½ cup canola oil	
1 or 2 very ripe Roma tomatoes, diced	1 pound flounder, plaice, sole, herring, or trout, cut into large chunks
½ cup catsup or tomato paste	Rye bread crumbs
2 tablespoons white wine vinegar	¼ cup canola oil
½ tablespoon sugar	Chopped dill
1 teaspoon salt	Salt, sugar, & vinegar to be served at the table
Salt & pepper	

Sauté onion in hot oil, using a small sauté pan, until soft. Add tomato and sauté until soft, then add catsup and seasonings, and simmer about 10 minutes, covered. Meanwhile, season fillets, dredge with rye crumbs, and sauté in oil on both sides until golden brown and done. Place half the sauce in a glass dish, just large enough to hold the fish, and then cover fish with remaining sauce.

Cover, and refrigerate a day or so, at least, for exceptional flavor. At the table, everyone adjusts the salt, sugar, and vinegar, to taste. Serves 4.

Meat cookery in northeastern Europe is generally quite simple, made up of mostly stews, pot roasts, and the ubiquitous meatball or meat pattie, of which there are endless varieties. Danish Frikadeller have soda water in them; Estonian patties contain the spices that make up Chinese 5-spice powder; Russian Kotletti are made with chicken; Swedish Lindstrom have beets; and Norway likes to include mashed potatoes.

SCANDINAVIAN MEAT PATTIES

This is my composite of some of the best I've savored, especially at the Operakälleren in Stockholm, at a friend's house in Stockholm, and on the Swedish Islander cruise. If desired, a combination of beef and veal may be used.

1 pound ground veal	½ -1 teaspoon Chinese 5-spice powder
4 egg yolks	
1/3 cup cream	Rye or white bread crumbs
1 tablespoon chopped capers	¼ cup butter
2 teaspoons white wine vinegar	1/3 cup white wine
	4 fried or poached eggs (optional)
1 teaspoon salt	Lingonberry Preserves (optional)

Process veal, yolks, cream, and seasonings in a food processor until well mixed. Form into 4 patties, dredge with crumbs, and chill. Sauté on both sides in butter until golden brown and done as desired. Remove, deglaze pan with wine and pour over patties. Top them with eggs or preserves.

Serves 4.

NORWEGIAN ROAST LAMB WITH GJETÖST SAUCE

The Norwegian method of roasting a not-so-tender cut of meat is quite ingenuous and frugal: dry roasting is followed by covered roasting, resulting in a flavorful and yet meltingly tender roast. Again, I use the caramel-flavored Gjetöst cheese in a delicious sauce.

3 pounds lamb or veal shoulder, boneless & trimmed of excess fat	1 cup veal stock
	½ tablespoon lingonberry preserves or currant jelly
Salt & pepper	1 cup sour cream
2 tablespoons butter	¼ - ½ cup shredded Gjetöst cheese
3 or 4 juniper berries	

Rub lamb with seasonings and butter. Place on a rack in a roasting pan, and roast at 450° about ½ hour, or until golden brown. Reduce heat to 350°, add berries and stock, and roast about 1 to 1 ½ hours, covered, or until very tender. Pour pan juices into a saucepan, skim fat, and reduce until thickened, about ¼ cup. Whisk in preserves, cream, and cheese, until smooth. Slice roast and nap with sauce.

Serves 6.

SWEDISH ROAST BEEF WITH COFFEE GRAVY

This old Swedish method of roasting beef with gravy can also be prepared in the pot roast style, and lamb, veal, and pork are equally good. For a more modern version, substitute pork tenderloin or beef, and sauté in butter. Then add remaining ingredients, and cook only until meat is tender. Reduce remaining liquid until lightly thickened, and serve with meat. Stockholm's oldest restaurant, Stallmastersgarden, was the first place enjoyed this very flavorful dish.

3 pounds top round of beef	1 cup coffee
Salt & pepper	2/3 cup veal stock
2 tablespoons butter	1/3 cup cream
2 onions, sliced	2 tablespoons molasses
1 bay leaf & 4 juniper berries	Chopped dill

Rub beef with seasonings and butter. Place on a rack in a roasting pan, and roast at 450° about 45 minutes, or until well browned. Add remaining ingredients, lower heat to 350°, and roast, covered, about 1 ½ hours, or until tender. Strain cooking liquid, and reduce to desired consistency. Slice beef, nap with sauce, and sprinkle with dill.

Serves 4-6.

LATVIAN ROAST PORK WITH SAUERKRAUT

This traditional Christmas recipe was given to me by family members, Astrida Kippert and Linda Olson, who make an annual pilgimage back to Riga, Latvia. They serve it with mashed potatoes and lettuce salad with a sour cream dressing. They tell me that one of the "in" foods now is a reincarnated classic of crêpes filled with a ground roast beef and onion mixture, then folded, sautéed in butter until well browned, and served in broth. My granddaughter, Lindsey, loves the one with a cheese filling.

3 pounds Boston butt pork roast	2 pounds sauerkraut in a cryovac bag, drained & rinsed
Salt & pepper	Salt & pepper
½ pound sliced bacon	Bay leaves, caraway seeds, or juniper berries, optional
1 onion, chopped	
2 large garlic cloves, crushed	

Season pork, and roast in a 350° oven 3 hours, or until meltingly tender. Sauté bacon until half done, add onion and garlic, and sauté until soft. Add kraut and brown well. Season as desired, add only a small amount of water, cover, and simmer slowly about 2 to 3 hours. Add pork drippings, if desired, and make gravy with remaining drippings.

Serves 6.

KARELIAN PASTIES WITH SOUR CREAM PASTRY

These wonderful and versatile little pirakka from Karelia in eastern Finland have been taken by workmen for their lunch, like the Cornish pasties in England, since olden times. There are also versions known as piroshki in Russia, pierogi in Poland, and pirragi in Latvia. They can be made in any size, and make wonderful appetizers, as well as an accompaniment to main courses. The filling is traditionally rice, but can be mashed potatoes, which is my favorite, or any meat or vegetable leftover. The pastry is traditionally made from rye flour, mixed with white, but I prefer flaky and rich sour cream pastry.

1 pound Yukon potatoes, peeled & cooked	½ cup melted butter
3 tablespoons butter	3 hard-cooked eggs
3 tablespoons sour cream	¾ cup soft butter
Salt & pepper	½ teaspoon salt
1 teaspoon curry powder	½ teaspoon curry powder, or to taste
Sour Cream Pastry (see below)	Chopped dill

Crush or whip potatoes, stir in butter, sour cream, and seasonings. Roll out pastry thinly, and cut into 24 3-inch rounds or 12 5-inch rounds. Place about half a tablespoon on small pastries and about 2 tablespoons on large ones. Make small pleats or crimps around the edge, then fold 2 sides over the filling, leaving it partially exposed. Crimp the ends together, so that you have a boat-shaped pastry. Brush with butter, and bake at 400° about 10 minutes, or until pastry is done. Dip briefly in melted butter. Crush or mash eggs, and beat in butter and seasonings. Mound on top of the pastries, sprinkle with dill, and enjoy a most delicious and unusual appetizer, or serve as an accompaniment to meat or fish.

Sour Cream Pastry:

1/3 cup cold butter	1 egg yolk
1 cup flour	¼ cup sour cream

Using a food processor, cut butter into flour only until crumbly. Add yolk and sour cream, mixing briefly. Roll out as desired. I have also substituted rye flour for half the amount of white flour when making pirakka.

Makes 24 3-inch pastries or 12 5-inch pastries.

DANISH CARAMELIZED POTATOES

Potatoes in every guise are found in this part of the world, but my favorites are the previous curried mashed potatoes and the unctuous Norwegian potatoes with sour cream and butter, which are found in my Culinary Classics. These simple caramelized potatoes are wonderful with everything, and I first experienced them at the venerable Krogsfiskerestaurant in Copenhagen.

12 small red new potatoes	¼ cup butter
¼ cup turbinado or white sugar	Salt & pepper
	Chopped chives

Peel 2 wide crisscross strips off potatoes with a vegetable peeler, and boil in salted water until done, drain and dry well. Melt sugar in an iron skillet until caramelized, add butter off the heat, and when mixture is smooth, add potatoes, turning until caramelized, using low heat, about 15 minutes. Season well.

Serves 4 to 6.

SWEDISH SWEET & SOUR BROWN BEANS

These beans were a part of the wonderful smorgasbord on Lindblad's Swedish Islander cruise, and are remarkably similar to the Dutch Brown Beans and Bacon (see Index.)

1 ½ cups dried brown or cranberry beans, soaked overnight 1/3 red wine vinegar	1/3 cup dark corn syrup 2 tablespoons molasses Salt & pepper

Drain beans, add fresh water to cover by an inch, and simmer, covered about 1 ½ hours. Add remaining ingredients, and let simmer, uncovered about ½ hour, or until tender and thickened. Add more water if too much evaporates, or boil if too much water remains.

Serves 4.

NORWEGIAN RED CABBAGE with SYRUP

Red cabbage is prepared in an infinite number of ways in this part of the world, more so than green cabbage, and frequently is a sweet and sour dish.

1 ½ pounds red cabbage, coarsely shredded, tough stems removed 1 cup black currant or blackberry syrup	1/3 cup black currant or blackberry preserves or jam 2 tablespoons red wine vinegar 2 tablespoons butter Salt, pepper, & cinnamon stick

Place all ingredients in a sauté pan, cover, and simmer about 1 ½ to 2 hours, or until cabbage is very tender and glazed. Add water, if necessary while cooking to prevent sticking to the pan and burning.

Serves 4.

SWEDISH GRIPSHOLM EGGS

One of my favorite dishes for a buffet or simply as comfort food, it is apparently named after Gripsholm Castle, which I visited in the quaint and charming town of Mariefred, on the sea, and south of Stockholm.

¼ cup butter	7 or 8 hard-cooked eggs, shelled
¼ cup flour	
3 cups milk	6 slices bacon, cooked & crumbled
Salt & pepper	
¾ cup Parmesan cheese	Chopped dill or parsley

Make a roux with butter and flour, whisk in milk all at once, and cook until thickened. Season and add cheese. Sieve 3 yolks, reserving for the garnish, and chop remaining whites and eggs. Fold them into creamed mixture, heat well, and pour into a 12-inch serving dish or deep platter. Garnish with diagonal rows of sieved yolks, bacon, and dill or parsley.

Serves 6-8.

GRIPSHOLM WAFFLES

These waffles are named after the charming Gripsholm Värdshus & Hotel in Mariefred, where I stayed while on the Swedish Islander. I actually poured the batter into an old waffle iron by candlelight at my table. With a view of Gripsholm Castle, it was undoubtedly the most enchanting breakfast ever.

1 ½ cups flour	2 cups sour cream
1 ½ teaspoons baking powder	¼ cup melted butter
½ teaspoon baking soda	3 egg whites
½ teaspoon salt	¼ cup sugar
½ -1 teaspoon cardamom	Maple syrup, melted butter, strawberries, & whipped cream
3 egg yolks	

Sift dry ingredients together, and stir in mixed yolks, sour cream, and butter. Whisk whites until foamy, gradually add sugar, and whisk until stiff but not dry. Lighten whites by whisking in a small amount of batter, then gently fold into remaining batter. Bake in a preheated waffle iron until steaming stops, and serve with your choice of toppings, any or all of them.

Makes about 12.

SWEDISH SAFFRON COFFEECAKE

I really enjoyed the bounteous breakfast buffet at the Victory Hotel in Gamla Stan, Stockholm's old city. Wonderful granolas and sweet breads, especially this coffeecake which I have duplicated, were the best.

1 envelope yeast	¾ cup golden raisins
1 tablespoon sugar	¼ cup ground almonds
2 tablespoons warm milk	¾ cup warm milk
1 teaspoon powdered saffron or cardamom	½ cup soft butter
	½ cup light brown sugar
1 tablespoon brandy	1 egg
1 teaspoon orange flower water	1 egg yolk mixed with 1 tablespoon milk
½ teaspoon salt	Turbinado sugar & sliced almonds
3 cups all-purpose flour	

Mix yeast with sugar and milk, and let stand until bubbly. Add seasonings, then alternately add flour, mixed with raisins and nuts, and milk. Cream butter with sugar, and beat in, kneading until smooth. Cover and let stand about 45 minutes and until almost doubled in bulk. Divide into 2 long ropes, about 1 inch thick, then braid them, forming into a circle, if desired. Brush with egg yolk glaze, then sprinkle with sugar and almonds. Let rise again, covered, until almost doubled. Bake at 350° about 45 minutes, or until golden brown, and it tests done. Serve for breakfast or as an afternoon treat with coffee.

Makes 1 long braid or wreath.

SWEDISH PLÄTTAR

These delectable and popular pancakes can be served for breakfast or as a dessert. They are made with crêpe batter and can be made the same way.

½ recipe crêpes (about 18), see index	2 tablespoons butter
	Powdered sugar
1 cup lingonberry preserves	18 butter balls
1 tablespoon turbinado sugar	½ cup cream, whipped (optional)

Spread crêpes with preserves, roll up, and arrange on a large stainless steel platter (which I prefer) or on a jelly roll pan. Sprinkle with sugar, dot with butter, and bake at 350° about 10 minutes. Place 2 or 3 on each plate, sift with powdered sugar, and top with a butterball. If desired, form a rosette of whipped cream, using a pastry bag, on each plate.

Serves 6-8.

STRAWBERRIES WITH PASSION FRUIT SAUCE

Norway has exceptional berries, and with the advent of new and lighter cooking, they are destined for delicious desserts with eye appeal, instead of the old way of smothering them in cream. Enjoy with a glass of champagne.

1 ½ cups milk	6 egg yolks
½ cup passion fruit juice	1 pint small strawberries, sliced
1 vanilla bean, slit lengthwise	Sour cream
¾ cup sugar	Small mint leaves
½ tablespoon cornstarch	

Combine milk, juice, and vanilla bean in a medium saucepan, and bring to a boil. Whisk sugar, cornstarch, and yolks together, add a little hot mixture, then whisk back into saucepan, cooking over low heat until lightly thickened. Remove bean, scraping seeds into sauce. This is particularly effective if you have the modern square or rectangular dessert plates, but round ones are fine. Pour sauce onto plates, tilting them to cover with sauce. Arrange overlapping rows of berries, diagonally, about 1 inch apart. Pipe fine lines of cream diagonally, in the opposite direction. Scatter with small mint leaves.

Serves 4-6.

PASCHKA

(Russian Easter Cheese Mold With Fruits and Nuts)

A very rich traditional Easter dessert in both Russia and Finland, it is usually made with a pot-cheese, but I love this version. A mold shaped like a pyramid is used, but any 6-cup mold will suffice.

1 ½ pounds soft cream cheese	½ cup mixed, diced crystallized fruits
½ pound soft butter	
2 egg yolks (optional)	½ cup chopped almonds or hazelnuts
1 cup powdered sugar	
½ tablespoon vanilla	Diced crystallized fruits, to garnish
½ cup golden raisins or currants	
	Lingonberry or Black Currant preserves or syrup

Cream the cheese, butter, yolks, and sugar together in an electric mixer until smooth. Add vanilla, fruits, and nuts. Line a 6-cup mold with damp cheesecloth, pour in the cheese mixture, and chill until firm, about 3 or 4 hours. Unmold onto a platter, remove cheesecloth, and garnish with the fruits. Serve with preserves or syrup.

Serves 8.

ALEKSANDER TORTE

It was with not a little trepidation that I proffered this luscious raspberry pastry from Latvia at my son's pre-wedding dinner party. To my relief, it received much praise and approval, quite a feat when you consider that my son's fiancée and her family are excellent Latvian cooks, and they requested the recipe.

3 cups flour	2 cups powdered sugar
½ pound cold butter	2 tablespoons water
2 tablespoons sugar	1 ½ tablespoons each orange & lemon juice
1 egg, beaten	
1 ½ cups seedless raspberry preserves	Powdered sugar, for sifting

Using an electric mixer, blend flour, butter, and sugar only until crumbly. Add egg, mixing briefly. Chill, divide dough in half, and roll each half into a 10- by 15-inch rectangle on a floured surface. Place on baking sheets, and bake at 350° about 20 minutes, or until golden. Cool, then spread preserves over 1 pastry layer, and top with the other.

Whisk sugar with water and juice until smooth. Pour and spread evenly over pastry, then chill until set. Cut into small squares or rectangles. Place on a doily-lined platter, and sift powdered sugar over top.

Makes about 4 dozen.

NORGE TÖRTA with STRAWBERRIES

Strawberries highlight this delicate mélange of tender cake, meringue, and whipped cream, which is a summer treat in Norway.

½ pound butter, softened	2 teaspoons vanilla
1 cup sugar	6 egg whites
6 egg yolks	¾ cup sugar
¾ cup unbleached flour	1 cup cream, whipped
2 teaspoons baking powder	½ cup strawberry purée
2/3 cup milk	1 pint small ripe strawberries

Cream butter with sugar until fluffy, using an electric mixer. Beat in yolks, then add dry ingredients alternately with milk. Add vanilla. Line 2 9-inch cake pans with wax paper cut to fit. Butter pans, and pour in batter.

Beat whites until almost stiff, then gradually add sugar, beating until stiff. Spread over batter not quite to the sides of the pan, and bake at 350° about 30 minutes, or until cake tests done. Cool, invert layers onto plates, then invert again. Place 1 layer on a cake platter, spread with cream, top with other layer, and spread remaining cream over entire cake. Drizzle with purée, letting it run down sides of cake. Arrange whole berries around bottom of cake. They may be brushed with melted currant jelly in the French style, if desired.

Serves 8.

OPERATÖRTA WITH CARAMEL AND CHOCOLATE FROSTINGS

Many years ago, this was a dessert specialty at Stockholm's venerable Operakälleren Restaurant, owned by Tore Wretman, one of Europe's most renowned restaurateurs. The name is derived from the unique layering which resembles the steps of the opera house, and I especially love the flavoring juxtaposition of the chocolate and caramel frostings.

Chocolate Genoise:	½ cup unbleached flour
4 whole eggs	3 tablespoons cocoa
4 egg yolks	2 tablespoons sugar
½ cup sugar	¼ cup melted butter
1 teaspoon vanilla	

Whisk eggs and sugar over hot water until double in volume, and add vanilla. Sift combined flour, cocoa, and sugar over mixture, folding in gently. Fold in butter, and pour into a buttered and floured 12- x 16-inch jelly roll pan, lined with buttered and floured parchment paper or wax paper. Bake at 325° about 20 minutes, or until firm. Cool briefly, turn out onto wax paper, and cool.

Caramel Frosting:

¾ cup butter	2 ½ -3 cups powdered sugar
1 cup light brown sugar	1 teaspoon vanilla
1/3 cup milk	

Melt butter, add sugar, and dissolve. Add milk, bring to a boil, and remove from heat. Beat in sugar and vanilla.

Makes about 2 ½ cups.

Chocolate Buttercream Frosting:

2 egg yolks	½ cup soft butter
½ cup sugar	3 ounces semisweet chocolate
Dash of cream of tartar	1 ½ tablespoons cream
¼ cup water	1 tablespoon Tiramisu or Frangelico

Whisk yolks until thick and pale. Boil sugar, cream of tartar, and water to 238°. Add gradually to yolks, beating constantly until cool. Beat in butter gradually, then beat in chocolate melted in cream, and liqueur. Makes about 1 ¼ cups.

To assemble, cut cake into a 9- x 12-inch rectangle, a 7- x 7-inch square, and a 5- x 5-inch square. Frost large rectangle with caramel, top with large square in one corner, frost it, and place remaining square on top, frosting it and all sides. Using a pastry bag, decorate each layer with rosettes, at the base and on top. If desired, melt 14 ounces of white chocolate, and write "Operatörta" across large portion of bottom layer.

Serves 8-10.

CHOCOLATE BEET CAKE

Although it is of Scandinavian origin, I obtained this best chocolate cake ever from the Farmer's Inn in Havana, North Dakota when attending my husband's family reunion. The grated beets seem to melt into the luscious cocoa cake batter and intensify the flavor.

1 ½ cups sugar	½ cup cocoa powder
3 eggs	1 ¾ cups unbleached flour
1 cup canola oil	1 ½ teaspoons baking soda
1 teaspoon vanilla	½ teaspoon salt
1 ½ cups cooked, grated beets, or canned beets	½ cup water

In an electric mixer, beat sugar, eggs, oil, and vanilla until blended and lightly thickened. Add beets and cocoa, then alternately add mixed dry ingredients with water until just blended. Pour into a greased and floured 9- x 12-inch cake pan or 2 8-inch round pans, and bake at 350° about ½ hour or until it tests done. Invert, and frost with following frosting while still warm.

Chocolate Nut Frosting:

½ cup soft butter	1 pound powdered sugar
3 tablespoons cocoa	½ tablespoon vanilla
1/3 cup milk	1 cup chopped walnuts or pecans

Bring butter, cocoa, and milk to a boil, and whisk in sugar until smooth. Whisk in vanilla and nuts.

Serves 8.

Eastern Europe

POLAND CZECHOSLOVAKIA
AUSTRIA HUNGARY THE BALKANS

These East European countries have cuisines with a close and significant rapport, yet they were influenced by Russia in the north and Turkey in the south, not to mention other influences through wars and marriages. Traveling through these countries, I was amazed by travelers who were finding their own dishes far from home and wondering how they got there. This area, of course, was the bridge between the east and the west; thus, the food, architecture, religions, and the people themselves are a result of these vast influences wrought by several empires.

Poland, land of Chopin, Paderewski, and Rubenstein, once was the largest country in Europe when its union with Lithuania stretched from the Baltic to the Black Sea. This expansive territory was almost constantly being torn apart and rendered with new neighbors who left their culinary legacy.

As in the Baltic states, Polish cooking thrives on dark bread, cabbage, beets, cucumbers, dill, pork, and herring. Russia has contributed borscht, pierogi, and sour cream to Polish cuisine, while Austria, Hungary, France, Italy, and Germany have also left an indelible influence, along with Jewish cookery.

But the pride of Polish cooking is its outstanding and diversified yield of mushrooms and game from the extensive forests. Also, kielbasa (Polish sausage) is renowned, and barley soup (krupnik) is an outstanding example of Poland's proliferous grain crops. Warsaw's restaurants offered these as well as great pastries.

I can honestly say I have never had better pastries than those from Blikle's, the venerable pastry shop on Nowy Swiat Street near the

Bristol Hotel. My husband and I bought at least a dozen kinds, took them back to the Bristol, sat on the bed, and savored every last crumb. And this was after lunch!

Czechoslovakia, once part of the Austro-Hungarian Empire, is now two countries—Czech Republic in the west and Slovakia in the east. The former was once called Bohemia and sent its skilled cooks to Vienna to cook for the Habsburgs. This was part of my legacy as my maternal grandmother, Maria Riha, emigrated from Prague and passed on her dumplings, strudel, and streusel.

The heavy and robust cooking is also dominated by pork and ham, always served with sauerkraut, noodles, or potatoes. This is always washed down with the famous Pilsner beer which should be imbibed at Prague's oldest beer hall, Ü Fleku, founded in 1499. The sausages, however, were the highlight for me.

Slovakia, the eastern part, shares the same specialties, but its Hungarian and eastern influence is evident in the various goulashes and other spicy foods. While the cooking in the Czech Republic is becoming more contemporary, Slovakia and its capitol, Bratislava, have remained delightfully unchanged in every way, and its fourteenth century St. Martin's Cathedral, towering over the Danube, is the resting place of my mother's ashes. A short bus ride from Vienna's airport, Bratislava has numerous cellar restaurants and cafés where you can sample roast goose and potato dumplings topped with bacon and cheese.

Austria, the land of the Blue Danube and the waltz, may also be considered the land of the original fusion cuisine, as the 600-year Austro-Hungarian Empire once covered most of Europe—from Prague to Belgrade and from Trieste to Lvov—and the famous international marriages included culinary influences in their dowries from as far away as Mexico.

Vienna was the center of the opulent Baroque period during the golden age of the eighteenth and nineteenth centuries, and its palaces hosted lavish banquets equal to those of Paris. Outstanding meats were and still are the centerpiece of the cuisine.

The eastern Tyrolean region in the Alps near Italy has been an important culinary influence, as have Hungary and Turkey to the east, with the introduction of coffee and pastry (which led to the establishment of coffee houses and a fabulous array of cakes, tarts, and at least six dozen tortes). Demel's is still the star of this national institution, and the stately Hotel Sacher still serves its glorified Sacher Torte.

The heavy cuisine is now becoming lighter as Europe's mother of fusion cuisine is introducing new ingredients and healthier cooking techniques. And the excellent Austrian Rieslings and Veltliners are the perfect companions. One of the best is the 1993 Ruster Grauburgunder Heidi Schrock, which was introduced to me by Charlie Trotter at his eponymous Chicago restaurant. The place to enjoy these wines is at a heuriger, a wine tavern owned by the vintner. The village of Grinzing near Vienna is famous for its heurigers, and I have sampled excellent whites as well as reds such as Gumpoldskirchner and Lippizanner. Simple food and gypsy music accompany the wine and the Austrian camaraderie.

Hungary, a major part of the Austro-Hungarian Empire, also had a strong French culinary presence, but its invasions by Ghengis Khan and especially the Turks, who introduced paprika, stuffed vegetables, and fillo pastry, left the most indelible mark on the cuisine, which is based on the world's best paprika, onions, and lard. Lard, by the way, is purported to be healthier than butter, according to many Italian culinarians.

A boat ride from Vienna is the way to arrive in the charasmatic city of Budapest on the Danube which separates Buda, the old part with cobbled streets and ancient buildings, from Pest, the commercial area. The national dish, goulash (gulyas), in its many forms can be enjoyed in many restaurants, accompanied by the enchanting gypsy music. Fogash, a wonderful white fish from Lake Balaton, central Europe's largest lake, was the focal point of one of my favorite meals at Matyas Pince, a cellar restaurant renowned for its gypsy music.

The full-bodied red wines make great companions to the food, especially Egri Bikaver from the area around Lake Balaton. The

Badacsony whites from the east are pleasantly dry, but Tokay, one of the world's greatest wines and from the Carpathian mountains, is a sweet wine, similar to Château d'Yquem of France, and made from overripe grapes, the "noble rot" of Hungary.

The place to enjoy the best wines and the ultimate in Hungarian cuisine is at Gundel's, reincarnated by George Lang, the renowned authority on Hungarian cooking. Karoly Gundel was Hungary's answer to Escoffier before World War II.

The pride of Hungary is its lavish pastries, tortes, and cakes, as in Austria, whom it rivals in this respect. The many layered Doboschtorte, with its unctuous chocolate buttercream filling and caramel glaze, is the epitome of a great dessert. This can be savored in numerous coffeehouses, which are an integral part of Hungarian social life, such as Café Hungaria, Vorosmarty (formerly Gerbeaud's), and Ruszwurm, Hungary's oldest, since 1500. I've tried them all.

The Balkans are my favorite places to visit in this part of the world, as there is a definite déjà vu feeling reminiscent of the Middle East in the people, architecture, and food. The area consists of the former Yugoslavia, Albania, Romania, and Bulgaria. The southern part of Macedonia, in northern Greece, is included.

Yugoslavia, formed in 1918 without regards to ethnicity, is now seven separate countries—Slovenia, Croatia, Serbia, Bosnia, Montenegro, Kosovo, and Macedonia. While I was traveling through them I noticed a distinct similarity in the food, but each has its own specialties. Slovenia has Italian and Austrian overtones with an emphasis on fish and potatoes. Croatia and Montenegro feel and taste like Italy, especially the wonderful prsut ham and an abundance of fruits and vegetables. Serbia specializes in hearty soups and stews with a strong Hungarian influence, while Bosnia, Kosovo, and Macedonia feel and taste like Turkey with their baklava, yogurt, and skewered grilled meats. They all share a passion for slivovitz (plum brandy), sweets, and Turkish coffee.

Albania, a wild mountainous country on the southern Adriatic, has a somewhat primitive cuisine, because it was virtually cut off from the world for many years while it endured the most severe form of despotism under Communist rule. What remains of the cuisine is mostly pasta, yogurt, and bread, with Turkish, Italian, and Greek influences. They do make red and white wines and have an interesting fish from Lake Ohrid called Koran, apropos for a Muslim country.

Romania and Bulgaria share a similar cuisine, which was mostly the legacy of 500 years of Turkish rule, but the Roman conquest left the Romanians with an important dish, mamaliga, almost identical to polenta, as well as its name and an Italianate personification. Also, there is a Russian influence because a large part of Moldavia was taken from Romania and made a part of the Soviet Union, and Ukraine is also a neighbor. Ciorba, a sour soup made in infinite ways, is striking in its resemblance to the Solyanka that appears in the Russian section.

Bulgaria, more rural with many peasants, has remained very Turkish in many ways and also has a strong Armenian and Greek influence. Yogurt, garlic, saffron, and walnuts are an integral part of the cooking, as well as small, pointed red peppers which are stuffed, breaded, and fried. They remind me of the Basque peppers in Spain, and the strong resemblance in the people make me wonder if possibly this is where the Basques originated.

Both countries share the wonderful sheep's milk cheeses, kaskaval and brinza, and a wonderful array of fruit including cherries, quinces, plums, grapes, figs, apricots, and chestnuts. To accompany these cheeses and fruits, there are an astonishing number of wines produced throughout most of both countries. They have Chardonnay, Cabernet, Pinot, Riesling, Muscat, and many others. The whites are the best, and the best vineyards in both countries are along the Black Sea coast and near the Danube delta in Romania.

RECIPES FROM EASTERN EUROPE

BANITSA (BULGARIAN FILO ROLLS)
QUINCE PRESERVES
LIPTOI (CZECHOSLOVAKIAN CHEESE SPREAD)
HERBED TOMATOES WITH FETA
WARM WALNUT GREEN BEAN SALAD
KRUPNIK POLSKI (POLISH BARLEY SOUP)
TYROLEAN BEEF SOUP
BOHEMIAN SAUERKRAUT AND SAUSAGE SOUP
SERBIAN BEAN SOUP
TIROLER FLEISCHSTRUDEL MIT SPECKSAUCE
(TYROLEAN MEAT STRUDEL WITH BACON SAUCE)
SHRIMP WITH RED RISOTTO AND DILL SAUCE
SUPRÊMES BADACSONYI
ROAST CHICKEN WITH OLIVES AND YOGURT SAUCE
BUTTER SCHNITZEL WITH SAUCE SMETANE
ALBANIAN LAMB WITH TOMATO AND EGGS
RAZNJICI (GRILLED SKEWERED MEAT, YUGOSLAVIAN STYLE)
POLISH KIELBASA WITH SAUERKRAUT
CZECH BOILED BEEF WITH ROOT VEGETABLES
AND SOUR CREAM SAUCE
SAUCE SMETANE
BULGARIAN EGGPLANT WITH MINTED YOGURT
POLISH SAUERKRAUT WITH WILD MUSHROOMS
CZECH NOODLES WITH POPPY SEED
BRAISED SWEET AND SOUR RED CABBAGE
HUNGARIAN POTATO STRUDEL
BALKAN SCRAMBLED EGGS
CZECH SCRAMBLED EGGS
SLATKO (YUGOSLAVIAN CHERRY PRESERVES)

LINZERTORTE

GLAZED APPLE TORTE

VANILLA CRESCENT COOKIES

ARANYGALUSKA (GOLDEN DUMPLING COFFEECAKE)

One of the best arrays of appetizers I've had was at a very humble home in a tiny village near Nessebur, Bulgaria, which was founded by the Greeks in 500 BC and is home to several dozen Byzantine churches.

A group of us from Swan Hellenic's Black Sea cruise were warmly welcomed and served the following Bulgarian specialties in the garden: cheese filo rolls, quince preserves, wonderful coarse country bread, kaskaval cheese, and a platter of marinated olives, roasted peppers, and cucumbers (I recommend a garlicky lemon vinaigrette to be served with these). Also served were a bowl of walnuts and local fruit, along with plenty of good local homemade wine.

BANITSA

(Bulgarian Filo Rolls)

These traditional filo pastries with a cheese filling are almost identical to the Tiropeta in Greece. In Bulgaria they are usually twisted into an S-shape.

½ pound Feta cheese or brynza	Finely chopped mint (optional)
¼ cup yogurt	16 half sheets of filo pastry
1 egg	½ cup melted butter

Blend cheese with yogurt and egg in a processor until smooth. Add mint. Brush a filo sheet with butter, add another sheet, and brush again. Pipe a strand of cheese mixture, using a pastry bag, along the long edge of the filo, and roll up. Brush again with butter, and repeat with remaining filo sheets, making a total of 8 pastries. Our hostess left them in a cigar shape, as they do in Turkey, but you may curve them into an S-shape. Bake at 400° about 15 to 20 minutes, and let cool before serving.

Makes 8 pastries.

QUINCE PRESERVES

These wonderful preserves, which I ended up eating with a spoon, are traditionally spread on country bread or eaten with brynza or kashkaval cheese. The quince, Which originated in the Caucasus, is one of Armenia's contributions to the Balkans. This is the way our Bulgarian hostess makes it.

6 ripe yellow quince, scrubbed, cored, and chopped into small pieces 2 cups water	2 to 3 cups sugar 1 tablespoon lemon juice 1 tablespoon orange blossom water

Place quince, water, and sugar in a large pan, bring to a boil, and simmer until thickened. Flavor with juice and flower water, if desired.

Makes 1 quart.

LIPTOI

(Czechoslovakian Cheese Spread)

This is the zesty cheese spread that I savored at Ü Fleku in Prague along with the wonderful sausages and beer. It is very similar to Hungary's Liptauer, and is made in infinite ways.

4 ounces feta cheese 2 ounces cream cheese ¼ cup butter 1 teaspoon Dijon or other mustard 1 teaspoon paprika 2 tablespoons beer	½ teaspoon caraway seeds, crushed 2 tablespoons minced scallions or chives Garnishes: pickles, radishes, and rye bread

Blend cheeses with butter in a mixer or processor until smooth. Beat in seasonings and beer until light and fluffy. Garnish as desired.

Serves 6 to 8.

Salads are not a major part of Polish, Czech, Austrian, or Hungarian cooking except for the ubiquitous cucumber salad, which is also popular in the Balkans. They are all quite similar to the Swedish version in the Scandinavian section. The Balkans also have a number of marinated vegetable salads that make use of their excellent tomatoes, beans, peppers, carrots, and eggplants. Topped with feta and walnuts, they are also good appetizers.

HERBED TOMATOES WITH FETA

A new way to present an old classic from the Balkans.

½ pound feta, cut into cubes	Butter lettuce leaves
1 teaspoon dried oregano	3 cups halved cherry tomatoes
½ cup diced red onion	1/3 cup chopped mint & parsley
¼ cup olive oil	Black or Kalamata olives

Mix feta with oregano, onion, and oil, let stand about 2 hours. Line a platter with lettuce, top with tomatoes, and spoon feta mixture over them. Sprinkle with herbs, and place olives around base of salad. Serve with crusty bread.

Serves 4-6.

WARM WALNUT GREEN BEAN SALAD

This is an excellent way to feature Bulgaria's beans and walnuts.

½ cup walnut halves	Leaf lettuce
1 small red onion, thinly sliced	2 tablespoons each lemon juice & red wine vinegar
1 small red bell pepper, roasted (see index)	1 teaspoon Dijon mustard
½ cup olive oil	Salt & pepper
½ pound young green beans	

Marinate walnuts, onion, and pepper in oil about an hour. Meanwhile, boil beans in plenty of salted water until barely tender. Drain, refresh under cold water, and drain well. Arrange lettuce on platter. Drain marinade from walnut mixture, heat in a skillet, and toss beans in the oil until warm, and arrange on lettuce. Whisk remaining ingredients into oil, pour over beans, and sprinkle walnut mixture over all.

Serves 6.

Hot robust soups are found throughout the east European countries and are especially welcome during the bitter cold winters. All varieties of meat, vegetables, and grains are used in infinite combinations.

KRUPNIK POLSKI

(Polish Barley Soup)

Polish barley soup is so good I have even found it in Jerusalem, but the best was probably at Warsaw's Bristol Hotel, which was the only building not bombed during the war, because it was Nazi headquarters. The hotel has been completely restored to its former elegance.

½ cup pearl barley	1 medium potato, peeled & diced
1 ½ quarts chicken or veal stock	1 cup heavy cream
½ cup each finely chopped carrot, celery, and leeks	Salt & pepper
	Chopped dill & parsley
2 tablespoons butter	

Simmer barley in stock, covered, until tender, about 1 hour. Meanwhile, sauté vegetables in butter until almost tender. Add to barley with potatoes and continue simmering, uncovered, until soup is done. Gradually add cream, season, and garnish with herbs.

Serves 6.

TYROLEAN BEEF SOUP

This Austrian soup from the mountains near the Italian border is very similar to Goulash soup in Hungary, except that this one is thickened with flour.

4 medium onions, chopped	1 tablespoon tomato paste
¼ cup butter, lard, or oil	2 tablespoons flour
1 ½ pounds beef chuck or shoulder, cubed	2 quarts beef stock
1 tablespoon paprika	1 pound potatoes, peeled & diced
2 garlic cloves, crushed	Salt & pepper
	Spaetzle (see Index, optional)

Sauté onions in fat until translucent. Add beef and paprika, stirring until beef is lightly browned. Add garlic and tomato paste, blend well, and add stock. Cover, and simmer at least an hour, or until beef is tender. Add potatoes, and simmer until tender. Season to taste. Add spaetzle, if desired.

Serves 6 -8.

BOHEMIAN SAUERKRAUT AND SAUSAGE SOUP

This is an easy version of a Czech classic that my mother made during the winter. Short ribs of beef were roasted with aromatic vegetables at high heat until browned, then deglazed as the base for the soup. If you have leftover roast beef, this is the place for it, otherwise sausage is fine.

½ pound Kielbasa or other sausage, sliced	6 cups beef stock
1 cup chopped onion	1 bay leaf
2 garlic cloves, crushed	2 tablespoons sugar
2 tablespoons bacon fat or lard	2 tablespoons lemon juice
1 pound sauerkraut, in a cryovac bag, rinsed & squeezed dry	Salt & pepper
	2 cups diced roast beef (optional)
1 16-ounce can tomatoes, undrained	

Sauté sausage, onion, and garlic in fat until lightly browned, add kraut, and cook about 5 minutes. Add tomatoes, stock, and bay leaf. Cover, simmer about 1 ½ hours, then add remaining ingredients, and simmer another ½ hour. Serve with lots of sour cream.

Serves 6.

SERBIAN BEAN SOUP

During a three-day flight delay from Belgrade to Ohrid, Macedonia, during the Yugoslavian civil war, I had the great fortune to have a virtual education in Yugoslav cooking. A dear, sweet lady who answered my room service calls was so flattered that I requested Yugoslav dishes, she made sure that I would have all the best along with cooking instructions. And this was at the Hyatt! There are many variations, she explained, such as the use of ham or pork, borlotti beans, sauerkraut, potatoes, or tomatoes. This simple version is my favorite.

1 cup chopped onions	1 teaspoon dried marjoram
2 large garlic cloves, crushed	1/3 cup tomato purée
2 tablespoons lard or olive oil	1 pound dried white beans, soaked overnight
1 pound smoked sausage, sliced	4-6 cups rich chicken stock
1 tablespoon Hungarian paprika	Salt & pepper & red wine vinegar
1 bay leaf	

Sauté onions and garlic in fat until translucent, add sausage and seasonings, and sauté about 5 minutes. Add purée, beans, and enough stock to cover beans. Simmer, covered, about 1 ½ hours, adding more stock if necessary. When tender, the beans should form a very thick soup. If not thick enough, mash beans against side of pan. Season well, and pass red wine vinegar at the table. Serves 6.

TIROLER FLEISCHSTRUDEL MIT SPECKSAUCE

(Tyrolean Meat Strudels with Bacon Sauce)

When I travel, normally I know in advance where I'll eat every meal, if not what it will be, but the cold and rainy night that I took the train from Venice to Innsbruck through harrowing mountain passes, I didn't even know where I would stay for the night. As I came out of the station I saw the Hotel Europa across the street, and for dinner I had the best pasta dish ever and savored every bite with a bold Austrian red.

½ pound ground beef	1 teaspoon salt
½ pound ground pork	2 tablespoons flour
2 tablespoons lard or oil	1 cup beef stock
¾ cup chopped onion	1 egg, beaten
1 tablespoon paprika	1 recipe Pasta Dough, rolled, cut into 6 equal lengths, & cooked (see Index)
1 tablespoon chopped parsley	

Sauté meats in fat until golden, add onion, and sauté until tender. Add seasonings and flour, stir until blended, and add stock. Simmer until thickened, remove from heat, and beat in egg. Spread pasta sheets thickly with filling, roll, cut in half, place in a shallow baking dish, and cover with Specksauce. Bake at 350° about 10 minutes, or until hot.

Specksauce:

2 slices bacon	1 bay leaf
2 tablespoons minced onion	1 tablespoon white vinegar
1 ½ tablespoons flour	½ teaspoon sugar
1 cup beef stock	Salt & pepper

Sauté bacon until done, remove from pan and crumble. Sauté onion until tender, blend in flour, add stock, whisk until smooth, and add bay leaf. Simmer about 5 minutes, and add remaining ingredients and crumbled bacon.

Serves 4-6.

Main courses in Eastern Europe are primarily robust and heavy in keeping with long cold winters, and include veal, pork, lamb, and beef. Wild game is very popular, especially in the northern countries, and chicken is the bird of choice in the South. Surprisingly, fish is not a common dish except for herring in the North.

SHRIMP WITH RED RISOTTO AND DILL SAUCE

I have had great meals at the Imperial, Bristol, and Sacher hotels, but my best meal was at Hotel Im Palais Schwarzenburg, located in a Baroque eighteenth century palace in its own large park. While rich, this is an example of the new and lighter cooking in Vienna, with an Italianate touch.

¼ cup each julienned carrots, celery and shallots, steamed until tender	1 cup heavy cream
	1 cup shrimp or fish stock
1 ½ pounds shrimp, peeled	3 egg yolks
¼ cup butter	¼ cup chopped fresh dill
¼ cup Riesling wine	Salt & pepper
	Risotto Rosso (see Index)

Sauté shrimp in butter until done, and remove from skillet. Add wine and deglaze. Add cream and stock, reducing to 1 ½ cups. Whisk yolks with some of the hot cream mixture, then whisk into skillet to cook until lightly thickened, and add most of the dill, season to taste. Unmold a small cup of rice in center of each plate. (Small custard cups or ice cream scoops work well.) Arrange shrimp and vegetables around rice, drizzle with sauce, and sprinkle all with remaining dill. A very colorful and beautiful presentation!

Serves 4 to 6.

SUPRÊMES BADASONYI

This Hungarian specialty made with the delicious young Badacsonyi wine from Lake Balaton, where there are wonderful restaurants, is given a lighter remake here while retaining its outstanding flavor.

3 slices bacon, diced	1 teaspoon fresh thyme
¼ cup butter	4 suprêmes
¼ pound wild mushrooms, sliced	¼ cup brandy, preferably plum
4 medium shallots, thinly sliced	¾ cup Badacsonyi or other young wine
1 bay leaf	Salt & pepper, to taste

Sauté bacon until almost done, add butter, mushrooms, and shallots, cooking until transparent. Add herbs, chicken, and brandy. Cover, and simmer lightly about 5 minutes to imbue the chicken with the flavor of the brandy. Add wine and simmer uncovered, until wine has reduced and thickened slightly, removing chicken when tender. This is wonderful with Puliszka, the polenta of Hungary.

Serves 6.

ROAST CHICKEN WITH OLIVES AND YOGURT SAUCE

When I arrived in Bucharest I went straight to La Doi Cocosi (the two cocks) from the airport. This old country restaurant is renowned for its chicken, but I especially remember when I was presented with a beautifully wrapped gift. It was a ceramic cock, which I still display in my kitchen, even though the check included a steep charge for my gift! My rendition of their roast chicken is enhanced with Kalamata olives and roasted bell peppers.

3-pound whole chicken	¼ cup white wine
Salt & pepper	1 cup chicken stock
½ cup Kalamata olives, pitted	½ cup olives, pitted
1 lemon, halved	1 tablespoon each chopped mint & parsley
4 garlic cloves, crushed	
1 each red, yellow, & orange bell peppers, roasted (see Index)	1 tablespoon chopped marjoram
	½ cup yogurt
½ -1 teaspoon saffron, crushed	

Season chicken, place in a small roasting pan, and fill cavity with olives, lemon, and garlic. Roast at 350° about 1 ½ hours or until done. When done, remove chicken, and degrease juices remaining in pan. Add wine and stock, deglazing, and reduce until lightly thickened and glazed. Add olives, seasonings, and yogurt, whisking until smooth. Season, and serve with the chicken, cut into sections and topped with the peppers. This is perfect with Mamaliga, the Polenta of Romania.

Serves 4 to 6.

BUTTER SCHNITZEL WITH SAUCE SMETANE

Very similar to the Cotleti Pojarski, made with chicken, in my first book, this is a rich but lighter rendition of the classic breaded Wiener Schnitzel fried in copious amounts of lard. I discovered this at Villa Bled in Bled, Slovenia, a short train ride from Vienna. Formerly part of Austria and the site of a Habsburg palace before being demolished by the Germans, Villa Bled was built for President Tito in 1947 as a place for entertaining heads of state; thus, 13 acres of trees and shrubbery were not trimmed for their protection. Now a small elegant hotel, on the shores of enchanting Lake Bled, the Kitchen is noted for its Yugoslav specialties with a strong Austrian and Italian influence.

½ cup chopped onion	4 slices white bread, crusts removed
2 tablespoons butter	1/3 cup cream
1 egg, beaten	1 cup sliced wild mushrooms
1-2 teaspoons paprika	¼ - ½ cup butter
Salt & pepper	Sauce Smetane (see Index)
1 pound ground veal	

Sauté onion in butter until translucent, and add to egg with seasonings and veal. Soak bread with cream, then work into meat mixture until smooth. Form into 4 oval patties, and sauté with mushrooms in butter, using a large sauté pan. Serve with Sauce Smetane.

Serves 4.

ALBANIAN LAMB WITH TOMATO AND EGGS

I arrived in Ohrid, Macedonia, after midnight. After clearing immigration, I was warned not to take a taxi driven by an Albanian, such is discrimination around the world. So my very helpful Albanian driver took me to Struga and not only woke up the Macedonian border guards, but also waited to be sure I made it to the other side with no problems; I had to wake up the Albanians also. During my very brief visit I learned about this wonderful and easy dish.

1 pound ground lamb	¼ cup red wine
½ cup chopped onion	1 teaspoon dried oregano
2 garlic cloves, crushed	Salt & pepper
1 cup chopped tomatoes	4 fried or poached eggs
½ cup tomato purée or catsup	Chopped dill & mint

Sauté lamb until browned and crusty, adding onions and garlic briefly. Add tomatoes, purée, and wine, simmering until thickened and your kitchen is redolent with Albanian aromatherapy. Top with eggs, sprinkle with herbs, and pour plenty of good strong red wine.

Serves 4.

RAZNJICI

(Grilled Skewered Meat, Yugoslavian Style)

Grilled meats are the essence of Yugoslav cooking, and I gave you Cevapcici (skewered meat) and Pljeskavica (grilled meat patties) in my previous book. Raznjici are grilled skewered cubes of veal or pork. I enjoyed this version at Dubrovnik's Excelsior Hotel, perched on the edge of the Adriatic and with a great view of the old city. Its restaurant, the Taverna, was rustic, with a fireplace and musicians.

¾ pound each veal & pork, cut into 1 ½ inch cubes, or all veal or pork	2 large garlic cloves, smashed
	½ teaspoon paprika
¼ cup olive oil	½ teaspoon oregano
¼ cup wine vinegar or lemon juice	Salt & pepper
	1 dozen bay leaves, broken in half
1 small onion, thinly sliced	

Marinate meats in oil mixed with vinegar, onion, garlic, and seasonings about 4 hours or overnight, refrigerated. Thread onto skewers with bay leaves, and grill over charcoal, turning until done, and basting, if desired.

Serves 4-6.

POLISH KIELBASA WITH SAUERKRAUT

This delightfully simple dish is probably the most typical of all. I enjoyed it with rye bread at Kameralna, reasonable and popular with the locals.

1 pound sauerkraut, in a cryovac bag, drained & rinsed	1 onion, chopped
6 bacon slices, chopped	1 ½ pounds kielbasa, cooked & sliced

Sauté bacon until half done, add onion, and cook until translucent. Add kraut and kielbasa and cook until browned.

Serves 4 to 6.

CZECH BOILED BEEF WITH ROOT VEGETABLES AND SOUR CREAM SAUCE

The national dish of Czech Republic is simple to make and has a pure, honest savoriness. It is a dish of the people especially to enjoy at home or at Koruna, a simple Prague restaurant where we stood at a counter to eat it.

2 pounds beef brisket	2 bay leaves
3-4 cups beef stock, beer, or water	Parsley stems, tied into a bundle
	2 tablespoons red wine vinegar
2 medium red onions, peeled	1 cup sour cream
4 parsnips, peeled	1 tablespoon flour
4 carrots, peeled	1 tablespoon horseradish (optional)
4 small potatoes, peeled	
Salt & pepper	1 cup reserved stock

Cover brisket with choice of liquid in a large Dutch oven, add vegetables and seasonings, and bring to a simmer. Skim foam from top, cover, and let cook about 2 ½ hours, or until tender, removing as they become tender. Blend sour cream with flour and horseradish in a saucepan, and whisk in reserved stock, bringing it to a boil. Simmer until thickened, and serve over sliced brisket with vegetables on the side.

Serves 4-6.

SAUCE SMETANE

This simple and versatile sauce is good with many of these main courses and any simply cooked chicken or meat dish.

1 ½ tablespoon minced shallots	1/3 cup white wine
2 tablespoons butter	1 cup sour cream
	Chopped dill, mint, or parsley

Sauté shallots in butter until soft, add wine, and reduce briefly. Whisk in sour cream, and bring to a boil. Add herbs, to taste.

Makes 1 ½ cups

BULGARIAN EGGPLANT WITH MINTED YOGURT

The Balkans are fortunate to have a much wider variety of vegetables than the others in this part of the world.

1 pound eggplant, peeled & sliced	1 garlic clove, crushed
1/3 cup olive oil	½ tablespoon dried mint, crushed
1 cup yogurt	Salt, to taste

Sauté eggplant in oil until tender and golden brown on each side. Cut into large cubes when cool and mix with yogurt and seasonings. Serve cold.

Serves 4.

POLISH SAUERKRAUT WITH WILD MUSHROOMS

This unique kraut dish is not fried, and the browned flour adds an earthy flavor which complements the mushrooms.

1 pound fresh sauerkraut, rinsed	2 bay leaves
1 cup chicken stock	2 tablespoons flour
4 ounces dried mushrooms	1/3 cup sour cream

Simmer kraut with stock, mushrooms, and bay leaves about ½ hour. Heat and stir flour in a skillet over medium heat until it is beige in color. Whisk in sour cream, add to kraut, and simmer about 20 minutes. Serve hot.

Serves 4-6.

CZECH NOODLES WITH POPPY SEED

Poppy seeds are used extensively in savory and sweet dishes, especially in Poland, Czechoslovakia, and Hungary. This is the way I remember my mother making it, and it is a great accompaniment for most of the main courses.

½ pound wide egg noodles	2 tablespoons butter
¼ cup milk or cream	1 tablespoon turbinado sugar
¼ cup poppyseeds	¼ cup raisins or sultanas
2 tablespoons honey, preferably chestnut	Salt & pepper, to taste

Cook and drain noodles well. Mix remaining ingredients, bring to a boil, and add to noodles.

Serves 4.

BRAISED SWEET AND SOUR RED CABBAGE

This is a wonderful companion dish for the Czech noodles, and with rye bread, it would be a typical dinner in Poland, Czechoslovakia, and Austria.

1 large onion, thickly sliced	½ teaspoon ground cardamom
2 red apples, thickly sliced	1 bay leaf
2 tablespoons duck or bacon fat	1/3 cup red wine vinegar
1 large garlic clove, crushed	¾ cup red wine
1 pound red cabbage, thinly sliced	1/3 cup dark brown sugar

Sauté onion and apples in fat, using a large sauté pan, until soft. Add cabbage and garlic, and sauté until well blended. Add the rest and simmer, covered, at least an hour. Boil uncovered until juices thicken.

Serves 4-6.

HUNGARIAN POTATO STRUDEL

Potatoes, the ubiquitous vegetable in Eastern Europe, are truly a comfort food when they become a strudel. Diced ham or sausage may be added.

1 pound Yukon potatoes, cooked & peeled	½ tablespoon chopped dill
4 slices bacon, diced	½ tablespoon chopped marjoram
1 cup diced red onion	Salt & pepper
1 tablespoon chopped parsley	12 half-sheets of filo pastry
1 tablespoon chopped chives	Melted butter

Mash potatoes, leaving them slightly lumpy. Sauté bacon until half done, add onion, and sauté until translucent. Add to potatoes with herbs and seasonings. Brush 1 filo sheet with butter, top with another sheet, and brush with butter. Spoon about 1/3 cup of potatoes over narrow end of pastry, turn in sides, roll up, brush with butter, and place seam-side down on baking sheet. Repeat with remaining filo sheets, filling, and butter. Bake at 375° about 20 minutes, until golden. Slice into thick rounds.

Serves 6.

Scrambled eggs are frequently eaten as a main course in humble homes in eastern Europe or as an accompaniment to left-over roast chicken or grilled meats. There is usually a vegetable or meat (such as sausage or ham) sautéed in the skillet before adding the eggs. My mother was known to add a small amount of leftover poppyseed noodles to the eggs.

BALKAN SCRAMBLED EGGS

Tomatoes, peppers, eggplants, herbs, spicy ground meats, and Brynza cheese are frequently added to eggs in Bulgaria and Romania and may be made into an omelet instead of scrambling the eggs. I always save a bit to garnish the top.

½ cup Roasted Bell Peppers (see Index) cut into strips 2 tablespoons butter or olive oil	4 large eggs, whisked ¼ cup crumbled feta or brynza cheese Salt & pepper

Sauté peppers in oil briefly, using a large iron skillet. Add eggs and cheese, lifting edges to let uncooked part of egg to run underneath, using medium heat. Gradually lift edges onto top to produce lightly cooked eggs.

Serves 2-4.

CZECH SCRAMBLED EGGS

In Poland, Czech Republic, Austria, and Hungary, you are likely to find heavier fillings such as leftover spaetzle or dumplings, Polish sausage, potatoes, and even sauerkraut.

¼ cup diced bacon, ham, or sausage	¼ cup cottage cheese or sour cream
1 cup diced rye bread	Salt & pepper
2-3 tablespoons butter, if needed	Paprika, chopped dill & chives
4 eggs, whisked	

Sauté your choice of meat until fat is rendered, using a large skillet. Add bread, and butter if more fat is needed, and sauté until bread is crisp. Remove a few tablespoons of bread and meat for topping the eggs. Whisk eggs with cheese or cream, and add to skillet, lifting edges to let uncooked part of eggs run underneath, using medium heat. Gradually lift edges onto top to produce lightly cooked creamy eggs. Season, top with reserved meat and bread, and sprinkle with paprika and herbs.

Serves 2-4.

East European desserts are legendary, especially those of Austria and Hungary, and the infinite variety includes crêpes, soufflés, filo, strudel, tarts, cakes, tortes, cookies, meringues, and many extravaganzas. Sacher Torte and Dobosch Torte were in my Culinary Classics, and now it's time for other favorites.

SLATKO

(Yugoslavian Cherry Preserves)

For some reason, the cherry and plum preserves taste better in Serbia and Croatia, and although good enough as a dessert on its own, it is an integral part of many of my desserts. Wrap the fruit pits in cheesecloth to cook with the fruit and it will add flavor as well as thickening.

2 pounds cherries or black plums, pitted, pits tied in cheesecloth 3 cups sugar	½ cup water or fruit juice 1-2 tablespoons lemon juice

Place fruit, sugar, and water in a large saucepan, stir well over medium heat, bring to a boil when sugar dissolves, and cook briskly until juices thicken, about ½ hour. Add lemon juice, cool, and freeze, if desired.

Makes about 4 cups.

VANILLA CRESCENT COOKIES

Cookies are not among my favorites, except for these, which are mandatory at Christmas, and they are known as kipferln in Czech Republic.

½ pound butter	1 ½ teaspoons vanilla
½ cup powdered sugar	1 cup finely chopped hazelnuts, almonds, walnuts or pistachios
2 cups flour	Powdered sugar, for sifting

Cream butter with sugar until fluffy, gradually adding flour, vanilla, and nuts. Blend well, chill briefly, and form into several dozen crescent shapes. Bake at 350° about 20 minutes, until still bisque-colored. Transfer to cake racks, and sift powdered sugar over them. Store in tins several weeks.

Makes about 3 dozen.

ARANYGALUSKA

(Golden Dumpling Coffeecake)

This delicious coffeecake contains lots of butter, brown sugar, nuts, golden raisins, and preserves. In Hungary, it is eaten in coffeehouses with coffee at any time of day or night, rather than for breakfast or dessert.

2 packages dry yeast	½ cup melted butter
1 tablespoon sugar	1 cup walnuts or hazelnuts, finely chopped
½ cup warm milk	
½ cup soft butter	½ cup each brown sugar & white sugar
½ cup sugar	
1 teaspoon salt	1 teaspoon ground cardamom
4 egg yolks	1 tablespoon grated lemon zest
½ cup hot milk	½ cup golden raisins
4-5 cups unbleached flour	½ cup cherry or apricot preserves

Proof yeast by mixing with sugar and warm milk, letting it stand until bubbly. Cream butter with sugar until fluffy, add salt, yolks, and yeast mixture, beating until blended. Beat in ½ cup flour and hot milk, then gradually beat in remaining flour until smooth and elastic. Cover, let rise until doubled, about 1 hour. Punch down, let rise again until doubled. Form dough into 1-inch balls, dip in melted butter, then roll them in mixed nuts, sugars, and cardamom. Place half of them in a single layer in a buttered 10-inch springform pan. Sprinkle with raisins and preserves, add remaining balls of dough, and sprinkle with any remaining nut mixture and butter. Cover, let rise about 45 minutes, and bake at 350° about 45 minutes. Remove sides of pan, let cool slightly, pull apart, and serve with coffee.

Serves 8-12

LINZERTORTE

This is my version of an old Austrian classic, which traditionally has a raspberry filling. I prefer a very rich chocolate nut pastry with a cherry filling (another use for Slatko, the Yugoslav cherry preserves), but also try quince, fig, or apricot with your choice of pastry. The tart is from Linz, also known for its warm flannel nightgowns.

1 ½ cups unbleached flour or 1 cup flour & ½ cup cocoa powder	¼ teaspoon nutmeg
	10 tablespoons cold butter, cut up
¾ cup almonds, hazelnuts, or pistachios, finely chopped	2 egg yolks
½ cup sugar	1 tablespoon vanilla
1 teaspoon ground cardamom	1 ½ cups cherry preserves
	Powdered sugar, for sifting

Mix all dry ingredients in electric mixer bowl, add butter, and mix only until crumbly. Add yolks and vanilla, beating briefly. Press ¾ of the dough on the bottom and sides of a 4- x 13-inch fluted pan with a removable bottom. Fill with preserves, and chill. Roll out remaining pastry, cut into strips, and form a lattice design on top of torte. Bake at 350° about 45 minutes, or until pastry is golden. Sift top with powdered sugar, and remove from pan. When cool, cut diagonal strips.

Serves 6-8.

GLAZED APPLE TORTE

All-American apple pie has never held much appeal for me. Give me the famous and fabulous Hungarian apple torte any day! Four rich and flaky pastry layers sandwich a thick apple glaze, and the top is spread with lemon icing.

Pastry:

1 ¾ cups unbleached flour	½ cup ground almonds or walnuts
½ pound cold butter, cut up	¾ cup powdered sugar

Blend all together in a processor only until crumbly. Chill, divide into 4 portions, and roll between sheets of wax paper placed over 8-inch square pans or 9-inch round pans. Remove paper, invert onto baking sheets, and bake at 375° about 15 minutes or until golden.

Glazed Apples:

1 ½ cups sugar	½ cup sliced almonds or walnuts
¾ cup apple or orange juice	1 tablespoon grated lemon zest
2 pounds apples, peeled & thinly sliced	2 tablespoons lemon zest

Bring sugar and juice to a boil, add the rest, and cook until thickened and transparent. Cool, then spread on all pastry layers, stacking them.

Lemon Icing:

1 cup powdered sugar	1 tablespoon warm water
2 tablespoons lemon juice	

Whisk together until smooth and shiny. Cover top of torte with glaze, letting it run down the sides. Chill well.

Serves 6.

Greece, Cyprus, Turkey & the Caucasus

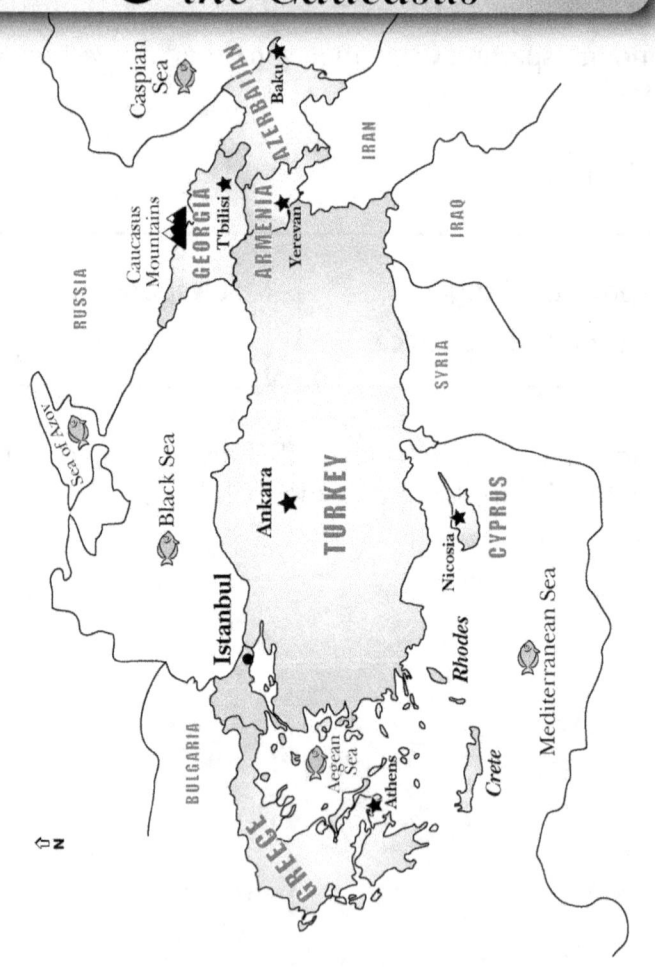

GREECE CYPRUS TURKEY
ARMENIA GEORGIA AZERBAIJAN

The charismatic, warm, hospitable, and sometimes fiery traits of these people are reflected in their cooking, which was influenced by numerous empires and invaders, from Russia to Persia. Borders changed, people migrated, and they now claim many of the same dishes. This fascinating and historical area which stretches from the Mediterranean to the Black Sea and the Caspian Sea is one which I will never tire of exploring.

Greece, land of Homer, Socrates, and Alexander the Great (who spread his control to Asia Minor, Egypt, Persia, and India), has a cuisine with vast influences and has had an impact on other cuisines as well, such as the Balkans'. Situated on the end of the Balkan Peninsula, Greece is divided by the Corinth Canal, a great marvel of engineering, and the presence of more than 2,000 islands in the Ionian and Aegean Seas. Corfu, the sea gateway to Albania, has Italian, French, and English culinary influences, while Crete and Rhodes have an Arab influence. Fish and spices prevail in the islands, while Mykonos and Santorini also add seaside tavernas with bouzouki music and plate smashing.

The cooking is rather simple and is based on olive oil, olives, feta, filo, eggplant, lamb, and superb Greek lemons and oranges, which flavor many of the dishes. The mountains have a cold climate and a more robust cooking style with potatoes and meat. Oregano and honey are the national flavorings.

Retsina and ouzo are the drinks to have with the mezze, a vast array of appetizers, which is an influence from the Levant. Red and white wines are made throughout the country and on the islands, but are not remarkable. The crowning glory, however, is the superb Metaxa brandy.

The island of Cyprus in the eastern Mediterranean, only about sixty miles from Syria, has been divided since 1974 into the Turkish north side and the Greek southern side. Long before that, it had been invaded by Egypt, Persia, Macedonia, Rome, Byzantines, Arabs, Venetians, Turks, Greeks, and the British, who occupied it until 1910, when it became a Greek colony. Of course, this makes for an interesting cuisine with major overtones of Greek, Turkish, Lebanese, and Syrian.

Stews of lamb and pork seasoned with cumin and coriander are popular, as are dolmas, beans, greens, and the mezze specialties from the East—hummus, kibbeh, and tabbouleh. The dark red wines, grown in the Troodos Mountains, are perfect with the zesty food, which is similar on both sides of the green line. The Greek side is quite international with its resort cities of Larnaca, Limassol, and Paphos, and it has excellent cafés and restaurants.

But it is the Turkish side which enchanted me, as it has not been spoiled by tourism and it is safe and friendly. My first attempt to visit was foiled by immigration upon arrival in Larnaca, on the Greek side, when I was asked where I would be staying and my reply was in Kyrenia, a town on the Turkish side. A bell rang and I was whisked away to an interrogation office. I was detained overnight, but I made it to Istanbul the following day for my flight to Alma Ata, Kazahkstan. Such is the plight of a recipe and country collector.

Never to be thwarted, I eventually flew from Istanbul to Ercan airport near Kyrenia. I arrived around midnight without a hotel reservation, and the helpful taxi driver recommended the Jasmine Court, where I had a four-room suite overlooking the sea. The town has numerous atmospheric cafés on the waterfront with great inexpensive food and outdoor dining. I found it was easy to take a bus in any direction, and everyone had great advice on where and what to eat. Did I mention that my suite was $80.00 a day?

Istanbul is the world's only city that straddles two continents, Europe and Asia, separated by the Bosphorus, which has the longest suspension bridges in Europe. They lead to Scutari on the Asian side of Turkey. Surrounded by the Mediterranean, Aegean, and Black Seas, Turkey has been invaded by Alexander the Great, as well as Mongols, Persians, Romans, and Greeks, all of whom left their mark on the people and the cuisine, not to mention the great architecture of the Byzantine and Ottoman Empires.

China, central Asia, and the Mediterranean have played the most important role in the formation of the cuisine, and the exchange was mutual, with Turkish cooking having a great influence on the entire region. Similar to Greek cooking, the Turks also have excellent lamb, rice pilafs, vegetables, and rich pastries made with filo. This is the home of Turkish coffee, always served in places of business, and the heavy sediment in the bottom is used to tell one's fortune. Flat breads and yogurt are especially Turkish also, as are the liqueurs made from the wonderful apricots, figs, nuts, and cherries.

To experience the history, food, and scenery of the Black Sea coast, I took Swan Hellenic's educational Minerva voyage from Thessaloniki, Greece to the ancient Hellenistic sites in Greece, then on to the Dardanelles, Troy, Gallipoli, and Bursa, by the Sea of Marmara, where I bought a supply of genuine saffron for a nominal amount. At Sinop, a former Greek shipping settlement, I was not surprised to find Borek, so similar to Greek Tiropeta, in a remote mountainous area filled with dense forests. Port calls are also made in Trabzon; at Batumi, Georgia; and Sochi, Russia; site of the highest tea plantations in Europe, where I bought wonderful chestnut honey that I am now addicted to. A visit to a dacha and teahouse for local refreshments was followed by intriguing visits to Yalta and Sevastopol, Russia, with much emphasis on the Crimean war and Levadia Palace, site of the famous Yalta Conference in 1945. A visit to Stalin's dacha, Massandra Palace, is a chance to sample the famous wine of the same name. The highlight of the north coast is a visit to the grand old city of Odessa, designed by the Duke of Richelieu from France. The 192 Potemkin steps lead from the port up to the tree-shaded promenade, where the old-world Londonskaya Hotel provided me with a traditional Ukrainian meal in their beautifully maintained dining room with an aura of bygone days. Afterwards, I attended a performance at the magnificent Odessa Opera House, designed in Louis XIV style, and where Pavlova, Caruso, and Bernhardt once performed. Ukrainian champagne was served at intermission. The remainder of the voyage made visits to the peaceful Danube Delta, where delicious local pastries were served on the boat, and to Nessebur, Bulgaria, which I included in the Balkan section. This is a voyage to repeat.

Georgia, at the eastern end of the Black Sea, is part of the rugged and sometimes violent Caucasus Mountain region, along with Armenia and Azerbaijan. The delicious cuisine was influenced by the invasions of Tamerlane, the Persians, and Russians, as well as its prime location on the silk and spice routes between Baghdad, Venice, and Constantinople.

There are definite Balkan and Mediterranean similarities, with extensive use of herbs and spices, especially mint, coriander, sumac, garlic, and marigold petals. The cooking also is highlighted with distinctive sauces containing butter, walnuts, and pomegranate syrup; and the fragrant warm Khachapuri cheese bread is the highlight of the meal for me.

Georgians have long been known as the bonne vivants of food and wine in the former Soviet republics, and the beautiful and hospitable people in Tbilisi take great pride in their food and wine. Tsinandali is a popular white, and Kindzmareuli was a favorite of Stalin. The champagne is excellent.

My visit to this captivating city of stone houses on hilly, winding streets with views of the mountains was far too short, but I had quite an interesting departure. After being seated on the flight to Odessa, I noticed that the flight attendants were throwing the cabin baggage out onto the tarmac, but it was only after a long delay that I discovered the reason—bribery. If the passengers did not pay, off went their belongings. Several hours later and after deplaning, we finally departed, not to Odessa but to Kiev. The silver lining in this escapade was the great Georgian food and wine that my seatmates shared with me and the abundant help I had in acquiring a visa and hotel after arriving in Kiev after midnight.

Armenia, one of the world's oldest Christian countries, has the same culinary influences as Turkey with its vegetables, herbs, flat breads, honey, yogurt, lamb, and dried fruits. I arrived in Yerevan on Armenia Airlines from Istanbul on an old Russian Tupelov and within five minutes I had acquired a visa for only $7.00. (The other passengers had paid almost $80.00 in their home countries.) Hotel Armenia, a stately old-world hotel, has a wonderful restaurant overlooking the majestic square with its exquisite architecture, and I learned much about the delicious food as well as the necessity of checking the prices charged. They seldom matched those on the menu!

Azerbaijan, like Armenia and Georgia, is part of the Caucasus, but here you know you are definitively in the Middle East, as you can detect it in the people, food, architecture, and even the smells. Like Armenia, Azerbaijan has been invaded by Romans, Persians, Arabs, Mongols, and Turks, but the main culinary influence is Turkish, Georgian, and Iranian. The main difference is the plate of neatly overlapping herbs on the table to nibble on while waiting for your meal, which is likely to be flavored with dill, mint, saffron, sumac, or quince paste. The best difference is the caviar, which is from the Caspian Sea, which borders the old city. I relished being able to eat my fill of this top-quality caviar for a mere pittance. The best place to enjoy this delicious delicacy is at your hotel and at the Caravanserai Restaurant in Baku's medieval walled old city. The sturgeon from which the caviar comes is quite popular here also. There is nothing more rewarding than strolling through the cities of the unspoiled Caucasus, and it was a powerful force in my predilection to travel to Iran.

RECIPES FROM GREECE, CYPRUS, TURKEY, AND THE CAUCASUS

CAUCASUS SALAD WITH YOGURT AND FETA

GEORGIAN BEAN SALAD WITH WALNUT SAUCE

POMEGRANATE DRESSING

POMEGRANATE MOLASSES

EGGPLANT ROLLS WITH WALNUT FILLING

SHRIMP PLAKI

ARMENIAN EGGS WITH LAMB

BASTURMA AND POTATOES WITH EGGS

GREEK FILO PIE WITH SAUSAGE AND POTATOES

YOGURT CHEESE

KHACHAPURI (GEORGIAN CHEESE BREAD)

GREEK OLIVE BREAD

AZERBAIJANI BOZBASH (LAMB AND FRUIT SOUP)

KHINKALI SOUP (GEORGIAN MEAT DUMPLINGS)

YOGURT SOUP WITH BARLEY

RED LENTIL AND BULGUR SOUP

GREEK SPAGHETTI WITH SHRIMP

BAKED FISH FILLETS WITH VEGETABLES

CIRCASSIAN CHICKEN

SATSIVI (GEORGIAN CHICKEN WITH WALNUT SAUCE)

ARMENIAN ROAST CHICKEN WITH POMEGRANATE GLAZE

ARMENIAN LYULA KEBABS

GREEK SOUVLAKIA

TURKISH SHISH KEBABS
(KOFTA KEBABS WITH TOMATOES AND YOGURT)

GREEK LAMB STEW WITH TOMATOES AND FETA

AFELIA (CYPRIOT BRAISED PORK WITH CORIANDER)

YOGURT-GARLIC SAUCE

SKORDALIA (GREEK POTATO-OLIVE OIL SAUCE WITH GARLIC AND LEMON)

AZERBAIJANI PILAF

EGGPLANT CREAM WITH LEMON AND CHEESE

TURKISH STUFFED VEGETABLES

BAKLAVA WITH CRYSTALLIZED FRUIT AND HONEY SYRUP

TURKISH YOGURT CAKE WITH MINTED ORANGES AND STRAWBERRIES

Appetizers in this part of the world are usually a salad composed of raw or cooked vegetables in any combination, or simple egg dishes, or the ubiquitous Middle Eastern mezze, which can be as many as several dozen simple cold dishes. Filo pastries, such as Tiropeta and Borek, are popular also.

CAUCASUS SALAD WITH YOGURT AND FETA

From Corfu to Baku, I always had a salad in a myriad of presentations, but this is the way I have created my own, with deference to each country.

6 ripe Roma tomatoes, sliced	Salt & pepper
1 English cucumber, scored & sliced	1 cup yogurt
	1 garlic clove, crushed
¼ cup chopped fresh mint	Salt, to taste
2 tablespoons lemon juice	¼ pound feta cheese, crumbled
1 garlic clove, crushed	Kalamata olives
¼ cup olive oil	

Arrange alternate rows of overlapping tomatoes and cucumbers on a platter, and sprinkle with mint. Make a vinaigrette with juice, garlic, oil, and seasonings. Drizzle over ingredients. Mix yogurt with garlic crushed with salt, and dollop over salad, saving some for the table. Sprinkle with feta and olives, and more mint if desired. Eat with lots of crusty country bread or Flat bread.

Serves 4 to 6.

GEORGIAN BEAN SALAD WITH WALNUT SAUCE

Beans, or lobio, of all kinds are very much a part of the Georgian cooking, as are walnuts, which make a delightful dressing that can be used on many salads-even a simple lettuce salad.

½ pound small red beans, soaked overnight and cooked	¼ teaspoon paprika
	¼ teaspoon ground saffron or marigold
¾ pound small grean beans, cooked & refreshed under cold water	
	½ teaspoon salt
	Pinch of sugar
1/3 cup chopped fresh herbs, such as basil, coriander, & mint	1 garlic clove, crushed
	½ cup walnut or olive oil
¼ cup rice vinegar	½ cup finely chopped walnuts
½ teaspoon ground coriander	2 cups chiffonade of Romaine

Mix beans with herbs. Mix vinegar with seasonings in food processor, and gradually add oil until emulsified. Walnuts may be ground with the dressing or simply added when dressing is ready to pour over salad. Place beans on romaine, pour dressing over, and taste for seasoning.

Serves 4 to 6.

POMEGRANATE DRESSING

Pomegranates are essential to Georgian cooking, and this dressing is ideal on most salads and with grilled meats. The juice itself is used in many soups and stews, and the seeds are used as a garnish.

2 tablespoons pomegranate molasses (see below) 2 tablespoons lemon juice	2 garlic cloves, crushed 1 teaspoon salt 1/3 cup olive oil

Whisk ingredients together, adding oil slowly, until emulsified. Makes about 1 cup.

POMEGRANATE MOLASSES

This is one of those staples I keep in the freezer along with roasted garlic, oven-dried tomatoes, and pesto. This unctuous Georgian molasses will add a fillip to many sauces, soups, vegetable dishes, and even desserts.

3 cups bottled pomegranate juice ½ cup sugar	1/3 cup lemon juice 1 cinnamon stick (optional)

Place all in a non-reactive saucepan, and stir until sugar dissolves. Reduce slowly, simmering until reduced to 1 cup. Freeze until needed, and use in recipes as is, or reconstitute to juice by using 1 teaspoon per cup of water.

Makes 1 cup.

EGGPLANT ROLLS WITH WALNUT FILLING

1 pound eggplant, sliced ¼-inch thick, or 6 to 8 Japanese eggplants, halved	2 garlic cloves, crushed
	1/3 cup chopped cilantro
¾ cup olive oil	1/3 cup chopped parsley
¾ cup walnuts	1/3 cup chopped basil
½ teaspoon paprika	1 tablespoon red wine vinegar
¼ teaspoon powdered saffron	Pomegranate seeds or tomato concasse
Pinch of fenugreek	Leaf lettuce

Sprinkle eggplant with salt, let stand 1 hour, rinse and dry well. Sauté in oil on both sides until tender. Grind walnuts with seasonings in processor until a paste forms, then add garlic, herbs, and vinegar, processing briefly. Spread on eggpant, roll up, and chill. Sprinkle with seeds or concasse, and arrange on lettuce. Serve as an appetizer or salad.

Serves 6 to 8.

SHRIMP PLAKI

This is a popular appetizer that I have had in various forms in the eastern Mediterranean, from the Greek Islands to Turkish Cyprus. It is usually made with mussels, but I much prefer shrimp or scallops. An Armenian or Georgian chef might splash with a little pomegranate molasses.

1 medium red onion, thinly sliced	2 garlic cloves, crushed
2 tablespoons olive oil	4 large Roma tomatoes, seeded & chopped

1/3 cup white wine	Salt & pepper
1 tablespoon pomegranate juice	1 pound shrimp, peeled, or scallops
1 tablespoon lemon juice	1 lemon, quartered
¼ cup chopped mint or parsley	¼ pound feta, crumbled

Sauté onion in oil until soft, add all but shrimp, lemon, and feta. Cook until thickened, arrange shrimp on top, and cook until done. Chill, and garnish with lemon and feta.

Serves 4.

Egg dishes are a surprisingly important part of the cooking in this region. Any vegetable or meat can be combined in an omelet or scrambled eggs. The most typical way is to pour the eggs over the cooked mixture and then finish it in the oven. I prefer the stovetop method or simply frying the eggs separately and then placing them on the top. The following are my favorites.

ARMENIAN EGGS WITH LAMB

At Hotel Armenia in Yerevan, the eggs were scrambled and cooked on top of the meat mixture, but I prefer fried or poached eggs on top.

½ pound ground lamb	½ cup canned crushed tomatoes
1 small onion, chopped	Salt & pepper
1 garlic clove, crushed	4 eggs, fried or poached
¼ cup chopped pistachios	¼ cup chopped mint or cilantro
½ teaspoon Five-Spice Powder	Yogurt Garlic Sauce (see Index)

Sauté lamb in a skillet until almost done, then drain off extra fat. Add onion, seasonings, and tomatoes, simmering until done. Top with eggs, and add mint and dollops of sauce. The very best way to start the day in the Caucasus.

BASTURMA AND POTATOES WITH EGGS

This is a lusty Mediterranean and Middle Eastern dish not unlike what you might have at Katz Deli in New York, because the Armenians took it wherever they went. It is quite similar to pastrami, a spiced and dried beef.

4 purple potatoes, thinly sliced	Salt & pepper, to taste
2 tablespoons olive oil or butter	Pinch of ground sumac
4 thin slices pastrami	¼ cup crumbled feta or haloumy cheese
4 eggs, beaten	Chopped cilantro & mint

In a large skillet, sauté potatoes in oil until tender, pressing down and turning once until browned. Arrange pastrami on top, and add eggs with seasonings. Cook over very low heat, raising the edges like an omelet, and when almost done add cheese and herbs.

Serves 4.

GREEK FILO PIE WITH SAUSAGE AND POTATOES

This typical meat and potato pie from northern Greece was given to me by a Greek God on my trip to the South Pole. This savory pastry can be made small or large with your choice of fillings, and it can be an appetizer or a main course.

Global Culinary Adventures

4 half sheets filo pastry	¼ cup chopped onion
¼ cup melted butter	1 tablespoon olive oil
2 or 3 small purple potatoes, boiled & sliced	½ cup tomato sauce
	¼ cup crumbled feta or kefalotiri cheese
5 ounces garlic sausage, chopped	Salt & pepper

Brush 2 sheets of filo with butter, stacking them. Overlap potatoes on top, season well. Sauté sausage with onion in oil, add sauce, and cook until thick. Spread over potatoes, sprinkle with cheese, and top with remaining 2 sheets of filo prepared as before. Pinch edges together, and bake at 375° about 20 minutes until golden and crisp. The pie may be formed in an 8-inch cake pan.

Serves 1 or 2 with a Greek salad.

YOGURT CHEESE

Known as khacho in Georgia and labneh in most of the Middle East, it is widely eaten as part of the mezze, drizzled with olive oil and sprinkled with mint leaves and olives. It is also an integral part of the breakfast, and it is excellent for your health. To make, simply place yogurt mixed with a little salt in a strainer lined with cheesecloth, and drain to half its volume, or more if you want it even thicker. The whey is especially excellent for your health. If you reconstitute it with an equal amount of water or milk (fat-free is fine), it is an ideal substitute for crème fraîche or sour cream.

KHACHAPURI

(Georgian Cheese Bread)

When I arrived in Tbilisi from Baku on a not very serene flight, I haggled with drivers for a ride to Metechki Palace Hotel. My first Georgian meal began with this divine bread, which can be made with many different fillings and with different doughs, depending on the part of the country. This is the most typical. For a light lunch, divide dough into 2 to 4 pieces, roll thinly into ovals and top each with an egg, over the cheese, when about half done, then continue baking until egg is just set. Top with butter for a truly soul satisfying meal.

Dough:

½ cup yogurt	¼ teaspoon ground coriander
1 tablespoon olive oil	Pinch of salt
½ teaspoon baking soda	1 cup unbleached flour

Filling:

¼ pound Emmenthaler, grated	¼ pound Monterey Jack, grated
	1 egg, beaten

Mix yogurt with oil, soda, coriander, and salt. Add flour gradually, kneading until soft and smooth. Roll on a floured surface into a 12-inch circle about ¼-inch thick. Mix cheeses with all but 1 teaspoon of the egg, and spread on dough to within 2 inches of the edge. Bring edges together on top, pinching them to adhere, and turn over onto a baking sheet. Glaze with reserved egg, and cut a ½-inch hole in the center. Bake at 400° about 5 minutes, reduce to 350° and bake about 15 minutes. Serve hot, cut into wedges.

Serves 4 to 6.

GREEK OLIVE BREAD

I also love this rich aromatic bread, which I've had not only in Greece, but also in Macedonia, Turkey, and Turkish Cyprus.

1 package dry yeast	¼ cup butter or olive oil
1 teaspoon salt	4 cups bread flour
1 tablespoon sugar or honey	1 cup oil-cured olives, pitted & halved
¼ cup warm water	1 ½ teaspoons dried oregano
1 cup milk	¼ cup butter or olive oil

Dissolve yeast with salt and sugar in warm water, using a mixer with a dough hook. Heat milk with butter or oil until lukewarm. When yeast is bubbly, add warm milk mixture and gradually knead in flour until smooth and elastic. Knead in olives and oregano by hand. Cover and let rise until doubled, about 1 ½ hours. Punch down, let rise again, then punch down, and divide into 2 loaves. I always like to use the French technique of rolling out the dough, then rolling it up and placing it in a French bread pan to rise again. Otherwise, form the bread into 2 round loaves or oval ones in the Greek style. In either case, oil the pan and dust with cornmeal. Bake at 375° about 45 minutes, or until golden brown. Brush with butter or olive oil, and cool on racks.

Makes 2 long or round loaves.

Soups are a mainstay of the cuisine in this region and are closely related. The addition of lemon juice and eggs, as in the Greek Soupa Avgolemono, is found all the way over in Armenia and Azerbaijan. Turkey and Armenia incorporate yogurt and mint into many of their soups, and they are eaten from breakfast to bedtime, especially tripe soup.

AZERBAIJANI BOZBASH

(Lamb and Fruit Soup)

Preceded by a substantial amount of Caspian Sea caviar, this terrific and unusual soup with a Greek touch was set before me. Although Hotel Baku was inhabited with many homeless refugees, the chef still prepared excellent meals. Bozbash is also prepared with many kinds of vegetables.

1 pound tender lamb	1 tablespoon turbinado or brown sugar
6 cups chicken or veal stock	
1 medium onion, chopped	2 eggs
2 tablespoons butter	2 or 3 tablespoons lemon juice
2 purple potatoes, peeled & cubed	Salt & Pepper to taste
	Chopped fresh mint
1 cup dried mixed fruit, such as apricots, apples, peaches, prunes	

Simmer lamb in stock, covered, until tender, about 1 hour. Meanwhile, sauté onion in butter until translucent, add potatoes, and sauté briefly. When lamb is tender, add to onion and potatoes, and sauté briefly until golden. Add fruit and sugar, and simmer until potatoes and fruit are very tender. Whisk eggs with juice, add a small amount of hot soup, and whisk back into soup, cooking briefly to thicken slightly. Season, and add mint. A little pomegranate juice may also be added.

Serves 4 to 6.

KHINKALI SOUP

(Georgian Meat Dumplings)

A most memorable part of my first meal in Tbilisi was a clear broth filled with these delightful dumplings. The word "dumpling" is actually a misnomer, as they are more similar to ravioli, pot stickers, wonton, pelmeni, and manti, all of which find their home between Japan and Italy. The Mongolian-Chinese influence is quite apparent. They are also an excellent appetizer with yogurt.

Filling:

12 ounces ground lamb, beef, or pork or a combination	Salt, pepper and coriander
1 small onion, chopped	¼ cup warm meat stock or water

Dough:

2 cups flour	6 cups beef or chicken bouillon
½ teaspoon salt	Chopped dill or mint
½ cup water	

Blend filling ingredients together thoroughly. Mix dough ingredients in a processor, and roll thinly using a pasta machine. Cut circles about 3 or 4 inches in diameter, and top each with a tablespoon of filling. Moisten edges, draw together at top, pleating tightly, and twist to make a small stem. Poach in simmering bouillon until they rise to the surface, about 6 to 8 minutes. Serve as soup or as an appetizer.

Makes about 2 dozen, serving 4 to 6.

YOGURT SOUP WITH BARLEY

There are numerous versions of this Turkish-Armenian classic. Some are simply yogurt, broth, and barley like this one, or without the barley, or with the addition of beef or lamb. Some of the best have been at Pandelli in Istanbul's Spice Bazaar, at an humble restaurant in the hills of Turkish Cypress, and at Hotel Armenia in Yerevan.

½ cup pearl barley	1 tablespoon dried mint, crushed
4 cups meat or chicken stock	2 cups yogurt or more
1 medium onion, finely chopped	Salt & pepper
1 egg, beaten	4 tablespoons butter & 1 teaspoon paprika

Simmer barley in stock about 1 ½ hours, or until tender, covered. Add onion, simmer briefly. Whisk egg with mint, yogurt, and seasoning, and then whisk a small amount of hot soup into it. Whisk back into hot soup. Melt butter with paprika, and drizzle over soup with more dried or fresh mint, if desired.

Serves 4 to 6.

RED LENTIL AND BULGUR SOUP

Another Turkish-Armenian classic with many variations. I enjoyed a similar version many years ago at Istanbul's Liman Lokantasi.

1 cup chopped onion	3 tablespoons butter
2 garlic cloves, crushed	Pinch of turbinado sugar

3 tablespoons tomato paste	Salt & pepper
1 tablespoon paprika	1 tablespoon dried mint, crushed
1 cup red lentils	
6 cups chicken or meat stock	1 teaspoon paprika
1/3 cup fine bulgur wheat	2 tablespoons butter

Gently sauté onion and garlic in butter with sugar, using a soup pot, until caramelized. Add tomato paste and paprika, cooking gently until glossy and deep red. Add lentils, stock, and bulgar, cover, and simmer about 1 hour, or until lentils are tender. Season well. Add mint and paprika to butter, melt, and drizzle over each serving.

Serves 4 to 6.

Main courses in this part of the world are dominated by lamb, the meat of choice from Greece to Azerbaijan, especially when grilled or roasted. Seafood is eaten extensively in the Greek islands, Cyprus, and Turkey, while chicken is prominent in the Caucasus.

GREEK SPAGHETTI WITH SHRIMP

This light but delicious pasta is still as appealing as when I savored it long ago at Gerofinikas, a colorful local luncheon spot in a garden setting in Athens. Another good Greek pasta is Pastitsio, similar to Moussaka, and Greece has its own orzo pasta, a good side dish to meat.

1 ½ pounds shrimp, peeled	1 tablespoon ouzo or anise liqueur
1 tablespoon lemon juice	
	1 medium onion, chopped

2 garlic cloves, crushed	¼ cup chopped fresh basil
3 tablespoons olive oil	½ cup white or red wine
2 cups canned crushed tomatoes	Salt & pepper
	¼ pound feta cheese, crumbled
¼ cup chopped fresh oregano, or 1 tablespoon dried	12 ounces Pasta Dough or Pasta Verde (see Index), cut into spaghetti & cooked

Marinate shrimp in juice and ouzo about 20 minutes. Sauté onion and garlic in oil, using a skillet, until soft. Add tomatoes, herbs, and wine, and simmer until thickened, about 15 minutes. Season, add shrimp and feta, and simmer about 5 minutes. Pour over cooked spaghetti.

Serves 4 to 6.

BAKED FISH FILLETS WITH VEGETABLES

I've enjoyed many variations of this easy fish preparation from Italy to Cyprus, and especially enjoy making it in individual gratin dishes. In the Turkish Cypriot mountains it is prepared in a rustic manner, using a large roasting pan and whole fish. My version is quite elegant.

4 fillets of turbot, sole, or basa	2 small zucchini, thinly sliced
1/3 cup Lemon Vinaigrette (see Index)	4 small Rona tomatoes, thinly sliced
½ teaspoon paprika	Olive oil
¼ teaspoon powdered saffron	Salt & pepper, to taste
4 small purple potatoes, peeled & thinly sliced	Chopped chervil or cilantro

Marinate fish in vinaigrette, with paprika and saffron added to it, while preparing vegetables. Oil 4 individual gratin dishes, and place overlapping layers of potatoes in them, then drizzle with oil and seasonings. Repeat with zucchini and tomatoes with oil and seasonings. Bake at 450° about 15 to 20 minutes, or until potatoes are tender. Place drained fish on top, and bake about 5 minutes, or until done, adding drained vinaigrette if desired.

Serves 4.

CIRCASSIAN CHICKEN

Claimed by both Turkey and Armenia, this wonderful cold chicken dish was always a cooking class favorite. It can be served as part of a mezze, a buffet, or a main course with the Caucasus Salad in hot weather.

1 3-pound chicken or 2 pounds suprêmes	1 teaspoon paprika
3 cups water	½ teaspoon ground coriander
1 carrot, cut into chunks	1 garlic clove, crushed
1 leek, cut into chunks	1 cup reserved stock
Cilantro or parsley stems	2 tablespoons walnut oil
1 ½ teaspoons salt	1 teaspoon paprika
1 ½ cups walnuts	2 hard-cooked eggs, sliced
3 slices stale multi-grain bread	Chopped cilantro & black olives

Simmer chicken in water with seasonings, covered, about 1 hour for whole chicken or ½ hour for suprêmes. Let cool in stock, then remove, and reduce stock to 1 cup. Remove skin and bones from whole chicken, and pull meat into small pieces. Grind walnuts and bread with seasonings in processor, adding reserved stock gradually until fairly smooth. I like it to have a little texture. Mix half of it into chicken, form into a loaf on a platter, and mask with remaining nut mixture. Mix oil and paprika, drizzle over the top, and garnish with cilantro and olives.

Serves 6 to 8.

SATSIVI

(Georgian Chicken with Walnut Sauce)

Georgia's version of Circassian Chicken is different in that it is thickened with egg yolk instead of bread, and it has Georgia's favorite seasoning, ground marigold, as well as wine vinegar. Also, I prefer this one hot, served with pilaf containing golden raisins and saffron. Since Satsivi is so rich, it is also good with a pilaf cooked in pomegranate juice, and the contrasting color is very appealing.

1 3-pound chicken or 2 pounds suprêmes	2 tablespoons butter
3 cups water	1 cup walnuts
1 carrot, cut into chunks	1 ½ cups reserved stock
1 leek, cut into chunks	½ teaspoon ground coriander
Cilantro or parsley stems	½ teaspoon paprika
1 ½ teaspoons salt	½ teaspoon ground marigold or saffron
1 medium onion, finely chopped	1 or 2 egg yolks
2 garlic cloves, crushed	2 tablespoons red wine vinegar
	Chopped cilantro

Simmer chicken in water with seasonings, covered, about 1 hour for whole chickens or ½ hour for suprêmes. Let cool in stock, then remove, and reduce stock to 1 ½ cups. Remove skin and bones from chicken, and cut into small pieces. Sauté onion and garlic in butter until tender, then grind with walnuts, part of the stock, and seasonings in a processor. Add yolks and blend well. Add to remaining simmering stock gradually with vinegar. Simmer about 10 minutes until as thick as desired, and pour over chicken. Garnish with cilantro.

Serves 6 to 8.

ARMENIAN ROAST CHICKEN WITH POMEGRANATE GLAZE

Every country has its roast chicken, and Armenia is no exception. They have a wide variety of stuffings, including rice, bulgur, and bread.

1 3-pound chicken	¼ cup dried currants
Salt & pepper	¼ cup chopped pistachios
¼ cup melted butter	2 tablespoons chopped mint
6 to 8 ounces ground lamb	½ cup fine bulgur wheat
½ cup chopped onion	1 cup hot chicken stock
2 tablespoons butter	2 or 3 tablespoons pomegranate juice
½ teaspoon Five-spice powder	
1 teaspoon salt	¼ cup pomegranate molasses (see Index)
½ cup diced dried apricots	

Season chicken, rub with butter, and roast in a small roasting pan at 350° about 15 minutes. Meanwhile, sauté lamb and onion in butter until partly cooked, add seasonings, fruits, mint, and bulgur which has been softened in hot chicken stock. Add pomegranate juice, and stuff chicken. Baste with butter and molasses about every 10 to 15 minutes until done, about 1 hour. Mix any remaining molasses and juice with a little stock and serve as a sauce.

Serves 4.

ARMENIAN LYULA KEBABS

Yerevan's Hotel Armenia serves wonderful lamb kebabs which they call Lyula, and they have their own presentation which sets them apart from Georgian Shashlik, Turkish Shish Kebab, and Greek Souvlakia. The kebabs are placed on soft squares of lavash, their flat bread, with the top folded over them, and then served with a cucumber and tomato salad and fried eggplant.

1 ½ pounds ground lamb or beef	Salt & pepper
½ cup finely chopped onion	¼ cup finely chopped mint
½ teaspoon ground coriander	4 squares soft lavash

Mix lamb with seasonings until very smooth. Wet hands and form into 4- or 5-inch long sausage shapes, or you may form them onto long skewers instead of running the skewers through them. You should have about 16. Grill over charcoal until done, about 10 to 15 minutes, turning them. Place on lavash, fold top over them, and serve hot. Wonderful!

Serves 4 to 6.

GREEK SOUVLAKIA

There is nothing like sitting in a Mykonos café by the waterside and dining on these succulent Greek kebabs.

2 pounds boneless lamb leg, cubed	½ cup white or red wine
½ cup lemon juice	½ cup olive oil
	1 medium onion, thickly sliced

2 garlic cloves, lightly crushed	1 teaspoon oregano
2 bay leaves	1 teaspoon salt

Marinate lamb in combined remaining ingredients overnight. Thread onto skewers, and grill over charcoal, turning until done to your liking, about 15 minutes.

Serves 4 to 6.

TURKISH SHISH KEBABS

(Kofta Kebabs with Tomatoes and Yogurt)

Turkish kebabs are ubiquitous and come in a myriad of ways, but my favorite is this beautifully executed and flavorful dish. I prefer lamb cubes, marinated in yogurt, but you may make kofta (meatballs, like those in the Armenian section). The highlight of this dish is the luscious combination of grilled, buttered bread topped with juicy grilled lamb, tomatoes, and yogurt-garlic sauce.

1 ½ pounds boneless lamb leg, cubed	1 ½ tablespoons butter or olive oil
1 ½ cups yogurt	1/3 cup tomato pure
2 garlic cloves, crushed	1 teaspoon salt
½ teaspoon coriander	4 slices country bread or pitas
½ teaspoon cumin	2 tablespoons butter or olive oil
Salt & pepper	1 cup Yogurt Sauce (see Index)
1 ½ cups chopped ripe tomatoes	Chopped mint & cilantro, to garnish
2 garlic cloves, crushed	

Mix lamb with yogurt and seasonings, and marinate overnight. Sauté tomatoes and garlic in butter until softened, add purée and salt, then simmer until thickened and it is rich in color. Spread bread on both sides with butter, and place on grill with lamb, cooking until golden brown and not too crisp. Cut bread into quarters, if desired, and place on individual plates, top with juicy hot lamb, cooked about 10 minutes and turning frequently. Pour tomato sauce over lamb, spreading it to cover bread, and divide yogurt over tomatoes. Garnish with herbs.

Serves 4.

GREEK LAMB STEW WITH TOMATOES AND FETA

When I visited Cyprus I discovered the similarity of their Tavas, a lamb and tomato stew cooked in a terra cotta casserole, and the Greek stew cooked in the traditional manner. If you have a terra cotta casserole, simply place the lamb, without sautéeing, and the remaining ingredients, using only a small amount of the water, in it, and bake at 275° about 3 hours, or until tender.

2 pounds boneless lamb, cubed	1 tablespoon oregano
½ cup olive oil	2 to 3 cups chopped ripe tomatoes
1 teaspoon oregano	1 cup water or meat stock
1 onion, chopped	Salt & pepper
4 garlic cloves, crushed	½ pound feta cheese, crumbled

Marinate lamb in oil and oregano overnight. Sauté lamb in the same oil until brown, using a large skillet. Add onions and garlic, sauté and add all but feta. Simmer, uncovered, about 1 ½ hours, until tender. Add feta to melt.

Serves 4 to 6.

AFELIA

(Cypriot Braised Pork with Coriander)

Probably the most important dish on Greek Cyprus, I was able to enjoy it at the Golden Sands Hotel after I was detained at Larnaca Airport for trying to go to the Turkish side, and this was definitely a silver lining.

2 pounds boneless Boston butt pork, cubed, or whole pork tenderloin	2 tablespoons butter
	½ pound mushrooms, halved
1 cup red wine	2 teaspoons ground coriander
1 ½ teaspoons salt	¼ cup chopped cilantro
1 pound purple potatoes	

Marinate pork in wine about 2 hours. Sauté seasoned potatoes in butter until golden, using a large skillet. Add mushrooms and pork, sautéing until brown. Add wine, deglazing, and simmer, covered, about 1 hour for Boston butt, and no more than ½ hour for the tenderloin. Add coriander, and season if necessary. Remove solid ingredients, and reduce cooking liquid to a syrupy glaze. Pour over pork and potatoes, and garnish with cilantro.

Serves 4 to 6.

The following sauces are excellent with many of these main dishes, especially grilled or fried entrees.

YOGURT-GARLIC SAUCE

This is a popular sauce from the Balkans through the Middle East, and can be used on salads, soups, vegetables, and meats.

1 cup yogurt	2 tablespoons melted butter
1 garlic clove, crushed	1 tablespoon paprika
½ teaspoon salt	

Mix yogurt with garlic, crushed in the salt, then pour combined butter and paprika over the top.

Makes about 1 cup.

SKORDALIA

(Greek Potato-Olive Oil Sauce with Garlic and Lemon)

A very old and unctuous Greek sauce for fish and vegetables, it is made with mashed potatoes or bread with lots of garlic, olive oil, and lemon juice.

1 pound Yukon potatoes, peeled, boiled & mashed	2/3 cup olive oil, or more
3 large garlic cloves	¼ cup lemon juice
½ tablespoon salt	½ cup walnuts, ground (optional)

Using an electric mixer, beat potatoes until very smooth. Crush garlic in salt, using a mortar, and beat into potatoes. Add oil gradually, then add juice, and walnuts if using.

Makes about 1 ½ cups.

Grains and vegetables are an intrinsic part of Greek, Turkish, and Caucasian cooking. Rice and bulgar wheat are both made into pilafs and also used in stuffings. Eggplant is probably the favored vegetable throughout the area, but there is also an abundance of artichokes, green beans, tomatoes, grapevine leaves, and spinach, frequently used in a meat dish.

AZERBAIJANI PILAF

There is a definite hint of Iran in this most unusual and flavorful pilaf, which I discovered at the Caravanserai in Baku. It is traditional to rinse the rice in cold water over and over until it runs clear, but not necessary. There are hundreds of pilaf combinations using fish, meat, poultry, fruits and vegetables, not to mention seasonings. Dried fruits and nuts are among the best, and bulgar wheat can also be a pilaf with the same ingredients.

¼ cup chopped onion	1 cup chopped tomatoes
¼ cup pine nuts or pistachios	1 cup chicken stock
¼ cup dried currants	Pinch of saffron
3 tablespoons butter	Pinch of sumac
1 cup long-grain rice	Salt & pepper, to taste

Sauté onion, nuts, and currants in butter until onion is translucent. Add rice, stirring until coated with butter. Add tomatoes, and cook until shiny and thickened. Add stock, saffron, and sumac, cover, and simmer about 20 minutes, or until liquid is absorbed. Season to taste.

Serves 4.

EGGPLANT CREAM WITH LEMON AND CHEESE

Reminiscent of a French puréed vegetable, this grilled and puréed eggplant is an ideal accompaniment to roast chicken or lamb, kebabs, and stews.

2 1-pound eggplants	¾ cup milk or light cream
2 tablespoons lemon juice	Salt & pepper
3 tablespoons butter	Lemon juice, to taste
3 tablespoons flour	1/3 to ½ cup grated Parmesan or kasseri

Prick eggplants all over, and grill over charcoal, turning, until collapsed, about 15 to 20 minutes. I have also successfully grilled them on my ridged iron grill from Le Creuset. Peel, and place in a bowl of water acidulated with lemon juice to preserve the whiteness, about 20 minutes. Make a roux of butter and flour, whisk in milk all at once, and whisk until thick. Add eggplant, drained and mashed. Whisk until smooth, and season. Add cheese.

Serves 4 to 6.

TURKISH STUFFED VEGETABLES

The Greeks and Turks stuff everything from grapevine leaves to onions and peppers, but I especially like stuffed eggplant and tomatoes. The following stuffing may be made without the meat, and it may have only rice or bulgar instead of both. Also, the vegetables may be cooked on the stove or in the oven. Feel free to season as you like.

2 medium eggplants, about ¾ pound each, halved	¼ cup bulgar wheat
4 medium tomatoes, ½ inch sliced off top	3 tablespoons tomato paste
1 pound ground lamb	2 tablespoons chopped mint
½ cup chopped onion	1 ½ teaspoons salt
2 garlic cloves, crushed	½ cup water
2 tablespoons olive oil	¼ cup olive oil
Reserved tomato pulp	2 tablespoons lemon juice
½ cup dried currants or golden raisins	Yogurt-Garlic Sauce (see Index)
¼ cup rice	Chopped cilantro
	¼ cup chopped walnuts or pistachios

Scoop out eggplant and tomato pulp, leaving a shell about ½-inch thick. Reserve tomato pulp for stuffing. Salt vegetables and invert to drain. Sauté lamb, onion, and garlic in oil until partially cooked, add reserved tomatoes, nuts, currants, rice, bulgar, and seasonings. Simmer briefly, and fill eggplants and tomatoes about ¾ full to allow rice to expand. Place in a large baking dish and pour water, oil, and juice around them. Bake, covered, in a 350° oven about ½ hour or until vegetables are tender. Serve with Yogurt-Garlic Sauce, and sprinkle with cilantro.

Serves 4 as a vegetable or a light meal.

Desserts in Greece and Turkey are characterized by syrupy filo preparations, rich nut cakes, puddings, and fruit compotes. Probably the most highly respected dessert component is Kaymak, the ultra-rich cream with a solid texture, made by cooking it over low heat.

BAKLAVA WITH CRYSTALLIZED FRUIT AND HONEY SYRUP

I knew I had arrived when my Greek students praised my Baklava and even requested private lessons. This version, not as well known, is also great.

2 eggs	8 half-sheets filo
¾ cup powdered sugar	½ cup melted butter
1 ½ cups walnuts, almonds, or a combination, finely chopped	½ cup chopped pistachios
	¾ cup water
½ pound crystallized fruit, preferably cherries, orange, & lemon peel, finely chopped	1/3 cup sugar
	1/3 cup honey
1 teaspoon orange flower water	1 tablespoon lemon juice

Whisk eggs until fluffy, adding sugar gradually until lightly thickened. Fold in nuts, fruit, and flavoring. Brush a 9- x 13-inch pan with butter. Place a buttered sheet in pan, sprinkle with pistachios, add another buttered sheet, and spread about 1/3 of filling on it. Repeat with remaining sheets of filo, butter, pistachios, and filling, ending with 2 buttered sheets. Cut into diamond-shaped pieces almost to the bottom, and bake at 350° about 45 minutes, or until crisp and golden. Make syrup by boiling remaining ingredients to 220°, cool, then pour over hot filo.

Makes about 30.

TURKISH YOGURT CAKE WITH MINTED ORANGES AND STRAWBERRIES

This deliciously moist and flavorful cake was also a cooking class favorite. Serve with the sauce or fruit of your choice.

¾ cup soft butter	2 teaspoons baking powder
1 cup sugar	½ teaspoon baking soda
5 egg yolks	Pinch of salt
1 cup yogurt	5 egg whites, stiffly beaten
1 teaspoon orange flower water	1 cup sugar
Grated zest of 1 orange	¾ cup water
2 ½ cups unbleached flour	Grated zest of 1 orange
	½ tablespoon orange water

Cream butter with sugar, beat in yolks and yogurt, then add seasonings. Add flour, baking powder and soda gradually. Fold in whites gently. Tour into a buttered and floured bundt pan, and bake at 350° about 40 minutes, or just until it tests done. Meanwhile, combine remaining ingredients in a saucepan, and simmer briskly 10 minutes, and cool. Invert cake while hot, place on a platter, and pour syrup over it slowly.

2 cups yogurt	1 teaspoon orange flower water
1 tablespoon turbinado sugar	½ teaspoon vanilla

Drain yogurt several hours, then stir in sugar and flavorings. Pour into center of cake.

Minted Oranges and Strawberries:

4 oranges, zested & sectioned	2 tablespoons grenadine
1 pint strawberries, quartered	½ cup mint leaves

Mix oranges, zest, and strawberries with grenadine. When ready to serve with cake add mint leaves.

Serves 8 to 10.

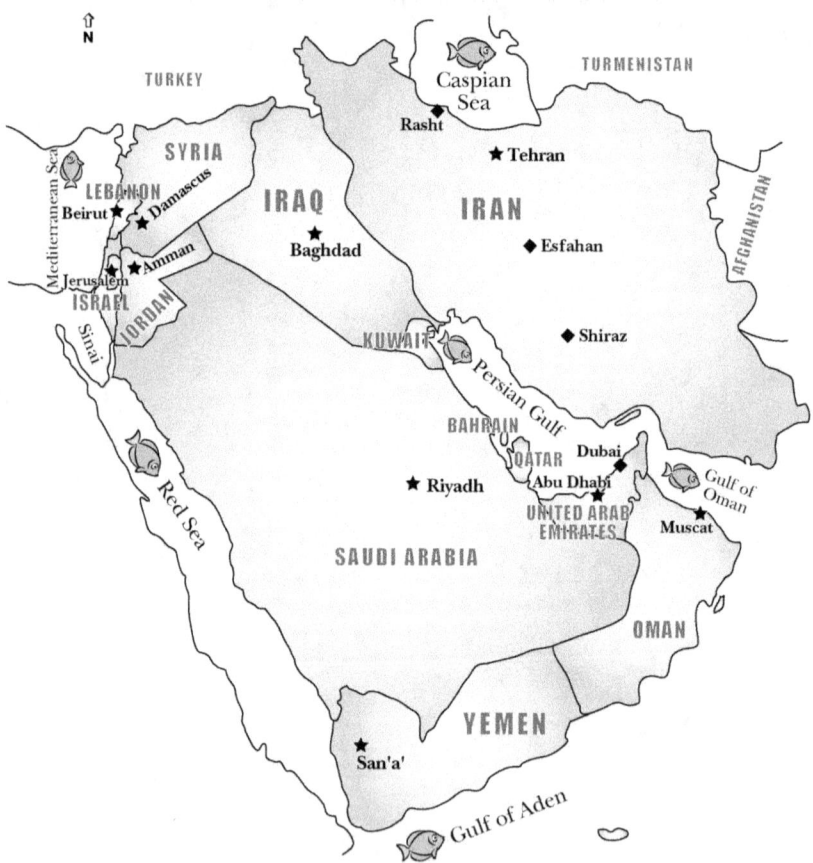

MIDDLE EAST
IRAN IRAQ SYRIA JORDAN LEBANON ISRAEL PERSIAN GULF YEMEN

The mystery and magic of the Middle East has lured me back many times since my first visit in 1974. The stunning Persian architecture in Iran and the eerily beautiful mud-brick buildings in medieval Yemen, not to mention the fascinating history and exotic foods, are not to be missed.

But just how do you define the Middle East, once known as the Near East? Historians, geographers, culinarians, and many others have diverse ideas. Also, there are different opinions as to who is an Arab. Many include North Africa in addition to the ones above, and they do share the presence of mosques and souks, and the absence of pork and alcohol in most of the countries, but liberalization is spreading throughout the region. I separate North Africa because their history and cuisines, as well as the people, are somewhat dissimilar. Also, theoretically, Arabs are those from the area near the Arabian Sea. The ancient caravans on the trade routes from China to Yemen affected the cooking of the entire area, and the influences were reciprocal as we shall see.

Iran's Persian Empire covered most of Asia, and its trade routes influenced even the Caucasus and Eastern Europe. Now, with the current emigration to the United Kingdom, Scandinavia, Canada, and other countries, their culinary influence is still having a distinct effect.

The year was 1979, and I was thrilled to be landing in Iran, but the Shah was on his way out, and Ayatollah Khomeini was on his way in, so the visit was not to be. Many years later, however, I finally experienced this outstanding cooking, which is considered to be the mother of Middle East cusine, and the exceptional hospitality of the Iranian people. My arrival was well after midnight, and I passed speedily through immigration with welcoming smiles and was then met and driven to the deluxe Laleh Hotel.

I soon discovered that Iranian cooking differs from the rest of the Middle East in that the Caspian Sea provides it with sturgeon and the world's best caviar (which I was invited to see being processed, but more about that later). Also, the Iranians shy away from garlic. Rice, rather than burghul, is the foundation of its cuisine, especially the numerous pilaus with Kebabs. Iranians frequently add its luscious bounty of fruits—cherries, apricots, pomegranates, quince, and dates, which were first dried in ancient Persia—to its cooked dishes. The enormous melons are legendary.

They also make much use of herbs, especially mint, coriander, saffron, and sumac, as well as the same spices used by neighboring countries. The Iranians also have wonderful lamb, eggplant, spinach (which is native to Persia), and an abundance of pistachios and almonds. Yogurt, in many forms, and tea are the drinks of choice.

The food is lighter and spicier in the southern cities of mystical and enchanting Isfahan, and Shiraz, the city of wine, roses, and poetry, and the gateway to Persepolis, the 2,000-year old archaeological site.

Iraq was the site of greater Mesopotamia 9,000 years ago, when the first food was grown and animals were raised for food, and it is said that the first laws, science, and literature originated here. It is also the site of ancient Babylon and Ali Baba.

Again, I managed to fly into Baghdad after midnight due to a delay in Kuwait, but the hospitable Iraqis found a safe ride to my hotel with a Serbian family who was fleeing the Yugoslavian atrocities. It was also just prior to the Persian Gulf War, and I had seen the newspaper headlines on the plane—Americans Are Dogs. During my entire stay, however, I was treated like a queen.

The food was similar to that of Iran and Turkey, with Chinese,

Indian, and Persian influences. Although my visit was limited to Baghdad, I learned that the people in Kurdistan to the North eat mostly hearty soups and stews, and the people in the South eat plenty of rice and fish, even catfish, and, of course, dates. Iraq grows the majority of the world's dates, and uses them in many different ways; they are frequently made into a paste and into vinegar. I have duplicated the latter by macerating chopped dates in white wine vinegar, much as we do with berries. My fondest culinary memory will always be the simple native-style dinner that I savored in an outdoor café on the banks of the Tigris River. Abu Nawas Street is lined with vendors who barbecue shaboot, a large, firm fish, on sticks over a fire. The dinner is called Masgoof and includes a simple accompaniment of tomatoes and onions with vinegar. A night to remember!

All too soon it was time to depart, and the friendly hotel staff actually took up a collection to pay my taxi fare to the airport so that I would not have to change money again. They even went outside and waved me off.

Jordan, Syria, and Lebanon share a very similar cuisine, but they also share differences. Jordan is a new country by comparison, as it was founded after World War I. Amman is a rather lenient and modern city built among seven hills and was my gateway to Petra, the ancient rose-colored city carved from sandstone. My favorite meal in Jordan was room service breakfast, Arab style. It consisted of eggs, sausages, yogurt, flat bread, and warm, garlicky favas.

I obtained a visa to Syria in a few hours and was on my way to Damascus in a red velvet Mercedes bus. An ancient and exotic city, Damascus exudes a mysterious atmosphere. Its food specialty is definitely the honey cakes with candied fruit, rose water, and almonds, much like is found in Turkey. Aleppo, close to the Turkish border, is the culinary center of the country, and also the center of the friendliest people.

Lebanon is definitely the most westernized country in the Middle East, and it is half Christian and half Muslim. Fortunately, after its 20-year war, it is now well on its way to being like it was when I visited in 1974. Beirut was the Paris of the East with its Casino du

Liban and belly dancers. It was also an important fashion capital and banking center. Byblos, up the coast, is one of the world's oldest cities, and is where I had my first mezze, the most important part of the meal. Sitting by the sea, I had a variety of about three dozen appetizers, dominated by the now well-known Tabbouleh, Hummus bi Tahini, and Baba Ghanoush. Kibbeh, a mixture of burghul and ground lamb, is the national dish of Jordan, Syria, and Lebanon, and is baked, broiled, or fried. These countries also have a fondness for Shawarma, lamb that is grilled on a vertical rotating spit, then thinly sliced.

Israel, the land of milk and honey, is the youngest country in this group, but it can boast of the Middle East's finest cooks. A melting pot of at least 100 ethnic groups, the main influences have been Russian, Oriental, and that of the Yemeni Jews. This, of course, has resulted in Israel's own fusion cuisine, especially in the restaurants. Home cooking is still very much like that of Jordan, with an emphasis on lentils, burghul, and a plethora of luscious fruits, which they have used in unique combinations with other foods. My first Israeli meal, in 1979, was a delicious fish dish with the famous Jaffa oranges.

The dairy products are outstanding but are not eaten with meat or poultry, and neither pork nor shellfish are eaten. The national dish is Felafel, deep-fried balls of ground chickpeas and burghul, a traditional Arab dish. Traditional Jewish dishes such as Tzimmes, Challah, and gefulte fish are still eaten, and the best place for them is at a kibbutz, a communal agricultural settlement that is an important part of the Israeli culture. They have been providing Israel's produce for nearly 100 years and hire thousands of people.

It is ironic that wine was first produced in the Middle East and was popular until the advent of Islam in the eighth century, but Israel is the only major wine-growing country in the region. Its Carmel wines are excellent and Sabra brandy is also quite good.

The Persian Gulf is comprised of Kuwait, Bahrain, Qatar, Oman, the United Arab Emirates, and Yemen, as well as Saudi Arabia. Yemen does not border the Gulf but it is part of the Arabian

Peninsula, and is the only such country that does not luxuriate in oil wealth. Traveling through them, I was quite amazed at the westernized luxury hotels and cultures. Saudi Arabia, however, is extremely Islamic in spite of its excessive wealth, but its thirty-five million dollar bridge to Manama, Bahrain, transports them to the cosmopolitan realm of wine, women, and song on the weekends.

Spice is the common denominator in all of these countries, as the spice route extended into Yemen. Cardamom, coriander, and cumin predominate in the earthy cuisine, as do dried limes. As in the rest of the Middle East, rice, dried beans, kebabs, lamb, yogurt, dates, and Baklava play an important part in the cooking. A multitude of fish includes grouper, mullet, pomfret, bream, and prawns. The national dish throughout most of the area is generally considered to be Khouzi, a whole lamb stuffed with a chicken, rice, eggs, onions, and Baharat, the spice mixture endemic to this region; the place to enjoy it is at a Mansaf, an Arabian feast held in a tent out in the desert.

My foray into Arabia began with a flight to Abu Dhabi, one of the seven emirates, and I was immediately mesmerized by the flamboyant style of the airport. The beautifully landscaped streets were bordered with a bounty of flowers and trees, and the palatial Intercontinental Hotel was awash in gold decor and crystal chandeliers.

The highlight of my first meal was a super-fresh mullet coated with date purée, grilled, and served on aromatic saffron rice with a classic vegetable garniture. I could already detect the culinary influences of India, Iran, and the Horn of Africa. The next morning I enjoyed a typical Arab breakfast of yogurt with olives and dates, and then drove off in my rental car to see the rest of the Emirates.

There are seven Emirates: Abu Dhabi, Dubai, Sharjah, Ajman, Umm al Quawain, Ras al Khaimah, and Fujairah, and the area is so small that the drive can be done in one day, but I wanted to spend the night at Hatta Fort, a Relais & Châteaux hotel in the foothills of the Hajar Mountains, in Dubai, near the Oman border. It was not with a little trepidation, considering that it was during Ramadan that I drove across the desolate moonscape of the

Arabian desert, with its burnished sand dunes and more camels than I had ever seen. It looked like the end of the world, but I was back in reality when greeted by Sergio Magnaldi, the gracious and charming Italian manager. It is difficult to meet a genuine Arabian, because they are too wealthy to hold public jobs, which are mostly held by Indians and Filippinos.

The candle-lit Jeema restaurant, with its panoramic view of the oasis and mountains, offered European and Middle Eastern dishes. Fusion was already evident here in 1989, as I perused the menu featuring fanned avocado slices with Gulf prawns and caviar, and the Burgundy escargots were enhanced with pistachio butter, while the fresh crab was flavored with ginger and soy sauce. My main course was Machbous, a dish indigenous to the Gulf region, and which is composed of succulent Gulf shrimp baked in an aromatic tomato sauce seasoned with Baharat, the prerequisite Gulf spice mixture.

It was with great reluctance that I left this oasis of peace and tranquility, but Sergio serviced my car wearing his silk Gucci suit, and provided me with plenty of drinking water and a light box lunch to sustain me while driving around the peninsula to the other Emirates. Since it was Ramadan, I had to be sure no one but the camels saw me drinking and eating.

Dubai, the Pearl of the Gulf, is now the world's most glamorous and luxurious resort with phantasmagorical hotels, elegant restaurants, and a renowned gold souk, which is a shopper's paradise.

The destination of choice, however, is Oman's Arabesque walled city of Muscat with its original carved gates and sixteenth century Portuguese forts. The magnificent A1 Bustan Palace Hotel was built by the Sultan, and the food is exquisite. The Omani desert is also a great place to experience the Mansaf feast.

When I arrived in Yemen, I felt like I had been transported to another world. Originally known as Felix Arabia (Happy Arabia) and ruled by the Queen of Sheba, Yemen's hospitality has always been legendary. Even my white-robed taxi driver offered to share his qat, a mildly narcotic plant that is chewed in Yemen and the Horn of Africa.

Sanaa, the capital and considered by some to be the world's oldest city, has a unique architectural style of mud-brick buildings and a 1,000-year old souk, Bab-al-Yemen, the most archaic I've ever experienced. Many of the vendors were actually living in small cave-like areas in the rear of their selling spaces with their small camels. The alien and suspicious stares I received made me anxious to return to my deluxe hotel, the Taj Sheba, and meet with the Indian chef.

The cooking in Yemen has Arab and Indian influences, and South Yemen, now a separate country, has a distinict Ethiopian influence as well. Yemen has a special affinity for spice and their aromatic spice mixture called Hulbeh or Hilbeh is the essence of their cooking. Fenugreek, caraway, cardamom, saffron, and healthy doses of both black and hot red peppers are favored.

Yemeni honey is one of its culinary treasures, along with coffee, which was once one of the world's most famous, especially that from Moccha on the Red Sea. Tropical fruits, Middle Eastern vegetables, barley, dried beans, poultry, and meat are much used in the cooking, and Felafel is also the national dish here.

Yemen borders on both the Red Sea and the Indian Ocean which yield a large amount of seafood, but I lost my taste for it when I visited the fish market in Aden, South Yemen, which was once a British colony. My Seabourn cruise called at Aden, an antiquated, impoverished city, and our shore excursion lost a male passenger when we arrived at the fish market. The sight of raw sewage running onto the concrete landing that was covered with fish was just too much for some of us. In retrospect, the filthy fish market in Greenland was not so bad after all.

RECIPES FROM THE MIDDLE EAST

FATTOUSH (SYRIAN-LEBANESE BREAD SALAD)
BINT-AL-SAHN (YEMEN HONEY BUTTER PASTRY)
FATUT (YEMEN SCRAMBLED EGGS WITH CROUTONS)
TRUFFLED SCRAMBLED EGGS WITH CAVIAR
YEMEN PEASANT SOUP
SYRIAN LENTIL SOUP WITH SPINACH
WATERCRESS SOUP WITH CAVIAR
AVOCADO SOUP WITH SMOKED SALMON AND CAVIAR
ISRAELI FISH WITH HONEY AND FRUIT
GRILLED IRANIAN STURGEON
MACHBOUS (PERSIAN GULF SHRIMP AND RICE WITH BAHARAT)
MUSAKHAN (PALESTINIAN CHICKEN WITH SPICY ONIONS AND ARAB BREAD)
KHORESH E FESENJEN (CHICKEN WITH WALNUT AND POMEGRANATE SAUCE)
CRUSTY PELAU WITH YOGURT AND EGGS
CHELOU KEBABS
LAMB WITH SOUR CHERRY SAUCE
LAMB WITH LIMA BEANS AND DILL
ISRAELI FLANK STEAK WITH JAFFA ORANGES
PURÉED CHICKPEAS WITH GARLIC AND YOGURT
GREEN BEANS WITH GARLIC AND OIL
BULGAR PILAF WITH FRUIT
CHELOU (PERSIAN RICE)
YOGURT BEETS
JORDANIAN DATES AND BANANAS
MIDDLE EAST RICE PUDDING WITH FRUIT & NUTS
HONEY WALNUT CAKE

MEZZE AND CAVIAR

Mezze, the ubiquitous array of appetizers, could well be the national dish of the Middle East, except for Iran. There are infinite choices including raw, grilled, and puréed vegetables; sausages and kebabs; salads, olives, and savory pastries; as well as shellfish. Other than this, as if not enough, Iran offers the pearls of the Caspian Sea, caviar.

Caviar, the world's most delectable and exquisite delicacy, as well as the most expensive epicurean status symbol, provides us with the most sensual, ethereal, and irresistible tastes in life. The word, caviar, is derived from the Turkish word for roe—khavgah. Caviar is the salted roe of sturgeon.

Although also found in the Black and Azov Seas, it is the Caspian Sea that produces the finest caviar. Paradoxically, my first sublime caviar experience was on Aeroflot, many years ago. Russia once produced the best, but since the Soviet Union broke up, there has been excessive pollution, overfishing, poaching, and illegal fishing, mostly in the former republics of Kazakhstan, Turkmenistan, and Azerbaijan, all of which border the Caspian Sea. This has caused the sturgeon to be an endangered species, and the price has escalated. Iran, which has control of one-third of the Caspian coast, now produces the best and does not practice the Russian offenses. I had the honor of being invited to observe the entire processing of caviar at Shilat, the official state fishery. This was, indeed, my most ultimate culinary adventure.

I flew into Rasht from Tehran, and was driven to a Caspian Sea resort where I enjoyed a delicious seafood dinner in my spacious loft-style room. The next morning, after a typical Iranian breakfast of fruit, eggs, panir (sheep's milk cheese), and flat breads, I was driven to Shilat and welcomed with a cup of tea while watching a 200-pound sevruga, the medium-size sturgeon, being carted in from the sea. Then followed a sanitation ritual to equal that of the world's most sanitary hospital. I stepped into a pool of sanitized water, and once inside the building, I removed my shoes, put on slippers, and donned a white surgeon's coat (over my own coat, which is required by Iranian law at all times) and hat over my scarf.

The quite simple processing of approximately 20 pounds of caviar (usually a tenth of the sturgeon's weight) took only about 20 minutes, and the caviar would sell for probably $100.00 an ounce! First, the sturgeon was slit open from head to tail. The white-coated surgeon, wearing surgical gloves, then scooped out millions of eggs to put through a wide-meshed sieve to remove the membrane. After a thorough rinsing with water, the eggs were mixed with French sea salt and piled into tins. The lids were pressed on, the sides wiped, and they were ready to be shipped. The sturgeon was then taken to a large refrigerated room where they are processed to be sold as food, which I was soon to enjoy.

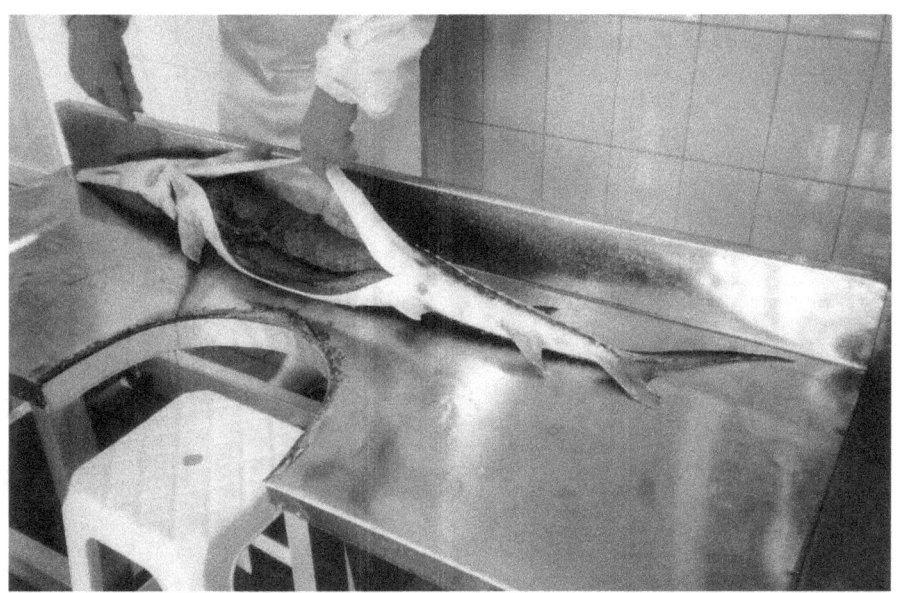

I was then taken to a simple room for the highlight of my visit and of all my travels. A white-clothed table displayed tins of all five kinds of caviar, and I was told to help myself, an offer which proved to be worth the cost of my business class ticket to get there. Gold spoons were used, not the customary mother-of-pearl, and not silver, which will oxidize. The only thing missing was champagne.

The five premium caviars that were served were Beluga, the queen of caviar, and the most expensive, coming from the largest sturgeon. It was said to be Picasso's favorite. The next tin held Osetra, the most variable type, which is preferred by the French and James Bond. The Sevruga has an intense flavor, is the least expensive of these three, and is preferred by Charles de Gaulle. Pressed caviar, made from broken and older eggs, is considered to be a Russian favorite. The highlight of this festive tasting was without a doubt the Golden caviar, from the Sterlet sturgeon, which is quite rare. It was originally reserved for the Czars and the Shah. Malossol caviar simply means that it is lightly salted.

Although I was completely mesmerized by then, my day was not over. Five of the Shilat associates took me and my guide to their restaurant on the property for a sturgeon lunch, where I was given the marinade recipe for the exceptional grilled fish. Rice and a simple lettuce and tomato salad accompanied the delicate but firm white fish. It is also boneless and low-fat.

It was interesting to note that two mullahs who came in to eat never even glanced at our table, even though I was with six men. It was necessary, however, to leave an empty chair between me and the man seated next to me. Also, we were not allowed to shake hands, even when in the Shilat building. Although caviar is preferred au naturel in Iran and by many purists, it is the perfect complement to many foods, especially creamy soups, egg dishes, canapes, seafood, and even some salads. I love to top purple potato chips with a little sour cream and a bit of caviar, as well as baked potatoes. Be sure to keep the recipe simple, as the caviar is the prima donna. My recipe for Pasta au Caviar is in the French section.

FATTOUSH

(Syrian and Lebanese Bread Salad)

This is the de facto salad of the Middle East. Many cooks soak the bread in water, and some add black olives and dried mint, and cos (Romaine) instead of cucumber. I like it as part of the mezze or with a main course.

4 large Romas, seeded & diced	¼ cup chopped basil
1 medium cucumber, peeled, seeded, & diced	2 garlic cloves
	1 teaspoon salt
½ cup chopped red onion	¼ cup lemon juice
¼ cup chopped parsley or cilantro	½ cup olive oil
¼ cup chopped mint	1 or 2 pita breads, split, toasted, & broken into small pieces

Mix vegetables with herbs in a large bowl. Mash garlic in salt, whisk in juice, then gradually whisk in oil. Add to salad with pita, and toss well.

Serves 6.

BINT-AL-SAHN

(Yemen Honey Butter Pastry)

This rich pastry cake is layered like filo pastry into a flaky, golden round. Normally eaten before the meal, I much prefer it for breakfast or as a comforting snack or dessert. Yemen's world-renowned honey is the one thing I bring home, very similar to Ethiopia's honey.

1 package dry yeast	4 eggs, beaten
¼ cup warm water	¾ cup melted butter
3 cups all-purpose flour	1 cup honey, or more
1 teaspoon salt	1 cup melted butter, or more
1 teaspoon cardamom	

Dissolve yeast in water, and let proof for a few minutes. Place flour, salt, and cardamom in a large electric mixer bowl, and add yeast mixed with eggs, gradually. Knead until smooth and elastic, then divide into 16 parts. Roll or press with your hands into 8- to 10-inch rounds, brushing each with butter, and layering 8 of them, pressing edges together as you layer each one. Repeat with remaining 8 sections, and finish with more butter on each stack. Let rise about 45 minutes. Bake on pastry sheets about 45 minutes at 375° or until golden brown. Place on a platter, and drizzle with extra honey and butter. Break pieces off or cut into wedges, and add more honey and butter.

Serves 6-8.

FATUT

(Yemen Scrambled Eggs with Croutons)

A popular breakfast dish or a light meal for any time of day, it bears a distinct resemblance to the Balkan Scrambled Eggs in the eastern Europe section. Like the Balkan eggs, these may also have a bit of leftover meat in them. Also, Yemenis have been known to pour their wonderful honey over these eggs.

2 small pita or other flat breads	1 teaspoon salt
¼ cup melted butter	1 tablespoon chopped cilantro (optional)
4 eggs, beaten	

Tear bread into small pieces and sauté in butter over medium heat until crisp and golden. Add eggs mixed with salt and cilantro, and lift edges to allow uncooked eggs to run underneath, as in making an omelet. Gradually fold edges onto top to make very soft, barely set eggs.

Serves 4.

TRUFFLED SCRAMBLED EGGS with CAVIAR

A pseudo-Iranian dish that I was inspired to make on my way home from Iran. When changing planes in Amsterdam, I always shop at their duty-free food shops, and this time I discovered caviar cream in a tube. It is great in eggs, or you can use real caviar and real truffles, but I use truffle oil or juice, which they also have.

4 eggs, beaten	1 tablespoon yogurt or crème fraîche
1 teaspoon caviar cream	
1 teaspoon truffle juice or oil	¼ cup melted butter

Whisk eggs with caviar cream, truffle juice, and yogurt. Cook gently in butter, lifting edges, and turning them until very soft and barely set.

Serves 4.

YEMEN PEASANT SOUP

While taking a tour of the Taj Sheba Hotel kitchen in Sanaa, Yemen, the Indian chef gave me a taste of fiery hot soup made of leftovers by every kitchen in Yemen on a daily basis. This is my version without the heat, and it is done as fast as you can add the ingredients. A great quick meal!

1 quart lamb or chicken broth	2 tablespoons chopped cilantro
1 cup chopped, cooked lamb or chicken	¼ - ½ teaspoon each fenugreek, cardamom, saffron, & curry powder
1 cup cooked rice	1 egg, beaten
1 cup cooked chickpeas or lentils	2 tablespoons butter or lamb fat
3 or 4 garlic cloves, crushed	Pita or flat bread
2 tomatoes, chopped	

Bring broth to a boil in a large soup pot and add meat, rice, beans, and all seasonings. Whisk a bit of hot mixture into the egg, and then whisk back into soup pot to thicken lightly. Finish with butter, adding salt, if necessary. It is eaten with pita, which is torn into pieces and dipped into the soup.

Serves 4.

SYRIAIN LENTIL SOUP WITH SPINACH AND NOODLES

Lentil soup is ubiquitous throughout the Middle East, and there are endless variations. I savored this at the bus station in Damascus. This soup is quick and easy, as well as delicious and wholesome.

1 ½ cups chopped onion	1 package frozen chopped spinach, thawed
2 garlic cloves, crushed	2 teaspoons salt
¼ cup olive oil	1 teaspoon allspice
1 cup lentils	1-2 tablespoons lemon juice
1 ½ quarts beef stock or water	½ cup yogurt
2 or 3 ounces linguine or other narrow pasta	Chopped cilantro

Sauté onions and garlic in oil, using a large soup pot, until softened. Add lentils and stock, and simmer until lentils are almost done, about ½ hour. Add linguine, spinach and seasonings. Cook briskly until pasta and lentils are tender, yet still slightly firm. Add juice, and dollop with yogurt and cilantro when serving.

Serves 4.

WATERCRESS SOUP with CAVIAR

If you should have a windfall of Iranian caviar, this is an easy, delicious, and beautiful soup to serve with an Iranian or French dinner. Based on the classic French Potage Parmentier, it is given an Iranian touch of dried mint and yogurt. Caviar cream in a tube, which is in the scrambled egg recipe in this section, makes an acceptable substitute for fresh caviar.

2 or 3 large shallots, finely chopped	2 cups shrimp or chicken stock
½ pound Yukon potatoes, peeled & finely chopped	1 cup packed watercress leaves
	¾ cup yogurt
½ to 1 teaspoon dried mint, crumbled	Salt & pepper
2 tablespoons olive oil	Caviar or 1 teaspoon caviar cream, or more, to your taste

Sauté shallots and potatoes gently with mint in oil until golden. Add stock, cover, and simmer until potatoes are tender. Add watercress, and puree with an immersion blender, adding yogurt. If not using fresh caviar, blend in caviar cream, otherwise, top each serving with caviar.

Serves 4.

AVOCADO SOUP with SMOKED SALMON and CAVIAR

Essentially an Israeli soup, similar to what I enjoyed at the American Colony hotel with Israel's superlative avocados, I have given it an Iranian touch as in the watercress soup. Again, feel free to use caviar cream if needed.

2 Hass avocados, peeled, peeled, pitted, & cut into chunks	½ tablespoon lemon juice
	½ cup yogurt
	Salt & pepper
2 cups shrimp or chicken stock	4 ounces smoked salmon, cut into strips
¼ cup white wine	
1 egg yolk	Caviar or caviar cream, to taste

Puree avocados with stock in a large saucepan, and add wine, bringing to a simmer. Whisk yolk, adding juice, half the yogurt, and seasonings, including the caviar cream, if using. Add to saucepan and simmer briefly to thicken lightly. Garnish servings with remaining yogurt, salmon, and caviar.

Serves 4.

Main courses are dominated by lamb throughout the Middle East, but the lamb is prepared in a myriad of combinations with fruit, vegetables, and grains, all quite pleasing to the palate. Fresh fish from the Mediterranean, Red Sea, Persian Gulf, and the Indian Ocean are plentiful and varied, and prepared in diverse ways, as are chicken and duck, frequently served with the luscious local fruit.

ISRAELI FISH WITH HONEY AND FRUIT

One of my favorite methods of preparing fish is this decades-old fusion recipe from the Sea Dolphin in Jerusalem. There are many variations, depending on what is in season, and any firm white fish may be used.

4-6 fish fillets: turbot, sole, basa, or sea bass	½ cup kumquats, halved
Salt & pepper	¼ cup each diced dates, golden raisins, & sliced almonds or pistachios
2 tablespoons butter or olive oil	¾ cup assorted grapes
2/3 cup orange juice	Saffron Rice
¼ cup lemon juice	Slivered Mint
1/3 cup honey	

Season fillets and sauté in butter or oil about 5 minutes until barely cooked through, on both sides, and remove to plates. Add juices, honey, and fruits and bring to a boil, reducing until lightly thickened and glazed. Pour over fillets, serve with saffron rice, and sprinkle with mint.

Serves 4-6.

GRILLED IRANIAN STURGEON

This was part of the enormous lunch which I had at Shilat Caviar Processing Corporation's restaurant on the Caspian, and they graciously gave me this wonderful marinade, which can also be used on lamb or chicken.

1 cup lemon juice	¼ cup melted butter
1 cup thinly sliced onion	½ teaspoon crushed saffron
1 teaspoon sea salt	Paprika or sumac, to taste
1 ½ pounds sturgeon or swordfish, cut into 1-inch cubes	Chelou (see Index)

Combine juice, onion, and salt in a shallow dish, add fish, turning to coat, and let marinate at least an hour. Thread onto skewers, and grill about 5 minutes on each side, basting frequently with mixed butter, saffron, and paprika. Serve with Chelou or plain Basmati rice. This is worth going back to the Caspian Sea.

Serves 4.

MACHBOUS

(Persian Gulf Shrimp and Rice with Baharat)

The remote Hatta Fort Hotel in Dubai, near the Oman border, was the setting for my memorable dinner which featured exotically seasoned Machbous, the national dish of the Persian Gulf. It was worth the long drive through the desert from Abu Dhabi! Baharat, a vibrant spice blend, is used extensively in this area and is the local answer to curry powder.

1 ½ pounds large shrimp, peeled	¾ teaspoon turmeric or powdered saffron
2 tablespoons butter	1 cup chopped tomatoes
1 medium onion, chopped	1 ½ teaspoons salt
2 garlic cloves, crushed	2 tablespoons chopped cilantro
2 teaspoons Baharat (see below)	1 2/3 cup water
	1 ½ cups Basmati rice

Sauté shrimp in butter until barely pink, remove from pan, and add onion and garlic. Sauté until translucent, add spices, tomatoes, and seasonings. Simmer 5 to 10 minutes to deepen flavor, add water, bring to a boil, add rice, and simmer, covered, about 15 minutes. Add shrimp and simmer, covered, about 10 more minutes, or until rice is tender. Let stand, covered, off the heat about 5 minutes. Serve with pita, pickles, and a lettuce and tomato salad.

Baharat:

2 teaspoons pepper	1 teaspoon nutmeg
2 teaspoons paprika	1 teaspoon coriander
1 ½ teaspoons cumin	½ teaspoon cardamom
1 teaspoon cloves	

Mix spices, store in a jar, and use in Persian Gulf recipes.

Makes 2 tablespoons.

Serves 6.

MUSAKHAN

(Palestinian Chicken with Spicy Onions and Arab Bread)

This rustic and moist specialty from the Levant was introduced to me at Hassan Effendi in Jerusalem many years ago, and can be prepared with a whole chicken or with parts with adjusted cooking times. Thin pita-style bread or lavash is used.

4 small broiler halves, wings tucked under	¼ cup olive oil
Salt, pepper, & sumac	1 tablespoon sumac
½ cup olive oil	1 teaspoon allspice or cardamom
3 cups thinly sliced red onion	2 small pita breads, lavash, or Khoubz Araby, split

Season chicken well, and sauté in olive oil, using a very large iron skillet or 2 smaller ones, until browned on each side, but only partially cooked. Sauté onions in olive oil with spices until very soft. Place bread in bottom of skillets in which chicken was browned, leaving drippings. Spread each with a bit of onions, arrange chicken on top, and spread with remaining onions. Roast chicken at 350° about ½ hour, drizzling with extra oil occasionally.
Serves 4.

KHORESH E FESENJEN

(Chicken with Walnut-Pomegranate Sauce)

Khoresh is an Iranian stew with lots of luscious sauce, and this one, my favorite, can be made with duck, chicken, or lamb. Also, it is usually made with a whole bird, but suprêmes are healthier and more elegant. This was the way I had it at the Laleh Hotel in Tehran, which has a quite good restaurant.

1 cup chopped red onion	½ teaspoon cardamom or allspice
¼ cup butter	4 suprêmes
¼ cup turbinado sugar	2 tablespoons butter
1 cup finely chopped walnuts	1 or 2 tablespoons lemon or lime juice
1 cup pomegranate juice	
½ -1 cup chicken stock	

Sauté onion in butter with sugar until very soft and caramelized, about 20 minutes. Add nuts, juice, stock, and spice, simmer until thick about 20 minutes. Meanwhile, sauté suprêmes in butter until about half cooked. Add to sauce with drippings, and simmer about 10 minutes, until chicken is done. Season with juice, to taste. Serve with Chelo (see Index), and garnish all with pomegranate seeds, if available, extra walnuts, and slivered mint.

Serves 4.

CRUSTY PELAU WITH YOGURT AND EGGS

Pelau is to Iran what Pilaf is to Turkey, but in Iran a steaming method is used whereby a doubled towel is placed over the pan. This recipe is a bit more complex because yogurt and eggs are added, and it is allowed to become crusty on the bottom. Aromatic Basmati rice is used to simulate the incomparable Iranian rice. My guide bought a 50-pound bag of Iranian rice when we were in Rasht, as Iranians eat copious amounts.

2 cups Basmati rice	½ cup chicken stock
¼ cup butter, melted	½ teaspoon powdered saffron
1 cup yogurt	1-2 cups leftover cooked chicken
2 egg yolks	

½ cup diced dried apricots	½ teaspoon cumin
¼ cup dried currants	Chopped mint & cilantro, for garnish
¼ cup golden raisins	
½ teaspoon cardamom	Melted butter & yogurt, for serving

Rinse rice in a sieve under cold running water, then add to a pan of salted water, and boil 5 minutes and drain. Rinse in cold water in a sieve. Mix yogurt with yolks, stock, and saffron. Mix chicken with about 1/3 cup of the yogurt mixture, and mix half the rice with remaining yogurt mixture.

Pour butter into a 2-quart casserole or saucepan and coat sides. Spread half the yellow rice on the bottom, and sprinkle with a third of the chicken, fruits, and spices. Add half the white rice, spreading it over the top, and spread another third of the chicken, fruit, and spice mixture over. Add remaining white rice, and then remaining chicken, fruit, and spice. Top with remaining yellow rice. Cover with a doubled towel, and place a lid on top. Cook over low heat about 40 minutes, or until rice is tender. Dip bottom of pan in cold water or place on a cold surface, then unmold, if possible. Otherwise, spoon ingredients onto a large platter, and arrange crusty portions of the bottom layer on top. Garnish, and pour extra butter and yogurt over each serving.

Serves 6.

CHELOU KEBABS

Iran's version of Shish Kebab is elevated to supremacy, with the rich addition of butter, raw egg yolks, and sumac served on top of the world's best rice. Normally, the lamb is marinated in the same lemon and onion mixture which is used on the grilled Iranian Sturgeon, but I prefer this yogurt marinade, which I have also had in Jordan and Lebanon. Chicken can also be used.

1 ½ pounds boneless lamb loin or leg, cut into ½-inch thick strips 1 ½ cups yogurt ½ teaspoon each paprika & turmeric Salt & pepper	2 large tomatoes, halved Chelou (see Index) 4 tablespoons butter 4 egg yolks Sumac

Marinate lamb in yogurt mixed with seasonings at least 12 hours, refrigerated. Thread onto flat skewers and grill over charcoal, turning and brushing with marinade, about 5 to 10 minutes or until cooked to taste. Grill tomatoes with kebabs until blistered. Serve with Chelou, placing the butter, yolks, and sumac on top. Mix these into the rice for a rich, buttery taste.

Serves 4.

LAMB WITH SOUR CHERRY SAUCE

The use of fruit with meat in both Iran and Israel is quite similar except for the Israeli use of wine. Sour cherries are generally used, but Morello or any black cherry will suffice. This recipe is my version of the way I think it should taste.

1 ½ pounds boneless lamb or veal shoulder, cubed ¼ cup butter ¾ cup chopped red onion Salt & pepper ½ teaspoon each cardamom & French 4-spice powder 1 ½ cups cranberry or cherry juice	½ cup pomegranate juice ¾ pound cherries, pitted 1-2 tablespoons lemon or lime juice 1-2 tablespoons turbinado sugar 2 tablespoons chopped mint

Using a skillet, sauté meat in butter over fairly high heat until golden on all sides, add onion and seasonings, and sauté until meat is browned and onions are soft. Add juices, cover, and simmer about 1 to 1 ½ hours, or until meat is tender. Lamb will take longer than veal. Add cherries and simmer uncovered about ½ hour, or until juices have reduced and thickened somewhat. It may be thickened with a bit of cornstarch and water, although that's not the authentic method. Correct the balance of sweet and sour with juice and sugar, depending on the kind of cherries and your preference. Garnish with mint and serve with rice.

Serves 4.

LAMB WITH LIMA BEANS AND DILL

In Baghdad's Al Rasheed Hotel I had a restaurant version of the popular Arab dish, Khouzi, and it included 2 familiar ingredients. The broad beans resembled limas, and the herb was like dill. This is the way I remember it, and it is quite simple compared to most rice dishes of the region.

1 ½ pounds leg of lamb steaks or 4 suprêmes	1 package baby lima beans, thawed
3 tablespoons butter	6 cups salted water
Salt & pepper	½ cup chopped dill
½ teaspoon each saffron and Baharat (see Index)	½ teaspoon saffron
1 large onion, chopped	½ cup butter, melted
1 ½ cups Basmati rice	1 cup lamb or chicken stock

Sauté lamb or chicken in butter, using a 3- or 4-quart casserole, until golden. Season, add onion, and sauté until soft. Cover, and let cook gently in the pan juices until lamb is half tender. Add rice and limas to rapidly boiling water for about 8 minutes. Drain, add dill and saffron, and pour over lamb or chicken. Mix butter and stock, and pour over rice. Cover, and bake at 350° about ½ hour, or until all liquid has been absorbed.

Serves 4.

ISRAELI FLANK STEAK WITH JAFFA ORANGES

This Israeli fusion steak dish was made with the incomparable oranges from Jaffa, which we probably don't have, so I have substituted mandarin oranges.

1 ½ pounds flank steak	1/3 cup catsup
2 tablespoons olive oil	¼ cup chestnut honey
1 medium red onion, sliced	2 tablespoons soy sauce
2 large garlic cloves, crushed	1 small can Mandarin oranges
1 ½ cups veal or beef stock	Chopped fresh mint

Sauté steak in oil, using a skillet, until golden, add onion and garlic, and continue to sauté until soft. Deglaze with stock, add catsup, honey, and soy sauce, cover, and simmer until steak is tender, about 45 minutes. Remove steak, add oranges, and boil until reduced and slightly thickened. Check for seasoning, and serve, garnished with mint. Burghul Pilaf is ideal with this rich fruity dish.

Serves 4.

In the Middle East, most main courses are accompanied by rice or burghul, if it's not already included in the poultry or meat dish itself, and the same is true of vegetables. An infinite variety of beans, both fresh and dried; eggplant; and spinach, which is native to Persia, are the favorites.

PUREED CHICKPEAS WITH GARLIC AND YOGURT

This versatile Lebanese comfort food can be a simple meal in itself, or it makes a great base for kebabs of all kinds. I always use dried beans, but canned will suffice if time is of the essence. There are many ways to season and serve, but I prefer this one. The olive oil helps tenderize the beans.

1 cup dried chickpeas, soaked overnight	Reserved chickpea liquid
3 or 4 cups water	French bread or pita, torn into pieces
¼ cup olive oil	Yogurt Garlic Sauce (see Index)
2 large garlic cloves	Olives
2 teaspoons salt	

Drain chickpeas, cover with water and oil, and simmer covered about 2 hours or until tender. Drain, reserving liquid. Puree chickpeas in processor with garlic and salt, adding reserved chickpea liquid to achieve desired consistency. I also like to add more olive oil. Pour enough reserved chickpea liquid over bread, placed on plates, to soak as desired. Pour pureed chickpeas over bread, then add sauce or plain yogurt, even more olive oil, if desired, and olives.

Serves 2.

GREEN BEANS WITH GARLIC OIL

Lebanon, Syria, and Jordan have a penchant for cooking vegetables in oil with plenty of garlic. Tomatoes are frequently added to the beans, but that is fairly ubiquitous throughout the world, so I prefer to leave them out.

1 pound small green beans	½ teaspoon salt
1 large onion, diced	¼ teaspoon allspice
¼ cup olive oil	¼ cup water
2 garlic cloves, crushed	2 tablespoons chopped parsley

Trim beans, but leave whole. Sauté onion in oil until very tender, add garlic and beans, tossing with oil. Add seasonings and water, cover, and simmer gently about 20 minutes, or until tender. Garnish with parsley.

Serves 4.

BURGHUL PILAF WITH FRUIT

Burghul wheat, like rice, has many variations, and is a staple of the Middle East. It is frequently mixed with lentils and vermicelli, as well as rice and even barley. This one includes rice, fruit, and nuts.

1 cup burghul wheat	¼ teaspoon allspice
¼ cup chopped onion	¼ cup chopped pistachios or almonds
¼ cup butter	
1 ½ teaspoons salt	¼ cup dried currants
¼ teaspoon crushed saffron	¼ cup chopped dates or figs
¼ teaspoon crushed dried mint	2 cups chicken stock
	1 cup cooked rice (optional)

Sauté burghul and onion in butter until golden. Add seasonings, nuts, fruit, and stock. Simmer, covered, about 20 minutes, or until stock is absorbed. Fold in rice, if desired, and check for seasoning. Serves 6.

CHELOU

(Persian Rice)

Persia can easily take credit for developing the world's best method for cooking rice, and the rice itself is exemplary. Basmati rice is widely available and is a good substitute. Chelou is also called Chelo, as I found in Iran.

2 cups Iranian or Basmati rice	½ cup water
2 quarts water, boiling	6 tablespoons butter
2 tablespoons salt	

Rinse rice well, drain and add to boiling water with salt. Boil about 5 minutes, drain well. Pour water and butter into pan, and add rice, mounding it in the center. Insert the handle of a wooden spoon in the center all the way to the bottom to allow steam to penetrate all the rice. Place a folded towel on top of the pan, cover, and let cook gently about 20 to 30 minutes, or until rice is tender and liquid is absorbed. No matter what I serve this with, I still like to stir in butter, egg yolks, and sumac as in the Chelou Kebabs recipe in this section.

Serves 6.

YOGURT BEETS

In Iran this is considered a salad, but I love to serve it as a cooling and slightly tart side dish to many of the previous main courses which do not include yogurt. On a hot day, it is a delight by itself.

1 pound beets, cooked, peeled, & diced (¼ cup reserved)	1 tablespoon lemon juice
2 cups lightly drained yogurt	¼ teaspoon powdered saffron
2 tablespoons olive oil	½ teaspoon crushed dried mint
Salt	Fresh slivered mint leaves

Mix beets with yogurt, oil, and seasonings. Serve in a glass dish, green if possible, and garnish top with reserved beets and fresh mint. The soothing freshening flavor and the red, green, and yellow combination make this a very special dish.

Serves 6.

Middle Eastern desserts are sweet and syrupy, much as in Greece and Turkey. Rice puddings abound, as do fruit desserts that make use of the plethora of dried as well as fresh fruits. Pastries and cakes of many kinds are found throughout the area, including the ubiquitous baklava.

JORDANIAN DATES AND BANANAS

There are many variations in this Jordanian specialty, and there are few desserts so good that are so easy.

6 bananas, sliced	1 cup heavy cream
12 ounces chopped dates	¼ teaspoon orange flower water
½ cup halved pistachios or slivered almonds	1/3 cup brown sugar

Place layers of bananas, dates, and nuts in a shallow baking dish. Cover with cream, mixed with orange flower water, and refrigerate several hours. Sieve sugar over cream, and caramelize under the broiler several minutes.

Serves 6.

MIDDLE EAST RICE PUDDING WITH FRUIT AND NUTS

Rice pudding is universal; thus, the flavorings and type of rice denote its ethnicity. This is my composite of Middle east rice puddings.

¾ cup Basmati rice	1 strip each, lemon & orange zest
6 cups milk	

½ teaspoon each cardamom & powdered saffron 1 cup sugar 4 egg yolks	½ cup dried apricots, diced 1/3 cup dried currants 1/3 cup chopped pistachio nuts

Simmer rice in milk with orange and lemon zest about 45 minutes, or until soft and thick. Whisk seasonings, sugar, and yolks until thick, and add to rice with about half the fruit and nuts. Simmer gently until lightly thickened, about 5 minutes. Sprinkle with remaining fruit and nuts when serving. This is good hot or cold. Serves 6.

HONEY WALNUT CAKE

This luscious syrupy cake, cut into diamonds, is one of the most popular in the Middle East, especially Syria and Jordan.

½ cup butter, softened ¾ cup sugar 3 eggs 2 teaspoons grated orange zest 1 ¼ cups unbleached flour 2 teaspoons baking powder	1 teaspoon cardamom or cinnamon ¾ cup finely chopped walnuts Honey Syrup (see below) Yogurt & sweetened apricots or cherries

Cream butter with sugar until fluffy, beat in eggs and zest. Fold in dry ingredients and nuts. Bake in a buttered 8-inch square pan at 350° about ½ hour, or until it tests done.

1 1/3 cups water	2 tablespoons lemon juice
¾ cup sugar	2 tablespoons chestnut honey

Boil all ingredients for 10 minutes, cool, and pour over hot cake. Cut into diamond shapes and serve with yogurt and fruit.

Serves 6.

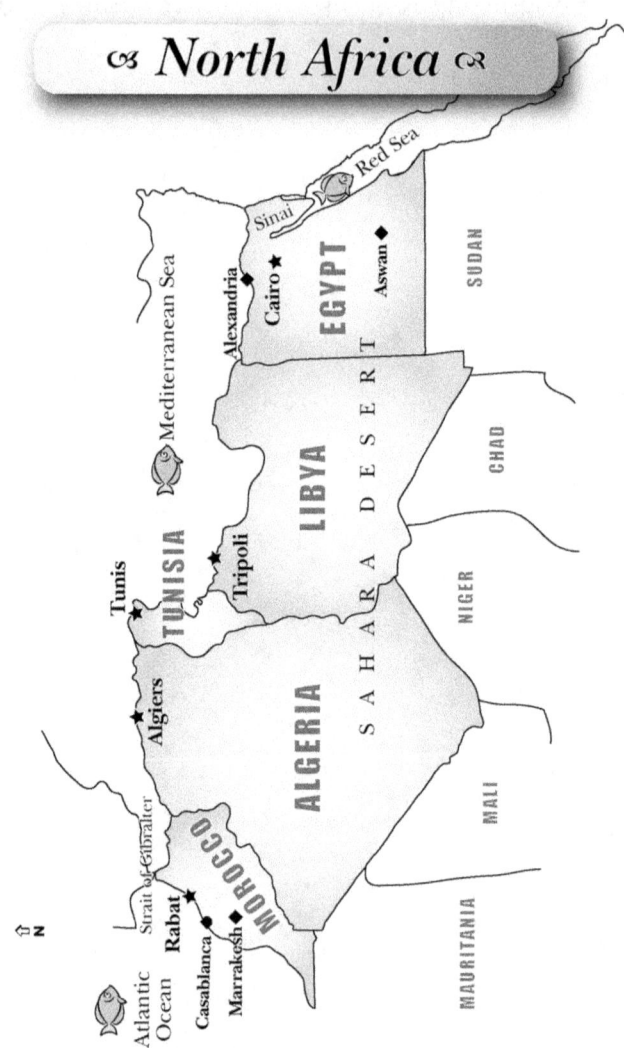

NORTH AFRICA
EGYPT LIBYA TUNISIA
ALGERIA MOROCCO

The ancient and exotic lands of North Africa form a cultural and gastronomical bridge between the Middle East and sub-Saharan Africa, as my journeys between Cairo and Casablanca have revealed. Although this is still Muslim territory, the governments are traditionally secular, and a more moderate form of Islam is practiced. Also, there is an intriguing blend of African, Arab, and European ethnology. The cooking also reflects this blend.

Egypt, the land of pyramids and pharoahs, should first be seen at night on a flight from Khartoum, Sudan to Cairo. The Nile, the longest river in the world, is bordered by more and more lights as the flight progresses and there are no lights to be seen to the east or west. This 4,000-mile stretch of river is where one of the world's earliest civilizations began about 7,000 years ago with the planting of crops. For a closer look, a cruise on the Nile to Aswan and Luxor is a most rewarding intellectual experience.

Cairo, the largest city in the Arab world, is one of astonishing diversity. The teeming streets are redolent with smoke from cigarettes and cooking fires, as well as spices and animal dung. A few blocks away are a myriad of luxury hotels and your choice of French, Italian, or other ethnic restaurants. For true Egyptian food, Felfela, a venerable favorite of the locals, specializes in ful medamis, a lusty fava bean dish pungent with olive oil, lemon juice, garlic, and cumin. I was so impressed I brought dried beans back home with me.

A visit to the Khan-el-Khalili Bazaar's narrow winding streets reveal the Arab, Turkish, and Persian influences. Hawkers offer kebabs, flat breads, and mezze dishes as in the Levant, as well as Fireek, the Egyptian form of couscous, and Milookhiyya, which is similar to spinach. Mint, dill, and okra, indigenous to Egypt, are ubiquitous. Sweet minted tea is the drink of choice, as it is from the Red Sea to the Atlantic. But I can never resist a glass or two of Omar Khayyam, a venerable red wine.

Libya, part of the Maghreb along with Tunisia, Algeria, and Morocco, is dominated by the sun-drenched Sahara and Moammar Ghadaffi. It was a political pariah until recently, and now its outstanding Greek and Roman ruins are ready to come out of obsolescence, as is the spicy food.

Under Ottoman, Spanish, and Italian rule for many decades, Libya has a yet-to-be-developed fusion cuisine. These influences blend beautifully and offer infinite possibilities, as I discovered on my brief visit.

I had flown to Djerba, a Tunisian island not far from the Libyan border, and was the lone American on the flight with French and Libyan business travelers. One's culinary interest can get one anywhere, I always say, and soon I was speeding toward the border in a Libyan publisher's private car. Since he was well known at the border, I was allowed to pass, and we drove to Sabratha, 45 miles from Tripoli. A humble restaurant served us a typical lamb, macaroni, and chickpea dish, highly seasoned and a perfect fusion of culinary influences. After this interesting afternoon, I was then driven back to Djerba. As I also say, "Anything goes in Africa." That's why I love it so much.

Tiny Tunisia, a jewel in the crown of North Africa, has an awe-inspiring legacy of invaders-Carthaginian, Roman, Byzantine, Arab, and Turkish. Then came the Spanish, Italian, and especially the French, who left their influences on the people, architecture, and food. From the great city of Carthage on the Mediterranean to the island of Djerba in the south, I found the always excellent food to be a cornucopia of these flavors.

Tunis, a cosmopolitan yet distinctly Arab-style city, has the best preserved medieval medina in the Islamic world as well as world-class restaurants. Farther south on the coast is Cape Bon, an area which supplies the country with an abundance of figs, olives, including excellent olive oil, citrus fruits, and quite good wine. I found a distinct Jewish influence on the island of Djerba, along with its very Muslim Houmt Souk, which displays all the Middle Eastern spices-anise, coriander, cumin, cardamom, cinnamon, mint, and saffron.

These spices flavor the ubiquitous lamb dishes, the abundant fish, and especially the many varieties of tagines, couscous, and the national dish of Tunisia-golden and flaky fillo pastry containing an egg, called Brik.

Algeria, the second largest country in Africa, is mostly Saharan desert, which is quite forbidding. Algiers, the capitol, is a most welcoming city in spite of its many years of civil strife. As a former French colony, it takes great pride in its cooking which is similar to Tunisia's and Morocco's, with an emphasis on tagines and couscous, as well as vegetables and citrus fruits.

The French influence was quite noticeable in the restaurants when French baguettes were brought to the table instead of the traditional Arab flat breads. And, of course, wine is a major part of the dinner. France has been the recipient of much inexpensive Algerian wine for blending, and the Pieds-Noirs (French expatriates) have always demanded it. A major exception is that the French culinary school of thought that no one seasoning should dominate is superseded by an aggressive use of seasoning.

Morocco, also a former French colony, is probably the most exotic and alluring country in North Africa, with one of the world's best and most developed cuisines. Lavish hotels and restaurants abound in Casablanca, a beautiful city planned by the French; the royal cities of Rabat, Meknes, and Fez; and, of course, magical Marrakech, a Berber city, which is on the ancient caravan route. Situated between the Atlas Mountains and the Sahara, the city has spectacular Moorish architecture reminiscent of Persian style. Djemaa el Fna, which means "place of the dead," is undoubtedly the most mysterious and occult square in the world, where one can visit the snake charmer, buy mystic potions, have dental work done "en plein air" then relax with the obligatory glass of hot, minted tea. Winding alleyways with markets and mosques lead off of Djemma el Fna to palaces and restaurants where you can have authentic Berber cuisine, as the Berbers were indigenous to this area.

With the same ethnic mix of invaders as the rest of the Maghreb, the cuisine is very similar, but with its own exceptional creations, such as Bastila. Also, seafood plays an important part in the cooking, with trout and pike from the mountain streams, and bass, skate, perch, mullet, and conger from the sea. And the tagines and couscous wouldn't be the same without preserved lemons.

RECIPES FROM NORTH AFRICA

MSIR (PRESERVED LEMONS)

MOROCCAN RADISH AND ORANGE SALAD

MOROCCAN OLIVE AND LEMON SALAD

MOROCCAN MIXED SALAD

TUNISIAN ROASTED PEPPER AND TOMATO SALAD

ALGERIAN COUSCOUS SALAD

HARIRA (MOROCCAN LAMB SOUP)

MILOOKHIYA (EGYPTIAN GREENS SOUP)

MOROCCAN ANISE BREAD

BASTILA (MOROCCAN FLAKY PASTRY WITH CHICKEN, ALMONDS, AND EGGS)

TUNISIAN LAMB AND EGG BRIK

MOROCCAN COUSCOUS

LAMB TAGINE WITH ARTICHOKES, LEMONS, AND OLIVES

ARTICHOKE MEATBALL TAGINE WITH TOMATO SAUCE AND EGGS

SHORBA (LIBYAN LAMB, PASTA, AND CHICKPEA STEW)

SFERIA (ALGERIAN CHICKEN WITH CHICKPEAS AND CROQUETTES)

FUL MEDAMES (EGYPTIAN FAVA BEANS WITH GARLIC, LEMON, AND PARSLEY)

ORANGE HONEY YOGURT

STUFFED DATES

HONEYED COUSCOUS WITH DATES AND PISTACHIOS

HONEYED FIGS WITH MADEIRA

First courses across North Africa are likely to begin with a cool refreshing salad composed primarily of vegetables or fruits, especially preserved lemons. The exceptional savory pastries, large and small, are ubiqitous, and the soups tend to be hearty. An outstanding meal can be made of a combination of these items alone.

MSIR

(Preserved Lemons)

The cornerstone of Moroccan cooking, preserved lemons are used in everything except desserts. Salads, tagines, and couscous reach new heights with this tart and salty addition. I have tried many methods of preparing them, but this is my favorite, and they last almost indefinitely.

6 large lemons 1 quart water	½ cup Kosher salt

Make 6 shallow lengthwise incisions in each lemon with a sharp knife. Boil in water with salt, using a stainless steel pan, about 10 minutes, or until slightly soft. Place lemons in jars, cover completely with the cooled brine, cover, and let stand 1 week. Refrigerate after opening, for up to a year. When using, discard pulp, and dice or slice peel.

MOROCCAN RADISH AND ORANGE SALAD

Moorish arches, colorfully tiled fountains, and exotically attired waiters were only a hint of the exotic dinner at Al Mounia in Casablanca. This salad was one of several we enjoyed with the Anise Bread.

¼ cup lemon juice	12 radishes, trimmed & grated
2 tablespoons sugar	6 oranges, peeled & sectioned
1 tablespoon orange water	Cinnamon
Dash of salt	Fresh mint

Mix dressing ingredients, add radishes and oranges, and chill. Sprinkle with cinnamon, and garnish with mint.

Serves 6.

MOROCCAN OLIVE AND LEMON SALAD

This is another of the classic salads served at Al Mounia.

2 tablespoons olive oil	¼ teaspoon sugar
2 garlic cloves, crushed	1 ½ cups mixed olives
½ teaspoon salt	2 preserved lemons, pulp removed, & rind diced
½ teaspoon paprika	
¼ teaspoon cumin	Chopped mint or cilantro

Whisk oil with seasonings, add olives and lemon, and garnish with mint.

Serves 6.

MOROCCAN MIXED SALAD

This contemporary salad is a mixture of all that composes a delicious Moroccan salad, and it is excellent with grilled or roasted meats. Various types of lettuce may be used.

2 tablespoons lemon juice 2 tablespoons orange juice 1 tablespoon orange flower water ¼ teaspoon cinnamon ¼ teaspoon salt 1/3 cup walnut oil	Mesclun, radicchio, arugula, or watercress (or a mixture) 3 oranges, peeled & sectioned ½ cup black olives 1 preserved lemon, pulp removed, diced ½ cup chopped walnuts

Whisk dressing ingredients together. Arrange lettuce on platter, mix with half the dressing. Arrange oranges and olives on top, and scatter lemon and walnuts over all. Drizzle with remaining dressing.

Serves 4-6.

TUNISIAN ROASTED PEPPER AND TOMATO SALAD

A classic salad that accompanied a variety of grilled meats and fish at a seaside restaurant in Hammamet, south of Cape Bon, and one which I have reinvented to give it a new twist.

3 orange or green peppers, roasted, peeled & julienned (see Index) 3 cups cherry tomatoes, halved ½ cup chopped parsley 1 cup black or brown olives 2 tablespoons lemon juice 2 garlic cloves, crushed	½ teaspoon cumin Salt, pepper, & paprika 1/3 cup olive oil 1 preserved lemon, diced, (optional) ¼ cup oven-dried tomatoes, sliced

Mix peppers, tomatoes, parsley, and olives. Whisk dressing ingredients together, add to salad, toss, and garnish with lemon and oven-dried tomatoes.

Serves 4-6.

ALGERIAN COUSCOUS SALAD

When I arrived at El Aurassi Hotel in Algiers, I was greeted by name and warmly welcomed. An appointment with the chef had already been arranged, and this was one of the great dishes on my kitchen tour.

½ pound couscous (1 1/3 cups)	2 tablespoons orange juice
1 ¼ cups hot chicken stock	1 teaspoon each grated orange & lemon zest
1 cup cooked chickpeas	1 teaspoon salt
½ cup chopped dates	½ teaspoon French 4-spice powder
½ cup golden raisins	
½ cup sliced roasted almonds	½ teaspoon powdered saffron
½ cup chopped parsley or mint	1 clove garlic, crushed
2 tablespoons date vinegar	1/3 cup olive oil
2 tablespoons lemon juice	

Add couscous to stock, stir, cover, and let stand about 5 minutes. Add chickpeas, fruits, almonds, and parsley. Whisk dressing ingredients together, and mix into salad. Serve at room temperature as a salad or as an accompaniment to roasted lamb or kebabs.

Serves 6.

HARIRA

(Moroccan Lamb Soup)

This is the famous soup eaten during Ramadan, the holy month when nothing to eat or drink is allowed from sunrise to sundown. It is very nourishing as well as delicious.

¾ pound lamb shoulder, cut into small chunks	½ teaspoon cardamom or cumin
2 tablespoons butter or olive oil	1 ½ teaspoons salt
½ cup chopped onion	1 teaspoon pepper
¼ cup chopped cilantro	6-8 cups water or lamb stock
2 large tomatoes, seeded & chopped	¼ cup lentils, orzo, or rice
1 cup cooked chickpeas	1 tablespoon lemon juice
½ teaspoon turmeric	2 eggs
	Cinnamon, for sifting

Sauté lamb and onion in butter until lamb is lightly browned, add cilantro, tomatoes, chickpeas, seasonings, and water. Cover, and simmer about 1 hour. Add lentils, and simmer about 4 hours, or until lamb and lentils are tender. Whisk juice and eggs, then whisk into soup, forming strands. Sift cinnamon over top when serving.

Serves 6-8.

MILOOKHIYYA

(Egyptian Greens Soup)

This traditional soup made with milookhiyya, Egyptian greens similar to spinach or chard, was prepared for me at Caroll Restaurant in Cairo, and is usually made with the meat and stock from a poached chicken. It is still great if you use a good strong stock, and you can add leftover chicken to it.

1 onion, thinly sliced	1 package dried milookhiyya (1 ½ cups) or 1 pound spinach or chard, shredded
5 garlic cloves, crushed	
1 teaspoon ground cardamom	Salt & pepper
2 tablespoons olive oil or butter	1 tablespoon lemon juice
4-6 cups strong chicken stock	Leftover shredded chicken (optional)
1 tablespoon tomato paste (optional)	1 cup rice, cooked

Sauté onion and garlic with cardamom in oil, covered, until very soft and translucent. Add stock, bring to a boil, add milookhiyya, and cook only a few minutes, until thick and floating on top. Add seasonings, juice, and chicken, if using. Serve over rice.

Serves 6.

MOROCCAN ANISE BREAD

This traditional North African bread can be formed into other shapes and have a variety of seeds, either in the dough, or on top. It is great with soups as well as with tagines and couscous.

1 package dry yeast	1 tablespoon salt
1 teaspoon sugar	1 tablespoon mixed anise, sesame, & cumin seeds, or all anise
¼ cup warm water	
2 tablespoons olive oil	
3 cups bread flour	1 ¼ cups warm water
1 ½ cups whole wheat flour	2 tablespoons honey
	Cornmeal

Proof yeast with sugar in water until bubbly. Add oil. Mix dry ingredients in large bowl of electric mixer with a dough hook. Add yeast mixture and remaining water and honey gradually, kneading until smooth and elastic. Cover and let rise about ½ hour in a warm place. Divide into 4 balls, flatten each into a round, place on a baking sheet sprinkled with cornmeal, cover, and let rise about 1 or 1 ½ hours, until doubled in bulk. Bake at 400° about 10 minutes, reduce to 350° and bake about ½ hour, or until they test done. Cool on a rack before cutting into wedges.

Makes 6 rounds.

BASTILA

(Moroccan Flaky Pastry with Chicken, Almonds, and Eggs)

This wild but heavenly pastry is well worth the effort as it can be a first course, part of a mezze, or a main course accompanied by a Moroccan salad. There are many variations, but this is the classic bastila, also known as bisteeya. It should be served hot.

2 2-pound chickens, cut up, or 4 squabs	4 garlic cloves, crushed
	1 cup chopped cilantro or parsley
½ cup butter	
1 cup chopped red onion	1 teaspoon ground cardamom

½ teaspoon ground cumin	¼ cup butter
¼ teaspoon turmeric	½ cup powdered sugar
¼ teaspoon powdered saffron	1 teaspoon cinnamon
Salt & pepper	15 half-sheets fillo pastry (9 x 14 inches)
1 cup chicken or veal stock	
3 tablespoons lemon juice	½ cup melted butter
8 eggs, beaten	Powdered sugar
1 ½ cups sliced or slivered almonds	Cinnamon

Sauté chicken in butter until golden, using a large sauté pan. Add onion and garlic, sauté until soft, then add remaining seasonings and stock. Cover, and simmer 1 hour, or until chicken is tender. Remove chicken, and reduce liquid to 1 ½ cups. Remove skin and bones from chicken, shredding the meat. Add juice to reserved stock, add eggs, and stir until soft-cooked. Taste for salt. Sauté almonds in butter until golden, chop coarsely, and add sugar and cinnamon.

Using a buttered 12-inch paella pan (or similar), overlap 9 fillo sheets, buttering each one, in a circle. Butter 6 more sheets, fold in half, and bake at 425° about half a minute, or until crisp. Lay 3 sheets in the center, side by side. Sprinkle almond mixture in the center, covering about half the pastry. Add half the egg mixture, draining if too much liquid remains, the chicken, and the remaining eggs. Lay remaining 3 sheets on top, side by side, and fold extended edges of fillo up over the top to form a neat package. Brush with butter, and bake at 425° about 15 to 20 minutes, or until golden and crisp. Place a large baking sheet over it, invert, and remove pan, and bake 10 more minutes, or until golden. Slide onto a large round platter, sift powdered sugar heavily over it, and using a small pastry tip, form a lattice design with cinnamon. Serve hot.

Serves 6 to 12.

TUNISIAN LAMB AND EGG BRIK

This is Tunisia's answer to Morocco's Bastila, which, although not as complicated, is every bit as delicious. There are many versions, but this is my favorite and the one I had at Hotel Abou Nawas Hotel in Tunis the night before all Americans and Europeans were told to leave the country because Yasser Arafat's top aides had been assassinated. But my final dinner was definitely one to remember. The Brik was followed by a savory tagine. You may find an uncanny resemblance between brik and Ravioli with Egg and Spinach in the Italian section, and it is likely that Brik was influenced by Italian invaders. Both may be made in any shape and with wonton wrappers instead of fillo for the brik and pasta for the ravioli.

½ pound ground lamb, veal, or chicken	¼ cup chopped mint or cilantro
2 large shallots, chopped	2 tablespoons butter or olive oil
¼ teaspoon cumin	2 tablespoons parmesan cheese
¼ teaspoon coriander or cardamom	4 fillo half-sheets, 9 x 14 inches
	Melted butter or olive oil
Salt & pepper	4 small eggs

Sauté lamb, shallots, and seasonings in butter or oil briefly, just until lamb is barely cooked through. Add cheese, cool. Brush fillo with butter, fold lengthwise into a 7- x 9-inch rectangle, brush again, and place filling in a shallow mound on lower half of the pastry width. Make a depression in the center, and break an egg into it. Fold upper half over filling, brush with butter again, and seal edges well. You will have 4 briks, about 4 ½ x 7 inches. Heat butter, oil, or a combination in a large skillet to a depth of about ¼ inch until quite hot, then fry briks a few minutes on each side, until golden and flaky. Serve with lemon wedges, if desired.

Makes 4.

North African main courses range from the Middle Eastern style kebabs and koftas in Egypt to hearty Libyan and Algerian stews to the flavorful tagines and couscous of Mahgreb. Egypt's roast pigeons are renowned as are roasted chickens and lamb throughout the region. Fish is eaten along the coast, of course, and vegetables play an important role in main dishes.

MOROCCAN COUSCOUS

Although the pride of Morocco, couscous is found as far away as Sicily and Brazil, and I have also had it in Ouagadougou, Burkina Faso and in Mali, where it is made with millet, maize, barley, and other grains instead of the typical wheat. Created by the Berbers in the Atlas mountains, it is traditionally cooked in a couscousière, a voluptuous-looking pan with the bottom part being used to cook the tagine (stew) and the perforated upper part used for steaming the couscous. I've had many decades of use with my French-made Bourgeat couscousière, probably the best. This recipe, a composite of the many that I have sampled from Marrakech to Tangier, gives the traditional method for regular couscous, but the instant variety is now ubiquitous, so I have given a method whereby it can be used in the couscousière. At least it does absorb some of the tagine's flavor and you will be aesthetically rewarded. Also, cubed lamb may replace the chicken with an adjustment of the cooking time, and optional ingredients that may be added are raisins, dates, almonds, honey, and butternut squash, all of which would be great with lamb. And although Moroccans eat copious amounts of couscous, as the Chinese eat rice, I opt for a more modest amount. I also love the fusion effect of the Italian cippolini onions, as well as the red onions, and the French 4-spice powder.

½ cup butter	1 red onion, thickly sliced
6 suprêmes or 1 3-pound chicken	1 large tomato, chopped

Global Culinary Adventures

2 teaspoons salt	2 cups cooked chickpeas
Pepper, to taste	3 carrots, peeled & sliced diagonally
1 teaspoon French 4-spice powder	2 small yams, peeled & sliced diagonally
½ teaspoon powdered saffron	1 small package lima beans, thawed
6-12 cups water	
2-4 cups couscous	1 pound zucchini, sliced diagonally
3-4 cups chicken or veal stock	
4-6 small cippolini onions, peeled	1- 1 ½ cups cream
	¼ cup butter

Melt butter in bottom of couscousière, add chicken, onion, tomato, and seasonings. Cover and let flavors meld about 15 minutes. Meanwhile, pour water over couscous, swish about, then drain. Place couscous in shallow pan to swell about 10 minutes, then rub between your hands to prevent lumps. Add stock and all vegetables except zucchini to bottom pan, and add couscous to top pan. Cover and let simmer and steam about 45 minutes until vegetables are tender and couscous is swelled, but not mushy. If chicken is tender before this, remove so that it is not overcooked. A whole chicken will take the entire 45 minutes.

If using instant couscous, simply pour water over it, drain, place in top of couscousière about 10 minutes before the lower pot is finished. Place vegetables around the edge of a large platter, I like to use a purple one, and reduce broth to about 2 cups. Add cream. Mix butter into couscous and mound in center of platter. Arrange chicken over it, and pour some of the sauce over all, serving the remainder separately.

Serve 6 to 8.

LAMB TAGINE WITH ARTICHOKES, LEMONS, AND OLIVES

This classic Moroccan tagine, or stew, is a composite of my favorite flavors and is quite versatile, as other vegetables may be substituted, as well as chicken. La Mamounia, the famous and exotic Marrakech hotel with dramatic high-ceilinged rooms and balconies overlooking the gardens and Koutoubia tower, was the setting for this light and delicious dish.

2-3 pounds lamb shoulder, cut into 1-inch cubes	1 teaspoon salt
¼ cup olive oil	1 fresh lemon, quartered
½ cup chopped red onion	1 cup water
2 garlic cloves, crushed	2 cups frozen artichoke quarters, thawed
1 teaspoon paprika	1 ½ cups assorted olives, pitted
½ teaspoon cumin	2 preserved lemons, quartered, and pulp removed
½ teaspoon powdered saffron	Chopped parsley or cilantro

Using a large sauté pan, sauté lamb in oil until golden, add onion and garlic, and sauté until translucent. Add seasonings, fresh lemon, and water, and simmer, covered, about 45 minutes or until lamb is tender. Add artichokes, olives, and preserved lemons, cover, and simmer about 10 minutes. Remove lamb, and reduce cooking liquid until lightly thickened and glazed. Pour over lamb, and serve with plain couscous or rice.

Serves 4-6.

ARTICHOKE MEATBALL TAGINE
WITH TOMATO SAUCE AND EGGS

After my brief foray into Libya, I returned to Djerba, Tunisia, and a secluded hideaway hotel (the name escapes me) at the end of the island on a private beach. This fantastic and unique meatball dish was my reward. It is actually somewhat similar to the Albanian Lamb with Tomatoes and Eggs in the East European section. After all, the Italian influence is evident in both places.

2 eggs, beaten	¾ pound ground veal or lamb
2 large garlic cloves, crushed	12-16 canned artichoke hearts, chopped
1 teaspoon paprika	¼ cup olive oil
1 teaspoon cumin	1 28-ounce can crushed tomatoes
1 teaspoon coriander	
1 teaspoon salt	1 teaspoon cumin
1 cup chopped parsley	4-6 eggs
1 cup bread crumbs	Extra artichoke hearts & parsley
½ cup Parmesan cheese	

Add to beaten eggs seasonings, parsley, crumbs, cheese, meat, and artichokes. Mix and knead well, then form into about 2 dozen meatballs. Sauté in oil, using a large sauté pan, until browned, add tomatoes and cumin, and let simmer about 10 minutes, or until done. Remove meatballs to a large shallow serving dish. Break eggs into sauce and poach until whites are set and yolks still runny. Some cooks poach the eggs in the sauce without removing the meatballs. Place eggs over meatballs with sauce. Garnish with extra artichokes and parsley.

Serves 4-6.

SHORBA

(Libyan Lamb, Pasta, and Chickpea Stew)

Shorba, frequently spelled sharba, chorba, ciorba, cherba, and other ways, is actually a Persian word for soup and is known throughout the Islamic world as such. It can be strictly soup or cooked down to a stew as this version was in Sabratha, Libya. My eternal gratitude goes to the prominent Libyan publisher who was able to make it possible for me to cross the border from the Tunisian island of Djerba to Libya, and who introduced this typical dish to me. This is the way he said to make it.

1 ½ -2 pounds cubed lamb shoulder	1 teaspoon cayenne (optional)
1 ½ large onions, chopped	1/3 cup tomato paste
3 tablespoons olive oil	2 cups lamb stock or water
½ cup chopped parsley	½ cup small macaroni
¼ tablespoon turmeric	1 ½ cups cooked chickpeas
½ tablespoon allspice	Chopped mint
½ tablespoon salt	Lemon slices

Sauté lamb and onion in oil until browned, add parsley, seasonings, and tomato paste, and simmer, covered, about 10 minutes to develop flavors. Add water, and simmer until lamb is almost done, about 45 minutes to an hour, covered. Add macaroni and chickpeas, cover, and simmer about 15 minutes, until all is tender and a wonderful aroma rises from the pot. Garnish each bowl with mint and lemon slices, and eat with lots of Arab flat bread.

Serves 6.

SFERIA

(Algerian Chicken with Chickpeas and Croquettes)

This is an humble and traditional dish that was part of my enormous dinner at La Baie Restaurant in El Aurassi Hotel, situated high on a hill overlooking the bay, and a great vantage point for listening to the enchanting call to prayer from the Imam's mosques. This was accompanied by several kinds of cigar-shaped fillo pastries, all very hot and spicy, and this was the same day I had my personal tour of the kitchen. A good rough red wine washed it down. I use suprêmes instead of a cut-up whole chicken, the typical way.

6 suprêmes	Salt & pepper
2 tablespoons butter or olive oil	1 cup dried chickpeas, cooked
	1 cup chicken stock or water
1 medium onion, chopped	1 egg
2 garlic cloves, crushed	1 tablespoon lemon juice
½ teaspoon cardamom or cinnamon	Chopped parsley or mint
	Croquettes (recipe below)

Sauté chicken in butter, using a sauté pan, adding onion, until both are golden. Add garlic and seasonings, cover, and simmer about 5 minutes to imbue chicken with flavor. Add chickpeas and stock, cover, and simmer about ½ hour. Remove chicken, reduce liquid to ¾ cup, and thicken with egg beaten with juice after croquettes are ready. Return chicken to sauce, keep warm and place in center of a large platter. Sprinkle with parsley.

Croquettes:

1 ½ pounds Yukon potatoes, peeled & boiled	Salt, pepper, & cardamom
	Flour, for dredging
2 egg yolks	2 eggs, beaten
½ cup parmesan cheese	1 cup bread crumbs
2 tablespoons chopped parsley	¼ cup olive oil

Drain potatoes, return to the heat to let dry, then whip them in an electric mixer. Add yolks, cheese, parsley, and seasonings to taste. Form into 1 dozen ovals. Dredge in flour, dip in egg to coat, then roll in crumbs. Sauté in hot oil until golden all over. Arrange around chicken and chickpeas.

Makes 12, serving 6.

FUL MEDAMES

(Egyptian Fava Beans with Garlic, Lemon, and Parsley)

A cousin of Lebanese Pureed Chickpeas with Garlic and Yogurt (see Index), this is probably Egypt's oldest dish and its national dish, as everyone, from the upper echelon to the street people, eats it regularly. I was taken to Felfela, a local mainstay for bean dishes, where I was taught the intricacies of making and eating this most satisfying dish. Favas or broad brown beans are used, and garlic, lemon, and parsley are traditional, but I love to add fried eggs and Labneh (see Index) or plain yogurt and then mash it all together, to be scooped up with flat bread. If none of these beans are available, small red kidney or cranberry beans make an acceptable substitute.

2 cups dried favas or broad brown beans, soaked overnight	4-6 hard-cooked eggs, quartered, or fried
6 cups water	2 lemons, quartered
4 garlic cloves, crushed	Olive oil
½ tablespoon salt	Chopped parsley
2 teaspoons cumin	Labneh (see Index) optional
	6 flat breads

Drain beans, add water, and cook, covered, until very tender-as long as 5 or 6 hours, if necessary. The beans I brought back from Cairo took that long. Drain beans, and add garlic, salt, and cumin. Serve whole, or mash. Pass bowls of remaining ingredients and bread for each diner to use as desired. This dish can be breakfast, lunch, dinner, or a snack, and it is the supreme comfort food.

Serves 4-6.

Desserts in North Africa include the ubiquitous Baklava and its many variations, rice pudding, sweet couscous, and especially many delightful fruit desserts that feature glorious oranges, dates, and figs. Morocco has numerous fried specialties, cookies, and cakes. Strong hot coffee is the drink of choice in Egypt and Libya, and the sweet minted tea is de rigueur all the way to the Atlantic.

ORANGE HONEY YOGURT

It was at the glorious and venerable Pullman Cataract Hotel in Aswan, Egypt, that the breakfast waiter told me that it is traditional to stir honey into the yogurt, and that is still the way I must have it. But for dessert, I can't think of anything better than this glorified version.

2 cups yogurt	1-2 teaspoons orange flower water
1/3 cup honey	
¼ cup orange juice	½ teaspoon ground cardamom
	Orange sections & mint (optional)

Whisk yogurt with honey, juice, and seasonings until blended. Pour into a bowl, I use a bright green glass one, or into individual glass bowls, and garnish with orange sections and mint, if desired. Serves 4-6.

STUFFED DATES

Throughout the Levant, the Persian Gulf, and North Africa, dates are used in a myriad of confectionary delights. In both Algeria and Libya, I had them stuffed with almond paste or marzipan, and also with whole almonds and pistachios. These are eaten like candy and make a nice accompaniment to the Orange Honey Yogurt (above). They are beautiful when displayed on a bed of mint.

2 dozen fresh dates, pitted	Pinch of cardamom
½ cup almond paste or marzipan	Pastel food colorings
	1 bunch of mint

Mix almond paste with a bit of cardamom and food coloring, using different colors. Fill each date in a slit in the side with about 1 teaspoon, allowing it to show. Arrange on a bed of mint. Enjoy with coffee.

Makes 24.

HONEYED COUSCOUS WITH DATES AND PISTACHIOS

I have discovered a number of sweet couscous dishes both for breakfast and dessert throughout North Africa, and this is my favorite.

1 cup orange juice or water	¾ cup couscous
2 tablespoons butter	1/3 cup chopped pistachios
½ tablespoon grated orange zest	¾ cup yogurt flavored with honey, orange flower water, & cardamom, to taste
¼ cup honey	
1/3 cup chopped fresh or dried dates	

Bring first 5 ingredients to a boil, add couscous, cover, and let stand about 5 minutes. Add nuts, and drizzle flavored yogurt over the top. Delightful!

Serves 4.

HONEYED FIGS WITH MADEIRA

Hannibal Palace near Sousse, Tunisia, served us a refreshing cold fig dessert.

1 pound ripe figs 1 cup Madeira 1/3 cup honey	¾ cup yogurt flavored with orange flower water, & honey Mint, for garnish

Simmer figs in Madeira and honey until soft, about 15 minutes. Reduce syrup, chill, and serve with yogurt drizzled over the top. Garnish with mint.

Serves 4.

EAST AFRICA
ETHIOPIA ERITREA DJIBOUTI SOMALIA KENYA TANZANIA ZANZIBAR UGANDA RWANDA BURUNDI

"Once you drink the waters of Ethiopia, you shall return again." This ancient proverb which I read on the trans-African flight into Addis Ababa will always be with me, as I have returned many times. No land is more mysterious, yet so welcoming. Part of the Horn of Africa, along with Eritrea, Djibouti, and Somalia, Ethiopia is the bridge between the Middle East and the rest of East Africa.

East Africa, the heart of the Great Rift Valley, has had a multitude of ethnic influences from Europe, India, and the Far East. This has provided a rich tapestry of beautiful people, excellent food, and dramatic music. The diversity of landscapes, from rugged mountains to exotic seashores to the world's best safari bush, also make this one of the prime areas in Africa.

Ethiopia's heritage is dominated by the Yemenites who came in ancient times with their renowned coffee, honey, and spices. The merging of Muslims, Jews, native animists, and Christians resulted in a beautiful people and cuisine.

The national dish is a stew, called wat in Amharic, and is saturated with berberé, a fiery pepper and spice paste. Spices widely used are cardamom, dill, chili, coriander, cumin, cloves, ginger, and fenugreek. Barley, millet, and numerous breads, including the staple, injera, made from the tef grain, are ubiquitous. Dairy products are important, and many exist on vegetarian dishes.

Addis has many excellent restaurants, including Chinese, Indian, and Italian. For typical native food, the Addis Ababa-the city's oldest-is a de rigueur culinary experience. But, more about that in the Doro Wat recipe. The Addis Ababa Sheraton, one of the most luxurious in Africa, offers at least half a dozen excellent restaurants. The authentic Italian and French restaurants transported me to Rome and Paris, with food, wine, and service to match. Ethiopian Airlines, one of the world's best, with new aircraft and outstanding service, will transport you in grand style directly from the United States.

Eritrea, at times part of Ethiopia, is a miniscule and friendly country on the Red Sea. The delightful capital of Asmara is a showpiece of Italian architecture, due to the former colonization. The people and the food also reflect this ambience. The coast reflects the days of Ottoman and Egyptian rule.

The cooking is similar to that of Ethiopia, but there is an abundance of seafood from the Red Sea. Prawns, lobster, snapper, sole, and trout are given special attention by the excellent chefs.

Djibouti, in contrast to Ethiopia and Eritrea, is an extremely hot little country on the Red Sea. Also, its French heritage dominates over the Arab and Oriental influence. The seafood is fresh from the sea and is well prepared. Otherwise, I have not found much of culinary interest except tropical fruit.

Somalia, the peak of the Horn of Africa, is actually two countries, Italian Somaliland in the North and British Somaliland in the South. There is also an Arab and Chinese influence here as in Djibouti, and while they have lobster, prawns, crab, tuna, and a plethora of other fish from the Gulf of Aden and the Indian Ocean, they eat meat and rice as well.

Kenya, best known for its great safaris and William Holden's famous Mt. Kenya Safari Club, has one of the best developed cuisines in Africa. By way of India, the British introduced curry and coconut, which are dominant in the cooking. Millet, corn, honey, bananas, and meat of all kinds are also widely eaten. The Carnivore Restaurant in Nairobi is enormously popular for its huge platters of meat, skewered and roasted.

Nairobi also has excellent ethnic restaurants, such as French, Arab, and Oriental. The chefs are also into enticing fusion cuisine, as well as French classics. The Grand Regency Hotel in Nairobi prepares the best Pommes Fondant (meltingly tender potato balls cooked in butter) I've ever had the privilege to savor, thus they are included in this section. The Delamere in the venerable British Colonial Norfolk Hotel is also among the best.

Located between Lake Victoria and the Indian Ocean, Kenya has a great supply of fresh seafood. Nile perch, trout, tilapia, and crab, lobster, and shrimp are all in great supply. Oysters from the coastal city of Mombasa are renowned.

It is here on the coast that the beautifully deformed baobab trees, proliferous throughout Kenya, give way to the fanciful and feathery casuarinas. They add a graceful air to the ancient Arab island of Lamu. The old town has no cars, only narrow streets with donkey carts, mosques, and Arab-style houses with intricately carved wooden doors. Delicious seafood and tropical fruit reign here.

Zanzibar, the exotic and mystical island off the coast of Tanzania (from where I easily reached it by hydrofoil), is known as the Island of Spice. Cloves, probably the world's largest supply, are used extensively in the cooking, along with nutmeg and cinnamon. Fish and tropical fruit abound.

Formerly part of the Sultanate of Oman, the old stone town has a very Arabic atmosphere with its palaces, forts, and stone aqueducts. Dr. Livingstone's house is here also.

Tanzania, once called Tanganyika, shares many of the same foods that the Kenyans eat, as they also have an Arab, English, and Indian legacy, and they also are located between Lake Victoria and the Indian Ocean. But on my first trip to Dar es Salaam, I immediately noticed the cleanliness and orderliness, which is a German legacy. It did not influence the cooking, however.

It is the talented and innovative safari chefs who are having a great influence on the cooking, as I discovered on a safari to the Serengeti. We were first taken to see the incredible produce on a farm in Arusha, near Mt. Kilimanjaro, where the climate is ideal for growing every conceivable kind of fruit and vegetable. Trees were dripping with citrus fruits, avocados, and mangoes. Acres and acres of land yielded numerous kinds of potatoes along with the tenderest of greens. Again, I noticed the German legacy when we were invited inside the farmer's immaculate house for tea.

The date was March 26, 1994, very significant for East Africa. This trip to Tanzania began in Addis Ababa, where I called the Burundi ambassador to inquire about the safety in Burundi and Rwanda. He assured me all was fine. Upon arrival in Bujumbura, Burundi, the Ethiopian flight crew advised that the passengers should not disembark except to retrieve their baggage because of the dangerous situation. So we were flown on to Kigali, Rwanda, a safe place. On the way into town I noticed there were no cars and no people on the streets, and it was Saturday afternoon. Very strange.

Early the following morning upon arrival at the airport, I was met by the Ethiopian station manager, who took me to his office, brought me some tea, and then after checking me in for the flight, personally escorted me out to the aircraft. Again, very strange.

Upon arrival at the New Africa Hotel in Dar es Salaam, I learned that the East Africa Peace Summit Meeting would take place in the hotel that evening with all East African presidents attending. After a delicious fish dinner at the rooftop Summit Restaurant overlooking the harbor, I joined other guests in the lobby, hoping to get a glimpse of the Presidents. When they emerged they shook hands with us and were quite happy and confident that peace would prevail.

The following morning I had an interesting Dr. Livingstone experience when I took the elevator down to breakfast. I asked a man who appeared to be a guard if he had been very busy the night before and he sadly informed me that the Burundi and Rwandan President's aircraft had been shot down when approaching the palace in Kigali, and that this was the beginning of the horrendous Hutu-Tutsi war. When he left the elevator, another man asked me if I knew whom I was talking with. It had been Boutros Boutros-Ghali, the Secretary General of the United Nations. Only in Africa do these things happen!

Although my stay in Burundi and Rwanda was cut short, I did manage to learn that the culinary influence here is Belgian and French, with fresh fish from Lake Tanganyika. As in the rest of East Africa the staple diet is a thick porridge of millet, maize, or other grains. And I collected two more countries and recipes.

Uganda, an exceptionally friendly country, is very peaceful, unlike its neighbor Rwanda. Once a British colony, Uganda was the recipient of many trout. Other fish figure prominently in the cooking, as do with millet and yams.

My very pleasant stay at the Windsor Lake Victoria Hotel in Entebbe was highlighted by the wonderful buffet breakfasts with hot dishes made to order and the lunches served on the terrace overlooking Lake Victoria.

Sudan, one of Africa's largest countries, is surrounded by nine countries, but does not share the same influences in cooking. The North is strictly Islamic while the South is Christian. Thus the cooking is Arab-style in the North and typical East African in the South. Again, civil war prevented me from visiting Khartoum, located at the confluence of the Blue and White Niles.

On my flight from Khartoum to Cairo, my seatmates, a Sudanese lawyer and a professor, informed me that in addition to the usual millet, yams, and cassava, there are many vegetables and that groundnuts (peanuts) are used as a sauce, as in West Africa.

It was quite interesting to note that both men denied that there was a civil war of long duration going on, and that extreme human rights offenses were taking place-the black Christians in the South were being killed or forced out of their burning villages.

RECIPES FROM EAST AFRICA

MANGOES AND AVOCADOS WITH SHRIMP
AND TROPICAL DRESSING

SERENGETI SLAW

CUCUMBER RAYTA

BANANA BEEF SOUP

ETHIOPIAN HONEY BREAD

MANGO SOUFFLÉED OMELET

MOUNT KENYA SAFARI CLUB SALAD

RWANDAN SHRIMP CURRY

LAKE VICTORIA BAKED FISH WITH ONIONS AND TOMATOES

HONEY CHICKEN KENYAN STYLE

ROAST DUCK WITH MANGOES

SIK SIK WAT (ETHIOPIAN STEWED BEEF WITH SPICE)

EAST AFRICAN OKRA

POMMES FONDANT (MELTING POTATOES)

SUDANESE PEANUT SAUCE

STRAWBERRIES WITH SWEET YOGURT SAUCE

CHOCOLATE BANANA DELIGHT WITH
CARAMEL SAUCE AND PECANS

TRIPLE CHOCOLATE CRÊPES WITH CHERRY SAUCE

African salads are usually cold, thirst-quenching dishes of fruit or vegetables that accompany hot and spicy main courses, but the new chefs are becoming very creative with them. Soups are rich and tend to be main courses.

MANGOES AND AVOCADOS WITH SHRIMP AND TROPICAL DRESSING

There are many versions of this salad throughout Africa, primarily avocados stuffed with shrimp. This is similar to one I enjoyed in Djibouti, and it reflects the French legacy.

2 tablespoons each butter, turbinado sugar, mango or guava nectar, catsup, and champagne vinegar or lemon juice 2 ripe hass avocados, peeled and pitted	1 ripe large mango, peeled and sliced ½ pound small shrimp, cooked and peeled Watercress or arugula

Simmer dressing ingredients until sugar dissolves and is reduced to about ½ cup. Arrange fruit and shrimp on cress, and pour warm sauce over.

Serves 4.

SERENGETI SLAW

Pascal Shemahonge, chef at the wonderful Serena Serengeti Lodge in Tanzania, is a very young culinary genius. This great slaw, now my favorite, is the most logical as well as the simplest example of fusion cooking ever, as it simply adds honey in place of sugar to American slaw. I have found that it doesn't matter whether your slaw dressing is creamy or otherwise. There are more of his creative recipes in this section.

1 cup mayonnaise or sour cream	1 teaspoon salt
½ cup honey, or more	½ cup black and golden raisins
¼ cup champagne or other vinegar	1 pound shredded cabbage
	1 large carrot, peeled and shredded

Whisk together dressing ingredients, and mix with raisins and cabbage. Sprinkle carrot on top or form a design, such as stripes.

Serves 4 to 6.

CUCUMBER RAYTA

The venerable Norfolk Hotel serves this refreshing salad with its wonderful curries, which are so popular in Nairobi.

1 cup yogurt	½ teaspoon salt
½ cup chopped cucumber	¼ to ½ teaspoon cumin
2 tablespoons chopped parsley or mint	1 small tomato, seeded and chopped

Mix yogurt with all but tomato, chill, and garnish with tomato. Makes 1 ½ cups.

BANANA BEEF SOUP

This surprisingly delicious and easy soup appears to be traditional all over East Africa, with many variations. You may also add cooked beef to the soup. This is another of Pascal Shemahonge's recipes from the Serena Serengeti Lodge in Tanzania.

6 small red bananas, turned black and ripe, or 3 large bananas, sliced	3 cups beef stock
	1 cup diced, cooked beef (optional)
2 tablespoons butter	Nutmeg, Chervil, and coconut (optional), to garnish
¼ cup chopped onions	

Sauté bananas in butter until very soft, and add onions, cooking until translucent. Add stock, simmer about 20 minutes, and puree until smooth. Add beef and garnishes, if desired.

Serves 4.

ETHIOPIAN HONEY BREAD

One of my favorites, this honey and spice bread was always a great hit in my cooking classes. It is quite a prominent showpiece, as it is baked in a 3-quart straight-sided casserole. I use my copper soup pot. It is great with soup, main courses, or even for breakfast with the following fruit omelet.

1 package dry yeast	½ tablespoon salt
¼ cup warm water	1 cup warm milk
1 egg, beaten	¼ cup melted butter
½ cup honey	4 cups all-purpose flour
1 tablespoon ground coriander	2 tablespoons melted butter
1 teaspoon 5-spice powder	Honey and Butter, for serving

Proof yeast in water until bubbly, then mix into combined egg, honey, seasonings, milk, and butter. Using an electric mixer with a dough hook, gradually add flour, and knead until smooth and elastic. Let rise, covered, until doubled, about 1 hour.

Spread a 3-quart casserole with melted butter, punch down dough, place in casserole, and let rise until double, uncovered, about 1 hour. Bake at 350° about 1 hour, or until it is golden and tests done. Turn out onto a rack to cool, and serve with lots of extra honey and butter.

Makes 1 large round loaf.

MANGO SOUFFLÉED OMELET

After a delightful buffet breakfast on the outdoor terrace of the magnificent hilltop Sheraton Luxury Resort in Addis Ababa, Ethiopia, I discovered this most unique and delicious fruit and almond souffléed omelet in the local morning paper. Great recipes can pop up anywhere, and this is a jewel.

1 ripe mango, peeled & diced	½ tablespoon rum
2 or 3 tablespoons orange marmalade	5 eggs (reserve 1 white)
	1 tablespoon turbinado sugar
2 tablespoons sliced almonds	½ tablespoon vanilla

Pinch of salt 3 tablespoons butter 1 kiwi, peeled & sliced	2 tablespoons toasted sliced almonds Mint leaves, for garnish Powdered sugar, for sifting

Combine mango, marmalade, almonds, and rum. Whisk eggs, reserving 1 white, with sugar and vanilla, until very fluffy. Whisk remaining white with salt until stiff but not dry. Fold into egg mixture. Melt butter in a 10-inch nonstick skillet (I use an iron skillet), and add omelet mixture. Cook over high heat until almost done, add fruit mixture, fold, and invert onto platter. Garnish with kiwi, toasted almonds, and mint. Sift powdered sugar over top.

Serves 4 to 6.

MOUNT KENYA SAFARI CLUB SALAD

Many, many years ago on my first trip to sub-Saharan Africa, I discovered how easy it is to do impromptu travel in Africa. The Norfolk Hotel concierge managed to get a last-minute reservation for me at William Holden's famed Mt. Kenya Safari Club, and also a ride up with a tour group. This delightful chicken and fruit salad has a true taste of Kenya, and was my first meal there. How did I return to Nairobi? In a metatu, against the advice of all who said I would lose my baggage, be robbed, and get in an accident. The driver was very considerate of me and parked so close to the Norfolk that he was fined by the police. But I wouldn't recommend it these days.

½ cup mayonnaise ½ cup whipped cream ¼ cup sour cream	¼ cup mango chutney 1 tablespoon lime or lemon juice

¼ teaspoon curry powder	1 cup diced pineapple
1 teaspoon salt	1 cup diced papaya or mango
3 cups diced, cooked chicken	Bibb lettuce

Gently whisk dressing ingredients together, and mix in chicken and fruit. Arrange lettuce on 4 plates, and top with salad.

Serves 4.

Main courses in East Africa include many fish preparations, usually with plenty of onion. Poultry and occasionally meat is eaten, but thick porridges are eaten by the masses, and especially ugali in Kenya, an African polenta.

RWANDAN SHRIMP CURRY

Since I had to leave Kigali early to avoid the Hutu-Tutsi conflict, this truly great and simple curry was the only meal I had at the Meridien. The Ethiopian flight attendants and I appeared to be the only hotel guests.

1 large red onion, thinly sliced	2 medium tomatoes, seeded & chopped
4 garlic cloves, crushed	1 ½ pounds shrimp, shelled
6 tablespoons butter	Salt, to taste
1 teaspoon curry powder	Saffron Rice
Chopped hot chilis (optional)	Chopped cilantro, for garnish

Using a large skillet, sauté onion and garlic in butter over medium heat until soft and translucent. Add seasonings and tomatoes, and cook over high heat until excess liquid evaporates and mixture is thickened. Add shrimp and cook a few minutes until barely done. Season, and pour over rice. Garnish with cilantro.

Serves 4.

LAKE VICTORIA BAKED FISH WITH ONIONS AND TOMATOES

The lovely Windsor Hotel on Lake Victoria in Uganda prepares a most flavorful baked fish with very few ingredients. I prefer to use salmon fillets, but halibut, haddock, or even cod would be great. This recipe taught me that superb flavor does not need a lot of ingredients, time, or effort.

1 large red onion, halved lengthwise, and thinly sliced	4 salmon fillets
2 tablespoons peanut oil	Salt and pepper
2 medium tomatoes, coarsely chopped	1/3 cup butter or peanut oil
1 large bay leaf	3 tablespoons catsup
	1 lemon, thinly sliced
	Chopped parsley or cilantro

Sauté onions in oil, using an iron skillet just large enough to hold fillets, until soft and translucent. Add tomatoes and bay leaf, and cook until most of liquid evaporates. Place fillets on top, season, and brush with butter or oil whisked with catsup. Bake at 350° about 15 minutes, or until just cooked through, brushing with catsup mixture until glazed and shiny. Garnish with lemon and parsley.

Serves 4.

HONEY CHICKEN KENYAN STYLE

On my first Kenyan safari I had some kind of game that was marinated in a spicy honey mixture at the Serena Lodge in Amboselli. I prefer to use suprêmes, and coat them with various kinds of seeds. Poppy seeds are my favorite but they aren't quite African. Honey is used extensively in East Africa with many kinds of meats and fowl, and I still prefer chestnut.

½ cup honey	Salt
½ tablespoon soy sauce or catsup	1 tablespoon poppy, sesame, or coriander seeds
4 suprêmes, halved lengthwise	

Mix honey with soy or catsup, add suprêmes, and marinate an hour or so. Remove and sprinkle both sides of each supreme with salt and seeds. Sauté in a lightly greased large iron skillet until cooked through. Remove, and add remaining marinade to skillet, reducing until syrupy. Serve over suprêmes.

Serves 4 to 6.

ROAST DUCK WITH MANGOES

Ducks in any country have a special affinity for fruit, and this classic from Nairobi's Norfolk Hotel is one of the best.

1 4-pound duckling	1/3 cup chopped celery
2 tomatoes, chopped	Bouquet Garni
1/3 cup chopped onions	1 quart strong chicken stock
1/3 cup chopped carrots	½ cup sugar

½ cup red wine vinegar	1 large mango, peeled and diced
2 ½ cups reduced duck stock	1 tablespoon cornstarch
½ cup mango or guava nectar	1 tablespoon water or nectar

Remove excess fat from duckling, render in a wide saucepan, and discard solid pieces. Remove wing tips and sauté in fat with neck and giblets until brown. Add vegetables, sauté briefly, add bouquet and stock, simmer about 2 hours. Meanwhile, prick duck well all over, place in a roasting pan with ½ cup water, and roast at 425° about 1 hour, or until done, pouring off fat after 45 minutes. Boil sugar and vinegar until lightly caramelized, add strained stock and nectar, and reduce until glossy. Add mango, season, and thicken with a mixture of cornstarch and water. Carve duck, and serve with sauce.

Serves 4 to 6

SIK SIK WAT

(Ethiopian Stewed Beef with Spice)

Ethiopia's national dish can be made with beef or with chicken (in which it's called Doro Wat). I first experienced this fiery creation at Addis Ababa, the city's oldest and most exotic restaurant. Colorful basket tables are overlaid with injera, the soft flat bread made with tef, to make a sort of tablecloth. Then the wat is poured onto the injera, which you tear off in pieces to wrap the wat and then eat with your fingers. It's really not as messy as it sounds. I have tempered the heat in my version, and you may serve it over rice or in pita breads. Also, I do not bother to make the fiery berberé spice paste, as Chinese 5-spice powder has virtually the same ingredients.

1 ½ cups chopped onion	½ cup beef stock or water
2 tablespoons butter or oil	½ cup canned crushed tomatoes
2 large garlic cloves, crushed	
1 tablespoon 5-spice powder	2 pounds boneless beef for stew, cubed
1 tablespoon paprika	
1 teaspoon ground cardamom	Salt, pepper, & red pepper, to taste
½ cup red wine	
	6 hard-cooked eggs, shelled & pricked

Using a 3-quart casserole, sauté onion in butter until soft and translucent. Add garlic and spices, sauté briefly, and add wine, stock, tomatoes, and beef. Simmer, covered, about 1 ½ hours, or until beef is tender. Season as desired, add eggs, and simmer about 10 minutes to color and flavor eggs. If sauce is too thin, cook uncovered until desired consistency is reached. I love to dollop yogurt over the beef, and the following okra dish is great with it.

Serves 6.

EAST AFRICAN OKRA

Those exotic ridged green pods known as okra are indigenous to Africa and are eaten throughout the continent. Many are put off by the mucilaginous texture, but that has never deterred me from this favorite vegetable. It should not be a problem if you use small pods and cut off only a small slice from the stem. Of all the myriad ways to prepare okra, this is my favorite. The use of balsamic vinegar along with the East African spices is a delicious fusion concept.

1 pound small okra	4 medium tomatoes, seeded & chopped
1 large red onion, finely chopped	1 teaspoon 5-spice powder
3 tablespoons butter or oil	½ teaspoon cardamom
2 large garlic cloves, crushed	Salt & pepper, to taste
1 tablespoon turbinado sugar	Balsamic vinegar, to serve

Cut a small slice off the stem end of the okra. Sauté onion in butter until soft, add garlic and sugar, cooking briefly. Add tomatoes and spices along with the okra, and simmer about 20 minutes, covered. Season and pass Balsamic for individual tastes. Wonderful at any temperature.

Serves 4.

POMMES FONDANT

Melting Potatoes)

Who would expect to see a French classic in East Africa? Room service at the Grand Regency in Nairobi served the best potato ovals drenched in butter I have ever savored. In fact, the entire meal was exceptional, and the green salad was of three-star Michelin quality. And yes, I always eat the salads and drink the tap water in sub-Saharan Africa. Without thinking, my husband, Howard, also indulged and lived to tell about it.

1 pound Yukon Gold potatoes, peeled	Water, to cover
	Fleur de Sel
6 tablespoons butter	Finely Chopped chervil or dill

Carve potatoes into small ovals about 1-inch long, or scoop out 1-inch balls with a melon baller as I do. They may now be boiled until half tender, about 5 minutes, or placed in skillet large enough to hold them in 1 layer. Add butter and enough water to cover, and cook over high heat until water evaporates and potatoes are golden brown on the bottom. Turn and shake the potatoes well until golden brown on all sides and tender, lowering the heat if necessary. Sprinkle with salt and herbs.

Serves 4 to 6.

SUDANESE PEANUT SAUCE

On the flight from Khartoum to Cairo, my Sudanese seatmates informed me that peanut (groundnut) sauce is a very popular topping for vegetables and fish. Peanut butter is a viable substitute for ground peanuts. The sauce is also added to many well-cooked tomato and onion mixtures, so it may be added to the recipes in this section with a base of tomatoes and onions. This is excellent on fish as well as chicken and meat. Each family has its own special mixture, but I prefer this one. It's so good I could eat it with a spoon.

¼ cup chunky peanut butter	1 garlic clove, crushed
2 tablespoons catsup	Spices or herbs of your choice
1 tablespoon citrus juice	

Whisk all ingredients together and serve on corn on the cob, grilled plantains, fried eggplant, or butternut squash, or mix into dried beans.

Makes about 4 cups.

Desserts in East Africa usually consist of fruit, especially mangoes, pineapples, bananas, and in Kenya, their incomparable strawberries. However, the young innovative chefs are creating some very special treats, as we will see.

STRAWBERRIES WITH SWEET YOGURT SAUCE

Kenyan strawberries are among the world's best. Chef Robert Warui prepared this when I was there many years ago, but I've added a few changes.

1 quart strawberries, halved, or quartered if large	½ cup cream, whipped
	¼ to ½ cup turbinado sugar
1 cup strawberry or raspberry yogurt	Mint Sprigs

Mix berries with yogurt. Whip cream with sugar, and fold into berry mixture. Garnish with mint.

Serves 4 to 6.

CHOCOLATE BANANA DELIGHT WITH CARAMEL SAUCE AND PECANS

Pascal Shemahonge, whose recipes for Honey Slaw and Banana Beef Soup are found in this section, also created scrumptious desserts when I was at the Serena Serengeti Lodge in Tanzania. You may use both chocolate and caramel sauce or only caramel. It's sort of a banana split without ice cream.

6 small red bananas, turned black and ripe, or 3 large bananas, sliced ¾ cup caramel or butterscotch sauce (see index)	2 ounces chocolate, melted ½ cup coarsely chopped pecans ½ cup grated coconut

Place bananas in a serving bowl and mix in sauce. Drizzle melted chocolate over top. It should harden. Sprinkle with pecans and coconut.

Serves 4.

TRIPLE CHOCOLATE CRÊPES WITH CHERRY SAUCE

The luxurious Kirawira tent camp, with Victorian decor and marble vanities in the private baths, also boasts of outstanding food and is nestled in the exotic backdrop of the Serengeti wildlife. This luscious and original crêpe dessert can be varied as you wish. You may substitute plain crêpes, vanilla pastry cream, or white chocolate sauce in various combinations.

12 crêpes (see index) 2 tablespoons cocoa powder French Pastry Cream (see index)	3 ounces semi-sweet chocolate 2 cups cherry sauce (see index) ¾ cup white chocolate curls

When making crêpes, add cocoa powder to flour to make them into chocolate crêpes. Also, when making pastry cream, add chocolate while cream is still hot. Spread crêpes with chocolate pastry cream, fold into quarters, and arrange on individual plates. Pour cherry sauce around them, and decorate with white chocolate curls.

Serves 6.

∾ Central & West Africa ⍺

CENTRAL AFRICA and WEST AFRICA
SENEGAL CÔTE D'IVOIRE TOGO
GABON SÃO TOME CONGO

Central and West Africa, not including the two Atlantic islands of Cape Verde and São Tome, are home to 22 out of the 52 countries on the continent, all of which I have visited (if only briefly for some that were at war). I have grouped all the West and Central countries together due to the culinary similarity.

Central Africa, in the culinary context, has always been a wasteland in the kitchen, although they were formerly French colonies, and thus should have been influenced as such. These are Chad, Niger, Central African Republic, and Republic of the Congo (formerly Zaire).

West Africa has been colonized by France, Belgium, England, and Portugal, and I have found that the best cooks are generally in the countries colonized by the French, not surprisingly, so these are the ones featured.

The cooking in all these countries is based on palm nut oil, peppers, yams, cassava, beans, greens, okra, rice, millet, groundnuts, and coconut. Fresh tropical fruit is also abundant, along with fish on the coast.

Mauritania, a Muslim country, has surprisingly good food in spite of its astounding poverty and the Sahara. There are definite shades of Moroccan cooking here, with an accent on couscous and roast lamb, as well as dates.

The remaining West African countries share several national dishes, especially Yassa Poulet, Mafé, Jollof, and to some extent,

Thieboudienne. Senegal can claim them all and has excellent chefs. I visited Guet Ndar at Pointe des Almadies, the restaurant owned by Baye M'Barick, the Bocuse of Senegal, many years ago, as well as others. Senegal surrounds tiny Gambia, a former British colony that claims the title of the smallest country in Africa.

Guinea and Guinea Bissau, with a Portuguese legacy, emphasize cashews and groundnuts in their cooking and have flights out to Cape Verde Island, which I have reached as a midway stop on South African Airways. The bean and Portuguese sausage stew is the meal of choice, even at Sal airport.

Sierra Leone and Liberia are frequently at war but have really good restaurants featuring Vietnamese, Armenian, and Lebanese cooking.

Côte d'Ivoire's main city, Abidjan, is the most cosmopolitan in West Africa and is quite international in every respect. Ghana, Togo, and Benin also have very good restaurants with a distinct Lebanese influence.

These countries are the gateway to Ouagadougou, Burkina Faso, and Bamako, Mali. The former, although a former French colony, has not advanced its culinary tradition as its neighbors to the south have. Mali, like Mauritania, has a North African influence and is home to part of the Sahara, which is experienced up in Tombouctoo, with its inimitable sandstorms.

Nigeria and Cameroon, with their French legacy, also have a Lebanese influence. It was in Douala that the best profiteroles ever were put on the plane which was operated by Jat, the Yugoslavian airline, which was chartered by Cameroon during the Serbian-Bosnian conflict.

Equatorial Guinea's capital, Malabo, is located on the island formerly known as Fernando Poo, now Bioko, and is actually a better place to dine. Far better is São Tome, a beautiful nearby island better reached from Libreville, Gabon. Although it has a Portuguese legacy, São Tome has a wonderful small French-style hotel with cottages and an informal yet elegant dining room, reminiscent of Burgundy, that serves wonderful food.

Gabon may be famous for Dr. Schweitzer's hospital, but the French food at the Meridien in Libreville is memorable, especially the baguettes, which are the best ever. I noticed many Chaîne des Rôtisseurs restaurants, as well as many ethnic restaurants featuring food from other parts of Africa. It was quite easy to buy my ticket to São Tome in this friendly and charming city.

Brazzaville, Congo, is also a lovely city with a distinct ambience of easygoing southern hospitality. The fish, oysters, and shrimp are outstanding and there are many international restaurants. I noticed the Belgian business travelers were eating the French green salads, as was I. Kinshasa, Zaire, now the other Congo, could be seen at night just across the Congo River. Their formerly excellent Greek, Chinese, and Tunisian restaurants have been hindered by war, unfortunately.

RECIPES FROM CENTRAL AFRICA AND WEST AFRICA

CREAMY CORN OMELET À LA BOUFFLIÈRE

WEST AFRICAN YAM AND AVOCADO SALAD

THIEBO DIENNE (SENEGALESE FISH AND RED RICE)

MAFÉ (WEST AFRICAN GROUNDNUT STEW)

YASSA AU POULET (WEST AFRICAN LEMON CHICKEN WITH ONIONS)

STEAK AND EGGS SÃO TOME STYLE

MANGO BUTTER SAUCE

MINTED LEMON COUSCOUS AND RED LENTILS

MANGOES FLAMBÉ BRAZZAVILLE

COCONUT HONEY ICE CREAM

My first day in sub-Saharan Africa began in Senegal with a delightful light luncheon of an omelet and a salad, imbued with the brilliantly contrasting colors of red, green, orange, and yellow. The setting was Gorée Island, off the coast of Dakar, and known for its somber House of Slaves Museum as well as the very French Hostellerie des Chevaliers du Bouffliére, where I had a déjà vu sense of Provence, but with an inimitable African flavor.

CREAMY CORN OMELET À LA BOUFFLIÈRE

This unusual omelet can be made with freshly cooked or frozen corn and can also be made into scrambled eggs. Throughout West Africa I discovered many egg dishes.

4 ounces lamb, beef, or pork sausage, crumbled or diced	½ cup crème fraîche or heavy cream
1 cup corn kernels, cooked	4 large eggs, beaten
	Salt and Pepper

Sauté sausage in a skillet, preferably iron, until done. Whisk cream into eggs, add corn, and seasonings. Pour into skillet with sausage, and cook over low heat, letting uncooked portion around edges run underneath. Fold, and invert onto a platter.

Serves 3 to 4.

WEST AFRICAN YAM AND AVOCADO SALAD

This colorful salad which I enjoyed at Bouffliére with the omelet is French in concept and typical of many variations and combinations in West Africa. This can be an humble or elegant presentation.

1 pound sweet potatoes or yams, cooked, peeled, and sliced 2 small Hass avocados, sliced	2 ripe Roma tomatoes, seeded and diced 1/3 cup Sauce Vinaigrette (see index) Chopped parsley, for garnish

Arrange overlapping slices of potatoes and avocados in alternating quadrants on 4 plates. Place a small mound of tomatoes in the center, and drizzle all with vinaigrette. Garnish with parsley.

Serves 4.

THIEBOU DIENNE

(Senegalese Fish and Red Rice)

Undoubtedly my most memorable meal in Senegal, if not all of West Africa, was this highly acclaimed Senegalese specialty. I arrived at dusk at the westernmost point in Africa, Pointe des Almadies, for my long-awaited dinner prepared by Baye M'Barick, the Bocuse of Africa. I remember his flowing robe and some sort of headpiece as this colossal restaurateur welcomed me to his exotic open-air temple of grand African cuisine. Seated on large floor pillows, I savored this dish with an excellent French wine. This is a simplified version based on a recipe from *La Cuisine Senegalaise*, a cookbook by Monique Biarnès that was given to me in Dakar.

1 medium red onion, chopped 2 tablespoons peanut oil 1 ounce smoked or dried herring or salmon	¼ cup canned crushed tomatoes ½ cup chopped parsley 2 garlic cloves, crushed

1 small red pepper, chopped	2 yams, peeled & quartered
1-1 ½ pounds grouper or snapper fillets	1 pound cabbage, quartered
1 quart water	12 ounces eggplant, halved & sliced
2 carrots, peeled & sliced thickly	½ pound okra, trimmed
2 turnips, peeled & quartered	1 ½ cups long-grain rice
	Salt & pepper

Using a 3-quart casserole, sauté onion in oil until soft and translucent. Add herring and tomatoes, cooking until thick and shiny. Using an immersion blender, process parsley, garlic, scallion, and pepper to a thick paste. Cut slits in fish, and fill with paste. Add fish to casserole, and cook briefly to imbue fish with the flavors. Add water, carrots, turnips, and yams, and simmer about 10 minutes, covered, until fish is done. Remove fish, add remaining vegetables, cover, and simmer about 20 minutes or until tender.

Strain vegetables, returning about 2 ½ cups water to the casserole. Add rice, cover and simmer about 20 minutes, or until water is absorbed. Traditionally, the rice is served on one platter and the vegetables and fish on another, but I prefer to mound the rice in the center, placing the fillets on top and the vegetables around the rice. The remaining cooking liquid is served, half of it enhanced with a hot chili pepper, if you so desire.

Serves 4.

MAFÉ

(West African Groundnut Stew)

Another great Senegalese specialty, I've enjoyed many versions in other countries as well. I prefer chicken rather than lamb or beef and I use chunky instead of creamy peanut butter. Also, I do not include vegetables, like yams, carrots, turnips, spinach, okra, eggplant, as I feel that they are not compatible with this glorious tomato-flavored peanut butter sauce. Do serve over rice.

4 to 6 chicken breasts, with skin and bone	2 cups chicken stock
Salt and Ginger	½ cup chunky peanut butter
¼ cup peanut oil	½ cup tomato paste
1 medium red onion, chopped	Salt and pepper
2 garlic cloves, crushed	Accompaniments: Sliced bananas, coconut, chutney, and chopped roasted peanuts

Rub chicken with salt and ginger, then sauté in oil, using a large sauté pan, until golden brown. Add onion and garlic, sauté until soft. Meanwhile, blend stock, peanut butter, and tomato paste in a food processor briefly, just to mix well. Pour over chicken, season, cover, and simmer until chicken is tender. Remove chicken and reduce pan liquid if too thin, or add more stock if too thick. Serve over rice with accompaniments.

Serves 4 to 6.

YASSA AU POULET

(West African Lemon Chicken with Onions)

One of my favorite West African classics, Yassa has an uncanny resemblance to Iranian cooking. Claimed mostly by Senegal, I enjoyed this at Chez Mamie, a small and elegant restaurant in Abidjan, Côte d'Ivoire. Mamie, a very charming lady and accomplished cook, took me on a tour of her kitchen and introduced me to African foods, as well as the Chaîne des Rôtisseurs, the prestigious gastronomic society founded in Paris in the thirteenth century, which she encouraged me to join. There are many Chaîne restaurants throughout West Africa, especially in the countries with a French legacy.

2 cups sliced onions	Minced chile pepper (optional)
2 large garlic cloves, crushed	4-6 chicken breasts, with skin and bone or 1 3-pound chicken, cut up
2 teaspoons salt	
¾ cup lemon juice	¾ cup water or chicken stock
3 tablespoons peanut oil	Hot cooked rice

Mix all marinade ingredients, add chicken and marinate several hours. Remove chicken and grill over hot coals, turning until lightly browned on all sides, but not cooked through. Strain marinade, reserve, and sauté onions in a large skillet until golden and translucent. Add chicken and reserved marinade along with the water. Cover and simmer about 20 to 30 minutes or until chicken is done. If sauce is too thin, remove chicken and boil to desired consistency. Serve with rice.

Serves 4 to 6.

STEAK AND EGGS SÃO TOME STYLE

The Marlin Beach Hotel may sound like Miami Beach, but it's on the Portuguese island of São Tome off the west coast of Africa. Very small and charming, with bungalows around the garden, their restaurant reminded me of Burgundy. Their Portuguese-inspired steak and eggs proved to be the best I've had.

2 slices beef tenderloin	Pinch of crushed saffron
Salt and cumin	1/3 cup cream
2 tablespoons butter	2 slices country bread, brushed with oil
1 garlic clove, crushed	3 eggs, beaten
1 tablespoon Madeira or port	2 tablespoons butter

Season tenderloin with salt and cumin, then sauté in butter on both sides until done as desired, adding garlic the last few minutes. Remove tenderloin and deglaze skillet with wine. Add saffron and cream, bring to a boil, and cook until lightly thickened. Toast or grill bread until golden and crusty. Add eggs to hot butter and scramble as desired. Place bread on 2 plates, top with steak, eggs, and then sauce. Great comfort food at any time of day.
Serves 2.

MANGO BUTTER SAUCE

Africa is not known for its sauces, but the Re N Dama Hotel in Libreville, Gabon, has a great French manager and chef. The baguettes are simply out of this world, and so is this versatile sauce, which I had with my perfectly fresh El Capitaine, a sublime white Atlantic fish. The sauce is also good with shrimp, chicken, and pork tenderloin, with an accompaniment of snow peas.

¼ teaspoon dried thyme	1/3 cup dry white wine
1 bay leaf	1/3 cup cream
2 shallots, finely chopped	¾ cup soft butter
¼ cup finely chopped mushrooms	1 large mango, peeled and halved.

Mix seasonings with mushrooms and wine, and boil until almost evaporated. Add cream simmer until thickened, and strain. Whisk in butter over very low heat. Purée half the mango, and whisk into butter sauce. Slice remaining mango half and use as a garnish.

Makes about 1 ½ cups.

MINTED LEMON COUSCOUS AND RED LENTILS

The outdoor terrace on the rooftop of Lomé, Togo's Palm Beach Hotel, overlooks the wide beach of the Atlantic, and was my favorite venue for dining on the intriguing creations of the French/Lebanese kitchen. The hotel owner is from Lebanon and has transported a bit of Beirut to Lomé.

2 cups water	½ cup couscous or burghal wheat, cooked
½ cup turbinado sugar	1 cup mint leaves, chopped or watercress
½ cup mint sprigs	
1 lemon, thinly sliced	½ cup pine nuts or pistachios, chopped
1/3 cup olive oil	
Salt, to taste	1 preserved lemon, diced (see index)
¾ cup red lentils, cooked and drained	

Boil water with sugar, mint, and lemon until liquid is reduced to about 1/3 cup. Remove solids, discard, and add olive oil and salt. Mix cooled lentils and couscous with mint, add syrup and toss. Garnish with nuts and lemon.

Serves 4 as an accompaniment to grilled fish, chicken, and meat.

MANGOS FLAMBÉ BRAZZAVILLE

A French kitchen prevails at the Meridien in Brazzaville, Congo. Brazzaville is a quiet, easygoing city with lots of shade trees across the Congo River from chaotic Kinshasa, Zaire. The Meridien's salads and French sorbets and ice creams were exceptional, as was this flaming mango creation.

¼ cup butter	1 cup orange juice
¼ cup turbinado sugar	¼ cup lime juice
Zest of 2 oranges and 2 limes, peeled into long strips	2 large ripe mangos, peeled and sliced
¼ cup orange liqueur	¼ cup rum

Melt butter in large skillet with sugar. Add zest, flame with liqueur, and add juices. Boil until reduced and thickened. Discard zest, add mango, simmer until hot, and flame with rum. I love this over the following Coconut Honey Ice Cream.

Serves 6.

COCONUT HONEY ICE CREAM

2 eggs, beaten	½ tablespoon lemon juice
¾ cup honey	¾ cup grated fresh coconut
3 cups light cream	1 small can crushed pineapple
½ tablespoon vanilla	

Mix all ingredients into beaten eggs, and chill well. Freeze in an ice cream maker, then transfer to freezer containers.

Makes 2 quarts.

SOUTHERN AFRICA
SOUTH AFRICA NAMIBIA BOTSWANA ZIMBABWE ZAMBIA MALAWI ANGOLA MOZAMIBIQUE AFRICAN ISLANDS

Southern Africa is anchored and dominated by South Africa, in its dramatic location at the tip of the continent between the merging waters of the Atlantic and Indian Oceans. It is a fascinating and colorful potpourri of English, Portuguese, German, Dutch, French, Indian, Arab, and Indonesian legacies, along with the indigenous Africans.

South Africa leads most of the continent with its burgeoning economy, scenic diversity-including game parks, mountains, seashores, and the Cape of Good Hope-and, of course, its outstanding food and wine.

Although the Portuguese were the first to round the Cape of Good Hope, the Dutch East India Company was responsible for the first settlement here. These Dutch and Germans, to be known as Boers and Afrikaaners, imported slaves, who eventually created Cape Malay cooking, from Indonesia and Malaysia. Indians, with their rice and spices, reached the East coast, thus establishing Indian cooking.

The British colonial period was the beginning of the Voortrekker's Great Trek inland, spreading these culinary influences. Then the Huguenots from Bordeaux came with cabernet vines and planted the vineyards in Franschoek. Stellenbosch, named after Governor van der Stel, and Paarl vineyards came later, and now, since the end of apartheid, the South African wine industry is ready to compete with the world's best.

The fertile Cape area has an astounding variety of fruits and vegetables, as I witnessed when I was served an array of fourteen vegetables, but more about that later. The Atlantic and Indian Oceans provide a vast array of seafood, the favorites being snoek (sea Perch), cod, shellfish, and rock lobster. The British island of Tristan da Cunha, which I reached on the St. Helena British mail ship with its yearly supply of mail, food, medical and school supplies, also has a surplus of rock lobster tails that it exports to the United States by way of South Africa.

The national dish is Bobotie, a spicy ground meat and custard casserole with dried fruits, which is a Cape Malay specialty, along with Sosaties and Bredies. Durban is the center of the Indian cuisine. The notable Dutch legacy includes preserves, the art of baking breads, pastry, and cakes, as well as the delicious tangerine Van der Hum liqueur.

The ideal place to enjoy these specialties and the innovative new cooking, as well as the wines, is at a grand trio of famous old hotels with spectacular Cape Dutch architecture located in the countryside. They are Groot Constantia's Alphen Hotel, the Grand Roche in Stellenbosch, and the Lanzerac in Paarl. The elegant luxury hotels in Capetown, especially the Cape Grace, Table Bay, and the Ellerman House, on the coast, also offer the best in food and wine, as do the luxurious Rovos Rail and the Blue Train.

South Africa's wide range of wines includes fortified, reds, and whites made from Cabernet, Hermitage, Gamay, Pinotage, Steen, and Riesling, among others. Brandy, also excellent, is a particular favorite of the locals. The most renowned vineyards are Nederburg and Bellingham.

Namibia, formerly Southwest Africa, is a friendly, beautiful, and peaceful land, one I would never tire of visiting, as it has all the necessary requisites for immense enjoyment. It shares most of South Africa's legacies and was a German colony. While on one of Namibia's incomparable safaris, I noticed the popularity of German names and foods. Natives named Otto, Hans, and Ursula ate plenty of potatoes, cabbage, and sausages.

As in South Africa, boerwors (sausages) and braaivleis (barbecue) are of great importance, as is Bobotie. I enjoyed these and creative new dishes at the luxury lodges and tented camps in the Namib Desert, where I climbed the world's highest sand dunes; at Windhoek's elegant Hotel Heinitzburg; and at a beach cookout on the Skeleton coast where the flying safari landed.

Botswana, another of Africa's most peaceful countries, also shares much of the same legacy, including safaris in the famed Okavanga Delta and Chobe National Park, where there is such an abundance of game, it frequently appears on the dinner table. While at Chobe, I especially savored gazelle, impala, ostrich, and springbok from the enormous buffet table. And for breakfast, my omelet was made with an ostrich egg that was large enough to make omelets for a dozen people.

Zimbabwe, formerly Rhodesia under British rule and known for its magnificent Victoria Falls, which it shares with Zambia, of Dr. Livingstone fame, also shares the culinary legacies of South Africa. Both countries have a quite British background, but the former is once again in deep political trouble. Aside from the braaivleis, fish is outstanding, The Zambezi River and the lakes and streams provide delectable Nile perch, bream, and salmon, among other fish.

Malawi, a beautiful country of diverse topography, also has a British legacy. Lake Malawi, a fisherman's paradise, makes up a very large portion of the country and supplies it with exceptional tilapia and other fish. Beef, chicken, and a vast array of fresh vegetables play a large part in the cooking.

Angola, on the Atlantic, and Mozambique, on the Indian Ocean, are both former colonies of Portugal, to which they are still very close, as they are to each other. This is not true of the other colonizations.

Angola's cooking is based on olive oil, chilies, corn, potatoes, tomatoes, chicken, goat, and shrimp, quite similar to that of Brazil, Portugal's former colony across the Atlantic. Sweet desserts, based on eggs, are of the Portuguese genre. Wracked by war almost incessantly, the cooking has suffered, and the best is found in

Luanda's hotels. Moamba, the national dish, is a chicken stew, which I enjoyed at the Presidente overlooking the ocean.

Mozambique's capital, formerly known as Laurenço Marques, is Maputo, and once again, is a beautiful city after extensive war. There is an Arab and Indian influence in the cooking not found in Angola. The cooking is based on olive and peanut oil, citrus fruits, rice, and spice. Piri-piri, a fiery pepper, is the essential ingredient. Both countries, however, thank Portugal for its pigs, chickens, salt cod, olives, coffee, tea, and the much beloved port wine. The elegant Hotel Polana, on a cliff overlooking formal gardens and the ocean, like Reid's Hotel on Madeira, was designed by the same architect and has simply divine food.

Madagascar, the world's fourth largest island and one of its largest producers of vanilla beans, is also renowned for its lemur population on Nosy Be. A former French colony, Madagascar boasts baguettes that are as ubiquitous as bananas, but they are also majorly influenced by South African cuisine. This can be seen in its international dish Romazava, very similar to South African Bredie, a meat and vegetable stew. The Middle East, India, and Southeast Asia have also influenced the cooking style of Madagascar and the other islands in the Indian Ocean, as is evidenced in much use of spice and rice. It was Madagascar, however, that introduced vanilla to the other islands.

The Comoros, an Islamic Republic, is a group of islands between Madagascar and Mozambique, and produces 85% of the world's perfume essence-Ylang-Ylang, which has become popular in aromatherapy. Couscous, spices, seafood, goat, and fruit all play a role in the cooking. The best food is probably in Dzaoudzi on the very French island of Mayotte, an exotic blend of Muslim mosques and French flair with much joie de vivre. I reached these islands by air from Mauritius.

Mauritius, the most glorious and delightful island in the entire world, has been colonized by the Dutch, French, and British. Although halfway around the world, the hide-away villas and small hotels are private, elegant, and personalized with outstanding service and food prepared by the best Indian, French, and

Chinese chefs. Tropical fruit, hearts of palm, prawns, and el Capitaine fish were all memorable. And Alain Ducasse's Spoon is now here.

The French Republic of Reunion and its capital of St. Denis remind me of an unspoiled town on the Côte d'Azur. It is a very small island of rugged beauty with volcanic valleys surrounded by mountains that plunge to the sea. The local Creole cooking is a mixture of African, Chinese, and Indian, but there is also pure French cooking in the hotels and the seaside cafe where there is a choice of local rum or French wine.

The Seychelle group of islands is quite verdant and scenic, but hot and humid in its proximity to the equator. In addition to African, Indian, and Chinese, there are also French and English influences. The lush vegetation on Mahé and Praslin Islands provide an abundance of produce, and the sea is rich in lobster, snapper, tuna, marlin, and other fish. Pork and chicken are popular and are prepared with curry, coconut milk, and rice. India can be sensed in the piquant flavor of the food, the fragrant aromas, and the misty night air.

RECIPES FROM SOUTHERN AFRICA

KIR HEINITZBURG

WARM PRAWN SALAD WITH HEARTS OF PALM

CURRIED LOBSTER SALAD SEYCHELLOISE

DURBAN FISH CURRY

AFRIKAANER CHICKEN POT PIE

MOAMBA (ANGOLAN CHICKEN AND OKRA STEW WITH PUMPKIN)

CHICKEN WITH BANANAS AND CASHEW IN COCONUT CREAM

DECONSTRUCTED LASAGNA WITH VEAL SCALOPPINE

BOBOTI (CAPE MALAY LAMB AND CUSTARD CASSEROLE)

SOSATIES (CAPE MALAY LAMB KEBABS)

ROMAZAVA (MALAGASY MEAT AND VEGETABLE STEW)

EGGS BENEDICT POLANA

SOSSUSVLEIS CARAMELIZED POTATOES

SWEET AND SOUR TOMATO CHUTNEY

ROVOS RAIL APPLE TART

PEPPERMINT CRISP PUDDING

AFRIKAANER BREAKFAST

COFFEE-WALNUT CAKE WITH MASCARPONE

KIR HEINITZBURG

Namibia's German influence was quite apparent in this apple-flavored Kir, which I enjoyed with the spectacular view of Windhoek's evening skyline. The setting was the cliffside terrace of Hotel Heinitzburg, a small gem of a hotel in the Relais et Châteaux group. The hotel is actually a castle built in the German style at the beginning of the last century. Its elegant dining room, with the same view, serves outstanding meals with a French and German influence. The chef had hunted for chanterelles that day and prepared an impromptu first course for me with German red wine and veal jus. The private wine cellar is Namibia's largest. The champagne breakfast buffet was also outstanding and was served in a quaint room furnished with German antiques. What a great way to begin and end a Namibian safari!

1 1/3 cup champagne or sparkling wine	1-1 ½ teaspoons grenadine
1 ½ tablespoons apple juice	1 small crabapple

Mix champagne with juice and grenadine, pour into a martini glass, and garnish with the crabapple on a cocktail pick.

Serves 1.

The ideal lunch in the African islands is a main course salad composed of all manner of tropical fruit, vegetables, seafood, chicken, and the chef's choice of African, Indian, or Chinese seasonings.

WARM PRAWN SALAD WITH HEARTS OF PALM

A unique blend of ingredients enhances the incomparable Mauritius prawns in this composed salad, which I had at the seductive Palm Beach Hotel at the north end of the island. The deluxe Oberoi is another deluxe small hotel.

1 shallot, halved	1 red bell pepper, julienned
1 teaspoon Honey Dijon mustard	1 tablespoon walnut oil
	1 tablespoon tamari sauce
½ teaspoon salt	4 hearts of palm, diagonally sliced
2 orange sections	
2 tablespoons raspberry vinegar	2 small avocados, peeled & sliced
2 tablespoons champagne	½ cup reserved vinaigrette
3 tablespoons walnut oil	1 bunch of watercress or mesclun
2 tablespoons peanut oil	
1 ½ pounds large shrimp, peeled	2 tablespoons chopped pistachios

Puree shallot with seasonings and orange sections, using an immersion blender. Add vinegar and champagne, then slowly add oils until emulsified. Sauté shrimp and pepper in oil until barely done, and add tamari and all but ¼ cup vinaigrette. Toss until warm. Toss palm hearts and avocados with remaining ¼ cup vinaigrette. Arrange cress on 4 plates, place shrimp in center, and arrange palm hearts and avocados around them. Sprinkle with pistachios. Serves 4.

CURRIED LOBSTER SALAD SEYCHELLOISE

At the end of Praslin Island in the Seychelles is Château des Feuilles, an exquisite tiny hotel and a member of Relais et Châteaux. Although I had no time to overnight, I savored this cooling and Indian-flavored salad. Shrimp is also good prepared this way, as is the ubiquitous Seychelle chicken.

2 medium lobsters, boiled or grilled, shelled, & cut into small pieces	1 tablespoon chutney
	1 teaspoon grated orange zest
1/3 cup yogurt	2 tablespoons dried currants or golden raisins
¼ cup coconut cream, the thick layer on top of the milk	¼ cup chopped toasted pistachios or cashews, reserving half
1 teaspoon curry powder, or to taste	1 bunch watercress or mesclun
1 tablespoon honey	

Chill lobster while preparing dressing. Mix yogurt, cream, and seasonings with currants and nuts. Stir in lobster, and serve over watercress. Sprinkle with reserved nuts.

Serves 4.

DURBAN FISH CURRY

Many decades ago on my first of many trips to South Africa, my visit to Durban's Maharani Hotel was highlighted by the comparison of its Indian chef's cooking styles with that of India, which I had visited a few years earlier. The main difference was an accent on tomatoes, tamarind paste, and fish. This is the way I remember the fish curry, which can be made with practically any kind of seafood or vegetable. The intensity of the seasoning is entirely personal. Also, coconut milk may be used for all or part of water.

1 cup chopped red onion	½ tablespoon tamarind paste, or to taste
2 tablespoons corn oil	1 cup water
3 large garlic cloves, crushed	½ pound small okra, top trimmed
2 medium tomatoes, chopped	
1 teaspoon paprika	½ pound yams, or butternut squash, peeled & cut into 1-inch chunks
1 teaspoon coriander	
½ teaspoon cumin	
½ teaspoon curry powder	4 fillets grouper, snapper, or halibut

Sauté the onion in oil, using a sauté pan, until soft and translucent. Add garlic, sauté briefly, and add tomatoes and spices. Simmer briskly a few minutes. Add water and vegetables, cover, and simmer about 10 minutes, or until almost tender. Add fillets, coating well with sauce, and simmer about 10 minutes or until done. If too much liquid remains, remove fish and reduce to desired consistency. Correct seasonings as desired.

Serves 4.

AFRIKAANER CHICKEN POT PIE

This terrific specialty must be the best thing the Afrikaaners ever did for South Africa. On my first trip there, I had this at Ouma's Kitchen, an ethnic standby in Johannisberg's Landdrost Hotel. It makes an impressive presentation and is a nice brunch dish.

1 3-4 pound chicken	1 carrot, cut in chunks
3 cups water or chicken stock	1 celery rib, cut in chunks
1 onion, quartered	1 teaspoon salt

½ teaspoon saffron or turmeric	2 tablespoons lemon juice
6 peppercorns	Salt & pepper
½ cup butter	1 cup cooked peas & diced carrots
½ cup flour	Rapid Puff Pastry (see Index)
¾ cup cream	1 egg yolk
2 egg yolks	1 tablespoon milk

Simmer chicken with water, vegetables, and seasonings, using a deep pan just wide enough to hold it, about 1 hour, covered. Uncover, let cool, remove chicken, strain stock, and reduce to 3 cups for the sauce. Remove skin and bones from chicken and cut into chunks.

Make a roux with butter and flour, add stock and simmer until thick. Add cream and yolks beaten with juice, cooking gently. Season, add chicken and vegetables, and keep hot.

Roll out about ½ pound of pastry, 1/8-inch thick and about the same size and shape of dish which chicken will be served in. Cut pastry scraps into fleurons or any desired shapes. Place pastry on baking sheet, brush with yolk beaten with milk to glaze. Arrange fleurons on top, brushing them also. Bake at 425° about 20 minutes, or until golden brown. Pour hot chicken into serving dish, and slide pastry on top.

Serves 6.

MOAMBA

(Angolan Chicken and Okra-Stew with Pumpkin)

Angola's national dish features that country's most popular foods, especially palm oil, but olive oil is an adequate substitute. Also, yams or butternut are sometimes used in place of pumpkin, which is the way it was served at the Presidente Hotel in Luanda. This was my reward for returning an inedible dish. Good ingredients were difficult to get so soon after the end of the 20-year war, but the Angolans still had their superb hospitality, Portuguese style.

4 suprêmes	½ tablespoon coriander
2 tablespoons olive oil	½ pound butternut squash, peeled & cubed
1 large red onion	
3 large garlic cloves, crushed	½ pound small okra, top trimmed
3 medium tomatoes, chopped	
1 tablespoon lemon juice	1 chile pepper, chopped (optional)

Using a sauté pan, sauté suprêmes in oil until golden. Remove, add onion and garlic, and cook until translucent. Add tomatoes and seasonings, and simmer briefly. Add chicken and vegetables, and simmer about 20 minutes, until all are tender.

Serves 4.

CHICKEN WITH BANANAS AND CASHEWS IN COCONUT CREAM

When I entered the Polana Hotel van with a red velvet interior, I knew I was in for an elegant stay in Maputo, Mozambique. As I registered at the antique desk I was served a flute of champagne. My room overlooked the terraced gardens leading down to the ocean, much like Reid's Hotel in Madeira, which was created by the same architect. The Polana has an excellent kitchen, and this is a great specialty.

4 suprêmes	2/3 cup coconut cream
2 tablespoons butter	2 cloves
1 tablespoon peanut oil	2 tablespoons lemon or lime juice
4 small red bananas, ripened & peeled	¾ cup chopped roasted cashews
2/3 cup chicken stock	Hot cooked rice

Sauté suprêmes in butter and oil until golden. Add bananas, sauté briefly, and add stock, cream, and cloves. Simmer, partially covered, about 10 minutes, or until chicken is tender. Remove chicken and bananas, reduce sauce until lightly thickened, and remove cloves, Add juice and cashews, return chicken and bananas to sauce to heat through. Serve over rice.

Serves 4.

DECONSTRUCTED LASAGNA WITH VEAL SCALLOPINE

High up on the Franschoek pass is the outstanding Haute Cabrière Cellar Restaurant, so reminiscent of those in Burgundy with an old-world ambience. Cabrière is the name of the village near Avignon, from where the original owner had come in 1694. The Haute Cabrière Vineyards produce some of South Africa's best Pinot Noirs, which I savored with this delectable veal entrée at my fireside table. As a world leader in gastronomical trends, this versatile recipe may be made with other meats and sauces as you desire.

4 thin veal scallops, about 3 or 4 ounces each	2 cups veal stock, reduced to 1 cup
Salt & pepper	6 ounces wild mushrooms, thinly sliced
Flour	
2 tablespoons each olive oil and butter	6 ounces zucchini, thinly sliced
	3 tablespoons butter
¼ cup Marsala	8 4- or 5-inch squares lasagna, cooked

Season and flour veal, then sauté in hot oil and butter, using a large sauté pan. When done to your preference, remove and keep warm. Deglaze pan with Marsala, add stock, and keep warm while sautéeing vegetables in butter. Place a square of lasagna on each of 4 plates, add veal and vegetables along with a spoonful of veal glaze, then top with remaining lasagna squares and sauce. These are also good with a slice of asiago or provolone, and they lend themselves nicely to being made in au gratin dishes. Serve hot.

Serves 4.

BOBOTI

(Cape Malay Lamb and Custard Casserole)

Although this dish, created by the Cape Malays, is the national dish of South Africa, the best was at Ongava Game Lodge in Namibia's Etosha National Park. Namibian cooks really know their way around the kitchen, whether it be the classics or creative new cooking. Boboti can be made with only lamb or combined with beef, and bay leaves are an acceptable substitute for the traditional lemon and lime leaves. Any kind of chutney may be used and seasoned as you wish.

2 medium red onions, chopped	1 tablespoon malt vinegar, wine, or tamarind paste
2 tablespoons butter or oil	1 tablespoon turbinado sugar or honey
1 large garlic clove, crushed	Salt & pepper
1 tablespoon curry powder	2 eggs
½ cup chutney + extra raisins	½ cup milk
1 pound ground lamb	

Sauté onions in butter until soft and translucent, add garlic and curry powder, sautéeing briefly. Add chutney with extra raisins and lamb. Cook until lamb is no longer pink, and stir in seasonings. Place in a shallow 1-1 ½-quart baking dish. Beat egg with milk, pour over lamb, and bake at 325° about 20 minutes or until custard is barely set.

Serves 4.

SOSATIES

(Cape Malay Lamb Kebabs)

Another Cape Malay classic, this dish's name is derived from Indonesian saté, yet another form of kebabs. Sosaties are an integral part of the braaivleis, or barbecue, throughout southern Africa. My first were at the Victoria Falls Hotel where there was a great fire, traditional dancers, and a terrific barbecue in the boma, a cleared area in the bush reached by foot. The marinade is usually based on cooked onions, lemon juice, and curry powder. The English chef liked to use a little malt vinegar also. Chicken is also prepared this way.

2 red onions, thinly sliced	¼ cup malt vinegar
2 tablespoons oil or butter	½ cup water
1 tablespoon curry powder	1 cup lemon juice
1 teaspoon ground coriander	2 pounds boneless lamb leg, cut into 1 ½-inch chunks
1 tablespoon turbinado sugar	
¼ cup apricot or plum preserves	3 large garlic cloves, crushed with salt

Sauté onions in oil until soft and translucent. Add seasonings, sugar, preserves, and liquids, bring to a boil, and let cool. Rub lamb chunks with garlic and let stand until marinade is cool enough to pour over it. Marinate at least 1 day, refrigerated. Thread onto skewers, and grill over charcoal or a fire, as they do in Africa, about 10 to 15 minutes, turning them until cooked to desired stage.

Serves 4 to 6.

ROMAZAVA

(Malagasy Meat and Vegetable Stew)

The greatest of African stews, Romazava is closely related to the bredies of South Africa and may have influenced them, although the Cape Malays are credited with their origin. Cooked greens, however, as in Romazava, were introduced by the Portuguese, probably in nearby Mozambique. Romazava is made with mixed meats, which may be browned or simply added to the pan with the onions and tomatoes. Also, your choice of greens includes collards, turnip, mustard, callaloo, or kale. I found that the hotels served a more sophisticated type in Antananarivo, known affectionately as Tana, than the native restaurants. I prefer the following method and serve it over yellow rice.

3 pounds mixed beef chuck, lamb and pork shoulder, and chicken parts	Finely chopped fresh ginger root
2 tablespoons olive oil	4 cloves
1 or 2 red onions, sliced	Salt & pepper
6 garlic cloves, crushed	1 pound collards, cut into chiffonade
1 ½ pounds tomatoes, coarsely chopped	

Using a large sauté pan, brown meats lightly in oil, add onions and garlic, and sauté until soft. Add tomatoes and seasonings, bring to a boil, cover and simmer about 2 hours, adding chicken about half an hour before meats are tender. Add collards, simmer about half an hour, adding water if necessary.

Serves 4 to 6

EGGS BENEDICT POLANA

The world's best and most elegant Eggs Benedict were found in Africa's most elegant hotel, the Polana in Maputo, Mozambique. They were actually part of the immense breakfast buffet, but would make a delightful brunch or lunch served with Mimosas. The orange-flavored Sauce Maltaise and the orange sections served over the eggs in their pastry shells were simply divine.

4 individual pastry shells, or rectangular pastry cases made with Rapid Puff Pastry (see index) 4 thin slices ham, such as Serrano 1 cup Hollandaise Sauce (see Index)	2 tablespoons orange juice 1 teaspoon grated orange zest 4 poached eggs 4 to 8 orange sections Mint sprigs

Place ham in bottom of pastry shells or cases. While Hollandaise is warm, whisk in juice and half the zest. Place warm eggs in pastry shells, pour sauce over them, and garnish top with remaining zest, orange sections, and mint.

Serves 4.

Vegetables are immensely important to all Africans, and the extensive variety in the Cape area has inspired South Africans to be excellent vegetable cooks, as I discovered when I ordered a vegetable plate at the venerable Town House Hotel in Capetown many years ago, the night before embarking on the British St. Helena mail ship's journey to Tristan da Cunha. The large white oval platter set proudly before me had an artfully arranged group of an astounding 14 vegetables, which were in their prime and perfectly prepared. They included stewed tomatoes, beets, yams, zucchini, turnips, carrots, spinach, green beans, corn, caramelized onions, okra, cabbage, cauliflower, and red beans. If only I could recreate that beautiful array of deliciously prepared vegetables which I remember so well.

SOSSUSVLEI CARAMELIZED POTATOES

These uniquely prepared fried potatoes were only a part of the really great food prepared at the Sossusvlei luxury lodge in Namibia's desert near the world's highest sand dunes. This method is of German origin.

| 1 pound Yukon potatoes, peeled & thinly sliced | 1 teaspoon salt |
| 3 tablespoons butter | 1 teaspoon sugar, or more |

Using a large non-stick skillet (I like iron), melt butter and layer potatoes, sprinkling them with salt and sugar. Fry over fairly high heat, tossing and turning until golden and tender.

Serves 4.

SWEET AND SOUR TOMATO CHUTNEY

Chutneys are one of India's greatest contributions to South African cuisine, and this one also has elements of French, German, and Italian influence. It is a must for Sosaties and Bobotie in this section, as well as many of the South American recipes, such as Chilean Pichanga and Ecuadorean Llapingachos. It is great on many of the potato dishes also. I make as much as possible, as it freezes beautifully.

3 pounds very ripe tomatoes, peeled and cut into chunks	2 tablespoons chopped crystallized ginger
½ cup chestnut honey	½ head garlic, peeled and chopped
1/3 cup brown sugar	
1/3 cup sherry vinegar	1 teaspoon cumin
1/3 cup balsamic vinegar	Salt & pepper, to taste
	¼ cup black or golden raisins

Mix all ingredients except raisins in a heavy stainless steel or enameled pan. Simmer, partially covered, about an hour, stirring occasionally. Add raisins, and cook until thickened, about 10 minutes. Serve cold.

Makes about 1 quart.

ROVOS RAIL APPLE TART

The Pride of Africa, the world's most luxurious train, is the pride of Rohan Vos, Rovos Rail's owner, who elegantly restored vintage rail cars. The all-suite accommodations are spacious enough for a queen-size bed, a sitting area with a chilled bottle of welcoming champagne, and a charming private bath. My trip from Capetown to Johannisberg stopped for a visit at the Victorian village of

Matjiesfontein and for lunch at the distinguished Kimberley Club in the famed diamond town. But the highlight of the trip was the retro dining car where one dresses for dinner, which is an elegantly served multi-course affair with excellent wines. The cuisine is a blend of the best South African products with French, Dutch, and other European influences. The luscious apple tart, for example, makes use of the Afrikaaner marmalade and Van der Hum tangerine liqueur. My rendition is quite similar and simple to prepare.

8 small Golden Delicious apples, peeled & thinly sliced	2 tablespoons Van der Hum liqueur
½ cup butter	2 tablespoons orange juice
½ tablespoon vanilla	Crème Chantilly (see Index), optional
1/3 cup turbinado suga	
½ cup orange marmalade	Pâte Sucrée(see Index) or pie pastry

Using a large sauté pan, cook apples, tossing and turning until golden, about 20 minutes. Add vanilla and cool. Line a 10-inch fluted tart tin with pastry. Place apples over pastry, and sprinkle with sugar. Bake at 375° about 45 minutes, or until pastry is golden brown. Mix marmalade with liqueur and juice, spread over apples, and garnish with Chantilly rosettes, if desired.

Serves 6.

PEPPERMINT CRISP PUDDING

This wonderful and original dessert recipe is from Namibia's Damaraland Camp, where I enjoyed it at the Boma, the cleared area in the bush where we had our superb dinner in grand style. The talented cook who gave me the recipe said she used Peppermint Crisp chocolate bars, which I cannot find, so I successfully used other mint-flavored candy, even chocolate mint patties and crushed peppermint candy canes. She also used Tennis Biscuits, which are a form of coconut cookies, but this is yummy whatever you use.

1 cup cream	2 Peppermint Crisp chocolate bars
1 cup Dulce de Leche	7 ounces coconut cookies or macaroons

Whip cream until almost stiff, then whip in caramel sauce. Mix in crumbled chocolate bars. Place half the caramel cream in an 8- or 9-inch square pan, add broken up cookies and remaining caramel cream. Chill at least 2 hours, or until set, and cut into squares.

Serves 6 to 8.

AFRIKAANER BREAKFAST

This luscious South African concoction is not only breakfast-it's good enough to be dessert, a midnight snack, or even a welcome treat before Christmas dinner. I've encountered it all over southern Africa, in north European countries, and even in the United States. Any kind of granola or muesli, homemade or not, and any kind of fruit is great. Serve in the traditional small glass or in a small bowl.

2 cups plain yogurt	1 cup or more of sliced strawberries, other berries, or sliced peaches, or diced mangoes
¼ cup honey, or more	
2 cups muesli or granola	

Spoon ½ cup of yogurt into an 8-ounce glass or bowl, mix in honey to taste, add ½ cup muesli or granola, and top with fruit of your choice. When eating, stir ingredients together as desired. Enjoy my daily breakfast!

Serves 4

COFFEE-WALNUT CAKE WITH MASCARPONE

A cake is a cake is a cake, but not this one-it's the world's best. The grand Sossusvlei Lodge near the highest sand dunes in the world in Namibia has terrific food, especially this glorious cake. I especially like it with a red wine syrup, and it's great for Thanksgiving.

½ pound soft butter	½ cup chopped walnuts
1 cup brown sugar	2/3 cup sugar
2 eggs	1 cup water
1 tablespoon instant coffee powder	1 tablespoon instant coffee powder
2 cups unbleached flour	3 tablespoons Tiramisu or Kahlua
1 ½ teaspoons baking soda	
1 teaspoon baking powder	½ pound softened Mascarpone cheese
1 teaspoon salt	
1 cup sour cream	½ cup chopped, toasted walnuts

Cream butter and sugar until light, and add eggs, beating well. Mix dry ingredients and fold in alternately with sour cream, ending with flour. Add walnuts, pour into a buttered and floured 10-inch cake pan, and bake in a 350° oven about 35 to 40 minutes, or until a skewer comes out clean. Cool before inverting onto a rack.

Meanwhile, boil sugar and water until thickened, about 5 minutes. Add coffee powder and liqueur. Chill, prick cake well, and pour half the syrup over it. Spread top of cake with mascarpone, and sprinkle with walnuts. Pass remaining syrup to spoon over cake.

Serves 8 to 12.

CENTRAL ASIA
INDIA SRI LANKA MALDIVES NEPAL PAKISTAN AFGHANISTAN
THE FIVE STANS

My adventurous travels throughout this vast area of central Asia have taken me to Indian Ocean islands, jungles, deserts, the world's highest mountains, and the northern steppes leading to Siberia. Russia, Turkey, Persia, and China have had vast influences on the people, religions, languages, customs, and above all, the foods that are encountered.

India, of course, was most influenced by the British, who introduced tea, the country clubs of Calcutta, hot water bottles for the cold beds in the North, and other genteel vagaries. It was Ghenghis Khan's Mongols, however, who introduced the most important cooking style of the sub-continent, Mughlai cuisine, which is characterized by rich and creamy sauces, flatbreads, kebabs, koftas, and the use of rose water, almonds, and pistachios. Saffron, notably from Kashmir, is the most important spice in this northern style of cooking and butter is the cooking medium. The tandoor, a clay oven below floor level, is used for cooking breads on its walls as well as roasting chicken and kebabs on long spits. Lamb is the meat of choice as Hindus reign throughout the north, which includes delightful Darjeeling and Gangtok, Sikkim, a most unique and mysterious semi-autonomous state, which some consider to be a separate country, between Nepal and Bhutan.

Since India is the birthplace of curry, it is ubiquitous throughout every region and is a different mixture in every household. Curry, the Anglicized word for Kari, is the actual mixture of spices while a masala is the sauce made with it. As many as two dozen spices can be used.

Southern Indian cooking, equally delicious, is spicier and makes much use of vegetables, lentils, coconut, fish, pakoras (vegetable fritters), and cooling raitas, made with yogurt and fruit or vegetables. There is also a strong Portuguese influence in the state of Kerala, especially in Goa and Cochin, the Venice of India, where Vasco da Gama was entombed in the cathedral.

Kerala, on the Malabar coast, which was the center of the trade route founded by da Gama, is also the only place in India which has both pork and beef, and I learned that it has the only safe drinking water from the tap and also no malaria. The enchanting islands, connected by boat, with their friendly people and outstanding food make this my favorite place in all of exotic India.

Sri Lanka, formerly Ceylon, is known as the pearl of the Indian Ocean and has a cuisine and people similar to that of nearby southern India. The Portuguese, Dutch, and English left their legacies of palm sugar, spices, coconut, and British tea plantations, located in the beautiful and misty mountains. I also sampled curries in the Andaman Islands, but it was in the Maldives that I enjoyed the most magnificent creamy masalas ever. Reached only by boat or helicopter, 200 low-lying islands on 20 coral atolls offer a private paradise of luxury hotels, with wonderful meals of freshly caught tuna, coconut curries, and an array of tropical fruit. My best meal was in a small hotel in Malé, the capital, which I flew into from Singapore.

Nepal, the Himalayan kingdom that separates India from Tibet, is home to Mt. Everest, the world's highest mountain, as well as the world's highest hotel, the Everest View, which I reached by taking a six-seat aircraft on a dizzying flight that landed on the world's shortest runway. And to think that the bearded and robed Sherpa pilot invited me to sit in the co-pilot's seat! A trek up to the hotel followed, as well as HMS (Himalayan mountain sickness), but at least I managed to sample yak and yak butter, which is highly prized by the Sherpas.

Back in Kathmandu, known for its Buddhist and Hindu shrines and temples in exotic Durbar Square, the cuisine is primarily regional Indian and is based on rice, lentils, potatoes, vegetables, and meat. There is a British, Indian, and Tibetan influence in the culture, people, and the food. Formerly, the best food in town was at the Yak & Yeti, owned by the illustrious Boris Lissanevitch, who invited me to his Easter dinner party attended by Kathmandu's cognoscenti, but more about that later in Boris's Yak Tail recipe.

Pakistan and Bangladesh, part of India until its independence from the British in 1947, have a cuisine similar to that of India with an emphasis on spicy curries, Basmati rice, flatbreads, lamb and chicken kebabs, and vegetable preparations. Pakistan also has an Iranian and Afghani influence. Its southern coastline offers great shrimp and barbecue specialties, while the rugged north in the Hindu Kush mountains and the Khyber Pass area have more of the Moghlai style with tandoori cooking as in northern India.

Bangladesh also shares the Moghlai cooking, but what impressed me was the great meal I had on Air Bangladesh, from Dhaka to Calcutta, a 45-minute flight. Upon entering the aircraft, each passenger was handed a box dinner that contained fresh fruit, imported cheese, freshly cooked flatbread, nuts, a large Toblerone bar, and a few other items. There was enough left over for my breakfast. To think the American carriers say there isn't enough time to serve food!

Afghanistan, a rugged land of mountains and caves, is best known for its Russian occupation and subsequent Al-Qaida terrorists led by Osama bin Laden. Its cooking is most influenced by India and Iran, but its national dish, Ashak, is a result of a brief Italian foray, when grape vines were also planted in this Muslim country. I had a most unexpected introduction to this cooking.

In late April, 1979, the elegant sales manager at the Maurya Sheraton in Delhi phoned the American Embassy to inquire about the safety in Afghanistan, due to the Russian problem and the American ambassador's assassination in February. No problem! So, at 38,000 feet my seatmate, a Cuban journalist, asked which publication I represented. The entire plane was filled with

Communist journalists going to Kabul to cover the first anniversary of the Russian coup. When I reached the Intercontinental Hotel, I asked the reception clerk to call the phone number I was given by the Sheraton sales manager, who asked me to contact her friend whom she knew at Brown, the prestigious American college. The friend was Mrs. S. K. Singh, wife of the Indian ambassador. The following morning, to the amazement of the hotel staff, the ambassador's chauffeured Mercedes picked me up to have a wonderful luncheon at their elegantly furnished home, after which Mrs. Singh took me shopping on Chicken Street, the Fifth Avenue of Kabul, where the owner of the shop gave me a lapis lazuli ring. That night the bridges were being blown up, but I was safely learning about Afghani cooking in the hotel kitchen. More about that in the Ashak recipe!

The Five Stans-Turkmenistan, Uzbekistan, Kazakstan, Tajikistan, and Kyrgyzstan, located on the central steppes of Asia-are former Russian republics and have an interesting and turbulent history, influenced by Turkey, Persia, India, and China, as well as Russia. The architecture and the food reflect this influence, as I discovered on my adventures throughout the area.

Turkmenistan proved to be the most difficult upon arrival when the immigration officer exchanged my dollars for obsolete local money in Ashkabad. Two Polish embassy officials graciously offered me a ride to my hotel, which informed me that I had no reservation (though I had prepaid). After a couple of hours, a small group of English-speaking Turkmen professors from Sweden and Scotland entered the hotel and solved my dilemma. And I learned that the national dish of all the Stans is Plov, a dish of fried mutton, turnip, and rice. In addition to Turkish, Russian, and Indian cooking influences, Chinese manty and pelmeni (pockets of dough, similar to ravioli, stuffed with meat) are popular. All these republics savor them, and they are quite good. Breakfast was another story, as I could not find the foreigner's breakfast room, but the professors invited me to join their entire group of several dozen professors who were there for a reunion. The breakfast consisted of very tough and strong-tasting mutton sausages and cold spaghetti covered with sheep tail's fat and some indiscernible blend of spices. But it was authentic! And the green tea and yogurt were quite good.

Uzbekistan, like Turkmenistan, is under the rule of a ruthless dictator, but its glorious ancient cities of Samarkand and Bukhara are reminiscent of the days of Tamerlane, Alexander the Great, and Ghenghis Khan. The Persian architecture is stupendously beautiful and was well worth the overnight train ride from Samarkand. In additon to Plov and manty, Uzbekistan has a fabulous array of Persian melons which I saw piled high in trucks and on streets. My pride and joy is the handmade birch rolling pin with decoratively painted handles that I bought at the Samarkand market for a mere fifty cents.

Tajikistan, less developed than Turkmenistan and Uzbekistan, is located in the rugged Pamir Mountains and has similar cooking, which I was able to sample in a small town near the Uzbek border where I had lunch.

Kyrgyzstan, also not well developed, is a land of mountains and lakes in the Tien Shan range. I visited Bishkek while I was in Almaty, Kazakstan. I hired a driver through my hotel, and he was an obstetrician who could not support his family without moonlighting on the weekend. He now has freedom but no money. This was a comment I heard over and over throughout all 16 republics.

Kazakstan, a huge republic stretching from the Caspian Sea to China, is quite famous for its apples, which its capital of Almaty, formerly Alma Ata, is named for. Russian and Chinese cuisine predominate, and the food here was better than in the other republics.

RECIPES FROM CENTRAL ASIA

MANGO LASSI

BORIS YAK TAIL (BLOODY MARY)

BANANA-COCONUT RAYTA

CHARD-TOMATO RAYTA

LEMON-MINT RAYTA

KARACHI CURRY

FISH WITH CREAMY COCONUT MASALA

MOTI MAHAL TANDOORI CHICKEN

BOMBAY CURRY

CURRIED LAMB KEBABS WITH SPICY SAUCE, PILAF, AND EGGS

ASHAK
(AFGHANI LEEK RAVIOLI WITH LAMB SAUCE AND YOGURT)

ORANGE LAMB BIRYANI

GARAM MASALA

NAAN

EGGPLANT BORANI

RED LENTILS WITH LIME

SHRIKHAND
(SAFFRON YOGURT WITH PISTACHIOS AND CURRANTS)

DATE HALWA

MANGO LASSI

One of India's most popular beverages, better than Coke, lassi is drunk as a cooling refreshment and also with meals. The drink can be salty, sweet, or spicy and with or without fruit. This is a delightful combination of all. It is traditionally served over ice cubes, which is the way I had a similar version at the Malabar Hotel on Willingdon Island in Cochin, Kerala, the Utopia of India. They also prepare magnificent vegetables.

1 very large, very ripe mango, peeled, pitted, & pureed	¼ cup turbinado sugar
2 cups yogurt	¼ teaspoon cardamom
½ cup passion fruit juice	Pinch of salt
1 tablespoon grated orange zest	1 cup small ice cubes, or crushed ice

Whisk puree into yogurt with remaining ingredients. Thin with more juice or water if too thick. Pour into glasses.

Serves 2 or 3.

BORIS'S YAK TAIL
(Boris's Bloody Mary)

The legendary Boris Lissanevitch, a former Russian Ballet Russes dancer, big game hunter, and famed Nepalese host and hotelier, has been the subject of at least two biographies, Tiger for Breakfast by Michel Peissel, and From Bali to Belly by Desmond Doig. Peissel wrote that Boris perfected the art of making total strangers feel important and accepted, and found a common bond with everyone. Although he has entertained kings, queens, and other luminaries, he invited me to his Easter dinner party at his famous

Boris Restaurant in 1979. Among the luminaries present were Douglas Heck, the American ambassador; Doig, the English author of From Bali to Belly; French embassy diplomats, a famous Burmese interior designer, and others. After imbibing these intense Yak Tails, or Bloody Marys, we dined on quail eggs, borscht, smoked bekti, and other delights. Boris is now over the horizon.

2 ounces each vodka, consommé, & V-8 juice	1 or 2 dashes each Worcestershire, Tabasco, & lemon juice

Shake ingredients together with ice, and serve cold.
Serves 1.

Salads, per se, are not an important part of this area's cooking style, but cold yogurt dishes known as raytas or sambals are ubiquitous. They can be made with practically any herb, vegetable, and seasoning, or simply yogurt with a little honey and golden raisins and walnuts. Try adding a little saffron to them. Think of rayta as a tossed salad: use what you have. Of course, cooked chutneys are great with curried dishes too, especially in western countries, so try the ones in this book in other sections.

BANANA-COCONUT RAYTA

This rayta is my favorite and is most at home with curried dishes from Sri Lanka, the Maldives, and southern India, especially with fish and chicken.

½ cup freshly grated coconut	1 teaspoon salt
2 tablespoons butter	¼ teaspoon turmeric
1 tablespoon honey	1 tablespoon chopped mint or cilantro
1 banana, peeled & sliced diagonally	1 cup yogurt

Sauté coconut briefly in butter. Add honey and banana, toss to coat, and add remaining ingredients. Chill well.

Makes about 2 cups.

CHARD-TOMATO RAYTA

This zesty red and green rayta has a special affinity for lamb dishes.

½ pound Swiss chard, cut into fine chiffonade	1 small tomato, seeded & diced
1 tablespoon butter	½ teaspoon salt
2 garlic cloves, crushed	½ teaspoon cumin
	1 cup yogurt

Place washed chard, still wet, into a skillet with butter and let steam until tender. Add garlic and tomatoes, cook briefly, and add seasonings and yogurt. Chill well.

Makes about 2 cups.

LEMON MINT RAYTA

Although this light rayta is excellent with fish, it is a natural with lamb.

1 cup mint leaves, packed	½ teaspoon salt
1 clove garlic, crushed	½ teaspoon sugar
1 tablespoon lemon juice	1 cup yogurt

Place all ingredients in an immersion blender, and puree until almost smooth.

Makes about 1 ½ cups.

KARACHI CURRY

Aggha's Grill in the Northwestern Hotel in Karachi serves a great but very simple shrimp curry that has many possibilities. I have used yellow tomatoes, which are visually stunning when paired with lots of cilantro, and I also like to add a bit of honey mustard infusion or a splash of balsamic to each portion.

1 large red onion, thinly sliced	2 large ripe tomatoes, cut into eighths
4 large garlic cloves, crushed	1 ½ pounds shrimp, shelled
¼ cup butter	Salt, to taste
1 teaspoon curry powder	½ cup chopped cilantro
½ teaspoon turmeric	Balsamic vinegar, to taste

Sauté onion and garlic in butter until very soft, add spices and sauté briefly. Add tomatoes, and simmer until lightly thickened, adding water if necessary. Add shrimp, salt, and cilantro. Cook about 5 minutes, then splash with balsamic. This is perfect on saffron rice.

Serves 4.

FISH WITH CREAMY COCONUT MASALA

Fish prepared with a creamy coconut masala in southern India, Sri Lanka, or the Maldives is the ultimate in taste appeal. My best meal in the Maldives was not at my private atoll luxury resort, but at the plebeian Nasandhura in the town of Malé. The chefs were from Kerala on India's Malabar coast, and their Maldivian food was outstanding.

½ cup chopped onion	1 cup heavy cream
2 tablespoons butter	1 cup coconut milk
2 garlic cloves, crushed	1/3 cup Japanese mirin
½ teaspoon turmeric	1 tablespoon lemon juice
½ teaspoon coriander	1 teaspoon salt
¼ teaspoon cumin	1 teaspoon turbinado sugar
¼ teaspoon ginger	4 fillets grouper, snapper, or sea bass

Sauté onion in butter until soft, add garlic and spices, and cook briefly to enhance flavor. Add milk and cream, simmer about 15 minutes, and add mirin, juice, and seasonings. Add fish and simmer gently about 15 minutes, or until done. This is ideal served over saffron rice.

Serves 4.

MOTI MAHAL TANDOORI CHICKEN

Without doubt, my most memorable meal in India was at old Delhi's famous Moti Mahal, which was originally in Peshawar, Pakistan, before the 1947 partition of India and Pakistan. But, alas, the humble Moti Mahal is now only a memory. My meal was served at an outdoor table in a pink-walled courtyard with musicians and gracious and hospitable service. I was taken on a tour of the kitchen with its tandoor ovens, which were sunk into the floor and manned by barefoot cooks wearing old-fashioned undershirts. The specialty, chickens marinated in a colorful and zesty yogurt mixture, were impaled on long skewers and roasted over hot coals and burning wooden embers. Naan and chapati, the flavorful flatbreads, were slapped against the oven walls to bake in the aromatic smoke. This is the original recipe, but I prefer to use only suprêmes, and lacking a tandoor, I cook them on a charcoal grill.

1 broiler chicken, skinned & halved, or 4 suprêmes	½ teaspoon ginger
1 teaspoon salt	½ teaspoon red food coloring
2 tablespoons lemon juice	2 large garlic cloves, crushed
¾ cup yogurt	2 tablespoons melted butter
1 teaspoon coriander	1 tablespoon lemon juice
½ teaspoon cumin	Salt & red pepper, to taste

Salad:

2 ripe medium tomatoes, sliced	1 lemon, quartered
1 small red onion, sliced	Tomato Butter Sauce (optional, see below)

Cut several gashes in chicken halves or suprêmes, rub with salt and juice, and let stand about ½ hour. Mix yogurt with seasonings, coloring, and garlic, and spread over chicken, letting it marinate at least several hours. Cook on a hot grill, turning and brushing with butter, about 20 minutes for halves and about 10 minutes for suprêmes. Sprinkle with juice and seasonings, and serve with salad ingredients. The following Tomato Butter Sauce may also be served with it:

¾ cup canned crushed tomatoes	2 tablespoons butter
1 teaspoon tomato paste	2 tablespoons cream

Mix sauce ingredients in a saucepan and simmer about 5 minutes. Serve warm.

Serves 4.

BOMBAY CURRY

Across from the magnificent Gateway to India arch on the Arabian Sea is the venerable Taj Hotel with its outstanding Indian restaurant, Tanjore. The service is Maharashtrian style, named for the state of Maharashtra. Large individual round trays made of silver or other metals are centered with rice pilaf, surrounded by small bowls of lamb and chicken curries, two soups, raytas, vegetables, and puri. The whole is garnished with silver leaf and a fried coiled banana leaf. Classical Indian entertainment accompanies this ethnic feast. This recipe, which has evolved over the years, is evocative of the Bombay style and can be made with chicken or lamb. Just as Bombay is India's melting pot, like New York is the US's, this curry is also a melange of flavors.

1 large onion, chopped	¾ cup water or chicken stock
2 large garlic cloves, crushed	¾ cup yogurt or heavy cream
½ cup butter	1 tablespoon tomato paste
4 to 6 suprêmes, cut into cubes	1 cup chopped mango, pineapple, or banana
1 teaspoon coriander	
½ teaspoon cumin	2 tablespoons chutney
½ teaspoon turmeric	2 tablespoons freshly grated coconut
½ teaspoon ginger	
Salt & pepper	1 tablespoon lemon juice

Sauté onion and garlic in butter, using a sauté pan, until golden. Add suprêmes, sauté until no longer pink and remove. Add seasonings, sauté briefly, return chicken to pan, and add water. Cover and simmer about 15 minutes, or until chicken is done. Remove chicken, add all but lemon juice, and simmer briskly until lightly thickened. Add juice and serve on pilaf.

Serves 4 to 6.

CURRIED LAMB KEBABS WITH SPICY TOMATO SAUCE, PILAF, AND EGGS

As much as I love Kerala in India's extreme south, Darjeeling-the Himalayan mountain retreat so loved by the British as a respite from Calcutta's heat-is a very special place. From Calcutta I flew to Shiliguri and took the Toy Train through jungles, tea gardens, and pine forests to the time-honored Windermere Hotel where I savored this outstanding Himalayan comfort food.

There are many versions, but I prefer mine. This fabled hotel extends comforts to the rooms, as I discovered after dinner when my turndown service included a hot water bottle tucked underneath the blanket, and there was a log blazing in the fireplace. This is a place to stay a while and definitely worth a detour.

1 cup thinly sliced onion	1 teaspoon salt
1 garlic clove, crushed	½ teaspoon powdered saffron
3 tablespoons oil or butter	Chelou Kebabs (see Index)
2 large tomatoes, chopped	Saffron rice
1 teaspoon oregano	4 fried eggs

Sauté onion and garlic in butter until soft, add tomatoes and seasonings, and simmer until thick, shiny, and oil or butter starts separating from the tomatoes, about 20 minutes. Place rice on platter, top with sauce, kebabs, and eggs.

Serves 4.

ASHAK

(Afghani Leek Ravioli with Lamb Sauce and Yogurt)

The first anniversary of the Communist coup in Kabul, per my anecdote in the preface to this section, was a blessing in disguise even though the bridges were being blown up. Since I was the only one for dinner in the Intercontinental's Pamir Supper Club, I had a virtual cooking course in the kitchen with the German chef. As we shared a bottle of Castellino, the best Afghani red, he explained the Italian influence on Afghani cooking and winemaking. Ashak is the national dish and is today's perfect fusion example: a combination of pasta and meat sauce with yogurt and mint. A simple lamb stew made with onions, garlic, tomato sauce, bell peppers, and oregano seemed quite Italian-until he added curry powder. The best of all was the golden flavorful naan, which is what the Afghanis have with tea for breakfast, as did I.

1 recipe Pasta Dough (see Index) or Wonton wrappers (about 2 dozen)	2 tablespoons olive oil
	1 teaspoon salt
2 whole large leeks, chopped in processor, about 3 cups	¼ teaspoon red pepper

Sauce:

1 pound ground lamb or beef	Red pepper, to taste
1 large onion, chopped	2 cups yogurt, drained about 2 hours
¼ cup olive oil	
½ cup tomato puree	1 or 2 large garlic cloves, crushed
½ cup water or red wine	
1 teaspoon salt	2 tablespoons chopped mint

Sauté leeks in oil with seasonings until very soft, covering the pan to let them steam. Brush edges of ravioli dough or wrappers with water, place about 2 teaspoons of cooled leek filling in center of each. Fold as desired, press edges firmly, and boil until they rise to the top, about 5 minutes. Drain. Sauté lamb and onion in oil until browned, add puree, water, and seasonings, then simmer, covered, about 20 minutes. Pour meat sauce over ravioli, top with yogurt and sprinkle with mint. A most delightful flavor combination.

Serves 4 to 6.

ORANGE LAMB BIRYANI

Biryani, the bountiful dish of layered saffron rice and aromatic lamb, is the crowning glory of Moghlai cuisine. Prepared from Bangladesh and northern India through the Khyber Pass, to Pakistan and Afghanistan, it has many variations. In my creation, I have made lavish use of oranges which gives it a very Persian aura. I have adjusted the recipe to serve from two to twelve with great success, although Biryani is considered to be a party dish. The much loved Orange Pilaf from *Culinary Classics* is the base of this recipe.

1 large orange, peel removed with a zester & orange segmented	2 tablespoons butter
	1 teaspoon salt
	¼ teaspoon powdered saffron
1 cup water	¾ cup water
½ cup sugar	¾ cup orange juice
½ cup orange juice	1 pound ground lamb
¼ cup sliced almonds	1 red onion, sliced
1 cup Basmati rice, rinsed	2 tablespoons butter
1 tablespoon grated orange zest	1 teaspoon cardamom

½ teaspoon cumin	3 tablespoons orange flower water
1 teaspoon salt	
½ cup orange juice	½ teaspoon crushed saffron threads
¼ cup yogurt	
¼ cup melted butter	¼ cup chopped pistachios
	Chopped mint

Boil zest in water about 5 minutes, drain and rinse. Add to sugar and juice, boil until syrupy, and add orange segments and almonds.

Sauté rice and zest in butter briefly, add seasonings and liquids, cover and cook about 10 minutes, or until half done, and drain, retaining liquid. Add drained liquid from orange zest.

Sauté lamb and onion in butter until onion is soft, about 10 minutes. Add seasonings and juice, and simmer about ½ hour, covered. Stir in yogurt and half the orange zest from syrup.

Pour melted butter into a 6-cup casserole (I prefer a clay pot) and add half the rice and half the combined orange syrup and rice cooking liquid. Add lamb and its juices, and then another layer of rice. Add remaining reserved liquids. Cover, and bake at 300° about 20 to 30 minutes. Spoon rice onto platter, make a well in center, add lamb, and spoon remaining rice around it. Drizzle with mixed orange flower water and saffron. Garnish with reserved orange zest, orange sections, almonds, pistachios, and mint. Of course, if you have silver leaf, you may add that also.

Serves 4 to 6.

GARAM MASALA

Spicing is a very personal choice, so if you like more than the amounts in these recipes, feel free to add this "hot spice" mixture, and keep it on hand if you make Indian dishes frequently.

1 tablespoon cardamom 2 teaspoons cinnamon	1 teaspoon each nutmeg, cloves, & black pepper

Mix and store in tightly covered jar. Use as desired.

Indian breads are the glory of Indian cuisine, which is one of the five best in the world. There are many types, including chapati, paratha, puri, and naan. Whole wheat flour is generally used, but I have not found that American whole wheat is the best, so I prefer unbleached white flour, and most Indian breads are not leavened.

NAAN

My favorite of all, naan is normally formed into the shape of a teardrop, but I prefer a simple round. Also, I have discovered that it can be baked, deep-fat fried, or cooked in a small amount of oil in an iron skillet. I flavor mine with cardamom, my favorite spice, which I have been known to add to my waffle batter and other baked items. This bread is great with practically everything and is absolutely delicious.

2-2 ½ cups unbleached flour	½ teaspoon baking soda
1 tablespoon cardamom	1 small egg, beaten
1 teaspoon turmeric or saffron	½ cup milk
1 teaspoon sugar	½ cup yogurt
1 teaspoon salt	¼ cup melted butter
1 teaspoon baking powder	Canola, corn, or peanut oil, from ½ to 2 cups

Mix dry ingredients together in a large bowl. Add milk, yogurt, and butter to egg, and stir in with a wooden spoon just until blended. Knead briefly, adding a little flour if necessary, cover, and let stand about an hour. Divide into 8 to 12 pieces, and roll into rounds about the thickness of pie pastry. Heat oil in an iron skillet to about 375°, lower a piece of naan, and gently ladle oil on top to cook and puff up, about a minute. Turn over and cook until puffed underneath and golden all over. Drain on paper towels and keep hot in a warm oven while cooking the rest. If you wish, you may use only enough oil to coat the surface in order to sauté them. They are even good reheated in a toaster oven or wrapped in foil.

Makes 8 to 12 naan.

EGGPLANT BOORANI

This superb eggplant dish is found in Pakistan as well as northern India and is prepared with sliced, diced, or pureed eggplant. It can be made with yogurt or sour cream, either mixed in or served underneath or over the eggplant. This one is similar to what I had in Kabul, and shows a Persian influence.

¾ pound small eggplants	¼ teaspoon turmeric
¼ cup butter	¾ cup sour cream or yogurt
1 garlic clove, crushed in salt	Chopped mint

Sauté eggplant in butter until soft and golden, adding garlic briefly. Mix turmeric with cream and stir into eggplant. Serve at room temperature or chilled with mint sprinkled over top.

Serves 4.

RED LENTILS WITH LIME

As I related in the foreword to this section, I was the guest of Ambassador S. K. Singh and his delightful wife, Manju, for lunch during the perilous Russian occupation in Kabul, Afghanistan, in April 1979. The Indian and Afghani staff served us campari and soda in the elegant living room of their 45-year old house. The memorable lucheon consisted of tandoori chicken, salads, kulfi, dal, local cheeses, yogurt soup, and gulab jamin for dessert.

Ambassador Singh selected a refreshing Pouilly Fuissé from the Maconnais to be poured during the lunch, after which Manju took me shopping for lapis lazuli on Chicken Street, the Fifth Avenue of Kabul. The dal, red lentils with lime, was a special dish, which I have recreated here, and lime is also the reason Indian women have a beautiful glow. Manju and other beautiful Indian ladies say they rub half a lime on their face every day.

½ cup chopped red onions	¼ teaspoon turmeric or saffron
1 garlic clove, crushed	2 cups water
2 tablespoons butter	1 tablespoon lime juice
1 cup red lentils, washed	Chèvre, or other fresh cheese, diced
1 teaspoon salt	
½ teaspoon cardamom	Chopped cilantro or parsley

Sauté onion and garlic in butter until soft, add lentils and toss to coat with butter. Add seasonings and water, cover, and simmer about 15 minutes. Lentils should be very soft and thickened. If not, reduce liquid by boiling. Add juice, and top with cheese and parsley.

Serves 4 to 6.

SHRIKHAND

(Saffron Yogurt with Pistachios and Currants)

Related to lassi, this refined yogurt dish is eaten from a small bowl instead of a glass. I had a version of this years ago at the Tanjore in the Bombay Taj Hotel.

3 cups yogurt	¼ cup each golden raisins & currants
1 cup turbinado sugar	
1 teaspoon orange flower or rose water	2 tablespoons rum or brandy
	1/3 cup chopped pistachios
¼ teaspoon powdered saffron	Nutmeg, freshly grated

Stir yogurt with sugar and flavorings. Pour into small bowls, and garnish with raisins, marinated briefly in rum, pistachios, and nutmeg.

Serves 6.

DATE HALWA

Halwa, usually made with carrots, is an unctuous sweet much favored by Indians and is similar to candy. Other forms are found throughout the Middle East.

½ pound pitted dates	¼ cup sliced almonds
10 tablespoons soft butter	½ teaspoon cardamom
½ cup hot milk or cream	1 lime, cut in fourths
¼ cup golden raisins	¼ cup chopped pistachios

Purée dates with butter in processor until smooth, slowly add milk, remove, add raisins, nuts, and cardamom. Serve hot, garnished with lime and pistachios.

Serves 4.

Far East

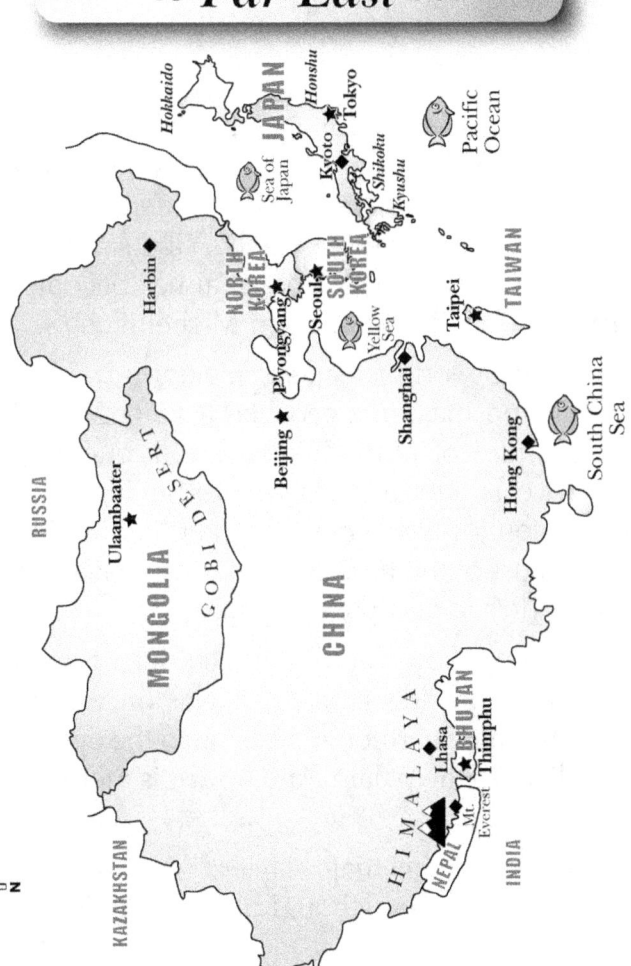

FAR EAST
CHINA HONG KONG TAIWAN
BHUTAN MONGOLIA KOREA JAPAN

The exotic and mysterious Far East brings us into the realm of Buddhism, soy beans, woks, bamboo steamers, cleavers, chopsticks, and hotpots. Yet there are vast differences between and within these countries. While Mongolia, Tibet, and Bhutan are still emerging from the Dark Ages, Shanghai has become as sophisticated as Paris with its couturiers and Michelin chefs.

China, one of the world's leaders, making up a quarter of the world's population, has emerged like a knight in shining armor since the departure of Mao. There were astounding changes in 1991, just 10 years after my first visit to Beijing. A freeway lined with high-rise condos led to my hotel, and cars and business suits had replaced most of the bicycles and Mao jackets on Tiananmen Square, the world's largest public square.

Unlike Russian food, however, Chinese cuisine never truly suffered, as it is one of the world's greatest. It was once described as an ancient art of ultimate harmony: pleasing to the eye, mouth-watering, and a delight to the palate. And now it is more delightful than ever.

In general, there are four major styles. The northern, or Beijing, style is highlighted by the rich and oily Peking Duck, which I ate copiously at a banquet held at the Great Hall of the People in 1981. At the time, ducks were served with their heads still intact, and it seemed that the other diners were quite repulsed by it, so it was offered to me, head and all. This took place at many other meals on the trip also, to my pleasure. Much bread and noodles are eaten and along with a lot of oil used in the frying, a heavier cuisine is encountered. There is a strong Mongolian influence in the use of lamb, barbecue, and the Mongolian hotpot.

The Shanghai style is noted for its "red cooking," which involves cooking meat in soy sauce, rice wine, and sugar-it's simply the best, especially with pork. Also, fish and rice are ubiquitous, and Bird's Nest Soup is a delicacy with bits of chicken and ham mixed with a gelatinous substance made of the saliva with which the swallows coat their nests. Simply divine and well worth the price.

Szechwan cooking, the inland style, is based on their famed hot peppers, but it is the moist and flavorful Hunnan ham that is a special treat. I had a great dish of ham, mushrooms, and rice, and not a few peppers, in Chengdu.

Cantonese, the best known Chinese cooking to Americans because of the first great immigration from that area, is subtler, sweeter, and more colorful than the other styles. Steaming and stir-frying are the most prevalent cooking techniques, and the renowned flavor is sweet and sour. Their dim sum, those little stuffed steamed breads, are consumed by all daily.

Remote Tibet, in the far West, mostly has a primitive diet of roots, rice, and fat, but with Chinese and Indian influences. Very cold and mountainous, Lhasa (City of Sun), has quite good Chinese and international cooking in the hotel restaurants, which were better than I anticipated.

Bhutan, although not part of China, is an agrarian society and quite similar to Tibet with its astounding Buddhist temples and monasteries. But nothing remains constant in this world, and even though Bhutan allowed only a limited number of visitors for many years, it is now cautiously entering the electronic world, and an Aman Resort is actually being built. The people have been protected from the world, and when I was there in the early nineties I was not allowed to leave the hotel for a walk. I had been driven from Bagdogra, India to Phuntsholing, Bhutan, and the next day I was treated to an immense luncheon prepared especially for me at a very humble roadside restaurant. Most of it was very hot and spicy, but well prepared and surprisingly tasty. An Indian influence was apparent and there was an abundance of dairy foods, as the cow and the yak supply the people with excellent cheeses. The food at my hotel, the best in Paro, was another story, except that the perfectly cooked green beans could compete with any in France. The chef said Yak butter was the secret. The recycled lamb chops, however, reminded me of those that I had in Srinagar, Kashmir, on a houseboat many years earlier.

Hong Kong, a great international city and now part of China again, has a new airport, Chek Lap Kok, that is simply the world's best; but after many scary approaches to the old Kai Tak, flying alongside hotel and condo windows will be missed. Dining is still among the world's best in Hong Kong, whether it be China's regional cooking or French cuisine. I would still go to Yung Kee on the Island for roast goose, the Luk Yu Teahouse for dim sum, Jimmy's Kitchen for American fried ice cream, and of course, Gaddis in the famed Peninsula Hotel for tea or an elegant dinner.

I would also take a ferry or hydrofoil to Macao, until recently a Portuguese colony and the oldest remaining European province in the Far East. On the edge of mainland China and once again part of it, Macao has a great cooking style combining Chinese and Portuguese foods and techniques. They prepare everything from dim sum to Brazilian Feijoada, which is Portuguese. Salt cod and caldo verde are as at home here as in Portugal.

Taiwan, formerly Formosa (the beautiful), features all styles of Chinese cooking, but their specialty is local fish dishes prepared with a soy sauce and garlic mixture, as well as spring rolls. I found the dim sum at the Grand Hotel to be the grandest ever, and the Ghenghis Khan serves authentic Mongolian barbecue. Taiwan also has a distinct Japanese influence.

Mongolia, wedged between Russia and China, is an unspoiled land of nomads who depend on their horses to move them and their gers (portable tents) seasonally. Ulan Batar, the capital, has so few visitors that I was regarded suspiciously. Beef, mutton, and dairy products are the staple diet and prepared in Russian and Chinese manners. Mongolia, however, has contributed two great culinary inventions to the world, the Ghengis Khan barbecue grill and the Mongolian hotpot.

The current dining scene is exploding with Chinese restaurants, as China has replaced Russia as a trading partner and is taking advantage of the economic possibilities in Mongolia. Let's hope the Chinese architectural flair will not change the traditional Ulan Batar skyline too much.

The Korean peninsula, still divided, juts off the coast of Manchuria, and has had virtually no cuisine in the north for decades, but the south has a highly developed one with Japanese, Chinese, and Mongolian influences. The national dish is Bulgogi, beautifully seasoned thin slices of beef which are barbecued, Mongolian style, on a convex grill. Kim Chi, a very zesty pickled cabbage dish, is eaten with Bulgogi and everything else, as well as at breakfast.

The hot and spicy cooking will be flavored with garlic, ginger, chili pepper, spring onions, soy sauce, sesame seeds, and vinegar. As in China, much fish and pork are eaten, but never lamb. The Japanese influence is apparent in the use of seaweed and the wonderful rice with Azuki beans, which I had for lunch while on a visit to the Demilitarized Zone. Rice and tea are consumed copiously with the meal where all dishes are served at the same time, as in the neighboring countries.

Japan, an isolated crescent of islands, reaching for Russia's Sakhalin Island, has a very original and unique cuisine of its very own. As in France, the presentation is of the essence, as well as supreme freshness of the food. Color, size and shape, texture, aroma, and flavor are prime considerations. The bento box with its beautifully arranged food is an anticipated highlight on Japan Airlines. Otherwise, all foods are served at the same time with plenty of sake and green tea, which was introduced by the Chinese. They also introduced soy beans, Buddhism, and art, while the Portuguese introduced tempura, and the Mongolians brought the firepot, renowned for its use in sukiyaki.

On my first visit to Tokyo, I endeavored to eat at those restaurants which featured each type of cooking, such as sushi and sashimi, so beloved by Americans; suimono, clear soups; sunomono, vinegared salads; nabemono, firepot cooking; and tempura restaurants, as well as others.

The cuisine is based on fish, rice, vegetables, and Kobe beef. There are also many wonderful noodle dishes made with udon, soba, and somen, mostly soups based on dashi, the simple stock made with kelp and bonito flakes. And as in Korea, rice cooked with Azuki beans is popular.

The unique flavoring agents in Japanese cooking are primarily miso and tofu. The former is now used globally in all sorts of fusion cooking and is a permanent part of mine. There are dozens of kinds, but the most important are saikyo miso-the mild white type also known as shiromiso from Kyoto, which is used in more delicate dishes such as fish-and aka-miso, the brown type, which is saltier and stronger and used in beef dishes and other sturdy types of cooking. I have found the best brand to be Shirakiku. They are made from fermented soy beans and rice and can be kept refrigerated for months.

Mirin, a sweet cooking wine which is also a staple of mine, and sake are other important flavoring agents. Wasabi and daikon, horseradish and radish, I can do without.

Tokyo is known for more than Japanese cuisine now, as the greatest of French chefs have restaurants there. Among these are Paul Bocuse and Joel Robuchon. Of course they have one of the world's greatest to contend with-Nobu, who has come home to share his exquisite fusion cuisine that has blazed a trail in Europe and the United States.

RECIPES FROM THE FAR EAST

ESCARGOTS GADDIS

CHINESE SHRIMP TOAST

STEAMED BARBECUE PORK BUNS

JAPANESE MISO SOUP WITH MUSHROOMS

CHINESE NOODLE SOUP

SZECHWAN STEAMED FISH

FISH WITH SWEET AND SOUR MISO

KOREAN BRAISED CHICKEN WITH BRAISED MUSHROOMS

CHICKEN WITH MANGO, SNOW PEAS, AND HONEYED WALNUTS

STIR-FRIED PORK WITH BLACK BEANS AND SHIITAKE

OYSTER SAUCE LAMB

HUNAN ORANGE BEEF

SHANGHAI RED-COOKED BEEF

CHINESE LEMON SAUCE

FIVE-SPICE BUTTER SAUCE

JAPANESE FUSION SAUCE

JAPANESE MISO GRAVY

KOREAN GREEN VEGETABLES

SUZHOU CAULIFLOWER AND MUSHROOMS

CHINESE/JAPANESE FRIED RICE

ESCARGOTS GADDIS

Dinner at Gaddis in Hong Kong's famed Peninsula Hotel is a special event. I have given this old classic an updated taste.

2 dozen escargots	1 ½ tablespoons rice wine
1 large shallot, minced	½ teaspoon Five-spice powder
3 tablespoons sliced almonds	1/3 cup cream
½ cup butter	Chopped chives
1 ½ tablespoons brandy	

Sauté escargots, shallots, and almonds in butter briefly. Add brandy, flame, and add wine and five-spice powder, reducing briefly. Add cream, simmer until hot and thickened. Serve in small pastry shells or in small shallow dishes. Garnish with chives.

Serves 4.

CHINESE SHRIMP TOAST

A perennial favorite in my cooking classes and a popular item in dim sum teahouses, this is a great hors d'oeuvre any time. Absolutely delicious!

12 slices white bread, crusts trimmed	½ teaspoon Five-spice powder
8-10 ounces shrimp, shelled and cooked	2 teaspoons salt
¾ cup water chestnuts	1 teaspoon sugar
¼ cup finely chopped shallot	1 egg, beaten
1 tablespoon cornstarch	Canola or peanut oil
	Chopped parsley

Finely chop shrimp and water chestnuts in processor, remove, and add shallot, cornstarch, seasonings, and egg. Spread on bread, cut into quarters or triangles, and fry in hot oil in a large skillet, shrimp side down until edges brown. Turn to brown other side, and drain on paper towels. You may use enough oil to be 1 inch deep or less. Sprinkle with parsley. These may be made ahead and reheated at 375° for 10 minutes.

Makes 48.

STEAMED BARBECUED PORK BUNS

One of my favorite Chinese creations and a traditional dim sum classic, which I especially enjoyed at teatime in Taipei's grand old Grand Hotel. They can be made without the filling or with a different kind. I also like steamed buns with Chinese and Japanese noodle soups.

2 ½ cups unbleached flour	½ cup water
½ cup powdered sugar	2 teaspoons rice vinegar
2 tablespoons baking powder	Chinese Barbecued pork (see below)
1/3 cup butter	

Mix dry ingredients, cut in butter, and stir in liquid ingredients. Mix only until dough holds together, then roll into a long rope about 1 ½ inches in diameter. Slice ½-inch thick, roll into 3-inch rounds, about 12 to 16, and put about ½ tablespoon of filling on each. Draw edges together, twist, and place on small squares of wax paper in a bamboo steamer, placed in a wok over boiling water. Cover and steam about 15 minutes.

Chinese Barbecued Pork:

1 tablespoon tamari soy sauce	2 tablespoons oyster sauce
1 tablespoon hoisin sauce	1 tablespoon soy sauce
1 tablespoon catsup	1 tablespoon honey
1 tablespoon honey	1 tablespoon dry sherry
½ teaspoon Five-Spice Powder	2 large garlic cloves, crushed
1 pound pork tenderloin	1 tablespoon black bean paste
	1 teaspoon cornstarch

Mix marinade ingredients in a shallow dish. Cut tenderloin in half lengthwise, then crosswise, forming 4 pieces. Place in marinade, and let stand several hours. Roast in the Chinese manner by hanging pork from the upper rack with drapery hooks. Place a pan of water beneath the pork to catch the drippings, and roast about ½ hour at 350° until done. While pork is cooling, mix remaining ingredients in a saucepan, and bring to a boil to thicken, adding a little water if necessary. Dice pork, add to mixture, and chill. After filling the above buns, there will probably be some leftover pork, much to the cook's advantage and delight. It is great added to omelets and fried rice.

Makes 12-16 buns and about 2 cups Chinese Barbecued Pork.

JAPANESE MISO SOUP WITH MUSHROOMS

Rich and hot miso soups are a cornerstone of Japanese cuisine, and they have great versatility. Normally made with dashi, a broth made with seaweed and bonito flakes, other stocks may be used depending on whether you include fish, chicken, or vegetables in your soup. Also, udon noodles are divine in a miso soup, and I like to slide whole eggs on top of the soup to cook gently. It's the ultimate comfort food.

2 cups assorted fresh mushrooms, thickly sliced	1 ½ tablespoons white miso (saikyo)
1 tablespoon sesame or canola oil	¼ cup mirin
4 cups dashi or chicken stock	Grated nutmeg
3 tablespoons brown miso (akamiso)	Chopped chives or chervil

Sauté mushrooms briefly in oil, add dashi or stock, bring to a boil, and whisk in miso and mirin. Simmer about 5 minutes, or until mushrooms are tender. Garnish with nutmeg and herbs.

Serves 4 to 6.

CHINESE NOODLE SOUP

In the darkened cabin of the Cathay Pacific *747*, which was gliding across the Pacific in the early morning hours, the flight attendants were quietly offering tall paper cups of noodle soup with a tantalizing aroma. Naturally, I persuaded the flight attendants to give me the recipe. As in the previous soup, there are variations, and you may add leftover barbecued or stir-fried pork or mushrooms to it, as well as leftover chicken.

¼ cup finely chopped shallots or scallions	2 tablespoons soy sauce
4 large garlic cloves, crushed	2 tablespoons rice wine
½ tablespoon peanut or canola oil	Salt & pepper
6 cups strong chicken stock	½ pound fettuccine or linguine, cooked

Sauté shallots and garlic in oil until soft and translucent, add stock, soy sauce, and rice wine. Simmer while cooking noodles, then add them to the soup. Season as desired.

Serves 6.

SZECHWAN STEAMED FISH

All Chinese know that steaming brings out the true flavor of fish. Practically any kind, whole or fillets, can be steamed, and with variable flavorings, as desired. Hunan ham is typical of the Szechwan style. I like to serve a sauce with it, such as Oriental Butter Sauce, Five-Spice Butter Sauce, or Chinese Lemon Sauce, which can be found in the index.

1 ½ pounds flounder, snapper, sea bass, grouper, halibut, or others (fillets)	2 tablespoons Chinese black beans
2 scallions, cut into pieces	1 tablespoon rice wine or sherry
2 garlic cloves, lightly crushed	2 tablespoons melted ham or duck fat
Hunan or country ham, thinly sliced	1 tablespoon light soy sauce
	½ teaspoon sugar

Place fish on a shallow plate or platter that will fit into a bamboo steamer. Scatter scallions, garlic, ham, and beans over them, and sprinkle with sherry. Steam over boiling water about 10 minutes, or until fish flakes. If not using a sauce recommended above, mix fat with soy sauce and sugar, and pour over fillets when serving.

Serves 4 to 6.

FISH WITH SWEET AND SOUR MISO

This divine dish, bursting with a triple miso flavor, was inspired by Nobu, the world famous guru of Japanese cuisine. I have used mild saikyo miso in a marinade, a sauce, and a topping. For beef, use aka-miso, and no sugar.

Sweet & Sour Miso:	½ cup sugar
¼ cup sake or rice wine	1 cup saikyo miso
¼ cup aji-mirin	

Bring sake, mirin, and sugar to a boil to dissolve sugar and evaporate alcohol. Whisk into miso, cool, and spread on fish, using about ¼ cup.

4 cod or sea bass fillets, about 5-or 6-ounces each	½ cup sweet & sour miso
	4 ounces mixed tiny shrimp and bay scallops
¼ cup saikyo miso	

After fish has marinated several hours, place on broiler pan with water in the bottom, and spread a mixture of ½ cup sweet & sour miso and shellfish on top of fillets. Bake at 400° about 5 minutes, then place under the broiler until glazed and golden, about several minutes. Serve on following sauce.

Sweet & Sour Watercress Sauce:

½ cup packed watercress with stems	1 teaspoon soy sauce
	¾ cup sweet & sour miso
¼ cup rice vinegar	

Remove tough stems from cress and discard. Puree cress with liquids in an immersion blender, then whisk into miso.

Serves 4.

KOREAN BRAISED CHICKEN WITH MUSHROOMS

This very flavorful homestyle dish is prepared in all parts of Korea and is quite similar to the Chinese versions. I enjoyed this at the venerable Presidente Hotel many years ago.

8-10 dried shiitake	2 tablespoons canola oil
4 suprêmes, halved diagonally	1 medium onion, cut into eighths
3 tablespoons Korean tamari soy sauce	4 scallions, cut into 1-inch pieces
1 tablespoon sesame oil	1 tablespoon toasted sesame seeds
4 garlic cloves, crushed	
Hot red pepper (optional)	

Soak mushrooms in hot water ½ hour, discard stems, and slice caps thinly. Marinate chicken in seasonings ½ hour, drain, and stir-fry in oil, using a wok, until golden. Add mushrooms, ½ cup of soaking water, and chicken marinade. Also add onion and scallions, cover, and simmer about 15 minutes, or until onions and chicken are tender. Sprinkle with sesame seeds.

Serves 4.

CHICKEN WITH MANGO, SNOW PEAS AND HONEYED WALNUTS

Chicken with walnuts is an old Chinese classic that is given an updated contemporary taste and presentation with mango and snow peas. The nuts taste of honey, but the honey is actually in the sauce.

Honeyed Walnuts:

1 cup water	¾ cup walnut halves
2/3 cup sugar	1 cup canola oil
½ teaspoon Five-Spice powder	Sea salt

Bring water, sugar, and spice to a boil until sugar dissolves. Add nuts, and simmer briskly about 15 minutes or until golden. With a flat whisk, place on a marble slab, and separate. Heat oil to 375°, add nuts and fry until shiny and a deep golden brown. Transfer to the marble slab, separate to dry, and sprinkle with salt.

1 pound suprêmes, cut into 1-inch cubes	1 cup chicken stock
2 tablespoons cornstarch	1 teaspoon cornstarch
½ teaspoon Five-Spice powder	2 tablespoons soy sauce
2 tablespoons soy sauce	2 tablespoons oyster sauce
2 tablespoons rice wine	1 tablespoon honey
¼ cup chopped onion	2 tablespoons peanut or walnut oil
2 garlic cloves, crushed	12 snow peas, cut diagonally into 1-inch pieces
1 tablespoon peanut or walnut oil	1 ½ cup cubed mango

Global Culinary Adventures

Toss chicken with cornstarch and spice, then add soy sauce and rice wine. Let marinate ½ hour. Sauté onion and garlic in oil until tender, add stock and cornstarch mixed with seasonings, and simmer 10 minutes. Drain chicken from marinade, and stir-fry in oil until white and firm. Add snow peas and mango, and stir-fry briefly. Add sauce and walnuts, and bring to a boil. Serve with plain rice.

Serves 4 to 6.

STIR-FRIED PORK WITH BLACK BEANS AND SHIITAKE

There are hundreds, if not thousands, of stir-fried dishes, but this is one of my favorites and it may be made with chicken or beef instead of pork. The flavor of the sauce is very similar to one that I had with garoupa fish and black mushrooms at the elegant Lai Ching Heen in the Regent in Hong Kong.

1 tablespoon Chinese black beans	1 pound pork tenderloin or loin
1 tablespoon rice wine or sake	½ tablespoon cornstarch
1 tablespoon sugar	3 tablespoons peanut oil
1 ½ tablespoons catsup	½ pound dried shiitake, soaked ½ hour
½ cup chicken or beef stock	3 garlic cloves, crushed
2 tablespoons soy sauce	

Crush beans in rice wine, stir in sugar, catsup, stock, and soy sauce. Cut pork into thin diagonal slices, toss with cornstarch, and stir-fry in very hot oil, using a wok, until barely cooked through. Remove from wok. Remove stems from shiitake, slice thinly, and stir-fry until tender, adding garlic briefly. Add black bean mixture, bring to a boil, and cook until lightly thickened. Add pork, and cook until hot.

Serves 4 to 6.

OYSTER SAUCE LAMB

While beef is the usual partner for oyster sauce, I think lamb has a definite affinity for it. Introduced to China by Mongolia, lamb is eaten primarily in the north, where I had a similar dish in Nanjing.

1 pound boneless lamb leg or loin, thinly sliced	½ cup chicken stock
	1/3 cup oyster sauce
2 tablespoons soy sauce	2 tablespoons soy sauce
2 tablespoons rice wine	2 tablespoons rice wine or sake
1 tablespoon cornstarch	1 tablespoon sugar
1 tablespoon sesame oil	2 tablespoons peanut or canola oil

Add lamb to mixed soy sauce, wine, and cornstarch, then toss with oil. Let marinate about an hour. Meanwhile, mix chicken stock with flavorings and sugar for sauce. Stir-fry in very hot oil, using a wok, until barely cooked through. Remove from wok, add sauce ingredients, and bring to a boil cooking until thickened. Return lamb, tossing with sauce.

Serves 4 to 6.

HUNAN ORANGE BEEF

This colorful amalgam of orange zest, black beans, and tomatoes is a daring fusion of a classic dish from the Szechwan area in central China, which is also the home of Hunan ham. This classic is also prepared with chicken, pork, and lamb. For flavor and color contrast, I like to serve it on watercress.

1 pound flank steak, halved length-wise and cut into ¼-inch diagonal slices	¼ cup soy sauce
	3 tablespoons rice wine or sake
	1 tablespoon cornstarch
½ teaspoon baking soda	¼ cup orange juice
½ cup cold water	1 tablespoon rice wine or sake
1 orange, zest julienned	1 egg white, lightly beaten
1 or 2 tablespoons minced ginger	1 teaspoon salt
	½ tablespoon cornstarch
1 or 2 tablespoons Chinese black beans	1 ½ tablespoons peanut oil
	½ cup peanut oil
2 scallions, cut into ½-inch pieces	1/3 cup oven-dried tomatoes (see Index)
2 large garlic cloves, crushed	
1 teaspoon sesame oil	

Put beef in a bowl with soda and water, and let stand about 2 hours. Meanwhile, mix dry seasonings and sesame oil in a small bowl. Mix soy sauce and wine with cornstarch, then add juice and set aside with other bowl of seasonings. Drain and rinse beef, dry well, and mix with wine, egg white, salt, cornstarch, and 1 ½ tablespoons oil, working in all ingredients. Heat oil in a wok until very hot, add half the beef gradually, and fry about 5 minutes, or until done. Remove to drain, and repeat with remaining beef. Pour off most of fat, and add seasoning mixture, stirring briefly. Add soy sauce mixture and meat, stirring briefly. Garnish with tomatoes.

Serves 4.

SHANGHAI RED-COOKED BEEF

In *Culinary Classics* I gave you a recipe for red-cooked pork, very similar to this one for beef, which is a very rich and robust country dish that I love and must have when I go to China. Fish, lamb, duck, and chicken are also prepared this way. This is wonderful on steamed buns, and a new way to serve it is in pita breads.

3 pounds boneless beef chuck roast	1 small knob of ginger
2 cups water	2 tablespoons sugar
½ to 1 cup soy sauce	1 tablespoon sesame oil
¼ cup rice wine or sake	1 tablespoon cornstarch
6 large garlic cloves, peeled	1 tablespoon water

Place roast, trimmed of all fat, in a casserole just large enough to hold it. Add liquids and flavorings, bring to a simmer, and cook about 3 hours, covered, turning occasionally. When very tender, remove beef and thicken the liquid with a mixture of oil, cornstarch, and water. Pull meat into chunks, family style, and serve with sauce poured on top. Great comfort food!

Serves 6 to 8.

CHINESE LEMON SAUCE

This simple, divine lemon sauce is perfect for steamed, grilled, or fried fish or chicken. When frying fish or chicken, I dust it with a mixture of ½ cup cornstarch and ½ teaspoon five-spice powder and then fry in a small amount of very hot canola or peanut oil. This gives an exceptionally crisp crust.

2/3 cup fish or chicken stock	2 tablespoons honey
¼ cup lemon juice	½ teaspoon Five-Spice powder
1 tablespoon rice wine or sake	½ tablespoon cornstarch
	½ tablespoon sesame oil

Bring stock, juice, wine, and honey to a boil, and simmer about 5 minutes. Mix spice and cornstarch with oil, and whisk into sauce to thicken.

Makes about 1 cup.

FIVE-SPICE BUTTER SAUCE

The zesty and lusty flavors of black beans, oyster sauce, and five-spice make a perfect marriage with the richness of butter. Pork, lamb, and beef are the ideal recipients of this sauce.

1 cup beef or veal stock	1 tablespoon Chinese black beans, diced
1/3 cup oyster sauce	2 garlic cloves, crushed
¼ cup rice wine or sake	½ teaspoon Five-Spice powder
1 tablespoon honey	½ cup cold butter

Combine all but butter in a saucepan and reduce by about half. Remove from heat, and gradually whisk in butter until lightly emulsified and thickened.

Makes about 1 cup.

JAPANESE FUSION SAUCE

Although the highly esteemed Explorer Club members are noted for exploring the world and not the kitchen, their daring and uninhibited double-sauce recipe is astoundingly excellent. Either sauce can be used on its own or combined in equal amounts, and they are good on salads or main courses of poultry, pork, or lamb. This is my version.

Lime Miso Sauce:

¼ cup lime juice	8 garlic cloves, lightly crushed
¼ cup rice wine vinegar	¼ cup grated ginger (optional)
¼ cup saikyo miso	1 cup sesame or canola or olive oil

Place all but oil in an immersion blender, and add oil gradually to emulsify.

Caramel Orange Butter Sauce:

3 tablespoons turbinado sugar	¼ cup Triple Sec or Grand Marnier
1 cup veal stock, reduced by half	½ cup butter
1 cup orange juice, reduced by half	

Caramelize sugar in a heavy saucepan until golden brown, add liquids, bring to a boil and stir until any hardened caramel dissolves. Remove from heat, and gradually whisk in butter until lightly emulsified and thickened. Mix sauces together while warm, or use separately, if desired.

Makes about 1 ¾ cup of each sauce.

JAPANESE MISO GRAVY

Miso, sake, and catsup (dearly loved by the Japanese) are added to a traditional American gravy to make one of the best ever. This gravy can be made in the pan drippings of sautéed steak, lamb, pork, or chicken.

2 tablespoons soft butter	1 tablespoon flour
2 tablespoons aka-miso	1 ½ cups beef or veal stock
3 tablespoons finely chopped herbs	¼ cup sake
	1 tablespoon catsup

Mix butter with miso, herbs, and flour until smooth. Bring stock to a boil, or add it to skillet in which meat was cooked, delazing it well. Whisk in sake and catsup with miso mixture, and boil until smooth and thick.

Makes about 2 cups.

KOREAN GREEN VEGETABLES

Although we hear only about kimchi, the ubiquitous pickled vegetables, the Koreans have a special way to enhance the flavor of their green vegetables, especially their superb snap beans, snow peas, cabbages, and spinach. Boil vegetables in plenty of salted water, only until done, as the French do. Then drain and toss in a mixture of hot melted butter and bacon fat. I like to add a dash of Korean tamari soy sauce for good measure. Enjoy!

SUZHOU CAULIFLOWER AND MUSHROOMS

On a tour of the canals and pagodas, I was taken to a very old restaurant in Suzhou, one of China's oldest cities. I found a jewel of a recipe for cauliflower, which I normally don't care for, and even went into the kitchen to see how they did it, as no English was spoken in those days. But they did use plenty of MSG, which I no longer use in my kitchen-the choice is yours.

1 medium cauliflower	1 teaspoon salt
2 scallions, chopped	1 teaspoon MSG (optional)
¼ cup peanut oil	1 teaspoon sugar
1 small can straw mushrooms or button mushrooms, undrained	½ tablespoon cornstarch
	½ tablespoon water

Cut cauliflower into small flowerets, parboil about 2 minutes, drain, and refresh under cold water. Sauté with scallions in oil until both are tender. Add mushrooms with their liquid and seasonings, bring to a boil, and thicken with a mixture of cornstarch and water.

Serves 6.

CHINESE/JAPANESE FRIED RICE

Fried rice is so ubiquitous that it has become a cliché, and even though I gave you a great and easy recipe in *Culinary Classics*, with bacon and eggs, I now include a composite of my favorites. It includes Indian, Japanese, and French influences as well as Chinese. Fried rice originated in the Shanghai region, and it was introduced to Japan, where curry and omelets are popular, many decades ago. If you have leftover fried rice, be sure to make an omelet and fill it with the rice for a special treat. Since all these countries love catsup, you might as well dollop that on top as well.

½ cup chopped red onion	3 tablespoons chicken stock
4 large garlic cloves, crushed	1 to 3 tablespoons soy sauce
¼ cup peanut oil or butter	½ tablespoon oyster sauce
3 cups leftover rice	½ tablespoon curry powder
¾ cup diced country ham, roast pork or chicken, or a combination	¼ cup dried currants
	¼ cup chopped parsley

Stir-fry onion and garlic in oil briefly, add rice and meat, and stir-fry briefly until hot. Add stock and seasonings, stir-frying until well mixed.

Serves 6 to 8.

Southeast Asia

SOUTHEAST ASIA
PHILIPPINES INDOCHINA THAILAND MYANMAR MALAYSIA BRUNEI SINGAPORE INDONESIA

The transition from the Far East to the tropical and equatorial countries of Southeast Asia brings significant changes in the culture and in the kitchen. Buddhists are gradually replaced by Muslims, and except for in Vietnam, chopsticks are replaced with finger-eating. Rice, fish, and noodles are the unwavering constant diet here also, but coconut milk, fish sauce, chilies, and tropical fruit add a new dimension to the vibrant cooking style.

The Philippines, composed of 7,000 islands in the South China Sea, is the only Christian country in Asia and the most westernized. It also has the most friendly people I've seen anywhere. As I was entering my hotel, the venerable Manila, one night after dinner, who should approach me and introduce themselves? Ferdinand and Imelda Marcos, who were most charming and gave me some great culinary tips on dining in Manila.

So, the following day I had lunch at Josephine Restaurant, owned by Josephine Sarayba, who insisted on giving me a palyok set, a very useful clay plate and covered casserole, which I lugged home and have used extensively since. That night, dinner at Jose Perez's Plaza Restaurant was not only an education in the local cooking, but a bonanza for me as he insisted that his daughter, a Lausanne hotel school graduate, pick me up in their chauffeur-driven car for lunch the next day. I was served a spectacular five-course lunch at their other Plaza Restaurant. And to think I was in Manila only three days!

I found the food to be a subtle blending of flavors and not too spicy. The culinary influence is a melange of Malay, Chinese, and Spanish, which is most noticeable in the breads and custardy desserts. In addition to the ubiquitous rice and fish, pork is very popular and the prime ingredient in Adobo, the national dish, which is a rich stew flavored with vinegar, garlic, and soy sauce. Other much used flavorings include coconut milk, fish sauce, and tropical fruit. Sour and salty are the words to describe this very tasty cuisine.

Indochina, comprised in a culinary context of Vietnam, Cambodia, and Laos, is a stunningly beautiful area of rugged mountains, steamy jungles, and Mekong Delta rice paddies. They share a past of savage wars as well as a cuisine based on the ubiquitous fish and rice flavored with garlic, ginger, spring onions, lemongrass, lime juice, fish sauce, and herbs.

Vietnam's cooking has a strong 1,000-year Chinese legacy and a 100-year French legacy. Chinese techniques and French finesse prevail, and omelets and baguettes are in profusion. Lettuce wraps are popular, and the national dish is Pho, a delicious beef and noodle soup that must have been perfected by the French.

I have visited Vietnam by air and by ship, the latter of which is preferable in order to visit the fascinating sights of Saigon (Ho Chi Minh), the chaotic French Colonial capital; Hue, noted for its imperial architecture; Da Nang, of China Beach fame and the rugged Marble Mountains; eerily beautiful Halong Bay with 3,000 chalk islands of bizarre cave formations and grottoes; and serene and elegant Hanoi, graced with many trees and lakes and the impressive Ho Chi Minh Mausoleum.

Cambodia and Laos also have Chinese and French influences, but the Thai and Burmese culinary style is more evident, and the soft-spoken, refined people immediately reminded me of the Thai and Burmese. The same flavorings and seasonings used in Vietnam are traditional here, but coconut milk and sticky rice are also important. Leaf-wrapping is a vital technique.

I found many wonderful French and Chinese restaurants in both countries, so it was not easy to find local food, although I stayed at traditional hotels in both Phnom Penh, Cambodia, and Vientiane, Laos. The prime focal point, of course, is Angkor Wat, the architectural wonder of massive and elaborate temples and the capital of the Khmer Empire.

Exotic Thailand is known for its warmth of hospitality, rich culture, and luxury hotels, epitomized by the legendary Oriental Hotel and the Aman resort in the trendy island of Phuket. The eternal gridlock and stifling heat of Bangkok is tempered by the stunning Buddhist temples of gold and jade; the klongs glutted with daily life and the floating market; great shopping; and the internationally famous Thai cuisine.

I have found that the best way to travel between restaurants is to take a tuk-tuk, or trishaw, which is small enough to weave in and out of the traffic. The cooking is hot and spicy with chilis, curry pastes, lemon grass, fish sauce, and herbs. Warm spices, such as cardamom, cinnamon, cumin, ginger, and coriander from their Indian legacy are prevalent in the curries. Sticky rice, coconut milk, palm sugar, leaf-wrapping, and tropical fruits are important aspects of the cooking. Fruit carving is an important part of the culture, and all young ladies are expected to master this art before marriage. Jackfruit, rambutan, mangosteen, pomelo, durian, and many others are to be found.

Mysterious Myanmar, formerly Burma, has had a history of severe political strife since the British left in 1948, but it is still an unspoiled country with a rich Buddhist culture, like Thailand. We are still dazzled by the 2,500-year old Schwedagon temple, glittering with gold, in Yangon, formerly Rangoon. The venerable Strand Hotel, designed by the architect of Singapore's Raffles and the Eastern and Oriental in Butterworth, Malaysia, is truly a destination in itself and serves admirable food. Pagan, in the north, has preserved thousands of its famous pagodas from the Middle Ages, and is famous for its lacquerware, while Mandalay, a former royal city, is proud of its Burmese arts.

The cooking is hot and spicy, as it is in Thailand, and has an Indian and Chinese legacy. The same seasonings are used here, but there is a greater array of curried dishes. Fish soups are legendary, especially along the Irrawaddy River. While at lunch in the Thiripyitsaya Hotel in Pagan, my table of six ordered this renowned local fish soup. I was the last to be served, fortunately, for I noticed live worms swimming in my bowl, after the others had sampled it. Mohinga, a very zesty and complicated fish soup, is the national dish.

Malaysia, the lovely, laid-back country at the end of the thousand mile Thai and Burmese peninsula is the Muslim frontier of Southeast Asia, and is a cultural potpourri of all these countries. KL, as Kuala Lumpur is affectionately called, is home to the world's tallest building, Petronas Towers (until Shanghai outdoes it). Also, one of the world's most beautiful railway stations built by the British in a dramatic Moorish design is here.

The Portuguese, Dutch, and English had a vast influence on Malaysia and surrounding areas, including Sumatra and Singapore, when they arrived to take control of the valuable Strait of Malacca and its spice trade. The Chinese and Indians came, leaving their culinary influence as well. But it was the Malays who created a delicious cuisine incorporating the best of all these ethnic legacies. Chili, shrimp paste, curry spices, and coconut milk enliven the fish and curry dishes, which are similar to Singapore's.

Penang, a lovely Malaysian island on the west coast, was developed by the British and has exceptional seafood restaurants on Batu Feringgi Beach, where the best hotels are. I have arrived there twice, once by air and once from Butterworth, the site of the venerable Eastern and Oriental Hotel, which was designed by the architect of Singapore's Raffles and Rangoon's Strand.

East of Malaysia, and at the southern end of the South China Sea, is another part of Malaysia well worth visiting. On the north coast of Borneo, sandwiching the Sultanate of Brunei in the middle, is Kuching, Sarawak, noted for its longhouses and a beautifully landscaped walkway and gardens along the river, and Kota Kinabalu, Sabah, noted for its longhouses and orangutans. I had marvelously fresh seafood in both places in restaurants on the beach.

Brunei, a tiny Muslim Sultanate, is said to be the richest country in the world. Its city, Bandar Seri Begawan, has restaurants serving Malay, Chinese, and Indian food, similar to that of its neighbors, Sarawak and Sabah. Although I didn't meet the Sultan on his home turf, he happened to be in the Beverly Hills Hotel gift shop where I was buying a terry robe, and being that he is the owner of the hotel (and numerous other luxury hotels around the world), I had a pleasant surprise when I arrived home-a note in the pocket reading, "Compliments of the Sultan of Brunei."

Singapore, the tiny city-state across the Strait of Malacca from Malaysia, is probably the cleanest and safest place in the world, and it is a cosmopolitan paradise of parks, gardens, and luxury hotels. Fabulous shops and restaurants abound in the Orchard Road area. Chinese, Indian, Malay, and English legacies prevail, but Nonya cooking, that of the housewives, is a blend of local and Chinese cooking styles which is highly regarded. Street food is served from stalls, especially at Newton Circus. When I first went to Singapore in 1973, the stalls were on Orchard Road in vacant lots used as parking lots in the daytime. All types of perfectly delicious and safe Asian foods are available at very low prices, so it is a great place to graze, and very educational.

One of the most famous hotels in the world is the legendary Raffles, opened in 1819 by the late Sir Stamford Raffles of the British East India Company. Leisurely dinners are still served in the courtyard after having a Singapore Sling in the Long Bar. Or, have one in the Writer's Bar, where Noel Coward, Somerset Maugham, and other luminaries once gathered.

The Malacca seaport is still the second busiest in the world and is where I embarked on the Song of Flower cruise to Hong Kong and Vietnam. Singapore (not that you need another reason to visit) is also the starting point for the wonderful Eastern & Oriental Express train trip that I took to Bangkok. The service and food were exceptional, especially the elaborate breakfast tray which was delivered to my suite. A trip to remember and to relive!

Indonesia, the world's largest Islamic country and one of the most populous, is composed of nearly 8,000 islands that meander along the equator for thousands of miles. The major islands are Java, with its teeming capital of Jakarta; Sumatra, known for its very hot curries and jungles; Kalimantan, the largest part of Borneo; Bali, the paradisiacal destination, and home to Hindus; Sulawesi, the friendly island which looks like a sea animal with a long tail; Ambon, in the Moluccas, and an area of strife; and Irian Jaya, on the island of New Guinea, which is shared with Papua New Guinea.

Numerous flights on Merpati Nusantara, the domestic carrier, were necessary to visit all these islands and sample their hot and spicy cooking. Portuguese, Indian, and some Chinese influence prevail. But the Dutch colonization, which lasted about 300 years, had a dramatic effect on the culture, and there are still very strong ties between the Dutch and the Indonesians. There were even Dutch business travlers in Pontianak, Borneo.

The Dutch colonists devised the famous rijsttafel, or rice table, which is composed of dozens of dishes that are eaten with rice. This specialty is easy to find in both Holland and Indonesia. The national dish, however, is satay, or sate, which is skewered meat, fish, or poultry, depending on the local religion, and it was created in Java. My favorite dish is Nasi Goreng, a variation of fried rice with a fried egg on top, and I recently saw it on a menu in a Point Reyes diner.

Fish and rice predominate, and they are seasoned with chilis, tamarind, lemon grass, spices, shrimp paste, soy sauce, and coconut milk, the cooking liquid of choice. Peanuts and a peanut sauce are very popular. My best meals were actually on Merpati Nusantara. On my flight from Medan, Sumatra, to Pontianak, Borneo, I was relishing my lunch with such gusto that my seatmate, the wife of a professor at the local university, invited me to dinner at their home. The service and food on Garuda, the international carrier, was also great.

RECIPES FROM SOUTHEAST ASIA

VIETNAMESE OMELET
THAI LEMON SHRIMP SOUP
BURMESE CHICKEN NOODLE SOUP
SHRIMP WITH PAPAYA SAUCE
STEAMED SCALLOPS WITH SAFFRON SAUCE
PENANG FISH CURRY WITH HERBED CURRY SAUCE
VIETNAMESE GRILLED LEMON CHICKEN
VIETNAMESE CARAMEL CHICKEN STIR-FRY
BURMESE DRY PORK CURRY
SUMATRAN COCONUT BEEF
THAI BEEF SALAD
FRIED MEAT PASTRIES WRAPPED IN LETTUCE
NUOC CHAM (VIETNAMESE FISH SAUCE)
KETJAP MANIS (INDONESIAN SOY SAUCE)
SWEET AND SOUR BUTTER SAUCE
INDONESIAN PEANUT BUTTER SAUCE
ORIENTAL MARINADE
INDONESIAN COCONUT RICE
BURMESE STIR-FRIED VEGETABLES

VIETNAMESE OMELET

The French legacy is quite apparent in this recipe, as the Vietnamese eat them frequently, but with a fusion of their own flavors, and with a baguette.

1 large shallot, chopped	1 teaspoon fish sauce
1 chili pepper, chopped (optional)	4 eggs, beaten
	Salt & pepper
1 tablespoon peanut oil	1 tablespoon peanut oil
½ cup chopped Chinese-style roast pork	Chopped cilantro
	Nuoc Cham Sauce (see Index)

Sauté shallot and pepper in oil until soft, add pork and fish sauce, cooking briefly. Season eggs, and cook in hot oil, using a 9-inch skillet, lifting edges to let uncooked eggs run underneath. When cooked as desired, fill with pork mixture, fold, and sprinkle with cilantro. Serve with Nuoc Cham Sauce.

Serves 2 to 4.

THAI LEMON SHRIMP SOUP

Known as Tom Yam Kung, this is a Thai classic that I enjoyed at the Oriental in Bangkok on their delightful riverside terrace where you can see the fruit-carving demonstrated.

1 pound shrimp	1 tablespoon minced lemongrass or zest
5 to 6 cups water or shrimp stock	4 dried Kaffir lime leaves
3 tablespoons lemon juice	1 to 2 teaspoons palm sugar
2 tablespoons fish sauce	Chopped cilantro, basil, or mint

Simmer shrimp in water until pink, remove, and shell them. Add seasonings, simmer, covered about 15 minutes, and add shrimp. Garnish with cilantro.

Serves 6 to 8.

BURMESE CHICKEN NOODLE SOUP

When I was at Boris Lissanevitch's Easter dinner party in 1979 in Kathmandu, Norman Moore, a noted Burmese interior designer, gave me this lusciously rich recipe, which can be a soup or a main course. Known as Pandey Coroswey in Burma, it is usually made with whole chicken parts and all coconut milk, but I prefer suprêmes and part chicken stock. I'm sure Norman would approve.

1 onion, cut lengthwise & finely sliced	2 teaspoons palm sugar
3 garlic cloves, crushed	8 to 12 ounces suprêmes, diced
3 tablespoons peanut oil	3 cups strong chicken stock
½-inch slice of ginger, finely chopped	2 cups coconut milk (see Index)
1 teaspoon paprika	2 tablespoons chickpea flour or potato starch
1 teaspoon turmeric or curry powder	8 to 12 ounces udon noodles, cooked
1 teaspoon salt	Lime wedges & chopped cilantro

Using a 2-quart soup pot, sauté onion and garlic slowly in oil until soft and beginning to brown. Add spices, and rub salt and sugar into chicken. Add chicken and sauté until white, about 5 minutes. Add stock, bring to a simmer, and add coconut milk (including coconut if you make your own) mixed with cornstarch. Simmer until lightly thickened, and pour over noodles in soup bowls. Garnish with lime and cilantro.

Serves 6 as a first course, or 4 as a main course.

SHRIMP WITH PAPAYA SAUCE

This delightful contemporary presentation of steamed shrimp with a coral-colored sweet and sour fruit sauce is typical of what the new Asian chefs are doing. I also like to use salmon in this dish.

1 ripe papaya, peeled, halved, and seeded	Salt & pepper
½ cup shrimp stock	18-24 large shrimp, peeled
2 tablespoons coconut cream	3 tablespoons butter
1 teaspoon lemon juice	Watercress or mint sprigs, to garnish
1 teaspoon palm sugar	

Purée enough papaya in processor to make ½ cup. Make about 18 to 24 papaya balls with remainder, using a melon ball cutter. Mix purée with stock, cream, and seasonings. Bring to a boil, and simmer briefly. Meanwhile, using a bamboo or other steamer, place shrimp over boiling water, cover, and steam about 2 minutes. Whisk butter into sauce gradually, off the heat. Divide among 4 to 6 plates, arrange shrimp and melon balls on plate, and garnish.

Serves 4 to 6.

STEAMED SCALLOPS WITH SAFFRON SAUCE

This divine and elegant entree was served for lunch aboard the Eastern & Oriental luxury train from Singapore to Bangkok. The chef used a superb delicate white fish called snowfish from Japan and served it on a bed of risotto perfumed with asparagus, which you achieve by cooking asparagus stems in the liquid with the rice. I have substituted large sea scallops.

12 sea scallops	½ tablespoon butter
1 tablespoon rice wine or white wine	1/3 cup white wine
	½ teaspoon roasted & crushed saffron
1 tablespoon grated orange zest	¾ cup shellfish stock
¼ teaspoon Five-Spice powder	1/3 cup cream or coconut cream
12 asparagus tips or small snow peas, cooked & refreshed in cold water	½ to ¾ cup soft butter

Marinate scallops in wine, zest, and five-spice about 15 minutes on a plate that will fit in your bamboo or other steamer. Steam about 10 minutes or until done, and keep warm. Meanwhile, place asparagus in a skillet with the butter to be tossed and reheated just before serving.

Make butter sauce by pouring liquid from scallops into a saucepan and reduce almost to a glaze, add wine and saffron, reducing almost to a glaze again. Add stock, reduce by half, and add cream, reducing by half. Gradually whisk in butter off the heat until emulsified. Cover plates with sauce, and arrange 3 scallops and 3 asparagus tips on each.

Serves 4.

PENANG FISH CURRY WITH HERBED CURRY SAUCE

Penang's Eden Seafood Village, on Batu Ferringhi Beach in Penang, Malaysia, is reputed to be the world's best seafood restaurant, and I agree. When I walked in, I passed a lineup of numerous glass tanks filled with every kind of fish and shellfish imaginable. The chef recommended pomfret, a popular local fish, with a light and delicate, but flavorful curry sauce. In the absence of pomfret, basa fillets are a good substitute, or use another mild white fish.

4 5-ounce basa fillets	1 teaspoon paprika
3 tablespoons lime juice	½ teaspoon turmeric
3 large shallots, finely chopped	¾ cup coconut milk
3 garlic cloves, crushed	¾ cup fish stock
2 teaspoons finely chopped lemongrass	1/3 cup chopped basil
	1/3 cup chopped mint
2 tablespoons peanut oil	1 tablespoon chickpea flour or potato starch mixed with water
1 tablespoon palm sugar	
½ tablespoon tamarind paste	

Marinate fillets in juice about ½ hour. Sauté shallots, garlic, and lemongrass in oil a few minutes. Add seasonings and cook until lightly caramelized. Add fish, turning in the spice mixture, and then add coconut milk and stock. Bring to a boil, and simmer about 5 minutes or until fish is done. Sprinkle with herbs, and if sauce is too thin, thicken with cornstarch mixture, or remove fish, and reduce as desired.

Serves 4.

VIETNAMESE GRILLED LEMON CHICKEN

Somewhat of an anomaly, this delicious and easy recipe seems to be more popular abroad than in its home country, but it will remain in my repertoire.

1 pound suprêmes, cut into 1- x 2-inch pieces (approximately)	1 tablespoon fish sauce
	2 tablespoons honey
1 tablespoon lemon juice	2 tablespoons palm sugar
1 tablespoon soy sauce	1 tablespoon grated lemon zest

1 tablespoon ground peanuts	1 teaspoon red pepper
½ tablespoon paprika	6 garlic cloves, crushed

Marinate chicken in combined remaining ingredients at least 2 hours. Thread onto bamboo skewers (soaked in water to prevent burning), and grill or broil until done. Serve with Nuoc Cham Sauce or Ketjap Manis (see Index).

Serves 2 to 4.

VIETNAMESE CARAMEL CHICKEN STIR-FRY

European chefs were the first to caramelize sauces; then the Asians perfected the technique which is so apropos with their ingredients.

½ cup water	2 large garlic cloves, crushed
½ cup turbinado sugar	3 tablespoons peanut oil
¼ cup fish sauce	1 teaspoon Five-Spice powder
¼ cup water	2 teaspoons chickpea flour or potato starch
2 tablespoons lemon juice	
1 cup thinly sliced shallots	1 ½ pounds suprêmes, cut into 1-inch cubes
¼ cup finely chopped lemongrass	
	¼ cup chicken stock, or more
1 teaspoon minced ginger	Chopped mint, basil, & cilantro

Boil water with sugar in a heavy saucepan until caramelized. Add fish sauce, water, and lemon juice, stirring until hardened caramel dissolves and a syrupy consistency is reached.

Using a wok, sauté shallots, lemongrass, ginger, and garlic in hot oil briefly, add spices and chicken tossed together, and stir-fry briefly. Add caramel sauce, tossing chicken until glazed, and then add chicken stock. Simmer briefly to reduce if necessary and until chicken is done. Garnish with herbs.

Serves 4 to 6.

BURMESE DRY PORK CURRY

Cooking meat slowly in a spicy onion purée without liquid is a typical pork preparation in Burma, and is prepared with other meats in the rest of southeast Asia. I enjoyed a version of this in Mandalay.

1 large onion, coarsely chopped	1 pound pork loin or tenderloin, cut into 2-inch cubes
2 large garlic cloves	1 stalk lemongrass, cut in chunks
1 teaspoon grated ginger	
2 tablespoons black bean sauce	1 tablespoon fish sauce
1 teaspoon paprika	1 tablespoon water mixed with 1 teaspoon tamarind paste
3 tablespoons peanut oil	

Purée onion, garlic, ginger, black bean sauce, and spices in an immersion blender. Add to hot oil in a heavy skillet just large enough to hold pork in 1 layer. Cover and cook, scraping bottom of pan frequently and adding a small amount of water if necessary, until puree is separating from the oil and is reddish in color. Add pork, cover and cook gently until tender, about 15 minutes. Add seasonings and cook until oil is separated. Discard lemongrass.

Serves 4 to 6.

SUMATRAN COCONUT BEEF

Known as Rendang in Indonesia, it is one of the most popular dishes and similar to the previous recipe. Although a liquid is used, it is allowed to evaporate, letting the beef brown in the oil that separates from the solids. A most elegant presentation of this was offered for lunch on the Eastern & Oriental Express, the luxury train that travels between Singapore and Bangkok. They served a medallion of beef tenderloin napped with this sauce and a sauté of wild mushrooms. This is absolutely delicious and very rich.

2 pounds beef chuck or round, or lamb shoulder, cut into 1- x 2-inch cubes	4 cups coconut milk
	1 tablespoon ground coriander
3 medium onions, coarsely chopped	2 teaspoons salt
	½ teaspoon turmeric
4 large garlic cloves, lightly crushed	2 or 3 red chilis, seeded (optional)
1 tablespoon chopped ginger	¼ to ½ cup tamarind liquid
2 tablespoons peanut oil	1 tablespoon palm sugar
	Cooked rice or pilaf

Purée onions, garlic, and ginger with oil, using an immersion blender. Add a little coconut milk if necessary. Place in a 2- to 3-quart casserole with the meat, coconut milk, and all seasonings except tamarind and sugar. Bring to a boil and simmer, uncovered, about 2 ½ to 3 hours, or until beef is tender. Stir frequently during last hour of cooking to prevent sticking, adding tamarind about ½ hour before beef is tender. When pan is almost dry and oil separates, add sugar, and let beef fry until mahogany brown. Serve with rice.

Serves 6.

THAI BEEF SALAD

There's nothing better for lunch in hot and steamy Bangkok than this gloriously refreshing salad with a tangy dressing. This is my modified version of classic Mee Krob, an elaborately composed salad with deep-fried rice stick noodles. You may add them to this new version if you wish.

1 pint cherry tomatoes, halved	¼ cup palm sugar
1 cucumber, scored & sliced	¼ cup water
1 small red onion, thinly sliced	¼ cup lemon juice
½ cup sliced radishes	2 tablespoons fish sauce
½ cup sliced scallions	2 tablespoons soy sauce
½ cup cilantro leaves	2 garlic cloves, crushed
½ cup mint leaves	1 pound flank steak
½ cup small basil leaves	Salt & pepper
Red leaf lettuce	Peanut oil

Toss all vegetables together and place on lettuce, using a large platter. Dissolve sugar in hot water, add remaining seasonings, and cool. Season steak, brush with oil, and grill until done as desired, about 5 minutes on each side. Slice thinly on the diagonal, and toss with sauce. Pour over vegetables, and garnish as desired. I like to place a tomato rose on top along with scallion brushes, and more herbs, as well as fried rice stick noodles if I'm ambitious. If it's a hot summer day leave well enough alone.

Serves 6.

FRIED MEAT PASTRIES WRAPPED IN LETTUCE

Leaf-wrapping is a phenomenon from the Philippines on through the Pacific, and these pastries are a Vietnamese specialty, often eaten as a snack. Considering the amount of work involved, I prefer to have them for dinner.

The Philippine versions are extremely diverse-some even include fruit as a filling-and are called lumpia. I have taken the liberty to add raisins to my Vietnamese meat pastries for a fusion dish.

1 ounce cellophane noodles, soaked in warm water 20 minutes, or cooked somen or ramen noodles	¼ pound finely chopped shrimp or crab
	½ pound ground pork
½ cup finely chopped red onion	10 sheets rice paper, spring roll wrappers, or 16 half sheets filo
2 garlic cloves, crushed	¾ cup mixed basil, mint, & cilantro
1 tablespoon fish sauce	16 Boston lettuce leaves, base of stems cut out
½ teaspoon salt	Nuoc Cham Sauce or Ketjap Manis (see Index)

Chop noodles coarsely and mix with onion, garlic, seasonings, shellfish, and pork. Blend well. Place about a tablespoon of filling along the bottom of the wrapper, fold in edges, brush with oil, and roll up tightly. Deep-fry at 350° about 5 minutes. To serve, let each diner place herbs of choice and a pastry on a lettuce leaf and roll up. Dip in sauce of your choice.

Makes 16.

NUOC CHAM

(Vietnamese Fish Sauce)

Also known as nuoc mam, this is a seasoned fish sauce that is a traditional part of the Vietnamese table, and is especially good on Vietnamese omelets and leaf-wrapped foods, as well as grilled meat.

¼ cup fish sauce (nam pla)	1 tablespoon sugar
1 tablespoon lemon juice	Minced chili pepper (optional)
1 tablespoon white wine vinegar	1 garlic clove, crushed

Mix all together, and serve in a small dish for dipping.

Makes about ½ cup.

KETJAP MANIS

(Indonesian Soy Sauce)

This luscious Indonesian creation is the answer to almost anything that doesn't have enough flavor. Use at the table or in the kitchen. Ketjap is the origin of our word "catsup." It will last indefinitely when refrigerated.

1 ½ cups soy sauce	1/3 cup palm sugar or dark brown sugar
½ cup molasses	½ teaspoon ground coriander

Mix well and store in a jar in the refrigerator.

Makes over 2 cups.

SWEET AND SOUR BUTTER SAUCE

This is not the first fusion butter sauce with an Oriental flair (see Beurre Blanc Orientale in the French section), but my sweet and sour version is great on practically any kind of seafood, poultry, or meat.

¼ cup palm sugar	2 tablespoons fish sauce
¼ cup butter	2 tablespoons lime juice
¼ cup soy sauce	½ teaspoon Five-Spice powder

Heat sugar and butter in a small saucepan until sugar is dissolved and almost caramelized. Add remaining ingredients and reduce until lightly thickened.

Makes about ¾ cup.

ORIENTAL MARINADE

This unctuous and delicious marinade is perfect for seafood, poultry, and meat of all kinds. Try adding a little fish sauce when marinating fish.

¼ cup palm sugar	½ tablespoon tamarind paste
2 tablespoons peanut oil	2 garlic cloves, crushed
1 tablespoon catsup	¼ teaspoon Five-Spice powder

Mix all together until blended and marinate 1 to 2 hours.

INDONESIAN PEANUT BUTTER SAUCE

There are many variations for this staple sauce, but the following is very simple and is a wonderful dipping sauce for satays and other grilled dishes. Try adding tamarind, fish sauce, coconut milk, shrimp paste, or palm sugar.

1/3 cup crunchy peanut butter	1 tablespoon soy sauce or Ketjap Manis (see Index)
¼ cup catsup	

Mix together until blended and serve at room temperature.

Makes about 2/3 cup.

INDONESIAN COCONUT RICE

Various versions of coconut rice are found throughout southeast Asia, especially from Burma on down to and throughout the Pacific islands. It may be varied considerably with curry spices, minced lemongrass, garlic, and tamarind liquid. My favorite is this simple yellow rice, which I first sampled in Bali at the Tanjung Sari's rijsttafel, or rice table, in Bali.

¾ cup coconut milk	1 teaspoon salt
¾ cup shrimp stock	½ teaspoon turmeric or saffron
1 cup rice	Fresh grated coconut, plain or toasted

Bring liquids to a boil, add rice and seasonings, and simmer about 20 minutes, covered. Garnish with coconut as desired.

Serves 4.

BURMESE STIR-FRIED VEGETABLES

The Burmese have a special talent for preparing vegetables, as do the French. It is important to cook them only until barely tender for the best flavor and color. The chefs in Mandalay also use okra, eggplant, zucchini, bean sprouts, celery, and spinach.

1 tablespoon peanut oil	Handful of thin green beans
1 small red onion, finely sliced	1 ½ cups shredded Chinese cabbage
2 garlic cloves, finely sliced	
2 small carrots, peeled & finely sliced	½ teaspoon turmeric
	½ teaspoon paprika
6 wild mushrooms, thinly sliced	Soy sauce, to taste

Heat oil in a wok until very hot. Add vegetables all at once and stir-fry until barely tender. Add seasonings, and serve promptly.

Serves 4 to 6.

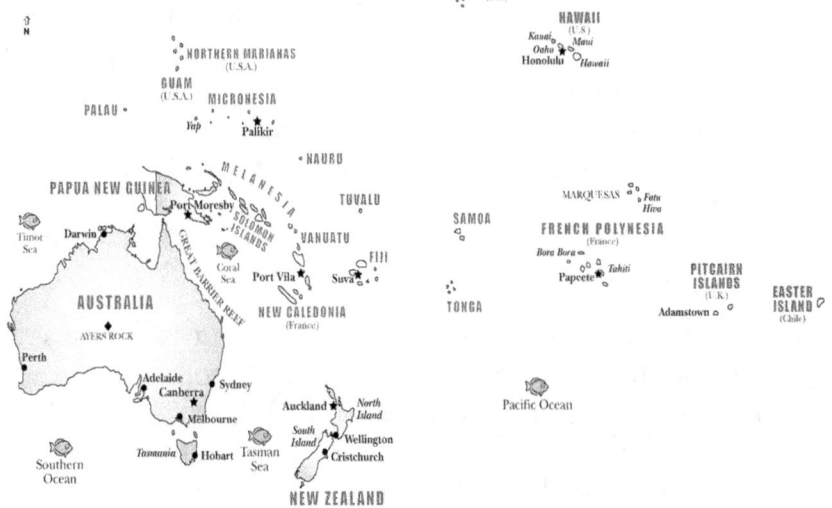

PACIFIC ISLANDS
AUSTRALIA NEW ZEALAND MELANESIA
MICRONESIA POLYNESIA

The vast Pacific, sparsely populated but with tens of thousands of islands, covers a quadrant of the earth. The earliest settlers probably came from Southeast Asia, and their cooking is still a vibrant part of the culture. Before the two world wars, more legacies were established when the Spanish, Dutch, Germans, Americans, and Japanese arrived, not to mention the English and French. The enterprising Indians have left their mark as well. This culinary melting pot shares a prodigious use for taro, breadfruit, yams, rice, cassava, coconut, bananas, pork, and fish. Kava, a form of firewater, is the drink of choice.

Australia, the smallest continent and the largest island, was first occupied by aborigines and then by British convicts and other rugged settlers. In fact, on my first visit in 1973, the people lacked finesse, especially the men. A decade later, even the bus driver was charming and gallant. He explained that travel in and out of the country had exposed the Australians to more refined cultures, and they learned from this experience.

The cuisine has also developed with the coming of many Orientals and Europeans, and the staid British-style cooking is found only in the Outback. When I heard that Ferrán Adrià, the world's most innovative and creative chef, had gone to this remote corner of the Pacific for inspiration, I knew that Australia's cuisine had become something special. Previously, only Carpetbag steak, filled with oysters, was the only ingenious creation.

The varied climates and growing conditions have always produced the best of vegetables, fruits, beef, lamb, pork, and veal. The extensive coastline yields the famous Sydney Rock oysters, bream, whiting, snapper, trout, and barramundi, a very special fish. Kangaroo can also be quite good.

Europeans brought their vines to Australia many years ago, but it is only recently that their wine industry is competing with the world's best. Wine is made from Brisbane to Perth, but it is the Barossa Valley, settled by German refugees, that is most noted for its fine quality of wines. I had a chance to sample many of these on the Indian-Pacific train, which travels 2,500 miles from Sydney to Perth in 68 hours, with 300 miles of straight track, the world's longest.

From Perth I flew out to Christmas and Cocos Islands, which are quite near Indonesia in the Indian Ocean, thus the Asian influence in the food. Tasmania, the island known for being a former penal colony, is known for its quail, venison, cheese, and honey liqueur, which I sampled in Hobart, the capital. The salmon, trout, and oysters are also outstanding in this quaint, unspoiled town. East of Australia are two more special islands. Norfolk is where many Pitcairners were sent when their island became too crowded with the British, but it is Lord Howe Island, a tiny paradise, that stole my heart. The people are as friendly as the Ansett pilot who let me ride in the cockpit so that I could see the spectacular view upon landing. When the aircraft door opened, the hotel owner's car was there waiting for me, to take me on a tour of the island.

New Zealand, composed of two small islands, is sometimes in the shadow of much larger Australia with its glamorous and sophisticated cities, but the stupendous scenery and glaciers on the South Island are reason enough to cross the Tasman Sea. The indigenous Maoris are still here in this far-flung part of Polynesia, but it is the British who left their culinary mark.

Still very much of a meat and potatoes society, New Zealanders are also known as proficient bakers, and their ethereal dessert, Pavlova, is legendary. I had delicious meals throughout the country, although they were simply cooked. The many rivers, streams, and seacoast yield the best of grouper, snapper, John Gory, and trout, which has become renowned through the popularity of fly-fishing, especially at Huka Lodge, a deluxe Relais & Châteaux property on the Waikato River on the North Island. The Lodge is a destination in itself, with memorable food.

Melanesia, which means "black islands" because of the color of the people, is in the southwest Pacific below the equator. New Caledonia is a French territory, and its capital, Noumea, appears to be transported from the south of France. Fine French food and wine, with a South Pacific flair, are available in the excellent restaurants. Vanuatu, formerly New Hebrides, has a French and Chinese legacy. Port Vila, the capital, is a delightful and friendly town with outstanding seafood. The Iririki Island Resort, on its own island with farés over the water, is adjacent to town.

Fiji, also in Melanesia, is predominantly Fijiian and Indian, with the economy being driven by the savvy Indians. The delicious national dish is Kakoda, fish with coconut milk, and curries are as abundant as in India. The Solomon Islands, best known for Guadalcanal, also has a strong Indian influence. Papua New Guinea, which is on the eastern end of the island shared with Irian Jaya, is also a wild and wooly place with many tribes and clans. The Sepik River and the rugged mountains are prime destinations, along with the Bismarck archipelago, comprised of New Britain and New Ireland. Fish is the meal of choice.

Micronesia, or "little islands," is in the northwest Pacific above the equator, and the most thrilling way to see these mostly tiny coral atolls is on Continental's Island Hopper. The flight from Honolulu to Guam makes seven exciting landings, the world record. Johnston is strictly a U.S. military base with chemical warfare, and all residents must wear a gas mask outside. Next are the tricky landings on runways so narrow a pebble could be thrown into the water on either side. After several stops in the Marshalls and Carolines, the big island city of Guam has plenty of ethnic restaurants with very good chefs. The primary flavor is definitely Oriental, as it is in Saipan, a short hop by plane from Guam.

The prime destination is Pelau, at the end of the Micronesian line, and its idyllic beaches. Not far from the Philippines, I was not surprised to find similar food and an abundance of tropical fruit.

Another Micronesian island I especially enjoyed was Nauru, once as wealthy as Brunei due to its phosphate, which is now depleted. Only twelve miles around the island, the people live on the perimeter and are supported by the government. I was invited to the home of the president of Air Nauru (which has only one plane) for pre-dinner drinks and hors d'oeuvres before dinner at Hotel Nauru with its excellent seafood prepared by Indian and Tongan chefs.

Polynesia, aptly named for its many islands, stretches from Midway Atoll in the North Pacific to New Zealand in the South Pacific, with most of the islands east of the International Date Line. Hawaii, discovered by Captain Cook, has a culture and culinary style heavily influenced by the East and the West. Its cultural melting pot includes Japanese, Chinese, Koreans, Southeast Asians, and Americans, as well as Europeans. It was not surprising to find that the assorted pupus (hors d'oeuvres) at the elegant Halekulani Hotel's cocktail reception included platters of wonton and satay along with Norwegian smoked salmon and chèvre.

The luau, native to Polynesia, is still a celebration with the pig and leaf-wrapped vegetables cooked in the underground oven called an imu. Hawaii is renowned for its macadamia nuts and Kona coffee, as well as its great chefs who have created a magnificent Pacific Rim or East-West cuisine. Alan Wong is the Bocuse of Hawaii.

A long flight from Honolulu to the now-closed Midway Atoll provided me with a startling welcome when a huge albatross fell out of his bed on the roof of the airport hangar and grazed my head. However, the excellent chef and his wife from Carcassone provided me with outstanding French dinners.

Western Samoa, near Fiji, has Chinese and German influences, noticeable in the people as well as the food. A distinct German orderliness and cleanliness is apparent. American Samoa, on the other hand, is one of the dirtiest and poorest islands I've seen anywhere, but it was the setting for Somerset Maugham's Rain. Robert

Louis Stevenson's home, Vailima, is in Apia, the capital of Western Samoa. Aggie Grey's renowned hotel is still serving its Samoan feast, called fia-fia, and is near other good restaurants.

Nearby Tonga is the only kingdom in the Pacific and is known for its excellent cooks, whom I have come across in many other islands. British and Chinese culinary influences prevail. On the island of Niue, known for its lush forests of ancient ebony trees, New Zealand cookery is dominant. The Cook Islands, also a New Zealand territory, has similar cooking with its strong English legacy.

French Polynesia, known for its paradisiacal islands of Bora Bora and Moorea, with their romantic over-the-water bungalows, is also a paradise for French cooking with an island accent. Papeete, on the island of Tahiti, has a raffish charm and is the gateway to the stunning beauty of the Tuamotus and the Marquesas. Paul Gauguin's grave site is in Hiva Oa. Chinese restaurants also offer great food in all these islands, but when you reach Pitcairn, the British influence prevails once again. Easter Island, farther to the east, begins to take on the flavor of Chile in South America.

RECIPES FROM THE PACIFIC ISLANDS

HONEYED PINEAPPLE-BEET SALAD WITH BABY SPINACH
TAHITIAN HEARTS OF PALM SALAD
CREAMY CAMEMBERT VINAIGRETTE
JOY'S CRAB SANDWICH
GRILLED GROUPER WITH AVOCADO BUTTER
SAMOAN LEAF-WRAPPED CHICKEN
POLYNESIAN MANGO CHICKEN OR PORK
HAWAIIAIN KALUA PIG
NEW ZEALAND LAMB WITH BEER SAUCE AND PESTO LINGUINE
FOO YOU HOW
FIJIIAN CURRIED VEAL AND PINEAPPLE
BROCHETTES OF BEEF TENDERLOIN FLAMBÉE WITH PINEAPPLE
PINEAPPLE FRIED RICE
WILD RICE WITH YAMS PACIFIC STYLE
PINEAPPLE-COCONUT CORNBREAD
NEW ZEALAND PASSION FRUIT SCONES
PASSION FRUIT PAVLOVA
TAHITIAN POE
MACADAMIA NUT TARTS
TROPICAL FRUIT TARTS
HAWAIIAN RAINBOW OF MACADAMIA CLUSTERS

TAHITIAN HEARTS OF PALM SALAD

Chef Jean, of Auberge du Pacifique in Papeete, once cooked at the illustrious La Tour d'Argent in Paris and is now serving its famed Pressed Duck in the Pacific. A kitchen tour revealed an impressive array of copper and memorabilia from his culinary career. After a delightful lunch of this salad, made with fresh hearts of palm and the freshest of grilled fish, this hospitable chef gave us a ride back to our hotel.

1 garlic clove, crushed	½ cup walnut or peanut oil
1 teaspoon Dijon honey mustard	1 can hearts of palm, drained, rinsed, & diagonally sliced
1 teaspoon salt	Bibb lettuce or mesclun
2 tablespoons lemon or lime juice	1 bunch watercress
	2 hard-cooked egg yolks, sieved

Whisk seasonings with juice, and whisk in oil gradually until emulsified. Add sliced palm and marinate about an hour. Arrange lettuce on a platter or individual plates, and add palm with dressing. Garnish with cress and yolks.

Serves 6.

CREAMY CAMEMBERT VINAIGRETTE

A simply magnificent buffet luncheon on the ocean terrace at the grand old Mauna Kea Hotel on the big island of Hawaii was the source for this most unusual salad dressing. I thought I didn't like camembert until I tried this. Their lamb chops were so succulent and meltingly tender that I actually ate 21 of them! The chef said that the best lamb comes from Iowa.

2 tablespoons camembert	2 tablespoons beaten egg, (optional)
2 tablespoons walnut vinegar	¾ cup walnut or olive oil
½ teaspoon lemon juice	Assorted salad greens
¼ teaspoon soy sauce	½ cup roasted broken macadamias
1 small garlic clove, crushed	
Salt & gray pepper	

Blend cheese, seasonings, and egg in processor or with an immersion blender until smooth. Gradually add oil until emulsified. Serve over greens, and garnish with roasted macadamias.

Serves 6.

JOY'S CRAB SANDWICH

On the way back from Midway Atoll I stayed at the exceptional Halekulani in Honolulu, and the turn-down service included this exceptional recipe on the pillow. What a great idea!

½ cup Dungeness crab meat, drained	4 slices whole wheat bread
3 tablespoons finely diced celery	Mayonnaise
	½ avocado, peeled & thinly sliced
3 tablespoons Thousand Island dressing	4 slices bacon, cooked
	4 leaves Bibb lettuce

Mix crab, celery, and dressing. Spread mayonnaise on bread, then add crab mixture. Add avocado, bacon, and lettuce. Add top slices of bread and cut diagonally. Garnish as desired.

Makes 2 sandwiches.

HONEYED PINEAPPLE-BEET SALAD WITH BABY SPINACH

This especially delightful and delicious salad is typical of the new breed of creative Australian chefs who are inspiring the super chefs of Europe. Pineapple, one of Australia's newly prominent ingredients, provides an intense contrast to the beets and spinach in color, taste, and texture. The dish is also typical of the Samoans, who are creating new dishes with the influence of the German legacy, which is also evident in Australia's Barossa Valley.

3 to 4 cups half-slices of beets, baked or canned, well-rinsed	3 tablespoons olive oil
3 to 4 cups pineapple wedges, preferable fresh	3 tablespoons honey or Lyle's Golden Syrup
3 tablespoons malt or sherry vinegar	Salt and gray pepper
	3 cups baby spinach

Combine beets and pineapple an hour or so before serving. Whisk vinaigrette ingredients together, and add with spinach. Toss well and serve at room temperature. Especially good with grilled pork, lamb, and chicken.

Serves 6 to 8.

GRILLED GROUPER WITH AVOCADO BUTTER

Noumea's seaside restaurants prepare excellent seafood dishes with a French and Chinese influence, as is evident in this flavorful combination of soy sauce, butter, and avocado.

4 grouper, snapper, or other firm fillets	¼ cup peanut oil
	3 tablespoons soy sauce

2 tablespoons lemon or lime juice	2 garlic cloves, crushed
1 garlic clove, crushed	2 tablespoon minced chives or parsley
½ cup puréed avocado	French Fleur de Sel
½ cup soft butter	Lemon or lime wedges
¼ cup lemon or lime juice	Chopped parsley & cherry tomatoes

Marinate fish in mixture of oil, soy sauce, juice, and garlic about an hour. Whisk purée with butter, juice, and seasonings. Grill fish about 5 minutes on each side, basting with marinade. Top with avocado butter, garnish, and serve with hot rice, which is also wonderful with the avocado butter melting on top.

Serves 4.

SAMOAN LEAF-WRAPPED CHICKEN

Throughout Polynesia, fish, chicken, pork, and vegetables are wrapped in taro, ti, breadfruit, or banana leaves and cooked in the underground oven over hot coals. Whether called fafa as in Tahiti or lau-lau as in Hawaii, I have found them to be similar. I use collard greens in the absence of Polynesian leaves and cook them in a steamer. This is the version I had at Aggie Grey's fia-fia in Samoa.

¼ pound salt pork, diced	½ cup finely chopped scallions
6 suprêmes, cubed	¾ cup coconut milk
Salt & pepper	6 large ti, banana, collard, or other leaves, or large squares of aluminum foil
1 tablespoon lime juice	
1 pound bok choy or spinach, cut into a chiffonade	

Sauté salt pork in a skillet until crisp and golden. Add chicken and sauté only until firm, add seasonings, bok choy, and scallions, and cook until wilted. Divide mixture among leaves or foil, pouring a little coconut milk over each. Fold into packages, using the drugstore wrap method. Put into a bamboo steamer, placed over boiling water in a wok. Cover, and steam ½ hour. Typically, the leaf package is placed in front of you at the table, and then opened. Serve with rice.

Serves 6.

POLYNESIAN MANGO CHICKEN OR PORK

This outstanding dish is also very simple to make, and its versatility allows you to substitute fruits and seasonings. Pineapple would be great if you use pork.

6 suprêmes or 2 pounds boneless country style ribs or Boston butt	¼ cup orange or pineapple juice
Salt & pepper	1 tablespoon rice vinegar
Chinese Five-Spice powder	2 tablespoons lemon or lime juice
2 large garlic cloves, crushed	1 tablespoon soy sauce
2 cups mango preserves	¼ cup crushed garlic
1 cup peanut or canola oil	1 teaspoon celery seed
½ cup catsup	1 teaspoon paprika
¼ cup palm or brown sugar	1 cup cubed mango
	Indonesian coconut rice (see Index)

Rub seasonings and garlic into chicken or pork, and let stand while mixing sauce ingredients. Mix preserves with remaining ingredients except mango and rice. Place chicken or pork in a heavy 2-quart baking dish, pour sauce over, and bake at 325° about 45 minutes for chicken and 1 ½ hours for pork, adding water or juice if sauce is too thick. Add mango about 20 minutes before chicken or pork is done. Serve around a mold of rice, and garnish with chopped herbs if desired.

Serves 6.

HAWAIIAN KALUA PIG

Undoubtedly the most terrific tasting pork, this is the way to cook it without digging an oven in the ground. It may be seasoned as you wish and used in salads, sandwiches, omelets, and just about anything else requiring leftover pork. Collards are great with this Pacific-style barbecue.

4 to 5 pounds boneless Boston butt	1 or 2 tablespoons crushed garlic
2 tablespoons oyster or hoisin sauce	6 large ti, banana, collard, or other leaves, or large squares of aluminum foil
2 tablespoons liquid smoke	Extra wide foil for pan
1 tablespoon sea salt	
½ teaspoon Chinese Five-Spice powder	

Rub pork with blended seasonings, and line a roasting pan just large enough to hold the pork with heavy-duty foil. Cover foil with overlapping leaves, add pork, and cover with more leaves. Bring edges of foil up around pork, and cover with more foil, crimping edges together tightly to completely enclose the pork. Cover pan tightly with foil, and bake at 375° about 4 hours. Pull apart into chunks to serve.

Serves 8.

NEW ZEALAND LAMB WITH BEER SAUCE AND PESTO LINGUINE

Lamb and beer are ubiquitous in New Zealand, and when they are cooked together, the taste is incomparable. Linguine with pesto is an ideal partner for this dish, which was inspired by the lamb I had at the incomparable Huka Lodge on the North Island-but the Kiwis wouldn't mind mashed potatoes!

1 ½ pounds cubed lamb shoulder or leg	1 tablespoon brown sugar or honey
Salt & pepper	½ cup cream (optional)
2 tablespoons butter or olive oil	½ pound linguine, cooked
	2 tablespoons butter
1 cup beer	2 tablespoons Parmesan cheese
1 tablespoon malt vinegar	½ cup Pesto (see Index)

Season lamb and sauté in butter until brown. Add beer, vinegar, and sugar, bringing to a boil. Cover and simmer about ½ hour, or until lamb is tender. Add cream, if using, and reduce until thickened. Toss linguine with butter and cheese, and place on plates next to lamb in its beer sauce. Drizzle pesto over lamb and linguine. A fabulous taste treat with beer or red wine.

Serves 4 to 6.

FIJIAN CURRIED VEAL AND PINEAPPLE

Some of the world's best curries are to be found in the Pacific, especially in Fiji, with its large Indian population. With a profusion of creative chefs we discover that veal and pineapple marry well and that Chinese-style Pineapple Fried Rice is the perfect accompaniment.

1 ½ pounds cubed veal shoulder	2 tablespoons curry powder
Salt & pepper	2 cups veal stock
¼ cup butter	1 ½ cups fresh pineapple chunks
½ cup chopped onion	Chopped macadamia nuts & coconut
2 large shallots, chopped	Chutney & lime wedges
2 large garlic cloves, crushed	Pineapple Fried Rice (see Index)

Sauté seasoned veal in butter until golden brown, add onion, shallots, and garlic, cooking until translucent. Stir in curry powder and stock, cover, and simmer about an hour, or until veal is tender. Add pineapple about half way through. Reduce to desired thickness, garnish, and serve with rice.

Serves 4 to 6.

FOO YOU HOW

I don't know the translation, but years ago I had this at Maramamu Chinese Restaurant in Raiatea, one of the islands near Tahiti, and it's been a favorite ever since. I frequently substitute other vegetables, depending on my refrigerator and what's in season.

6 small carrots, peeled & thinly sliced diagonally	6-8 ounces tender beef, pork, or chicken, cut into strips
3 ribs celery or bok choy, thinly sliced diagonally	½ teaspoon Chinese Five-Spice powder
6 scallions, thinly sliced diagonally	¼ cup peanut oil
	½ cup chicken stock

1 tablespoon sherry or Madeira	1 teaspoon sugar
1 tablespoon soy sauce, or more	1 tablespoon cornstarch
1 teaspoon salt	1 tablespoon water

Stir-fry vegetables in hot oil, using a wok, until crisp-tender, adding the beef and five-spice just before vegetables are finished. Stir-fry briefly, add stock, and seasonings. Simmer, covered, briefly, and thicken with cornstarch and water mixture. Serve over rice.

Serves 6.

BROCHETTES OF BEEF TENDERLOIN FLAMBÉE WITH PINEAPPLE

This dish was inspired by one that I had at the highly acclaimed Berowa Waters, which was reached partially by boat from Sydney. This was where the new Australian cuisine began, and is a good blend of old and new.

½ cup soy sauce	½ teaspoon Chinese Five-Spice powder
3 tablespoons brown sugar	2 pounds beef or pork tenderloin, cubed
2 tablespoons Madeira	
2 tablespoons Balsamic vinegar	1 ½ cups fresh pineapple chunks
1 tablespoon catsup	
1 tablespoon sesame oil	¼ cup Macadamia liqueur
1 garlic clove, crushed	Pineapple Fried Rice (see below)

Mix marinade ingredients together, and add beef, tossing to coat. Let stand about 2 hours, then thread onto skewers alternately with pineapple, allowing about 2 beef cubes between each pineapple cube. Broil or grill, basting with marinade and turning, about 10 minutes. Place on a bed of pineapple fried rice, using a stainless steel platter. Pour flaming liqueur over skewered beef.

Makes 4 to 6 brochettes.

PINEAPPLE FRIED RICE

This luscious dish was inspired by Paul Wade, the master of innovative Oriental and Pacific cuisine. His sensational pupu platter at Montagna in the Little Nell Hotel, the queen of Aspen Mountain, is worth the detour.

2 cups Basmati rice, cooked	½ cup golden raisins
2 shallots, finely chopped	2 tablespoons peanut oil
½ teaspoon Chinese Five-Spice powder	2 tablespoons sesame oil
	2 to 4 tablespoons soy sauce
1 ½ cups diced fresh pineapple	¼ cup chopped mint or cilantro

Using a wok, stir-fry shallots, seasoning, and fruits in hot peanut oil. Add rice, and stir-fry until golden. Add sesame oil, soy sauce, and mint.

Serves 6 to 8.

WILD RICE WITH YAMS PACIFIC STYLE

Wild rice from Australia is very compatible with Pacific flavors, and this orange version is a must for Thanksgiving.

1 cup wild rice	½ teaspoon Chinese Five-Spice powder
3 cups cold water	¼ cup butter
1 cup orange juice	12 ounces cooked yams, cubed
1 teaspoon salt	¼ cup roasted macadamias or walnuts

Wash rice in several changes of water. Add water, cover, and simmer about ½ hour or until water is absorbed. Add juice, seasonings, and butter, and simmer until juice is absorbed and rice is tender. Add yams and nuts.

Serves 6 to 8.

PINEAPPLE COCONUT CORNBREAD

Breads are not eaten much in the islands, except for French bread in French Polynesia and the other French islands, but this luscious creation is great with many of the island dishes as well as with our ham and barbecue.

1 cup yellow cornmeal	2 eggs, beaten
1 cup unbleached flour	1 ¼ cups coconut milk
½ cup sugar	8-ounce can crushed pineapple, drained
1 tablespoon baking powder	½ cup melted butter
1 teaspoon salt	Honey-Pecan Butter (see Index)

Whisk dry ingredients together in a large bowl. Whisk remaining ingredients together, and lightly stir into dry ingredients. Pour into an oiled and heated 10-inch iron skillet, and bake in a 375° oven about ½ hour. Serve with Honey-Pecan Butter, substituting macadamias for the pecans.

Serves 6.

NEW ZEALAND PASSION FRUIT SCONES

The great bakers of New Zealand have an endless variety of scones and none are better than those at Huka Lodge, where breakfast is prepared as you wish at the kitchen counter. This recipe is a composite of my favorites. You can buy very expensive passion fruit juice or easily squeeze the juice from fresh fruit. It will take about 4 to yield 1/3 cup of juice.

2 cups unbleached flour	1/3 cup dried currants or sultanas
2 teaspoons baking powder	½ cup light cream
½ teaspoon salt	3 tablespoons passion fruit juice
¼ cup brown sugar	Powdered sugar, for sifting
1 tablespoon poppy seeds	
½ cup cold butter, diced	

Using the flat beater of an electric mixer, combine dry ingredients and beat in butter until coarse crumbs form. Gently mix in remaining ingredients until dough barely holds together. On a floured surface, press dough into a ½-inch round and cut into triangles or cut with a biscuit cutter. They may be glazed by brushing with milk and sprinkling with sugar. Place on a baking sheet and bake at 375° about 20 minutes or until they test done. Sift powdered sugar over them, and serve with butter, preserves, and/or clotted cream.

Makes approximately 1 dozen.

PASSION FRUIT PAVLOVA

Claimed by both Australia and New Zealand, I have enjoyed many versions, including my rendition of the one I had at the fabulous Hayman Island Resort off the coast of Queensland.

4 egg whites	1 teaspoon vanilla
¼ teaspoon cream of tartar	¾ cup cream, whipped
¾ cup sugar	3 to 4 cups mixed fruit: sliced strawberries, sliced kiwis, and cubed mangoes
4 egg yolks	
½ cup sugar	
1/3 cup passion fruit juice	1/3 cup freshly grated coconut

Whip whites with cream of tartar until soft peaks form, then gradually beat in sugar until meringue is stiff and glossy. Place in a pastry bag, and pipe onto a baking sheet lined with parchment paper, forming a nest about 9 inches in diameter and 2 inches high. Bake at 225° about an hour or until almost dry. Remove to a rack to cool.

Beat yolks with sugar until fluffy, add juice and vanilla, then cook gently until thick. Cool, and fold in whipped cream. Pour into meringue nest and chill at least several hours. Fill with fruit, and garnish with coconut.

Serves 6.

TAHITIAN POE

Be assured this has nothing to do with the notorious Hawaiian poi made from taro root. This is simply a delicious fruit pudding.

1 ripe papaya, peeled	1 vanilla bean, halved lengthwise & seeds scooped out
2 ripe bananas, peeled	
1 can mangoes, drained, syrup reserved	2 tablespoons cornstarch
	Reserved mango syrup
13-ounce can crushed pineapple	½ cup cream, whipped
	1/3 cup sour cream
2 tablespoons lime juice	1/3 cup coconut
2/3 cup brown sugar	1 teaspoon vanilla
	1 teaspoon Macadamia liqueur

Cut fruit into large chunks, add pineapple, juice, sugar, vanilla seeds, and cornstarch mixed with reserved syrup. Pour into a shallow 6-cup buttered baking dish, and bake at 375° about 45 minutes, or until glazed and thickened. Chill, fold remaining ingredients together, and serve over poe.

Serves 6 to 8.

MACADAMIA NUT TARTS

Similar to southern Pecan Pie, this filling can be used in a 10- or 11-inch fluted tart pan with removable bottom. It is sinfully rich, but is complemented by the silky custard sauce.

Pâte Sucrée (see Index)	2 eggs
1 cup macadamia nuts, coarsely chopped	1 egg yolk
	2 tablespoons melted butter
½ cup freshly grated coconut	½ tablespoon vanilla
1 cup Lyle's Golden Syrup or light corn syrup	1/3 cup Macadamia liqueur or Frangelico
½ cup brown sugar	Crème Anglaise (see Index)

Double pastry recipe, roll out, and cut into rounds large enough to line 8 3 ½ - to 4-inch fluted tart tins. Divide nuts and coconut among them. Whisk filling ingredients together, and ladle over nuts and coconut. Place tins on a large baking sheet, and bake at 375° about ½ hour or until filling has set. Cool, mold, and serve with Crème Anglaise poured around them.

Serves 8 to 10.

TROPICAL FRUIT TART

The fabulous array of kaleidoscopic fruit tarts in the windows of Fauchon and other great food emporiums never cease to inspire and enthrall me, but the Japanese pastry chefs in Guam and Pelau leave nothing to be desired. The filling can be almost any kind-pastry cream, cream cheese, or lemon curd, which I have used here with passion fruit juice, or you may use the filling for Passion Fruit Pavlova. You will need about 3 passion fruits.

Pâte Sucrée (see Index) or pie pastry	½ papaya, seeded, peeled, & thinly sliced lengthwise
Lemon Curd, substituting passion fruit juice for lemon (see Index)	1 cup guava jelly or mango preserves, melted
½ ripe pineapple, peeled, halved lengthwise, cored, & thinly sliced	¾ cup mixed coconut & macadamias

Roll out pastry and line an 11-inch tart pan with removable bottom, and bake according to recipe. Cool, and fill with lemon curd. Arrange pineapple in concentric overlapping rows. Keeping papaya slices in original shape, fan slices slightly to resemble a shell, and place in center of tart. Brush jelly or preserves heavily over top, and sprinkle coconut and nuts around the edge. Chill well before serving.

Serves 6 to 8.

HAWAIIAN RAINBOW OF MACADAMIA CLUSTERS

The Hawaiian answer to French chocolate truffles for mignardises after the dessert. After I first saw these at the Mauna Lani, I couldn't wait to get home and make them. It is surprisingly simple, and you can make every color in the rainbow if you wish.

1 cup coarsely chopped macadamias	Pink, green, yellow, & orchid food coloring
12 ounces white chocolate, melted	

Place 16 tablespoons of nuts in small mounds on wax paper. Divide chocolate into 4 parts, and tint with coloring. Spoon over each nut mound, about 1 ½ tablespoons for each, until well coated, poking nuts a little to let it run underneath. Let set until firm, and arrange on white, gold, or silver doilies.

Makes 16.

SOUTH AMERICA
CHILE ARGENTINA URUGUAY PARAGUAY BRAZIL BOLIVIA PERU ECUADOR COLOMBIA VENEZUELA GUYANAS

South America's thirteen countries share a common bond-Indian heritage and European colonization. Leaving the giant stone men of Easter Island in Polynesia behind, this is now the realm of olive oil and indigenous South American ingredients, such as potatoes, corn, tomatoes, squash, lima beans, and avocados, which combine to form a delicious and practical cuisine with a profound European influence.

These countries also share a dramatic landscape of rivers, mountains, waterfalls, deserts, glaciers, jungles, and rainforests. Traveling from the Caribbean Sea on the north coast to Tierra del Fuego, where the Atlantic and Pacific meet, is similar to the transition from the Sahara to the North Cape.

Chile, almost 3,000 miles long, and only about 100 miles wide, is flanked by the Andes on its border with Argentina. The Atacama Desert, the world's highest and driest, dominates the North where nothing can grow, so the area is sparsely populated with people primarily of Indian and Spanish descent. The central valley around Santiago is Chile's garden and where its burgeoning wine industry is located. Farther south is Patagonia and Tierra del Fuego with its glaciers and fjords. The descendents of German and Spanish settlers populate this area, with many Yugoslavs, Norwegians, and Chinese in the extreme South.

The cuisine is based on cranberry beans, squash, corn, potatoes, lamb, pork, and seafood, probably the greatest catch on the continent. After six trips to Chile, I'm still discovering new varieties. Sea urchins are a true delicacy, and the congrio, salmon, tuna, sea bass, and cod are all quite good. All shellfish is plentiful, and when I went to Robinson Crusoe Island, about 400 miles off the coast of Chile, I was amazed to see the islanders casually catching their daily lobsters in front of the Villa Green Guest House. I stayed there and enjoyed you-know-what for dinner each night. No cars, TV, or telephones, (except for one out by the pier) and only about 200 inhabitants, make this an idyllic place.

Santiago has excellent ethnic restaurants of many kinds, but I have had some of my best meals in Punta Arenas, which is the jumping off point for Antarctica and where I had to stay for two weeks before taking off for the South Pole. On Sundays you can go to a Curanto, similar to the Pacific luau or fia-fia, where the pig, beans, and other items are baked in a pit with hot rocks.

Few oenophiles will dispute the fact that Chile produces the finest wines in South America. They use Bordeaux grapes and viticulture, as well as others, and make long-lived reds and dry whites as well. Concha y Toro and Undurraga are the ones we see the most, and we seldom get the best from Chile, where La Rosa is generally regarded as the best among connoisseurs. The drink of choice for most Chileans, however, is Pisco, a powerful brandy usually made into a Pisco Sour with lemon juice, syrup, and an egg white frothiness.

On one of my many trips to Chile, I traveled through the renowned Lake District on a series of buses and boats over the Andes to Bariloche, Argentina. The German legacy is quite apparent in this beautiful Andean resort city, as it is in Buenos Aires, along with a strong Italian influence. The fertile land and pastures were a perfect breeding ground for sheep and cows when the Spanish settled the area. The Atlantic coast also supplies excellent corvina, dolphin, salmon, and barracuda.

Parrilladas, or steak barbecues, are ubiquitous not only in Patagonia, but throughout the country, as beef is superb here. The

Spanish legacy is apparent in the countryside empanaderias and in the Spanish-style desserts. The Italian legacy is evident in the outstanding Italian restaurants and the pasta, which is enriched with the Parmigiana Reggianito produced here. Mendoza wine growers produce much better red than white, and unfortunately the emphasis is on quantity, not quality. Argentine tea, Yerba Maté, is outstanding and has medicinal properties. It is drunk daily and is also grown in other countries in the continent's southern part.

Uruguay, settled by Argentina, is probably the most stable, affluent, and safest country on the continent. Like Argentina, it has Spanish, Italian, and German influences, with virtually no Indian. I was amazed at the numerous mansions in Punta del Este, an enclave for the wealthy and the famous. As in Argentina, beef and lamb are superb, and there are about 10 of these animals to feed each person. Otherwise, the wine is quite poor, but the country imports the best vintages from France and elsewhere to accompany the well-prepared meats for which Uruguay is known.

Paraguay, on the other hand, is Indian to the core, but it does have some Spanish, Italian, and German influences. It is one of the two inland countries in South America, but does have plenty of fish in its mountain rivers and streams. Yerba Maté is the drink of choice here.

Bolivia, the other inland country, is also predominantly Indian in every way, including their dress. Most people live on the Altiplano, rather than in the eastern jungles. La Paz, at over 12,000 feet, is the world's highest capital, and its airport is the highest also.

The food is good and quite spicy with aji, their hot red pepper. Potatoes are the focal point of the diet and are prepared in many ingenious ways, especially with cheese and eggs. Beef and guinea pigs are favored, and corn is made into various types of tamales and porridge.

Brazil, the only Portuguese-speaking country on the continent, covers about half of it and borders every country except Chile and Ecuador. The vast terrain is mostly jungle and not a little water, as the mighty Amazon flows from the Atlantic on into Peru. Iguassu

Falls, one of the world's largest, shares its border with Argentina and Paraguay.

Once a Portuguese colony, this influence is shared with the African legacy that gives Brazil the reputation of having the best cooks on the continent. There are also French, German, and Italian influences.

Feijoada, the outstanding national dish, is made throughout Brazil, and reminds me of French Cassoulet in that it consists of many kinds of pork cooked with beans in a well-seasoned sauce. The similarity ends there, as black beans are used, and it is served with rice, kale or collards, orange slices, and toasted manioc meal.

The exceptionally beautiful state of Bahia is renowned for its cooks, the best in Brazil, and the fascinating cities of Salvador, Recife, and Fortaleza have an alluring ambiance not found elsewhere. A flight from Recife took me to Fernando do Noronja, a Brazilian island country where a traditional culture still exists. These areas have a cuisine based on African foods, such as dried shrimp, rice, okra, coconut, dende oil, peppers, and cashews. Tropical fruits are not better anywhere; nor are the dolphin.

The Portuguese influence is evident in the use of salt cod, olives, almonds, and very sweet desserts. Excellent Portuguese wines are imported, although Brazil does have a wine industry in the state of Rio Grande Do Sul, near Uruguay. Brazilian coffee is also outstanding.

The Indian culture is alive and well in Peru, the center of the Inca Empire, which included Chile, Ecuador, and Bolivia. Cuzco, the ancient capital of the Empire, is the gateway to the archeological wonders of Machu Picchu, which is reached by a thrilling switchback train ride. I have had excellent meals in both places, and detected a similarity to the food of Chile, which, like Peru, has a Spanish legacy.

On the coast, I have had memorable seafood meals, especially corvina, shrimp, and scallops. Ceviche is also quite popular. The Amazon also supplies fish, which I discovered when taking a boat from Iquitos to a lodge on the great river. Another interesting water trip is the hydrofoil from Bolivia to Peru on the world's highest freshwater lake, 2,000-foot Lake Titicaca.

The humble potato, however, is the backbone of Peruvian cooking, and there are countless varieties. The fashionable purple potato in the United States was eaten by the Incas hundreds of years ago. Sweet potatoes, pork, chili pepper (aji), and annatto powder and oil to season and color food are all quite popular. Pisco is definitely the drink of choice.

On my first trip to Ecuador, another very Indian country in the Andes, I took a bus to see the monument that is supposedly at the center of the world at this particular spot on the equator. It was dark when I returned to Quito and did not know where to get off the bus, and with little English spoken, the driver and all the passengers finally figured it out. The driver made an unscheduled stop, got off the bus with me, and pointed to my hotel. The warm and hospitable Ecuadorian Indians and their wonderful cooking will always be dear to my heart. I experienced the same genuine hospitality when I flew out to the Galapagos Islands, bleak and barren, but noted for wildlife.

Llapingachos, a wonderful composition of potatoes, cheese, avocado, and bacon, is the national dish. Hot aji, wonderful corn and potato soups, and banana desserts are typical of the cuisine.

Colombia, with a Pacific and Caribbean coastline, has an African influence in its coastal cities and a Spanish influence in the mountain valleys at the termination of the Andes. The ubiquitous potatoes, corn, rice, and cassava are still major elements of the cooking here, but there is also a fondness for capers, as is evidenced in its national dish, Ajiaco, a chicken stew with corn, potatoes, cream, and capers. Colombian coffee, of course, is renowned. Bogota, the capital, is very cosmopolitan, while 300 miles north of the coast is San Andres, an island that is still as strange as when it was headquarters for Captain Henry Morgan, a notorious English pirate. It can be reached from Costa Rica and Honduras.

Venezuela, close to Trinidad and Tobago, also has a very Caribbean influence, as well as Spanish. It was the first in South

America to be colonized, and Caracas, the capital, is quite cosmopolitan with a Spanish flair. I experienced Pabellon Criollo, the national dish, at El Cortijo in Caracas. Beef stewed in a cumin-scented tomato sauce is served with black beans and rice, and also fried plantains. My recipe for this is in Culinary Classics, my first book. Annatto and capers are quite popular here also.

The last three countries in South America are thoroughly Caribbean in every way except for their colonizers. The British took Guyana; the Dutch took Suriname; and the French took tiny Guiana, perched on the eastern corner of the continent.

Georgetown, Guyana, although very poor, has a British legacy in its 19th century colonial wooden buildings. There is also an Indian, African, and Chinese influence. I did note that vegetable cookery is truly outstanding here. Pepperpot Soup is a favorite dish.

Suriname, and its capital, Paramaribo, have a very Dutch and African influence. Restaurants serve the famous rijsttafel just as they do in Holland and Indonesia. Shellfish, tropical fruit, and okra are popular in all three of these countries. I had plenty of time to sample the food because I was stuck here for three days when the only aircraft owned by Suriname Airways didn't cooperate.

When I finally reached French Guiana, and its capital, Cayenne, it was like déjà vu. The French culture abounds here in the food, hotels, language, people, and even the airline, Air France. I felt as though I had come full circle in food research. And yes, this is the home of cayenne pepper.

RECIPES FROM SOUTH AMERICA

CHUPE DE CENTOLLA (CHILEAN LOBSTER CAZUELA)

CRÊPES DE CAMERONES

ENTRADA BRASALEIRO (BRAZILIAN APPETIZER)

PIQUEOS (PERUVIAN APPETIZER)

EL CASCO SALAD

ANDEAN MASHED POTATO SALAD WITH GARNISHES

SOPA CRIOLLO

ANDEAN POTATO SOUP WITH CHEESE AND CORN

SWEET AND SOUR FISH WITH PINEAPPLE

SALMON WITH SAUCE ANTIBOISE

AJI DE GALLINA (CHICKEN WITH BREAD SAUCE)

PICHANGA (CHILEAN LEFTOVERS)

LLAPINGACHOS (ECUADORIAN POTATO CAKES WITH EGGS, BACON, AND AVOCADO)

AVOCADO OMELET

PAPAS À LA HUANCAINA (HUANCAYA POTATOES WITH CHEESE)

BUCKWHEAT PASTA WITH SWEET RICE AND RAISINS

CRÊPES DULCE DE LECHE

TORTA DE MIL HOJAS (THOUSAND LAYER PASTRY)

TORTA DE CHOCOLATE Y DULCE DE LECHE

CHOCOLATE CARAMEL TRUFFLES WITH WALNUTS

CHUPE DE CENTOLLA

(Chilean Lobster Cazuela)

A dish I truly love, this is probably my most prized South American recipe. Chupe can be either thick soup or a luscious, comforting mixture of finely chopped lobster, bread, tomatoes, garlic, and olive oil baked in a cazuela. It can be either a first course or a main course. This is my re-creation of the one I had at the Finisterre Hotel in Punta Arenas during my two-week wait for the South Pole departure. Serve plenty of hearty red table wine. If used as a main course, only a fresh green salad is needed.

2 cups leftover lobster or scallops, or 1 pound fresh, finely chopped	½ teaspoon annatto powder
	2 cups coarsely chopped country bread
2 large garlic cloves, crushed	1 cup canned crushed tomatoes
1/3 cup olive oil	
1 teaspoon salt	Black olives or chopped parsley, optional

Sauté lobster and garlic lightly in oil, add seasonings and bread, and cook briefly. Add tomatoes, cook until bread is soft and well blended. If too dry, add more tomatoes or a little white wine. Pour into an oiled 1-quart cazuela or other shallow casserole, or individual gratin dishes, and bake at 350° about 10 minutes, or until golden brown. Garnish as desired.

Serves 4 to 8.

CRÊPES DE CAMERONES

El Cid, the elegant roof-top restaurant with a panoramic view in Santiago's San Cristobal Hotel, serves French cuisine with a Chilean touch, as do other restaurants in this cosmopolitan city. This is an elegant first course.

12 crêpes, 6 to 7 inches in diameter (see index)	1 tablespoon water
1 cup heavy cream	1 pound shrimp, cooked & shelled
1 teaspoon brandy	Salt & pepper
1 teaspoon soy sauce	½ cup heavy cream
1 tablespoon cornstarch	½ cup parmesan

Simmer cream with seasonings about 5 minutes, and thicken with a mixture of cornstarch and water. Add shrimp, and spread about ¼ cup filling on each crêpe, folding them to enclose filling. Place in a buttered au gratin dish just large enough to hold them or in individual au gratins. Pour cream over, sprinkle with cheese, and bake at 350° until hot, about 5 minutes.

Serves 6.

ENTRADA BRASALEIRO

(Brazilian Appetizer)

Spreads and dips have never appealed to me, but this flavorful cheese and butter mixture from Chalé, a Bahian restaurant since 1884 in Rio, is superb. A different blue cheese could be substituted.

4 ounces Roquefort cheese	Pepper, to taste
¼ cup soft butter	Paprika or powdered annatto
Brandy or cognac, to taste	Buttered country-style brad
	Assorted olives.

Cream the cheese with butter, brandy, and a little pepper until blended. Mold in the crock, and sprinkle with paprika, or spread on bread, and serve with olives.

Makes ¾ cup.

PIQUEOS

(Peruvian Appetizers)

Jose Antonio, a Creole restaurant in Lima's exclusive San Isidro suburb, has always been noted for its roasted meats and chicken, but I also had an interesting assortment of appetizers there. Tender skewered beef heart and braised pork fried in its own fat are served with marinated onion slices; thin, fried yam slices; and short pieces of corn-on-the-cob. The beautiful colonial dining rooms with dark wooden trim compete with the fine food.

1 pound beef heart or steak, cut into 1-inch cubes	1 chili pepper, minced
	1 teaspoon cumin
½ cup red wine or raisin vinegar	½ teaspoon annatto powder
	Salt & pepper
2 garlic cloves, crushed	2 tablespoons olive oil

Marinate beef in vinegar with seasonings, refrigerated, about 12 to 24 hours. Place on skewers, brush with oil, and grill over charcoal about 5 minutes or until done as desired. A combination of beef, chicken, and fish can be used.

Chicharrones:

1 pound pork butt, shoulder, or country-style ribs	2 garlic cloves, crushed
	Salt & pepper

Cut pork into chunky strips, cover with water, season, and simmer, covered, until tender. Uncover, and let pork continue to cook until water evaporates, and pork begins to fry in its own fat, becoming crisp and brown. Serve with anticuchos and the previously mentioned items, if desired.

Serves 6 as part of Piqueos.

EL CASCO SALAD

At the end of my Lake District crossing from Chile to Bariloche, Argentina, my destination was the elegant El Casco, a small hotel outside town owned by a German baroness, who was also an accomplished cook. She was so dedicated to offering her hotel guests fine food that she went back to Europe every year to learn the latest trends. The baroness and her lovely hotel will be long remembered by this simple and simply delicious salad.

1/3 cup red wine vinegar	1 pint grape or cherry tomatoes, halved
1 teaspoon salt	
1 teaspoon sugar	1 red bell pepper, sliced
1 cup olive oil	Bibb or Boston lettuce, torn into pieces
12 ounces roast beef, thinly sliced	
	1 Radicchio, torn into pieces
1 avocado, peeled, pitted, and sliced crosswise	1 carrot, peeled & shredded

Make a vinaigrette by mixing vinegar with seasonings, then whisk in oil. Add to beef, and marinate at least an hour. Also add avocado to prevent discoloring. When ready to serve, arrange beef in center of a large platter. Toss vegetables and lettuce with drained vinaigrette, and arrange around beef. Garnish with carrot.

Serves 6.

ANDEAN MASHED POTATO SALAD WITH GARNISHES

An elegant and new rendition of Causa, an ancient Incan dish, this is representative of the current creative cooking throughout South America. Originally, the mashed potatoes were piled in a dish, and garnished with the typical sweet potatoes, corn, and cheese. My version is made in the individual molds with a layer of your favorite egg, tuna, chicken, or ham salad and a kaleidoscope of colorful garnishes as delightful to behold as it is delicious.

1 ½ pounds Yukon or purple potatoes	½ tablespoon salt, or more
1/3 cup extra virgin olive oil	1 ½ cups egg, tuna, chicken, or ham salad
1 ½ tablespoons lemon juice	Watercress or mesclun, hard-cooked eggs, avocado wedges, olives, and grape tomatoes, halved.
1 ½ tablespoons capers	
Annatto or curry powder, to taste	

Simmer potatoes until tender, peel, and whip in an electric mixer until smooth, adding oil, juice, capers, and seasonings as you whip. Place a biscuit cutter or tuna can with lids removed on a salad plate, fill with a portion of potatoes, about 2 to 3 tablespoons, then add about 3 tablespoons of chosen salad, and another 3 tablespoons of potatoes. Smooth top, remove mold, and repeat with remaining salad plates. Chill well, overnight if desired, and place cress or mesclun around potato molds. Garnish with remaining ingredients, and drizzle more oil over all. This is a great first course or main course in hot weather.

Makes 4 to 6 3- or 4-inch molds.

SOPA CRIOLLO

Paltiti, a Creole restaurant in Cuzco, served this comforting and flavorful soup on a cold and foggy night before I went to Machu Picchu. There is a bit of Indian, Spanish, and Chinese influence.

½ pound chorizo, crumbled	2 large garlic cloves, crushed
1 large onion, chopped	2 teaspoons salt or soy sauce
2 tablespoons olive oil	6 cups light brown stock or rich chicken stock
1 teaspoon oregano	
1 teaspoon paprika	4 ounces soba noodles or linguine
1 teaspoon powdered saffron	
	6 fried eggs

Sauté sausage and onion in oil, using a 2-quart soup pot, until very soft. Add seasonings, cook briefly to imbue flavor, and add stock. Simmer about 15 minutes, add cooked noodles, and ladle into soup plates. Place an egg on each.

Serves 6.

ANDEAN POTATO SOUP WITH CHEESE AND CORN

A superbly rich and thick country-style soup which I have enjoyed from Colombia and Ecuador to Peru and Bolivia. Tiwanaku, a typical restaurant located in a small house in La Paz, Bolivia, inspired this version, which cost me only about $2.00 and included an Indian pork sandwich.

¾ cup chopped onions	2 cups chicken stock
2 large garlic cloves, crushed	2 cups milk
3 tablespoons butter	1 cup corn, fresh or frozen
½ teaspoon annatto powder	½ cup queso blanco or grated provolone
1 teaspoon thyme	
1 bay leaf	1 egg, beaten
1 ½ pounds Yukon potatoes, peeled & cut into chunks	1 avocado, peeled, pitted, & sliced
Salt, to taste	½ cup olives, pitted & halved
	Paprika

In a 2-quart soup pot, sauté onion and garlic in butter until translucent. Add seasonings and potatoes, toss to coat well, and add liquids. Cover, and simmer about 20 minutes. Mash potatoes against side of pan to thicken soup, and add corn. Simmer until desired consistency is reached, and gradually beat in cheese and egg. Garnish with remaining ingredients.

Serves 4 as a main course.

Gloria Preston Olson

SWEET AND SOUR FISH WITH PINEAPPLE

After exploring the entire world, I discovered the best Chinese restaurant of all, the superb Golden Dragon, perched high on a hilltop in Punta Arenas, Chile. Aside from the view all the way down to the Strait of Magellan, the red and yellow decor in the various rooms of this distinctive old home is just my cup of tea, as anyone who knows me will agree. Shirley Agnes De Silva is the very talented owner who came to the tip end of Chile via Singapore and Portugal, and her food is definitely worth coming back for, even though I have been to Punta Arenas many times. This is the way I remember it.

1 medium red onion, halved lengthwise, then sliced crosswise	½ cup rice vinegar
	¼ cup soy sauce
	½ cup sugar
4 small scallions, cut into strips	1 tablespoon cornstarch
¼ cup canola or peanut oil	¼ cup water
1 pound fresh pineapple, cut into short ¼-inch wide julienne	8 to 12 ounces congrio or sea bass, cut into large cubes
	½ cup cornstarch
1 tablespoon minced ginger	½ teaspoon Chinese five-spice powder
2 garlic cloves, minced	
½ cup chopped cilantro or parsley	Canola oil, for deep-frying

Using a wok, stir-fry onion and scallions in very hot oil briefly, then add pineapple, ginger, garlic, and cilantro, stirring. Add vinegar, soy sauce, and sugar, bring to a boil, and thicken with cornstarch mixed with water. Toss fish with cornstarch mixed with five-spice, and deep-fat fry only a few minutes, or simply sauté in a skillet, using a small amount of oil. Add to sauce, and serve with plain rice.

SALMON WITH SAUCE ANTIBOISE

The subdued but elegant decor of the restaurant in the Tierra del Fuego Hotel in Punta Arenas is the setting for some very serious and impressive dining. This classic French sauce is fairly involved, requiring two tomato preparations, but I have simplified it by using intensely flavored oven-dried tomatoes, which I always have in my freezer. The exquisite sauce is perfect with the freshest of Chilean salmon. For an even more impressive dish, place a small salmon fillet over a larger Basa fillet, then pour the sauce over the top.

6 large ripe Roma tomatoes, skinned, seeded & diced finely	1 to 1 ½ cups mixed olives, pitted
¼ cup oven-dried tomatoes, puréed	2 tablespoons lemon juice
	6 5-ounce salmon fillets
1 large roasted garlic clove, puréed	Salt & pepper
	¼ cup olive oil
½ cup extra virgin olive oil	1/3 cup chiffonade of basil

Place both kinds of tomatoes and garlic in olive oil, and barely simmer about 15 minutes to imbue flavor. Add olives and lemon juice, keep warm. Season fillets, and sauté in oil a few minutes on each side, or until cooked. Place on plates, and pour sauce over fillets, with basil to garnish.

Serves 6.

AJI DE GALLINA

(Chicken with Bread Sauce)

This may not sound very appealing, but the aroma, color, and flavor are simply magnificent. An old Bolivian mountain dish great for cold weather, I first had this at Yotala, a typical La Paz restaurant. I have taken the liberty to use suprêmes instead of whole pieces of chicken, as it is much easier to eat. Absolutely the best comfort food there is, especially in Bolivia where comfort is needed since coups are endemic there-well over 100 the last I heard.

4 slices white bread	½ cup chopped tomatoes, or canned crushed tomatoes
1 cup milk	
4 suprêmes	1 ½ cup chicken stock
¼ cup olive oil	¼ cup parmesan cheese
½ cup chopped red oinion	Salt & pepper
2 garlic cloves, crushed	Sliced Hard-cooked eggs, small baked sweet potatoes, & black olives
½ teaspoon annatto powder	
Minced chili peppers, to taste	

Soak bread in milk until soft, then mash with a large fork. Sauté suprêmes in a sauté pan on both sides until almost done. Remove, and sauté onion and garlic over medium heat until translucent. Add annatto, chili, tomatoes, stock, and bread. Bring to a boil, then simmer about 40 minutes, or until thick. Add suprêmes, cheese, and seasonings, and cook until chicken is hot. Serve in a cazuela, garnished with eggs, sweet potatoes, and olives.

Serves 4.

PICHANGA

(Chilean Leftovers)

During my two-week tenure in Punta Arenas, while waiting to go to the South Pole, I tried different restaurants for lunch and dinner every day, and Pichanga, which I had never heard of, is my culinary prize. It is a typical Chilean dinner using leftover fried potatoes and meat of any kind, depending on what there is. Just about anything else can be thrown in, as I discovered when I ordered this at several different restaurants for comparison. I absolutely love it and hope you will too. I even start from scratch sometimes.

12 ounces fried potatoes, sliced or like French fries	1 hard-cooked egg, cut into slices
6 ounces leftover meat	1 tomato, cut into wedges or slices
6 ounces cooked sausage	
¼ cup olive oil	Olives, pitted, or pickles
1 avocado, peeled, pitted, & cubed	Catsup and mustard, for serving

Using a wok, toss and stir-fry the potatoes and meats in hot oil until warmed through. Toss in remaining ingredients and serve with a red table wine. Some Chileños like to drizzle catsup and mustard over all, and so do I.

Serves 3 or 4.

LLAPINGACHOS

(Ecuadorian Potato Cakes with Eggs, Bacon, and Avocado)

At La Choza, a typical Andean restaurant in Quito, I discovered this favored homestyle potato dish. I like it almost as much as the previous Chilean potato dish. It could also be made with leftover mashed potatoes.

6 medium Yukon potatoes	2 teaspoons salt
6 slices bacon	½ teaspoon annatto powder
1 medium onion, chopped	3 tablespoons olive oil or butter
½ cup milk	6 fried eggs
1 to 1 ½ cups grated Muenster, Monterey Jack, or cheddar cheese	2 Hass avocados, peeled, pitted, and sliced
	Lettuce and Tomatoes, sliced

Boil potatoes until tender. Meanwhile, sauté bacon until done, remove, and sauté onion in bacon fat. Peel and mash potatoes in an electric mixer. Add onion, milk, cheese, and seasonings. Form into 6 thick cakes, and sauté in oil that has been added to pan in which onion was cooked. Cook until brown and crisp on each side. Top each with an egg and a strip of bacon. Serve with avocado, lettuce, and tomatoes. Again, catsup would be great.

Serves 6.

AVOCADO OMELET

The classic Ouro Verde Hotel in Rio has a Swiss/German kitchen which adds a Brazilian touch to European classics, as in this wonderful omelet, where the buttery avocado texture seems to melt into the eggs, butter, and cheese.

1 avocado, peeled, pitted and sliced crosswise 2 tablespoons butter 4 eggs Salt & pepper	2 tablespoons butter 1 cup grated Emmenthaler cheese Chopped parsley or mint

Sauté avocado in butter until soft and golden. Beat eggs with seasonings. Melt butter in a large omelet pan over medium heat, pour in eggs, and cook until barely set, lifting edges to let uncooked egg run underneath. Place all but a few slices of avocado on top, add cheese, fold, and slide onto a platter. Garnish top with reserved avocado slices and parsley.

Serves 2 to 4.

PAPAS À LA HUANCAINA

(Huancaya Potatoes with Cheese)

Huancaya, an Indian town high in the Andes, is famous for this versatile and attractive dish. It can be an appetizer, a light meal, or an accompaniment to meat. Beef is also served with this sauce.

1 cup queso blanco 1 tablespoon lemon juice ½ teaspoon turmeric or annatto ¼ cup olive oil ½ cup heavy cream	Salt & pepper 6 medium new potatoes or purple potatoes, boiled and peeled and halved Red leaf lettuce (optional) 2 hard-cooked eggs, sliced Black Olives

Purée cheese with seasonings, oil, and cream in a processor. Taste for seasoning, and if too thick add a little milk. If serving the dish warm, heat the sauce, otherwise serve it at room temperature. Arrange potato halves on a platter lined with lettuce. Garnish with eggs and olives. Purple potatoes are stunning and can be used in combination with new potatoes.

Serves 6.

BUCKWHEAT PASTA WITH SWEET RICE AND RAISINS

This unique dish from the Caribbean coast has a distinctive African influence in the rice, plantains, molasses, and bacon, and the Japanese pasta adds a bit of fusion to the dish. It makes a lusty main course served with a hearts of palm salad dressed with a sherry vinegar vinaigrette.

3 ounces Japanese soba noodles or other buckwheat pasta, broken into short pieces	1 ¾ cup beef stock
	½ cup dried currants or raisins
	4 slices bacon, sliced crosswise
2 tablespoons olive oil	1 tablespoon olive oil
1 cup Mexican Morello rice	1 small ripe plantain or 1 large banana, sliced diagonally
1 tablespoon molasses or sorghum	
1 teaspoon salt	Chopped chives or cilantro

Using a wide saucepan, sauté pasta in hot oil until golden, add rice, stirring until coated with oil. Add seasonings, stock, and currants. Cover, and let simmer about 20 minutes, or until stock is absorbed. Meanwhile sauté bacon in oil, and when almost done, add plantain, and sauté until golden. Mix into pasta and rice, and garnish with chives.

Serves 4 to 6.

CRÊPES DULCE DE LECHE

Chileños know how to eat breakfast if this luscious creation is any indication. The Hotel Finisterre in Punta Arenas has a breakfast buffet of adequate size but with great offerings. The crêpes are great for dessert too.

12 6-inch crêpes (see index)	Black currant preserves
Dulce de Leche (caramelized condensed milk)	

Spread as much dulce de leche as you wish on the crêpes, then add preserves. Fold in halves or quarters, and enjoy!

Serves 3 or 4.

TORTA DE MIL HOJAS
(Thousand Layer Pastry)

Hacienda Los Lingues, an elegant residence over 300 years old, is owned by German Claro-Lira, a descendant of one of Chile's earliest pioneers. As a guest in one of the ten rooms, I was privileged to have bacon and eggs served on a silver platter on the patio, a superb lunch in the wine cellar, tea and this luscious pastry torte served in the garden, and a divine multi-course formal dinner served in the period dining room with Baccarat crystal and fine china. Their luscious torte is composed of puff pastry with alternate layers of Dulce de Leche and a rich egg yolk icing. Definitely worth a detour!

8-10 round layers of Puff pastry baked and cooled (see index)	10 egg yolks
1 ¼ cups sugar	1 can or jar Dulce de Leche or caramelized condensed milk
1/3 cup water	½ cup sliced almonds

Dissolve sugar in water over heat until dissolved, then cool. Beat yolks until thick and pale, using an electric mixer, and add syrup gradually. Pour into a heavy saucepan and cook over medium heat until it forms a thick custard. Chill well. You will have about 1 ½ cups of icing and Dulce de Leche. Spread alternate layers of pastry with fillings, stacking them, and ending with caramel. Sprinkle top with almonds, and chill.

Serves 8 to 10.

TORTA DE CHOCOLATE Y DULCE DE LECHE

A chocolate pastry shell filled with layers of chocolate ganache and dulce de leche was one of the grand desserts served at teatime at Las Hayas, a mountain resort in Ushuaia, Argentina, the world's southernmost city. This visit followed the Silver Sea cruise which had just succeeded in rounding Cape Horn.

Chocolate Pastry (see below)	¼ cup butter
Chocolate Ganache:	1 can or jar Dulce de leche or caramelized condensed milk
1 cup cream, scalded	
12 ounces semi-sweet chocolate	Chocolate curls

Roll out dough to fit a 9-inch springform, and press about 2 inches high on the sides. Bake at 450° about 15 minutes, or until golden and crisp. Scald cream, add chocolate and butter, stirring until smooth, and chill. Pour ganache into pastry shell, and chill again. Then pour Dulce de Leche on top and smooth. Sprinkle with chocolate curls, and serve chilled.

Chocolate Pastry:

1 ½ cup unbleached flour	½ cup cold butter
1/3 cup cocoa powder	3 tablespoons sour cream
¼ cup sugar	

Mix dry ingredients into a processor, and blend in butter to form coarse crumbs. Blend in cream briefly, just until pastry holds together.

Serves 6.

CHOCOLATE CARAMEL TRUFFLES WITH WALNUTS

These luscious truffles would be a great addition to your mignardises selection after dinner or any time of day. They can be made in any amount and are well worth the sticky hands. This is an old Argentine recipe.

| 1 cup Dulce de Leche or caramelized condensed milk | 2 cups coarsely chopped walnuts |
| | ¼ cup cocoa powder |

Mix Dulce de leche well with walnuts. With wet or buttered hands, form small balls, then roll in cocoa. I find it easier to make all the walnut balls first and then roll them in cocoa.

Makes about 3 dozen.

‿ Caribbean Islands ‿

CARIBBEAN ISLANDS

The vast crescent of Caribbean islands, at least 2,500 miles long, stretches from Cuba to Trinidad, close to Guyana. One can eat well at the ethnic potpourri of tables in these sun-drenched islands, which have culinary influences from Carib and Arawak Indians, Spanish, English, Dutch, and French colonizers. Then thousands of slaves and laborers were imported from Africa, China, and India, which resulted in the zesty and colorful Creole cuisine, a beautiful fusion of European, African, and Asian cooking. I think of this as the world's first significant fusion cuisine.

Latin America's indigenous starchy roots, corn, potatoes, tomatoes, peppers, and chocolate; Europe's sugar, coffee, oil, beef, and pork; Africa's okra, callaloo, and ackee; India's curry and roti; and China's vegetables and rice cookery all meld to form this cookery style. Lard is ubiquitous.

Trinidad and Tobago, with British and Indian heritage, are known for their pepperpot soup and sancocho as well as their curries and roti. Port-of-Spain, Trinidad, was my first introduction to Indian culture and food, although my most profound impression was the cleanliness of the Indian people. Our guide was constantly dusting and polishing his immaculate car, and he wondered why we were going to the French islands.

Curacao's Dutch architecture and Indonesian Rijstaffel are most memorable, but stuffed Edam, goat stew, and Curacao orange liqueur are also popular. Aruba and Bonaire are also just off the Venezuelan coast.

Grenada and Barbados have a British lifestyle and elegant manor houses. I especially recall the unique flying fish, turtle soup, and conch fritters. St. Lucia and the Grenadines, also British, have the same type of cooking, but there is a French accent. The towering Pitons, lush and green volcanic cones, rise over the resorts on the beaches of St. Lucia.

Martinique was my first exposure to French culture and food, and it is still the destination for fine French cuisine in the Caribbean. The first island to have coffee, it was also the birthplace of Josephine, Napoleon's Empress. Along with Guadeloupe, these French islands have a Creole cookery that is quite spicy. Hearts of palm, blood sausage, dove, crab, turtle, and Blaffa (a delicious fish broth) are quite popular.

Antigua, quite British, is known for its lobster, pepperpot soup, and funchi (cornmeal pudding) as are its neighbors, St. Kitts and Nevis. These islands also have excellent French and Chinese cooking.

St. Barts, long known as the beautiful people's destination, is also a bastion of fine cooking that includes many ethnic styles as well as its own ethnic French. St. Martin and St. Maarten, French and Dutch island countries on the same island, are also quite upscale and have a variety of cuisines.

Anguilla, a flat and scrubby island with beautiful beaches and the Morroccan-style Cap Juluca, is sparsely populated with the Caribbean's friendliest people. With little traffic, this is where I learned to drive on the left side. Scilly Cay, my favorite restaurant, is a tiny island that you reach by waving your arms at the pier so that they will fetch you. The owner used to build tennis courts in Atlanta before he created Scilly Cay and became one of Anguilla's most successful entrepreneurs. The makeshift kitchen is taken over by boat every day, as cooking and eating are both al fresco. They catch your fresh lobster in the sea and grill it with your choice of fruits and vegetables, served in abundance on very large plates. Meanwhile, you read, sun yourself, take a dip in the water, or dance. This most enjoyable and unique lunch venue was about $40.00 in the '90s.

Tortola, a part of the British Virgins, along with Virgin Gorda and

Jost van Dyke, is true to its prim and proper heritage, and has a low emphasis on tourism, like Anguilla. Privacy is respected, and Virgin Atlantic's Richard Branson owns his own private Necker Island. Peter Island is an exquisite resort on its own island, reached by ferry from Tortola, and the food is excellent. Fish chowders are as popular in the Virgins as they are in Bermuda.

The American Virgins-St. Thomas, St. John, and St. Croix, the latter with a Danish legacy-have a blend of Creole and American cooking. Conch, callaloo, salt fish, and rice are part of the native cooking.

Puerto Rico, with its Spanish and American legacies, has an excellent cuisine with such specialties as land crabs, plantains with cracklings, and wonderful corn sticks known as surullitos. Asapao, a chicken and rice national dish, is especially good at San Juan's oldest restaurant, La Mallorquiña. San Juan, a very large and sophisticated city, also has excellent French, Italian, Spanish, Greek, and Oriental restaurants.

The Dominican Republic, which shares the island of Hispaniola with Haiti, was the site of the first sugar plantations, later spreading to Haiti, Cuba, and Jamaica. Sancocho, a hearty but tropical corned beef stew with yams, split peas, and coconut cream, is the most popular dish, as in Trinidad. Its Spanish heritage is reflected in its empanadas, known as pastelitos.

Haiti, the western side of Hispaniola, and its capital, Port-au-Prince, are the poorest in the Western Hemisphere and one of the poorest places in the world. The French and African legacies have created one of the finest Creole cuisines, with delicious specialties such as rice with black mushrooms, cod fritters, and the luscious pork dish called griots, which I savored at the Grand Oloffson Hotel, a Victorian gingerbread edifice. Known as a mecca for artists and writers and the barman's Cesar's Rum Punch, it is decorated in a wild potpourri of styles. Unfortunately, the continuous violence and political upheaval since Papa Doc's and Baby Doc's regime have deterred tourism.

Jamaica, known for its Blue Mountain coffee and Tia Maria

liqueur, is also the home of some very talented cooks. Saltfish and ackee, curried goat, pepperpot soup, jerk pork, escovitch, and cod fritters are a few of the specialties I've enjoyed there. Jamaica and the nearby Caymans have a British Legacy. And Myers's full-bodied dark rum has been produced since 1879.

Cuba, the Caribbean's largest island and undoubtedly the most fascinating, has been forbidden for quite some time. Known for Hemingway, cigars, Veradero Beach, the Tropicana, and its wonderful food, Cuba has it all. The famous Hotel Nacional is reminiscent of the past and has a great breakfast buffet. The best Cuban specialties are Piccadillo, a zesty ground beef dish with olives, raisins, and fried eggs; black bean soup; and the Cuban sandwich, all of which can be enjoyed in paladars, which are small restaurants in private homes.

RECIPES FROM THE CARIBBEAN ISLANDS

PETER ISLAND'S STRAWBERRY ALMOND SOUP
AVOCADOS WITH SHRIMP SALAD AND DEVILED EGGS
CUBAN BLACK BEAN SOUP
PORK AND PLANTAIN SOUP WITH ORANGE COCONUT CREAM
THE ULTIMATE CUBAN SANDWICH
REN SNAPPER WITH OKRA, PLANTAINS, AND TOMATOES
CUBAN FRIED CHICKEN WITH ORANGE, OLIVE, AND RAISIN SAUCE
TOMATO ROAST CHICKEN MARTINIQUE
DOMINICAN PINK BEANS WITH SPICY RABBIT
HAITIAN GRIOTS WITH SAUCE TI MALICE
PORK TORTA WITH ARTICHOKES, TOMATO, AND CHEESE
BANANA BRIOCHE WITH HOT BUTTER RUM SAUCE
CARIBBEAN FRUIT BRULÉE

Gloria Preston Olson

PETER ISLAND'S STRAWBERRY ALMOND SOUP

This delightful chilled soup was a perfect beginning to my first dinner at the luxurious private island resort of Peter Island, a short boat ride away from Tortola. Other fruit, such as mangoes, papayas, bananas, or other berries, may be substituted.

1 pint ripe strawberries	3 tablespoons chestnut honey
2 cups vanilla yogurt	½ cup sliced and toasted almonds or macadamias
2-4 tablespoons amaretto or fruit liqueur	

Purée berries in processor, and blend in yogurt, liqueur, and honey. Pour into small bowls, and garnish with nuts.

Serves 6.

AVOCADOS WITH SHRIMP SALAD AND DEVILED EGGS

La Samanna, a charming and typically French resort in St. Martin, is renowned for its presentation of excellent cuisine with a Caribbean flair. Their hillside terrace overlooking the long, curving beach was the ideal setting for the memorable avocado salad, a perfect luncheon dish or first course.

½ cup mayonnaise	2 tablespoons chopped parsley
2 tablespoons chili sauce or catsup	1 teaspoon lemon or lime juice
½ cup chopped celery	Salt & pepper
1 small tomato, seeded and chopped	1 ½ pounds shrimp, cooked and peeled

4 ripe Hass avocados, peeled, halved, and pitted 8 grape tomatoes, halved	8 Niçoise olives, halved Watercress 4-8 deviled eggs

Mix dressing ingredients, add shrimp, and fill avocado halves. Place tomato and olive halves on top, and arrange on cress with egg halves.

Serves 8.

CUBAN BLACK BEAN SOUP

Sopa de Frijol Negro, an indigenous Cuban classic, has had many evolutions since my recipe from La Zaragozana, a former Havana restaurant in San Juan, was published in *Culinary Classics*. Even Cuban chefs are recreating this very special soup. This is my flavorful update.

1 pound black beans, soaked overnight ¾ pound chorizo, sliced 1 large red onion, diced 1 large red bell pepper, diced 6 large garlic cloves, crushed ¼ cup olive oil 1 cup Madeira or sherry 2 quarts chicken or beef stock 2 bay leaves	½ tablespoon cumin ¼ cup olive oil 2-3 tablespoons sherry vinegar or lime juice Salt & pepper Garnishes: sour cream, sliced oven-dried tomatoes (see index), sliced baby red bananas, and chopped cilantro

Using a 4-quart soup pot, sauté chorizo, onion, bell pepper, and garlic in oil over medium heat until vegetables are soft. Add Madeira, reduce by half, add stock, seasonings, and beans. Simmer gently, uncovered, about 2 hours or until beans are tender. Mash about half the beans against the edge of the pot or purée in a processor. Stir in oil, vinegar, and check seasonings. Garnish as desired.

Serves 8.

PORK AND PLANTAIN SOUP WITH ORANGE COCONUT CREAM

Plantains are ubiquitous throughout Latin America and are usually eaten as a side dish with everything from fried eggs to fried fish. The East African Banana Beef Soup inspired this very Caribbean-flavored light soup, with orange and coconut.

1 pound pork tenderloin, cut into 1-inch cubes	1 cup chopped red onion
½ teaspoon annatto powder	1 cup chopped peeled carrot
1 tablespoon olive oil	2 large garlic cloves, crushed
Salt & pepper	1 cinnamon stick
1 ripe plantain, diagonally sliced	½ cup orange juice
1 tablespoon butter	2 cups chicken stock
1 tablespoon olive oil	¾ cup coconut cream
½ tablespoon brown sugar	2 tablespoons sherry or lemon juice
¼ teaspoon powdered saffron or turmeric	Chopped parsley or cilantro

Rub pork cubes with annatto, oil, and seasonings. In a 6-cup soup pot, sauté plantain in butter and oil with brown sugar and saffron until tender. Remove 4 slices and reserve for garnish. Add vegetables and reserved pork, and sauté until soft. Add cinnamon stick and juice, and bring to a boil. Add stock and simmer about 10 minutes. Remove pork when just cooked through. Add cream and simmer briskly a few minutes. Purée with an immersion blender, and add sherry or juice. Ladle into soup plates, and garnish with reserved plantain slices, pork, and parsley.

Serves 4-6.

THE ULTIMATE CUBAN SANDWICH

I am constantly in search of the best Cuban Sandwich, as well as the best Reuben. Actually, they are quite alike in that they are composed of meat, cheese, and something pickled, and they are both grilled until they are unctuously warm and soft. Among the places I have tried the Cuban sandwich are the Hotel Nacional in Havana and the fast-food outlet opposite the Northwest check-in counter in the Miami airport. This is my favorite.

4 slices country bread	4 ounces thinly sliced Emmenthaler, Muenster, or Idiazabal
Dijon Honey mustard	
4 ounces thinly sliced pork	
4 ounces thinly sliced ham or salami	1 Large Kosher dill pickle, thinly sliced
	Butter or olive oil

Spread 1 side of bread slices with mustard. Layer them with pork, ham, cheese, and pickle. Top with remaining bread slices, and spread butter or oil over both sides of sandwich. Press down and cook over medium-high heat until golden and cheese is bubbly. Turn and cook other side. There are now panini grills at an exorbitant price, but the waffle iron my children gave me many decades ago has reversible plates, with one side smooth and flat-perfect for making these.

Makes 2 sandwiches.

RED SNAPPER WITH OKRA, PLANTAINS, AND TOMATOES

Fish, although not as popular as meat in the Caribbean, is abundant and is the perfect partner for okra as in this version of a lusty dish I enjoyed in Trinidad. Fried plantains and curry add a dash of India.

½ cup chopped red onion	¾ pound okra, stem ends trimmed
2 garlic cloves, crushed	
2 tablespoons butter	2 tablespoons lime or lemon juice
2 tablespoons olive oil	
1 teaspoon curry powder	Salt & pepper
1 large plantain, peeled and sliced diagonally	4 5-ounce red snapper fillets
	Chopped cilantro
3 tomatoes, chopped	Hot cooked rice

Sauté onion and garlic in butter and oil with curry until soft and translucent. Add plantains, sauté briefly, add tomatoes, and simmer about 5 minutes. Add okra and juice, cover, and simmer about 5 minutes or until tender. Place fish fillets in pan, and cook gently, turning once, until done. Garnish with cilantro, and serve over rice.

Serves 4.

CUBAN FRIED CHICKEN WITH ORANGE, OLIVE, AND RAISIN SAUCE

Although seldom seen in print, this is a very popular Cuban dish for which I am frequently given the recipe. This one is based on La Mallorquiña's version in San Juan. The restaurant was once one of Havana's best.

4 suprêmes	¼ cup sherry
3 garlic cloves, crushed	¼ cup butter
1 teaspoon oregano	¼ cup sliced almonds
1 teaspoon cumin	¼ cup black raisins
¼ cup orange juice	¼ cup Spanish green olives
Flour	Salt & pepper
¼ cup olive oil	Fried potatoes

Rub chicken with garlic and seasonings, pour juice over and let marinate several hours. Dredge in flour and sauté in hot oil until golden brown on both sides. Remove, and deglaze pan with marinade and sherry until reduced by half. Return chicken to pan, add butter, almonds, raisins, and olives. Season, and let cook about 10 minutes, or until chicken is done. If more sauce is desired, add about ¼ cup more orange juice. Serve with Spanish-style fried potatoes.

Serves 4.

TOMATO ROAST CHICKEN MARTINIQUE

I could undoubtedly write an entire book on roast chicken, as every country has its own version. Around 1965, my husband and I stayed at Bakoua Beach Hotel at Trois Islets, outside Fort-de-France. It was a typical French Provençale inn, so much so that I noticed a lizard on my husband's head as we were going down to dinner. The food, however, was superb, especially this unique roast chicken.

1 3-pound chicken	½ teaspoon four-spice powder
3 or 4 ripe Roma tomatoes	2 tablespoons soft butter
2 garlic cloves, peeled	¼ cup white wine
Salt & pepper	Fresh chopped thyme, rosemary, & basil
Chopped herbs, optional	

Stuff chicken with whole tomatoes, garlic, seasonings, and herbs. Sprinkle chicken with four-spice, rub with butter, and place in a small roasting pan. Roast at 375° about 45 minutes, or until juices run clear. Remove from pan, and empty stuffing into the pan juices with white wine. Whisk to form an emulsion, and check for seasonings. Add fresh herbs.

Serves 4.

DOMINICAN PINK BEANS WITH SPICY RABBIT

Dried beans are proliferous throughout Latin America, but my favorite are the small pink beans that are found mostly in the islands with a Spanish legacy, especially Puerto Rico and the Dominican Republic. This rich and zesty stew can also be made with pork or chicken. This is reminiscent of the dish I had at Nicolas de Ovando, a 16th century Spanish Colonial edifice on Calle las Damas, the oldest street in the Americas. Blanquini, one of the oldest Dominican restaurants in Santo Domingo, serves Spanish-inspired home cooking on the porch in a pillared mansion.

1 cup dried pink beans	2 tablespoons sherry vinegar
4 cups cold water	3 tablespoons olive oil
2 tablespoons olive oil	1 teaspoon annatto powder
2 garlic cloves, crushed	½ cup chopped red onion
1 2-pound rabbit, cut into 6 pieces, or 1 pound boneless country-style pork ribs	2 garlic cloves, crushed
	1 teaspoon cumin
1 teaspoon cumin	1 teaspoon oregano
1 teaspoon salt	Salt & pepper
2 large garlic cloves, crushed	1 cup canned crushed tomatoes

Simmer beans, covered, in water with oil and garlic until tender, about 1 hour. Old beans will take longer. Do not drain liquid from beans. Meanwhile, rub rabbit or pork with seasonings, garlic, and vinegar. Let marinate several hours.

Sauté rabbit in oil with annatto until well browned and half cooked. Remove, and sauté onion and garlic until translucent. Add seasonings and tomatoes, and simmer about 10 minutes, or until thick and glossy. Add beans with their liquid and rabbit, cover and simmer until rabbit is cooked and beans are thickened.

If not thick enough, cook uncovered to desired consistency, or if too thick, thin with a little stock or water.

Serves 4-6.

HAITIAN GRIOTS WITH SAUCE TI MALICE

Probably my favorite Caribbean dish, this luscious, meltingly soft pork with a citrus flavor is Haiti's national dish. The Grand Oloffson Hotel, an eccentric old gingerbread edifice, was my destination for this special dish.

2 pounds boneless pork butt	½ teaspoon pepper
¼ cup orange juice	½ teaspoon thyme
¼ cup lemon juice	2 tablespoons butter
2 chopped shallots	Orange & lemon slices
2 teaspoons salt	Sauce Ti Malice (see below)

Marinate meat in juice with seasonings several hours. Cover with water, and simmer until tender and water evaporates, about 1 hour. Add butter and sauté until golden. Garnish with fruit and serve with sauce.

Sauce Ti Malice:

½ cup chopped onion	1 garlic clove, crushed
1 large shallot, chopped	1/3 cup lime juice
¼ cup chopped red bell pepper	2 tablespoons olive oil
	Salt & pepper

Mix ingredients and let marinate 6-12 hours.

Serves 6.

PORK TORTA WITH ARTICHOKES, TOMATO, AND CHEESE

Empanadas are synonymous with Spain and Latin America, and a torta is simply a much larger version. This deep pie is quite similar to the empanadas in the Spanish section and uses the same cheese, Idiazabal, which is Basque in origin, and artichokes, which are another Spanish favorite. While waiting to depart for the South Pole, I had a torta similar to this at the wonderful Asturias Restaurant in Punta Arenas, Chile. Asturias, known for its cooking, is just west of Basque country on the Bay of Biscay.

½ pound ground pork	½ cup oven-dried tomatoes, chopped
½ cup chopped red onion	
2 large garlic cloves, crushed	½ cup grated Idiazabal cheese
2 tablespoons olive oil	¼ cup parmesan
1 teaspoon each paprika, cumin, oregano, and salt	1 egg, beaten
	1 recipe Pie Pastry (see index)
½ cup marinated artichoke hearts, chopped	Tomato Chutney (see index)

Sauté pork in oil until golden brown, adding onion and garlic until translucent. Break up pork, add seasonings, hearts, tomatoes, and cheeses, and mix well. Stir in egg. Roll out 2/3 of pastry to fit a 7-inch springform pan. Press dough about halfway up the side, add filling, and roll out remaining pastry to fit the top. Press pastry edges together, and make a few slashes in the pastry. Any remaining pastry may be cut into fleurons to decorate the top. If using, brush pastry with milk, then press fleurons in place. Brush again. Bake at 350° about 45 minutes or until pastry is golden brown. This is wonderful hot, warm, or cold. Cut into wedges, and serve for lunch or a light dinner with a salad. Great for a picnic with a Chilean red! Serve with Tomato Chutney.

Serves 4 to 6.

BANANA BRIOCHE PUDDING WITH HOT BUTTER RUM SAUCE

Many years ago I savored this delightfully different bread pudding at Auberge de la Vielle Tour in Guadeloupe, and have made many adjustments to adapt it to today's culinary style. Mangoes are also quite good with it, as are caramel or butterscotch sauce.

4 large bananas, thinly sliced	1 tablespoon vanilla
1/3 cup passion fruit juice	1 cup light cream
¼ cup brown sugar or turbinado	¼ cup rum
	Freshly grated nutmeg, to taste
6 ounces leftover brioche, diced	Hot Butter Rum Sauce (see below)
1/3 cup melted butter	
2 large eggs, beaten	

Mix bananas with juice, sugar, brioche, and butter. Whisk eggs with liquids and nutmeg. Add banana mixture, mix well, and pour into a well-buttered 4-cup soufflé dish. Place in a larger pan, pour in hot water to come halfway up the soufflé dish. Bake at 375o about 45 minutes, or until pudding is almost firm. Cool on a rack, then invert onto a platter, and chill. Serve with the following sauce

Hot Butter Rum Sauce:

1 cup orange or passion fruit juice	1 tablespoon cornstarch
1 cup water	2 or 3 tablespoons rum
¾ cup sugar	1 tablespoon lemon juice
	2 tablespoons butter

Bring juice and water to a boil, and whisk in combined sugar and cornstarch. Boil until lightly thickened, and add rum, juice, and butter. Serve hot or cold with puddings, pies, and cakes.

Serves 6.

CARIBBEAN FRUIT BRULÉE

This very simple and delicious spin on the traditional crème brulée is my idea of a Caribbean dessert. You may use any tropical fruit, alone or in combination.

3 bananas, diagonally sliced	1 cup cream, whipped
1 mango, peeled, pitted, and sliced	1 teaspoon vanilla, or more
	½ cup brown or turbinado sugar

Place fruit in a buttered 9-inch round baking dish, and spread with cream whipped with vanilla. Chill 1 hour, then sieve brown sugar, or sprinkle turbinado on top. Broil about 4 inches below the heat until sugar melts and caramelizes. Serve hot or, preferably, cold.

Serves 6.

Central America & Mexico

CENTRAL AMERICA and MEXICO

Central America and Mexico have a common bond in the profound Indian and Spanish heritage that they share, as well as a terrain of jungles, beaches, mountains, and volcanoes. The Aztecs and Mayans, along with the Spanish Conquest, left deep roots throughout, but the African influence is of significance in the seven countries of Central America, due to its location on the Caribbean Sea.

An abundance of seafood, tropical fruits, rice, beans, meat, corn, and tomatoes are the basis of the diet and are seasoned with cumin, garlic, annatto, and coriander. But there are, of course, regional differences.

Panama, the most cosmopolitan country in Central America, was part of Colombia until 1903; thus it has a very Spanish influence, with American and also Oriental influences from the Andes. The Cuna Indian culture is quite prominent in the San Blas Islands, which is an idyllic, unspoiled beach destination that I reached by small aircraft from Panama City. Panamanian food is hot and spicy Creole with ceviche, empanadas, and tamales, along with fine international cuisine in its elegant restaurants.

Costa Rica has a very distinct Swiss influence, which was quite apparent in the Swiss chalet where I stayed and enjoyed the barley soup, perfect fare for the chilly rainforest setting. Other than its national parks, mountains, and beaches, Costa Rica takes great pride in its superb coffee and its burgeoning macadamia production. Gallo Pinto, a savory black bean and rice dish, is good any time of day with avocados, plantains, eggs, or meat.

Nicaragua, with a war-torn past, is one of the friendliest countries in Central America. The African influence is apparent in the culture, along with the Spanish and Indian elements. Meat, plantains, rice, and beans predominate.

Honduras and its bay islands have a distinct Mayan and Spanish influence in the cooking. Similar to that of Nicaragua, Honduran cuisine also has many Mexican-style tortilla dishes and wonderful fish.

El Salvador, the smallest country in this group and the only one only on the Pacific coast, has quite a cosmopolitan city, San Salvador, considering that half of the last century was dominated by dictators, coups, and a horrendous civil war. Riding on its Taca airline was an impressive experience. As in Nicaragua and Honduras, the people are primarily Mestizo, a mix of Spanish and Indian, and the cooking is similar. Pineapple and coffee are of great importance.

Guatemala, a virtual treasure in scenic beauty and historical sights, is predominantly Mayan Indian. Its coffee is renowned, and it is one of the world's leading producers of cardamom. European pastries with cardamom accompany the coffee; otherwise, the cooking is similar to that of the other countries in this region. The former capital, Antigua, is a lovely colonial town on the way to colorful Lake Atitlan, which is surrounded by mountains. Chichicastenango, the famous Indian town known for its Santo Tomas Church, with its celebratory incense swingers and the astounding marketplace, are all worth a detour and serve excellent food. I'll never forget the Tennessee-style country ham served at a roadside restaurant on the way from Guatemala City to Chichicastenango.

Belize, formerly British Honduras, was first settled by the British with their African slaves and later became a colony. There is still a very African influence and a bit of Asian as well. Belize City, about 300 years old, is known for its colonial architecture. Since Belize is only on the Caribbean coast, its cuisine leans heavily towards that of the islands and also Mexico.

From the Yucatan to the Baja peninsula, Mexico is a land of

deserts, jungles, mountains, and volcanoes, and its cuisine is almost as diverse. The Aztecs and Mayans, the Spanish, and other Europeans contributed to the fine art of Mexican cuisine. Chocolate and vanilla are indigenous to Mexico, as are turkeys, avocados, and some squash. Chilies are ubiquitous, as are tortillas and beans. These foods are seasoned with cumin, coriander, epazote, and many other spices. Lard has traditionally been the cooking medium, but butter and olive oil are favored in the sophisticated environs of Mexico City, one of the world's largest, and in the luxury resort areas of Acapulco and Cabo San Lucas. Flour tortillas are favored in the North; Veracruz cooks love to use capers, olives, and almonds; Monterey has a Jewish influence which favors cooking fruits with meat; central Mexico has a French flair with cream; and Puebla, as well as Oaxaca, make marvelous Mole sauce with chilies, spices, tomatoes, and chocolate. This is probably the national dish, but the area's Chilies en Nogada is a close second.

As with true love, fine cooking is reciprocal, and these Mexican culinary traditions were taken back to Spain and beyond to further develop European cuisine. Eventually, these traditions spread to California and across the United States, which had received its own European influences. Thus, the circle of fusion cooking is complete, or is it just beginning?

RECIPES FROM CENTRAL AMERICA AND MEXICO

OSTIONES SAN ANGEL (OYSTERS SAN ANGEL)

ENSALADA DE NOPALITOS (CACTUS SALAD)

TORTILLA SOUP

RED SNAPPER À LA VERACRUZANA

COSTA RICAN PORK WITH MADADAMIAS

CHILAQUILES (TORTILLA CASSEROLE WITH TOMATOES, SAUSAGE, CREAM, AND CHEESE)

CHILES EN NOGADA (MEAT-FILLED POBLANOS WITH CREAMY NUT SAUCE)

MEXICAN ORANGE CHICKEN WITH PASSION FRUIT

TACOS WITH POTATOES, CHORIZO, CHEESE, AND BEER SAUCE

MEXICAN TOMATO RICE

EL TIPICO DESAYUNO (THE TYPICAL BREAKFAST, PANAMA STYLE)

PAPAYA AND LIME COCONUT MOUSSE

MEXICAN KAHLUA CRÊPES

MEXICAN BROWN SUGAR FUDGE

OSTIONES SAN ANGEL
(Oysters San Angel)

Centuries-old San Angel Inn is probably Mexico City's oldest restaurant and is certainly the most nostalgic. Their signature oyster dish is my oldest and still my favorite for this noble shellfish. The main caveat, of course, is to obtain the freshest oysters possible. For easy opening, use the tough little oyster knife-one of my most useful kitchen tools.

2 dozen oysters	2 garlic cloves, crushed
¼ cup soft butter	Salt & pepper
2 tablespoons white wine	½ cup Parmesan or asiago cheese
2 teaspoons Maggi Sauce	
2 teaspoons Worcestershire	Rock salt

Place oysters in half shells. Cream butter, gradually adding wine and seasonings. Place a teaspoon on top of each oyster, and top with a teaspoon of cheese. Place shells on a layer of rock salt in a shallow baking dish, or, preferably on a large stainless steel platter, which can go straight to the table. Refrigerate until baking at 350° for 10 minutes.

Serves 4 to 8.

ENSALADA DE NOPALITOS
(Cactus Salad)

Cactus makes a quite good salad, and is now found fresh in many cities. If you do use fresh, buy the smaller pieces, as they are more tender, like most vegetables. Cut into small chunks and boil in salted water until tender. Drain, and refresh under cold water.

1 tablespoon sherry vinegar	2 medium tomatoes, seeded and diced
1 teaspoon salt	½ cup black olives, pitted
½ teaspoon cumin	2 tablespoons chopped cilantro
1 garlic clove, crushed	Watercress
¼ cup olive oil	¼ pound queso fresco, crumbled, or feta, or chèvre
1 1-pound jar nopalitos, drained and rinsed	

Whisk dressing ingredients together until emulsified. Add to mixed nopalitos, tomatoes, olives, and cilantro. Marinate about an hour, then arrange on cress, and garnish with cheese.

Serves 4 to 6.

TORTILLA SOUP

Tortilla soup was a central Mexican staple long before Dean Fearing, the celebrated chef at The Mansion on Turtle Creek in Dallas, introduced it to Americans. The typical Mexican version is made with lard, epazote, and Chihuahua cheese. The soup is typically thickened with tortillas, as in my version, and the choice of chili powder or fiery chilies is yours.

4 corn tortillas, coarsely chopped	1 tablespoon cumin
1 cup chopped onion	Chili peppers, chopped (optional)
6 garlic cloves, crushed	2 bay leaves
¼ cup olive oil or lard	¼ cup chopped cilantro
¼ cup tomato paste	2 cups canned crushed tomatoes
1 tablespoon dried oregano or epazote	

2 quarts chicken or brown stock 1 cooked chicken breast, julienned 1 avocado, peeled, pitted, & cubed	1 cup shredded cheddar or Monterey Jack, or crumbled queso fresco or Chihuahua 3 or 4 corn tortillas, julienned, and fried until crisp

Sauté tortillas with onion and garlic in hot oil, using a large soup pot, until soft. Add paste and seasonings, cook until well blended and aromatic, then add tomatoes and stock. Bring to a simmer, and cook about 30 to 40 minutes, uncovered, or until lightly thickened. Remove bay leaves and puree with an immersion blender. Pour into bowls, and garnish as desired.

Serves 8.

RED SNAPPER À LA VERACRUZANA

Veracruz, on the Gulf down near the Yucatan, is a haven for fish, and its red snapper has become the most renowned in Mexico. Bass or corvina may be used, and the fish may be poached, sautéed, or cooked in the sauce. Boiled potatoes are traditional, but I prefer fried potatoes in the Spanish style.

4 fillets red snapper ¼ cup olive oil Salt & pepper ¾ cup chopped red onion 2 large cloves garlic, crushed 1 tablespoon olive oil 1 tablespoon butter	2 cups chopped, ripe tomatoes 1 teaspoon dried oregano Pinch of sugar 1 tablespoon lemon or lime juice 2 tablespoons capers ½ cup green olives, pitted Fried potatoes

Sauté snapper in hot oil until almost done, season, and keep warm. Sauté onion and garlic in oil and butter until soft, add tomatoes, oregano, and sugar, and cook briskly until lightly thickened. Add juice, capers, and olives. Taste for seasoning, then add fillets, and cook briefly. Serve with potatoes.

Serves 4.

COSTA RICAN PORK WITH MACADAMIAS

Good Tico (peasant cooking) may be had at La Cocina de Leña San Jose, and good Swiss food can be found at Monte de la Cruz in the rainforest at Chalet Tirol, but Costa Rica is still learning the flavorful combinations of fusion cooking. Macadamias are now a Costa Rican alternative to those of Hawaii, and this is a beautiful blend of Pacific and Spanish flavors.

1 ½-2 pounds pork tenderloin	¼ cup butter
3 tablespoons soy sauce	1 cup veal or chicken stock
3 tablespoons Worcestershire	½ cup canned crushed tomatoes
2 tablespoons sherry	
2 tablespoons catsup	¼ cup cream
2 tablespoons lemon juice	2 tablespoons Madeira or port
2 tablespoons brown sugar	Salt & pepper
3 large garlic cloves, crushed	1/3 cup chopped Macadamias
	Chopped parsley or cilantro

Marinate pork in combined seasonings at least several hours. Slice thickly on the diagonal, and sauté in butter on both sides until just done, about 10 minutes. Remove from pan, add stock and tomatoes, and cook briskly until lightly thickened. Add cream, Madeira, check seasonings, and sprinkle with nuts and parsley.

Serves 6.

CHILAQUILES

(Tortilla Casserole with Tomatoes, Sausage, Cream, and Cheese)

An old classic, this has many versions and is the supreme Mexican comfort food. Try substituting tomatillos, green peppers, ground beef, and even corn and black beans.

3 large tomatoes, chopped	¼ cup olive oil, or more
1 small red onion, chopped	1 ½ cups crumbled or sliced cooked sausage, or leftover chicken
1 large garlic clove, crushed	
2 tablespoons olive oil or lard	
1 teaspoon salt	1 ½ cups mixed sour cream and heavy cream
3 roasted red bell peppers (see index)	1 cup grated Monterey jack or queso fresco
8 or 9 corn tortillas	

Sauté tomatoes, onion, and garlic in oil until thick and aromatic. Add salt and peppers, cut into strips. Fry tortillas in oil only until golden and softened. Cut into quarters, arrange in a buttered 10-inch shallow baking dish, and add half the tomato mixture, half the sausage, and half the cream and cheese. Repeat layers, and bake at 350° about 20 minutes, or until bubbly.

Serves 4 to 6.

Gloria Preston Olson

CHILIES EN NOGADA

(Meat-Filled Poblanos with Creamy Nut Sauce)

This important ceremonial dish, a specialty of Puebla and Oaxaca, both with great culinary esteem, is my favorite Mexican dish, and it has many variations. Patricia Quintana, the Julia Child of Mexican cuisine, uses over four dozen ingredients in her version. But you will find this is most delicious, and it has always been a tremendous success whenever I serve it. The filling is actually Piccadillo, the Cuban national dish. I use large bell peppers instead of the traditional poblanos, which are not usually available.

6 large roasted bell peppers (see index)	½ cup raisins
2 pounds ground chuck or pork	½ cup slivered almonds
2 tablespoons lard or olive oil	¼ cup sherry vinegar
1 cup chopped red onions	2 teaspoons salt
3 large garlic cloves, crushed	1 teaspoon sugar
1 ½ cups canned crushed tomatoes	1 teaspoon cinnamon or cardamom
	½ teaspoon saffron

After skinning peppers, cut in half and remove seeds and stems. Sauté meat in lard until browned, add onions and garlic, and sauté until soft. Add remaining ingredients, and cook until almost dry. Fill pepper halves.

Nogada topping #1:

2 cups cream, whipped	2 tablespoons chopped parsley
½ cup walnuts, ground coarsely	½ teaspoon cinnamon or cardamom
¼ cup almonds, ground coarsely	1 teaspoon salt

Nogada Topping #2:

½ cup walnuts	2 cups sour cream
½ cup almonds	6 ounces queso fresco
1 slice white bread, torn into pieces	1 teaspoon salt

Make the topping of your choice. For the first, simply fold all ingredients together. For the second, coarsely grind nuts in processor with bread, then pulse in remaining ingredients. Place peppers on a large stainless steel platter, and when ready to serve, pour topping over each one. Place under broiler until bubbly.

Garnish:

Pomegranate seeds or Roasted Red Bell Peppers, diced (see Index)	Chopped Italian parsley

Sprinkle above ingredients over hot peppers for a stunning presentation.

Serves 12.

MEXICAN ORANGE CHICKEN WITH PASSION FRUIT

Citrus juices, especially orange, are used in marinating and cooking everything from fish to fowl in Mexico, and throughout Latin America as well. Although not as well known as the tomato dishes, this is a very Spanish influence which is a result of the Spanish Inquisition, thus we see the same type of cookery in Israel. I also like to use pork tenderloin in this recipe, as the sauce has an intense fruity flavor and a brilliant deep orange color.

½ cup finely chopped red onion	1 small Mexican cinnamon stick
2 large garlic cloves, crushed	2 cups orange juice
1 tablespoon cardamom	2/3 cup passion fruit juice
Salt & pepper, to taste	2/3 cup strong chicken or veal stock
½ tablespoon veal or chicken base	1/3 cup turbinado or brown sugar
2 tablespoons olive oil	Salt & pepper, to taste
½ cup orange juice	3 tablespoons cold butter
½ cup passion fruit juice	Garnish: orange sections; roasted, sliced almonds; raisins; & mint leaves
4 suprêmes	
3 tablespoons butter	
1 bay leaf	

Mix marinade ingredients in a shallow dish just large enough to hold the chicken. Add chicken, and marinate several hours. Remove and sauté in butter on both sides until golden and almost done. Add marinade, simmer 5 minutes, and remove. Reduce marinade to a glaze, and add all but butter, and reduce to about 1 ½ cups glazed, thickened sauce. Whisk in cold butter, add chicken, turn to coat and warm through. Garnish as desired, and serve with hot, cooked saffron rice.

Serves 4.

TACOS WITH POTATOES, CHORIZO, CHEESE, AND BEER SAUCE

No cookbook of Mexican recipes is complete without at least one tortilla dish, whether it be tacos, enchiladas, burritos, tostadas, or quesadillas. This unusual taco variation can be made with fried or mashed potatoes, with or without any kind of leftover meat, and with your choice of sauce. This is great for a quick dinner when you have the leftovers.

1 pound Yukon potatoes, peeled	1/3 cup olive oil or lard
¼ pound cooked, crumbled chorizo	Beer Sauce (see below)
	Guacamole (optional)
¼ pound shredded Monterey Jack, mozzarella, or queso fresco	1 cup sour cream
	½ cup crumbled queso fresco, feta, chèvre, or other soft cheese
Salt, pepper, & cumin, to taste	Chopped cilantro or parsley
8 Corn or Flour tortillas	Black olives, pitted

Boil potatoes until tender, drain, mash, and add chorizo, cheese, and seasonings. Put about ¼ to ½ cup of potatoes on each tortilla, depending on the size. Fold or roll, secure with a wooden pick, and fry in hot fat on all sides, only until golden and slightly crisp. Keep warm.

Beer Sauce:

¾ cup chopped red onion	¾ cup canned, crushed tomatoes
2 tablespoons olive oil	¾ cup beer
1 large garlic clove, crushed	Salt & pepper

Sauté onion in oil until soft, adding garlic briefly. Add tomatoes and beer, bring to a boil, and cook until lightly thickened. Season, as desired. Mix cream with cheese and cilantro. Place 2 warm tortillas on each of 4 plates, pour beer sauce on one side of plate and guacamole on the other side. Top with cream sauce and olives.

Serves 4.

MEXICAN TOMATO RICE

This beautiful, coral-colored rice is as delicious as it looks, and is a great accompaniment to almost any Latin American main course.

½ cup finely chopped red onion	1 cup Mexican Morelos rice
2 garlic cloves, crushed	1 cup canned, crushed tomatoes
¼ cup olive oil	1 cup strong chicken stock

Sauté onion and garlic in oil until soft, add rice, and sauté until coated with oil. Add tomatoes and stock, and simmer, covered, about 20 minutes, or until liquid is absorbed. Season as desired.

Serves 4.

EL TIPICO DESAYUNO
(The Typical Breakfast, Panama Style)

When I saw this breakfast menu item, I was curious, and my first day in Panama City got off to a great start. It was also déjà vu, as I had the very same thing for dinner in Managua, Nicaragua, a few days earlier, at Antojitos, a charming and authentic local eatery with an al fresco patio. Antojitos, by the way, means "appetizers," but this is definitely a substantial meal. There are so many variations of this meal that I would call it the national dish of Central America.

3 cups cooked black beans, drained	Mexican Tomato Rice (see above)
1 small red onion, chopped	4 thick slices beef tenderloin
2 garlic cloves, crushed	Salt, pepper, & cumin
3 tablespoons olive oil	¼ cup olive oil
½ teaspoon cumin	2 plantains, peeled and sliced diagonally
½ teaspoon oregano	
Salt & pepper	4 fried eggs
2 tablespoons lime juice or sherry vinegar	2 small avocados, peeled, pitted, and sliced
	Lime juice or wedges

Sauté onion and garlic in oil until soft, add seasonings, juice, and beans, mashing them against side of pan to thicken slightly. Keep both beans and rice warm. Season beef, and sauté in hot oil until cooked as desired. Remove and sauté plantains, adding more oil if necessary, on both sides until golden and tender. Eggs need to be fried at the same time. Now, arrange beans, beef, rice, plantains, eggs, and avocados tossed with lime juice on plates. Enjoy!

Serves 4.

PAPAYA AND LIME COCONUT MOUSSE

This light and elegant fruit dessert is reminiscent of those I've had in many of the Latin American resorts. For coconut cream, I blend equal amounts of freshly grated coconut and milk in a processor and then strain it.

¾ cup lime juice ¾ cup sugar 1 cup cream or coconut cream	3 papayas, peeled, halved & seeded 6 thin lime slices Grated coconut

Blend juice and sugar with an inmersion blender until sugar dissolves. Whip cream until fairly stiff, then gradually add sweetened juice until it is of piping consistency. Place in a pastry bag with a large fluted tip, and pipe into papaya halves. Garnish with lime and coconut.

Serves 6.

MEXICAN KAHLUA CRÊPES

There is more to Mexican desserts than flans, puddings, and fritters. These delicious crêpes, a French legacy, are quite versatile, as they may be filled with French pastry cream, dulce de leche, or a fresh white cheese. The delicious Kahlua sauce is the quintessence of Mexico.

12 crêpes (see index) 6 ounces queso blanco, cream cheese, or other fresh white cheese ¼ cup butter ¼ cup sugar 2 tablespoons Kahlua liqueur	6 slices fresh pineapple, trimmed, and cut into 3 cups of small wedges 1/3 cup powdered sugar 1/3 cup Kahlua liqueur Kahlua Sauce (see below.)

Make crêpes about 6 inches in diameter according to the two-pan method in my recipe. Whip cheese with butter, sugar, and liqueur until smooth, and spread each crêpe with about a heaping tablespoonful. Fold or roll crêpes. Chill. Marinate pineapple with sugar and liqueur several hours.

Kahlua Sauce:

½ cup butter	¼ cup Kahlua liqueur
¼ cup sugar	4 egg yolks

Melt butter with sugar over low heat. Whisk liqueur into yolks, then whisk into butter. Cook gently until thickened, and serve warm. Makes about 1 cup. When ready to serve, place 2 crêpes on each plate, spoon pineapple around them, and serve sauce separately.

Serves 6.

MEXICAN BROWN SUGAR FUDGE

This wonderful Mexican candy, known as penuche or panocha, is a great addition to the trendy mignardises platter. Alone, it is a perfect ending to a Mexican meal, especially with a glass of Kahlua and a cup of Mexican coffee, stirred with a cinnamon stick.

3 cups light or dark brown sugar	1 ounce semi-sweet or dark chocolate
1 cup coconut or plan milk	½ tablespoon vanilla or almond extract
2 tablespoons corn syrup or molasses	1 ½ cups coarsely chopped pecans, walnuts, or almonds, or a mixture
2 tablespoons butter	

Mix sugar with milk, syrup, butter, and chocolate in a heavy saucepan. Stir to dissolve sugar, and boil to the soft ball stage, about 238°. Cool to lukewarm, and beat in flavoring and nuts until it becomes creamy and is no longer glossy. A heavy-duty mixer is an asset. Drop with a spoon on a buttered marble slab, or pour into a buttered 9-inch square pan. When set, cut into squares.

Makes 16 2-inch squares.

RECIPE INDEX

PRELUDES

Antipasto alla Swan 151
Barquettes de Chèvre 40
Bastila (Moroccan Flaky Pastry with Chicken, Almonds, and Eggs) 444
Blini with Caviar and Egg Salad 255
Boris's Yak Tail 524
Brazilian Appetizer 619
Bulgarian Filo Rolls 334
Carpaccio alla Cipriani 149
Cassolette d'Escargots Provençale 38
Chicken and Ham Croquettes 214
Chiffonade des Fruits de Mer 42
Chinese Barbecued Pork 550
Chinese Shrimp Toast 548
Crêpes des Camarones 619
Crespelle Caruso Belvedere 156
Eggplant Rolls with Walnut Filling 371
Empanadas con Idiazabal 213
Escargots Gaddis 548
Figs with Prosciutto and Gorgonzola 151
Galette de Mesclun, Tomato Confit, and Chèvre 44
Gravlax with Mustard Dill Sauce 301
Greek Filo Pie with Sausage and Potatoes 373
Herbed Chèvre 42
Kir Heinitzberg 500
Liptoi 335
Mango Lassi 524
Medallions of Avocado with Tuna and Lemon Vinaigrette 36
Noodles with Wild Mushrooms 276
Oysters San Angel 658

Palmiers with Prosciutto 40

Peruvian Appetizers 620

Prosciutto Roll with Paté 150

Quince Preserves 335

Roasted Red and Yellow Tomatoes with Caviar, Potato Purée, and Roasted Shallot Vinaigrette 43

Savory Herb Crêpes with Creamed Mushrooms 251

Serrano Ham and Idiazabal Terrine 215

Shrimp Plaki 371

Sicilian Fish Rolls with Couscous 155

Sizzling Garlic Shrimp 215

Steamed Barbecued Pork Buns 549

Tunisian Lamb and Egg Brik 446

Wild Mushroom and Escargots en Croûte 39

Yemen Honey Butter Pastry 410

Zen Radish Canapes 37

SAVORY SALADS AND DRESSINGS

Algerian Couscous Salad 441

Andean Mashed Potato Salad with Garnishes 622

Avocados with Shrimp Salad and Deviled Eggs 641

Banana-Coconut Rayta 526

Cactus Salad 658

Caucusus Salad with Yogurt and Feta 368

Chard-Tomato Rayta 527

Chicken and Gorgonzola Salad 153

Classic Vinaigrette 59

Cod Salad with Oranges 217

Creamy Camembert Vinaigrette 594

Cucumber Rayta 466

Cucumber Salad 302

Curried Lobster Seychelloise 502

El Casco Salad 621

Ensalada Valenciana 217

Georgian Bean Salad with Walnut Sauce 369

Harry's Bar Chicken Salad 152
Herbed Tomatoes with Feta 336
Honeyed Pineapple-Beet Salad with Baby Spinach 596
Lauswolt North Sea Salad 279
Lemon-Mint Rayta 527
Lobster Salad with Mango Sauce 280
Mangoes and Avocado with Shrimp and Tropical Dressing 469
Moroccan Mixed Salad 439
Moroccan Olive and Lemon Salad 439
Moroccan Radish and Orange Salad 438
Mount Kenya Safari Club Salad 469
Panzanella (Italian Bread Salad) 154
Pink Bean Salad with Artichoke Hearts 219
Pomegranate Dressing 369
Pomegranate Molasses 370
Potato Salad with Caviar Cream 60
Preserved Lemons 438
Roasted Purple Potato Salad with Tuna and Eggs 220
Russian Potato Salad 303
Salada Portuguesa 216
Salade Alsacienne 64
Salade Baumanière 62
Salade des Crudités 61
Salade de Pigeon 62
Salade des Tomates Provençale 61
Serengeti Slaw 466
Sweet and Sour Potato Salad 281
Syrian-Lebanese Bread Salad 410
Tahitian Hearts of Palm Salad 594
Thai Beef Salad 581
Tunisian Roast Peppers and Tomato Salad 440
Warm Bacon and Egg Salad 63
Warm Prawn Salad with Hearts of Palm 501
Warm Walnut and Green Bean Salad 337
West African Yam and Avocado Salad 484
White Asparagus and Serrano Ham Salad 218

SOUPS FOR ALL SEASONS

Andean Potato Soup with Cheese and Corn 624
Asturian Bean Soup 222
Avocado Soup with Smoked Salmon and Caviar 415
Azorean Fish Chowder 223
Banana Beef Soup 467
Bavarian Beer and Cheese Soup 278
Bohemian Sauerkraut and Sausage Soup 339
Braised Chicken with Vegetables and Basil 53
Burmese Chicken Noodle Soup 574
Chilean Lobster Cazuela 618
Chinese Noodle Soup 551
Cockaleekie Soup 256
Cream of Artichoke Soup 55
Creamy Chestnut Soup with Madeira 55
Cuban Black Bean Soup 642
Egyptian Greens Soup 443
Fish Soup Siberian Style 303
Japanese Miso Soup with Mushrooms 550
Khinkali Soup with Georgian meat Dumplings 378
Lamb and Fruit Soup 377
Moroccan Lamb Soup (Harira) 442
North Pole Cream of Garlic Soup 305
Peter Island Strawberry Almond Soup 641
Polish Barley Soup 338
Red Lentil and Bulgar Soup 379
Roasted Eggplant Soup 158
Serbian Bean Soup 340
Shrimp Bisque 51
Sopa Criollo 623
Soupe d'Escargots 278
Soupe en Croûte à la Bocuse 52
Soupe au Pistou 54
Syrian Lentil Soup with Spinach 413
Thai Lemon Shrimp Soup 573

Tomato Soup Berasategui 221
Tortilla Soup 659
Tsentralnaia Borscht 304
Tuscany Country Soup 156
Tyrolean Beef Soup 339
Watercress Soup with Caviar 414
Yemeni Peasant Soup 412
Yogurt Soup with Barley 379

FROM ALL THE SEAS

Baked Apulian Fish 174
Baked Fish Fillets with Vegetables 381
Baltic Herring with Red Onion Sauce 306
Bayonne-Wrapped Salmon with Endive Marmalade 69
Cod à la Flamande 281
Cod with Banana-Almond Sauce 230
Durban Fish Curry 502
Fillet of Sea Bass with Fingerling Potatoes, Haricots Vert, and Oven-Dried Tomatoes with Lemon Vinaigrette 259
Fish with Creamy Coconut Masala 528
Fish with Curry Sauce à la Mère Blanc 67
Fish with Sweet and Sour Miso 553
Fish Fillets with Tomato Butter à la Boyer 66
Gratin of Cod with Gjetöst Sauce 307
Grilled Grouper with Avocado Butter 596
Grilled Iranian Sturgeon 417
Israeli Fish with Honey and Fruit 416
Karachi Curry 528
Lake Victoria Baked Fish with Onions and Tomatoes 471
Marinated Tuna Steaks with Beet Purée 68
North Sea Fish with Potatoes and Onions 282
Orange-Baked Sea Bass with Orange Basil Butter 258
Penang Fish Curry with Herbed Curry Sauce 576
Persian Gulf Shrimp and Rice with Baharat 417
Poached Salmon 71

Poached Salmon with Garlic and Red Pepper Sabayon 70
Red Peppers Stuffed with Cod 229
Red Snapper with Okra, Plantains, and Tomatoes 645
Red Snapper à la Veracruzana 660
Rolled Tuna 227
Rwandan Shrimp Curry 470
Salmon with Sauce Antiboise 626
Sea Bass with Creamy Butter Sauce 260
Sea Bass Wrapped in Filo with Spicy Beurre Blanc 228
Sea Scallops with Lettuce Sauce à la Boyer 65
Senegalese Fish and Red Rice 485
Shellfish Medley with Creamy Basquaise Sauce 230
Shrimp with Papaya Sauce 575
Shrimp with Red Risotto and Dill Sauce 343
Sicilian Style Fish 175
Sole aux Nouilles Alsacienne 67
Steamed Scallops with Saffron Sauce 575
Sweet and Sour Fish with Pineapple 625
Sweet and Sour Fish with Tomato Purée Latvian Style 308
Szechwan Steamed Fish 552

FEASTING ON FOWL

Afrikaaner Chicken Pot Pie 503
Algerian Chicken with Chickpeas and Croquettes 452
Alsatian Chicken with Beer 77
Angolan Chicken with Okra Stew and Pumpkin 505
Armenian Roast Chicken with Pomegranate Glaze 384
Baked Chicken with a Salt Crust 176
Bombay Curry 531
Braised Chicken with Tarragon Cream 76
Canary Island Chicken 232
Chicken with Bananas and Cashews in Coconut Cream 506
Chicken with Bread Sauce 627
Chicken with Dried Beans 177
Chicken with Mangoes, Snow Peas, and Honeyed Walnuts 555

Chicken with Walnut Pomegranate Sauce 419
Circassian Chicken 382
Confit de Canard (Preserved Duck) 79
Confit de Canard with Shredded Brussels Sprouts and Peanut Pesto 264
Crusty Pelau with Yogurt and Eggs 429
Cuban Fried Chicken with Orange, Olive, and Raisin Sauce 646
Dominican Pink Beans with Spicy Rabbit 648
Duck with Mushroom Ragout 79
Georgian Chicken with Walnut Sauce 383
Grilled Chicken with Provençale Herbs 75
Honey Chicken Kenyan Style 472
Korean Braised Chicken with Mushrooms 554
Lemon Chicken 176
Mexican Orange Chicken with Passion Fruit 665
Moroccan Couscous 447
Moti Mahal Tandoori Chicken 529
Palestinian Chicken with Spicy Onions and Arab Bread 419
Polynesian Mango Chicken 598
Portuguese Chicken Moroccan Style 231
Roast Chicken with Herbs and Lemon Veal Sauce 78
Roast Chicken with Olives and Yogurt 344
Roast Duck with Mangoes 472
Samoan Leaf-Wrapped Chicken 597
Sautéed Chicken with Champagne Sauce and Fruit 72
Suprêmes au Badacsonyi 344
Suprêmes with Caramelized Vinegar Sauce 73
Suprêmes with Grapes 283
Suprêmes with Roasted Bell Peppers 74
Suprêmes au Sauce Verjus 74
Tomato Roast Chicken Martinique 647
Vietnamese Caramel Chicken Stir-Fry 578
Vietnamese Grilled Lemon Chicken 577
West African Groundnut Stew 487
West African Lemon Chicken with Onions 488

ALL MANNER OF MEAT

Beef:
Brochettes of Beef Tenderloin Flambée with Pineapple 602
Chilean Leftovers (Pichanga) 628
Chilies en Nogada 663
Czech Boiled Beef with Root Vegetables and Sour Cream Sauce 348
Daube de Bouef Provençale 81
Entrecôte de Bouef au Sauce Roquefort 82
Ethiopian Stewed Beef with Spice 473
Foo You How 601
Hunan Orange Beef 557
Israeli Flank Steak with Jaffa Oranges 424
Malagasy Meat and Vegetable Stew 510
Polish Kebabs with Sauerkraut 348
Sardinian Meatballs 179
Shanghai Red-Cooked Beef 559
Steak and Eggs São Tome Style 489
Steak with Eggs 83
Sumatran Coconut Beef 580
Swedish Roast Beef with Coffee Gravy 311
Tacos with Potatoes, Chorizo, Cheese, and Beer Sauce 666
The Typical Breakfast, Panama Style 667

Veal:
Artichoke Meatball Tagine with Tomatoes and Eggs 450
Butter Schnitzel 345
Fijiian Curried Veal and Pineapple 600
German Meatballs with Capers 286
Osso Buco Moderne 182
Osso Buco Orientale 183
Roasted Calf Liver 85
Scandinavian Meat Patties 309
Terra Cotta Roast Meat 180
Veal Scallops Wrapped in Savory Crêpes 84
Veal Stew with Nuts 679

Lamb:
Albanian Lamb Kebabs with Tomatoes and Eggs 346
Armenian Lamb with Potato Sauté 385
Boboti (Cape Malay Lamb and Custard Casserole) 508
Cape Malay Lamb Kebabs 509
Chelou Kebabs 421
Curried Lamb Kebabs with Spicy Tomato Sauce, Pilaf, and Eggs 532
Fried Meat Aragon Style 235
Greek Lamb Stew with Tomatoes and Feta 387
Greek Souvlakia 385
Grilled Skewered Meat Yugoslavian Style 347
Haggis 262
Haggis in Puff Pastry 263
Lamb with Balsamic 181
Lamb with Lima Beans and Dill 423
Lamb with Sour Cherry Sauce 422
Lamb Tagine with Artichokes, Lemon, and Olives 449
Libyan Lamb, Pasta, and Chickpea Stew 451
New Zealand Lamb with Beer Sauce and Pesto Linguine 600
Norwegian Roast Lamb with Gjetöst Sauce 310
Orange Lamb Biryani 534
Oyster Sauce Lamb 557
Provençale Lamb Sauté 87
Truffled Lamb with Potato Sauté 86
Turkish Shish Kebab 386

Pork:
Burmese Dry Pork Curry 579
Cassoulet Bourgeoise 88
Chilaquiles 662
Choucroûte Garni Alsacienne 89
Corsican Stew with Macaroni 90
Costa Rican Pork with Macadamias 661
Cypriot Braised Pork with Coriander 388
Dutch Brown Beans and Bacon 285
Fried Meat Pastries Wrapped in Lettuce 582

Glazed Asian Style Pork with Prunes and Grains 234
Haitian Griots with Ti Malice Sauce 649
Hawaiian Kalua Pig 599
Irish Ham with Whisky Sauce 261
Italian Sausage 178
Latvian Roast Pork with Sauerkraut 312
Medallions of Pork with Cherries 284
Pork Caramelized à la Basquaise 92
Pork with Clams Alentejana 233
Pork Cooked in Milk 179
Pork and Plantain Soup with Orange Coconut Cream 643
Pork Stew with Prunes 91
Pork Torta with Artichokes, Tomato, and Cheese 650
Roast Pork with Caramelized Beer Sauce 283
Stir-Fried pork with Black Beans and Shitake 556
York ham with Cumberland Sauce Hotel Savoy 261

SUMPTUOUS SAUCES AND MARINADES

Aioli (Provençale Mayonnaise) 98
Beurre Blanc 99
Beurre Blanc à l'Orange 99
Beurre Blanc Orientale 99
Caponata 188
Chinese Lemon Sauce 559
Coulis de Tomate (Reduced Tomato Sauce) 97
Creamy Pesto 184
Crème Fraîche 101
Cumberland Sauce 262
Five-Spice Butter Sauce 560
Garam Masala 536
Glace de Viande (Meat Glaze) 95
Greek Potato-Olive Oil Sauce with Garlic and Lemon 389
Honey-Balsamic Glaze 186
Indonesian Peanut Butter Sauce 585
Irish Parsley Sauce 257

Japanese Fusion Sauce 561
Japanese Miso Gravy 562
Ketjap Manis 583
Lemon-Orange Sicilian Marmalade 186
Mango Butter Sauce 489
Oriental Marinade 584
Pesto with Roasted Garlic 184
Red and Yellow Tomato Sauce 185
Roasted Garlic 187
Sauce Basquaise 96
Sauce Demi-Glace 94
Sauce Demi-Glace à la Crème 94
Sauce Espagnole (Brown Sauce) 93
Sauce Hollandaise 101
Sauce Smetane (Sour Cream Sauce) 349
Sauce Ti Malice (Haitian Lime-Onion Sauce) 649
Savory Sauce Caramel au Cassis 96
Savory Sauce Caramel à l'Orange 95
Sicilian Tomato Sauce 185
Sudanese Peanut Sauce 476
Sweet and Sour Butter Sauce 584
Sweet and Sour Tomato Chutney 513
Tapenade (Olive Paste) 98
Vietnamese Fish Sauce 583
Yogurt Garlic Sauce 389

TO ACCOMPANY THE FEAST

Azerbaijani Pilaf 390
Beans Cooked in Olive Oil 189
Belgian Endive with Orange Honey Butter 288
Braised Sweet and Sour Red Cabbage 351
Bulgarian Eggplant with Minted Yogurt 349
Burghul Pilaf with Fruit 426
Burmese Stir-Fried Vegetables 586
Chelou (Persian Rice) 427

Chinese/Japanese Fried Rice 563
Crusty Pelau with Yogurt and Eggs 420
Czech Noodles with Poppy Seeds 350
Danish Caramelized Potatoes 314
East African Okra 474
Eggplant Borani 538
Eggplant Cream with Lemon and Cheese 391
Ful Medames (Egyptian Fava Beans with Garlic, Lemon, and Parsley) 453
Gratin of Pumpkin and Butternut 106
Green Beans with Garlic Oil 426
Huancaya Potatoes with Cheese 630
Hungarian Potato Strudel 352
Indonesian Coconut Rice 585
Italian Borlotti Beans 190
Karelian Pasties with Sour Cream Pastry 313
Korean Green Vegetables 562
Le Puy Lentils 106
Macaroni and Cheese with Wild Mushrooms 105
Mexican Tomato Rice 667
Minted Lemon Couscous and Red Lentils 490
Norwegian Red Cabbage with Syrup 315
Pineapple Fried Rice 603
Polenta with Cheese 192
Polenta with Wild Mushroom Ragout 193
Polish Sauerkraut with Wild Mushrooms 350
Pommes Fondant (Melting Potatoes) 475
Potatoes with Sausage and Cheese 237
Pumpkin Risotto 194
Puréed Chickpeas with Garlic and Yogurt 425
Purée of Potatoes and Beets 104
Ratatouille Provençale 107
Red Lentils with Lime 538
Red Risotto 196
Risotto alla Pomodori e Olive 195
Roasted Peppers 235
Sautéed Potato Cakes 103

Sautéed Potatoes with Duck Fat 104
Sossusvlei Caramelized Potatoes 512
Spanish Fried Potatoes 236
Steamed Brussels Sprouts with Grapes 288
Stoemp (Belgian Potatoes with Spinach and Bacon) 287
Suzhou Cauliflower and Mushrooms 566
Swedish Sweet and Sour Brown Beans 315
Sweet and Sour Red Cabbage 290
Sweet and Sour Vegetables Sicilian Style 191
Swiss Chard Sauté 289
Tomato Confit 108
Turkish Stuffed Vegetables 392
Wild Rice with Yams Pacific Style 603
Yogurt Beets 428

THE BREAD BASKET

Azorean Cornbread 223
Baguettes 57
Bruschetta con Olio di Tartufi 159
Bruschetta con Pomodori 160
Currant Scones 249
Egg Salad Sandwiches 253
English Herb Bread 250
Ensaimadas (Mallorcan Sweet Rolls) 224
Ethiopian Honey Bread 467
Focaccia 160
Georgian Cheese Bread (Khachapuri) 375
Golden Dumpling Coffeecake 356
Greek Olive Bread 376
Grilled Vegetable, Pesto, and Mozzarella Sandwich 161
Gripsholm Waffles 317
Joy's Crab Sandwich 595
Maltese Tuna Sandwich 162
Moroccan Anise Bread 443
Naan 537

New Zealand Passion Fruit Scones 605
Pecan Pancakes 248
Pineapple Coconut Cornbread 604
Swedish Plattar (Pancakes) 318
Swedish Saffron Coffeecake 317
The Ultimate Cuban Sandwich 644
Tuna and Vegetable Sandwich Niçoise (Pan Bagnat) 58
Yemen Honey Butter Pastry 410

PIZZAS AND PASTAS

Afghani Leek Ravioli with Lamb Sauce and Yogurt 533
Buckwheat Pasta with Sweet Rice and Raisins 631
Deconstructed Lasagna with Veal Scalloppine 507
Farfalle with Eggs and Bresaola 169
Fettuccine and Scallops with Vanilla Chardonnay Sauce 48
Fettuccine Verde with Grand Marnier Sauce 49
Greek Spaghetti with Shrimp 380
Lemon Fettuccine 167
Linguine with Cream of Four Nuts 167
Pappardelle with Pepperoni and Sausage 170
Pasta au Caviar 48
Pasta Dough 164
Pasta with Lemon Cream 166
Pasta con Zucchini 168
Pizza Dough 163
Pizza Margherita 162
Ravioli with Chêvre and Basil Sauce 50
Ravioli with Egg and Spinach 173
Ravioli with Mushrooms and Spinach 171
Ravioli of Squash with Butter and Sage 172
Spaghetti alla Norma 165
Tagliolini with Fresh Tomato Sauce 165
Tyrolean Meat Strudels with Bacon Sauce 341

EPICUREAN GOLD-CHEESE AND EGGS

Armenian Eggs with Lamb 372
Avocado Omelet 632
Balkan Scrambled Eggs 353
Basturma and Potatoes with Eggs 373
Chèvre Soufflé on a Platter 46
Creamy Corn Omelet à la Boufflière 484
Czech Scrambled Eggs 353
Ecuadorian Potato Cakes with Eggs, Bacon, and Avocado 629
Eggs Benedict Polana 511
Frog Legs Soufflé 47
Mango Souffléed Omelet 468
Omelette Basquaise 45
Poached Eggs with Rice and Sauce Messine 257
Scrambled Eggs on Toast 251
Spätzle Omelet 277
Swedish Gripsholm Eggs 316
Tortilla El Transcantabrico 225
Truffled Scrambled Eggs with Caviar 412
Typical Breakfast Panama Style 667
Vietnamese Omelet 573
Wild Mushrooms, Scrambled Eggs, and Caviar 226
Yemen Scrambled Eggs with Croutons 411
Yogurt Cheese 374

GRAND FINALES

Sorbets And Ice Creams:
Caramel Ice Cream 242
Caramelized Nut Ice Cream 113
Caramelized Pineapple with Mascarpone Ice Cream 200
Cassis Sorbet 109
Chocolate Sorbet 110
Coconut-Honey Ice Cream 492
Olive Oil Ice Cream 240
Pears with Raspberries and Sorbet Cassis 128

Pistachio Ice Cream 111
Prune Sorbet 111
Raspberry Sorbet 110
Prune Sorbet 291
Vanilla Ice Cream and Chocolate Sorbet with Candied Chestnuts 128

Crêpes, Soufflés, Fruits, and Creams:
Afrikaaner Breakfast 515
Banana Brioche Pudding with Hot Buttered Rum Sauce 651
Caribbean Fruit Brulée 652
Chocolate Banana Delight with Caramel Sauce and Pecans 477
Chocolate Hazelnut Torte 202
Crêpes Dulce du Leche 532
Demitasse of Chocolate with Mascarpone Cream 269
English Summer Pudding 265
Flambéed Cherry Crêpes 294
Honeyed Couscous with Dates and Nuts 456
Honeyed Figs with Madeira 457
Jordanian Dates and Bananas 429
Lemon and Chocolate Soufflé 198
Mangoes Flambé Brazzaville 491
Marquise de Chocolat 129
Medley of Tiny Ambrosial Fruits 241
Mexican Kahlua Crêpes 669
Middle Eastern Rice Pudding with Fruits and Nuts 429
Monte Bianco 197
Orange Honey Yogurt 455
Papaya and Lime Coconut Mousse 668
Paschka 320
Passion Fruit Pavlova 606
Peppermint Crisp Pudding 514
Röte Grutze (German Red Fruit Pudding) 292
Rum Crêpes Palumbo 199
Shrikhand Saffron (Yogurt with Pistachios and Currants) 539
Sticky Date Pudding 268
Strawberries with Rhubarb 290

Strawberries with Passion Fruit Sauce 319
Strawberries with Sweet Yogurt Sauce 477
Stuffed Dates 456
Tahitian Poe 606
Triple Chocolate Crêpes with Cherry Sauce 478

Cakes, Tortes, and Meringues:
Butter Sponge Cake 266
Chocolate Beet Cake 324
Chocolate Genoise Cake 117
Coffee-Walnut Cake with Mascarpone 516
English White Fruitcake 253
Frozen Lemon Meringue Torte 114
Gâteau au Mousse au Chocolat 116
Gâteau Marjolaine 112
Genoise (French Sponge Cake) 115
Honey-Walnut Cake 430
Irish Flaming Grape Cake 266
Norge Törta with Strawberries 322
Operatörta 323
Torta de Chocolate y Dulce de Leche 633
Torta de Naranja (Orange Cake) 238
Turkish Yogurt Cake with Minted Oranges and Strawberries 394

Pastries, Pies, and Tarts:
Aleksander Torte 321
Apple Strudel 292
Baklava with Crystallized Fruit and Honey Syrup 393
Caramelized Nut and Chocolate Tart 125
Cream Puffs and Eclairs 130
Glazed Apple Torte 358
Linzertorte 357
Macadamia Nut Tarts 607
Napolean with Lemon and Prunes 122
Pastry with Figs and Raspberries 127
Pastry with Plums 126

Puff Pastry Horns with Cream 119
Puff Pastry Palm Leaves 120
Rapid Puff Pastry 119
Rovos Rail Apple Tart 513
Sour Cream Pastry 314
Sweet French Pastry 124
Swiss Plum Tart 293
Tartes au Citron 125
Tarte aux Kiwis et Fraises 121
Thousand Island Pastry 632
Torte Français 123
Tropical Fruit Tart 608

Frostings, Fillings, and Sauces:
Butterscotch Sauce 269
Caramel Frosting 323
Chocolate Buttercream Frosting 134
Chocolate Icing 118
Crème Anglaise (Custard Sauce) 137
Crème Chantilly (Flavored Whipped Cream) 137
Crème Patissière (Pastry Cream) 135
Fondant 135
Lemon Curd 134
Pralinée (Caramelized Nut Powder) 136
Raspberry Sauce 138
Royal Icing 136
Slatko (Yugoslav Cherry Preserves) 355

Friandeses-Truffles, Candy, and Cookies:
Amaretti 203
Chocolate Caramel Truffles with Walnuts 634
Date Halwa 540
Hawaiian Rainbow of Macadamia Nut Clusters 609
Mexican Brown Sugar Fudge 670
Scottish Shortbread 237
Truffles with Chocolate 131

Truffles with Fruit 133
Truffles with Mint 133
Truffles with Pralinée 132
Vanilla Crescent Cookies 355